Resource Conservation

Social and Economic Dimensions of Recycling

Edited by

David W. Pearce
University of Aberdeen

and

Ingo Walter
New York University

Longman Group Limited London

*Associated companies, branches and representatives
throughout the world*

*Published in the United States of America
by New York University Press 1977*

© New York University 1977

First published in Great Britain 1978

ISBN   0   582   46069.7

Manufactured in the United States of America

Preface

While working on a joint project on materials recycling in the summer of 1975, the editors of this volume realized that no standard reference work existed on the economic dimensions of materials recycling policy. Studies relating to specific industries do exist, and these demonstrate the extreme complexity of generalizing about the re-use of "waste" materials. Accordingly, we set about bringing together a group of international experts in the field of materials re-use, with the primary emphasis on economics. The result was a highly successful international symposium held at the Rockefeller Foundation's Study and Conference Center in Bellagio, Italy, during November 1976. This volume is the outcome of that conference.

Most papers contained herein have been revised in light of the forceful and occasionally heated discussion that took place. Additionally, we observed a "gap" in our planning of the various contributions and invited Robert C. Anderson to present us with a separate paper on the general economic problems faced when looking at recycling policy.

We are also conscious that, in speaking of "materials," we omitted highly important agricultural substances such as animal waste, the re-use of which can have important implications for the future world food supply. Equally, the disposal of such wastes creates significant pollution problems in many countries. Our excuse for this omission has to be that the book is already large, and even now many questions are raised and not answered. To have extended the discussion to cover agricultural wastes would have made the conference unwieldy and this volume too long.

We are deeply indebted to the Anglo-German Foundation for the Study of Industrial Society for their financial sponsorship and to that organization's Director General, Peter McGregor, for sympathetic and immediate understanding of the problems faced in funding a conference to be held in Italy at a time when exchange rates were changing daily. We owe an equal debt to the Rockefeller Foundation, both for financial support and for making available to us their unparalleled facilities at Bellagio. A special word of thanks is due Dr. and Mrs. William Olson of Villa Serbelloni and their excellent staff. Also as far as sponsors are concerned, we must thank the Organization for Economic Cooperation and Development, Paris, for financial support for some of the delegates to the conference. Lastly, we are indebted to Pat Greatorex of Leicester University and Marion Epps of New York University for typing, retyping, dealing with endless crises, and staying (most of the time) unperturbed by the whole process.

This volume attempts to draw together the salient features of recycling in its economic context, and, ultimately, that is the only proper context in which such problems can be legitimately analyzed. Two general messages seem to emerge rather clearly. First, vague generalizations about the desirability of a "total recycling society" merely indicate the naïveté of those who make such prescriptions for the future. Recycling is often a good thing, but it frequently generates as many problems as it solves. Second, there can be no such thing as "the" economics of recycling. There can only be detailed studies of individual secondary commodities—their interactions with primary commodity markets, their special technical attributes, and the particular problems involved in collection, reprocessing, and re-use.

Aberdeen, Scotland   David W. Pearce
New York City   Ingo Walter

Contents

About the Contributors

Robert C. Anderson is an economist with the Environmental Law Institute, Washington, D.C.

Robin Bidwell is an economist on the staff of Environmental Resources Limited, London.

Tayler H. Bingham is an economist with the Energy and Environmental Research Division, Research Triangle Institute, U.S.A.

Blair T. Bower is a consulting engineer-economist and Consultant in Residence, Resources for the Future, Inc., Washington, D.C.

John A. Butlin is a Lecturer in the Department of Agricultural Economics at the University of Manchester.

W. David Conn is an Assistant Professor of Environmental Planning at the University of California, Los Angeles.

Donald A. Fink is an economist with the Federal Energy Agency, Washington, D.C.

G. J. S. Govett is a Professor of Geology at the University of New Brunswick, Canada

M. H. Govett is an economist at the University of New Brunswick, Canada, and is interested in natural resource problems.

Richard Grace is a research associate at the University of East Anglia, Norwich, England.

William A. Irwin, is Institute Fellow, Environmental Law Institute, Washington, D.C.

Liselotte Lichtwer is an environmental economist with the Economic and Social Sciences Department, Battelle-Institut e.V., Frankfurt.

Talbot R. Page is Senior Research Associate, Resources for the Future, Inc., Washington, D.C.

David W. Pearce is Professor of Political Economy, University of Aberdeen, Scotland.

Rüdiger Pethig is associated with the Lehrstuhl für Volkswirtschafts-lehre und Aussenwirtschaft, Universität Mannheim, Germany

Michel Potier is Head of the Environment and Industry Division, Organization for Economic Cooperation and Development, Paris.

Fred Lee Smith, Jr., is an operations research and policy analyst with the Office of Solid Waste Management Programs, U.S. Environmental Protection Agency, Washington, D.C.

R. Kerry Turner is a lecturer in economics at the University of East Anglia, Norwich, England.

Ingo Walter is Professor of Economics and Finance, Graduate School of Business Administration, New York University.

Joan Wilcox is Economic Adviser to the United Kingdom Department of the Environment, London.

Bernd Wolbeck is an official of the Ministry of the Interior, Federal Republic of Germany, specializing in waste management.

List of Figures

xi

List of Tables

xiii

Economic Dimensions of Waste Recycling and Re-use: Some Definitions, Facts, and Issues

Blair T. Bower

Discussion of waste recycling and re-use in a national context often founders on the rocks of semantic confusion. The problem of communication is exacerbated when the discussion takes place in an international context. The first purpose of this (introductory) essay is to suggest some operational definitions, which will provide a common background for the papers that follow, even though different terms are used in different papers. The second purpose is to delineate some basic economic facts with respect to recycling (and re-use), facts which are relevant to all societies. The third purpose is to suggest some issues relating to recycling that underlie the specific topics addressed in the individual papers.

SOME DEFINITIONS

No production or use activity converts 100 percent of the material and energy inputs into desired products and services. There are five possible "fates" for these nonproduct outputs (NPOs): (1) material/energy recovery; (2) by-product production; (3) discharge into one or more of the three environmental media—land, air, water —with or without modification; (4) processing to obtain materials for use as subsequent inputs to production or energy conversion; and

1

(5) re-use in the same form. The last is simple and can be dispensed with easily. Re-use in the same form is exemplified by re-use of a pallet or a container to provide the same function or service as originally. Some processing often is involved, as in cleaning the container before refilling. The "second-hand" market—both for production goods such as used machinery and for domestic goods such as appliances and clothes—also exemplifies re-use in the same form.

Materials and/or energy recovery refers to recovery and re-use in the same production activity. In many, if not most, manufacturing activities it is economically necessary to recover and re-use substantial portions of the NPO materials and energy formed in producing the given product mix—chemical and fiber recovery in pulp and paper production, for example. This is true for many nonmanufacturing activities as well. The extent to which materials and/or energy recovery is practiced at any point in time in a plant is a function of the cost of recovered materials/energy relative to new (make-up) materials/energy, the latter usually being purchased in the market— or from another segment of the plant—at a price which may or may not be close to the open-market price. These relative costs are in turn affected by the technology of the production process, the technology of materials and energy recovery, the technology of production of the "new" inputs, and various governmental policies such as tariffs, depletion allowances, severance taxes. Trade-offs are possible between the design of the production process to increase physical efficiency (i.e., reduce the formation of nonproduct outputs) and utilization of material and energy recovery technology. In designing a plant, the objective is to optimize the *combination* of the production process *plus* the materials/energy recovery system.

By-product production refers to NPO material and energy which are used as inputs into another production activity, at the same location as, or at a different location than, the production activity which generated the original NPOs. The use of tomato pulp from the canning of tomatoes and tomato juice in the production of pet food and the use of peach pits to make charcoal briquettes exemplify by-product production.

In terms of profit maximization for an individual plant, for factor prices and the product mix/product specifications at a point in time— materials/energy recovery and/or by-product production are undertaken only to the level where the marginal value equals marginal cost.

Additional materials/energy recovery and/or by-product production might be undertaken if physical limits and/or charges were imposed on discharges to the environment. Under such conditions, additional materials/energy recovery and/or by-product production often provide the least cost alternative for the next increment of discharge reduction.

Discharge to the environment is obvious. Until recently, such discharge was often the least expensive option for the individual activity, given that any resulting externalities were borne by other activities. In many cases direct discharge—or discharge with minimal modification—is still the least expensive option, even in social terms.

Reclamation has been used as a generic term to include all types of recycling and re-use. For that purpose it is a more apt term than recycling, because only in the case of materials/energy recovery as defined above is the path of a material a *cycle,* where the cycle is defined as a closed path. A more limited, operational definition of reclamation is the *processing* of an NPO material in order to derive one or more elements as material inputs into some production or energy conversion activity. Thus, the output of reclamation is a *secondary* material rather than an *end-use* product. Cellulose fibers in used corrugated containers, copper in used insulated copper wire, and lead in automobile batteries are examples of *desired materials*. Similarly, municipal mixed NPOs are processed to produce so-called *refuse-derived fuel* (Ecofuel) for use in energy conversion.

Two other definitional points merit attention. First, if the NPOs have a zero price in existing markets—whether those prices are determined in a more or less competitive economy or centrally in a more or less directed economy—or if the prices are less than the variable costs of collecting and processing the NPOs for use, the NPOs are termed *residuals*. This is an economic definition, and emphasizes the dynamics of the context. The market at any point in time involves the current mix of installed technologies, the current final demand and related product specifications, the existing relative prices among alternative factor inputs, and the current spatial distribution of economic activities. A shift in any one of these factors can "move" a particular NPO into or out of the "residuals" category.

Other terms are *wastes* and *waste arisings*. Both of these are misnomers in that at least some of the materials to which they are applied have positive values (prices). *Waste paper* is a commodity, bought and sold in the market; thus, *paper stock* is a more apt term. The relevant point is that these "potential" raw materials are no different from so-called virgin raw materials. For both types of materials, demand depends on the quality of the material and its location, technology, and market conditions.

The other remaining definitional problem involves the terms *primary* or *virgin materials, secondary materials* and *secondary materials industry. Primary or virgin raw materials* can be defined as those which are directly extracted or harvested from "nature" (i.e., crude petroleum, copper ore, round wood, cotton). The definitions of *secondary material and secondary materials industry* are less straightforward. The implication of the term *secondary material* is that it has "been through" some end use, such as the packages containing parts shipped to a television assembly plant and the newspapers discarded from residences. A *secondary materials plant* (firm, operation) is one which processes secondary materials to produce a secondary raw material for input into production or energy conversion. Examples of processing include collection and baling of used corrugated containers, collection and stripping of copper wire, collection and processing of urban mixed solid residuals into fuel.

Two difficulties arise in connection with these definitions. First, NPOs generated in converting/fabricating activities—such as prompt scrap in steel fabrication, or cuttings from converting operations in production of paper products—are not the result of an end-use. However, because they are often, if not generally, handled organizationally in the same manner as NPOs from end-uses, including them under the rubric of secondary materials is operational.

The second difficulty stems from the fact that, in the United States at least, the term *secondary materials firm* has been applied *both* to firms engaged in processing secondary materials—as defined above— and, sometimes, to firms using secondary raw materials. Thus, an aluminum casting plant in which only secondary raw material is used could be considered in the secondary materials industry, which is confusing. Including such activities under the rubric of the secondary materials industry has an additional disadvantage in that a substantial number of plants in at least the pulp and paper and steel industries use both primary (virgin) raw materials and secondary raw materials.

Figure 1–1 depicts the definitions of materials and energy recovery, by-product production, and reclamation. Figures 1–2 and 1–3 depict the definition of residuals.

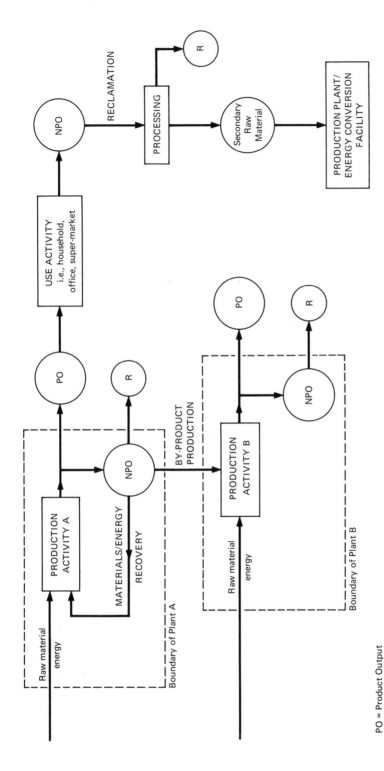

PO = Product Output
NPO = Nonproduct Output
R = Residual (gaseous, liquid, solid, energy)

Figure 1—1 Definition of materials and energy recovery, by-product production, and reclamation

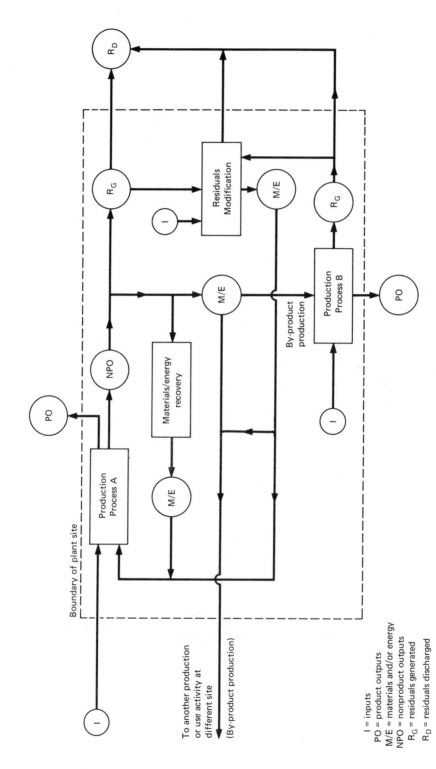

Boundary of plant site

Production Process A

PO

I

NPO

R_G

R_D

Residuals Modification

I

R_G

M/E

Materials/energy recovery

M/E

M/E

M/E

By-product production

Production Process B

PO

R_G

I

To another production or use activity at different site

(By-product production)

I = inputs
PO = product outputs
M/E = materials and/or energy
NPO = nonproduct outputs
R_G = residuals generated
R_D = residuals discharged

Figure 1–2 Definition of residuals generation

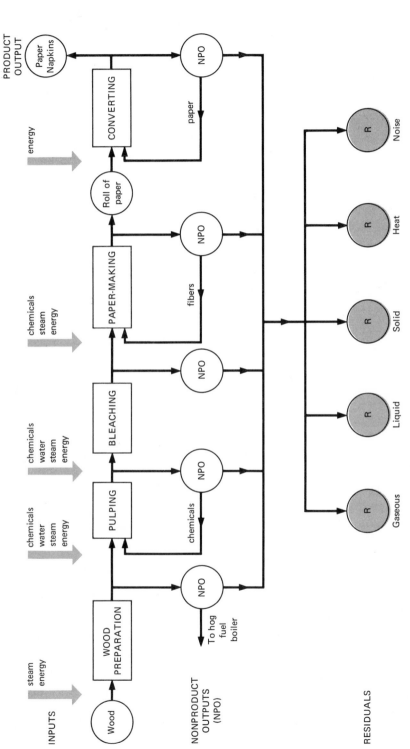

Figure 1–3 Illustrating the definition of residuals: simplified process flow chart for production of paper napkins

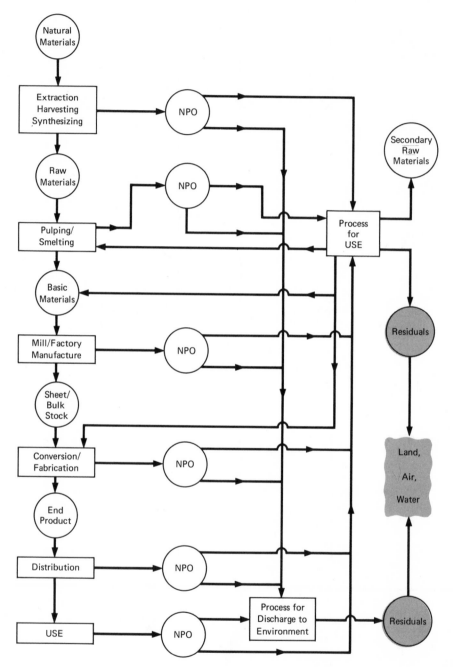

Figure 1—4 Illustration of sources of nonproduct outputs

In considering the economic dimensions of recycling, differentiating among the sources of NPOs is important, because the source is the major determinant of the characteristics of the NPOs. Figure 1–4 illustrates the various activities in which NPOs are generated in an economy.* Of the sources of NPOs depicted in Figure 1–4, the extractive and harvesting activities are not considered in this volume —mining, crude petroleum and gas extraction, agriculture, and silviculture. These activities are major sources of NPOs, most of which are residuals and some of which give rise to serious externalities— such as pesticides and manure from agricultural operations, uranium ore mine tailings, acid mine drainage from underground coal mining. As extraction involves increasingly "leaner" deposits of desired elements, and deeper and less accessible sources of petroleum and natural gas, and as agriculture and silviculture are intensified under pressure of producing more food and fiber for a growing world population, the residuals problems associated with such activities will be exacerbated. However, the same principles apply to these sources as to the others explicitly considered in the following papers.

SOME FACTS

At least four basic "facts of life" must be considered in the economic analysis of recycling—all of which merit explicit mention. First, the value of any raw material, primary or secondary, is a function of a number of factors. These factors are listed in Table 1–1. The important characteristics which affect the value of a raw material are location, quantity, and quality. Large mass of high quality (i.e., high concentration) close to the locus of production and/or market are desired characteristics. This is as true for a secondary material as it is for a virgin raw material. A high-grade iron ore in comparison to a low-grade iron ore is similar to the comparison of high-grade used newspapers with low-grade used newspapers. The quantity and quality affect the cost of processing and the quantity of residuals generated in that processing and hence the residuals management costs associated therewith. There is likely to be a wider variety of contaminants or nonusable materials in secondary materials than in many virgin materials. In some cases these contaminants, while small in quantity,

---

* Energy conversion is included under manufacturing in this schema; institutions such as schools and hospitals under USE.

TABLE 1–1

FACTORS AFFECTING VALUE OF SECONDARY AND VIRGIN MATERIALS

Secondary Material	Virgin Material
Quantity: amount in a single location *Quality:* nature and magnitude of contaminants *Accessibility:* where generated in activity in relation to physical configuration and physical structure in which activity is located *Technology* of processing, i.e., stripping wire, de-inking paper stock, shredding vehicle bodies *Residuals* management cost * with respect to processing secondary material *Transport* cost of secondary material and of secondary raw material *Technology* of producing final product *Product output specifications* *Transport* cost of final product to market	*Quantity:* amount in a single location *Quality:* concentration of ore *Accessibility:* depth of overburden, steepness of logging slope *Technology* of extracting virgin material, i.e., logging technique *Technology* of processing virgin material, i.e., pelletizing *Residuals* management costs * with respect to extraction and processing virgin material *Transport* cost of virgin material and processed virgin material *Technology* of producing final product *Product output specifications* *Transport* cost of final product to market

SOURCE:

*ResMgtCosts$=f(RM, T, PO, POS, E_c)$, where RM=quality of raw material; T=technology of production process; PO=product mix; POS=product output specifications; and E_c=effluent controls, i.e., standards, charges

may be difficult to remove and thus increase the cost of processing for use.

From the first fact of life follows the second, and obvious, fact. The extent of use of secondary materials (and the extent of recycling), in both national and international contexts, is a function of the relative prices of the alternative materials as factor inputs into economic activities. Relative prices are affected by the factors listed in Table 1–1, and, in addition, by such governmental policies as depletion allowances, expensing provisions, severance taxes, and capital gains tax provisions on virgin materials, tax credits for using secondary materials.

Third, there are economies of scale in materials/energy recovery and by-product production, just as in basic production processes.

Thus, for given prices of new materials and energy, more materials/energy recovery and/or by-product production will take place in a 1,000 tons per day (TPD) kraft linerboard mill than in a 400 TPD mill.

Fourth, because all of the factors affecting relative prices of secondary and primary materials are dynamic—even the quantity of ores and crude petroleum and natural gas "in place" vary with time, as a function of exploration and discovery—the extent of recycling changes with time, in both the short run and in the long run. In the short run, there is some flexibility, both in individual plants in an industry and for the given installed technological mix in an industry as a whole, to use different proportions of secondary and virgin materials. In the longer run this flexibility can shift, as old capacity is retired and new capacity is added—with the mix of new capacity based on estimated relative prices of secondary and virgin materials.

The economic dynamics of recycling can be illustrated by the steel industry in the United States over the last two or three decades, in relation to its two basic ferrous raw materials—iron ore and steel scrap, particularly obsolete steel scrap. Quite apart from fluctuating demand as a result of business cycles, the relative values of these two raw materials have fluctuated substantially as a result of the following: (1) changes in the technology of steel production; (2) changes in technology of ore processing; (3) changes in technology of scrap processing; and to some less clearly defined degree (4) the design of automobiles and changes in product mix and product specifications.

As the high-quality iron ore deposits in the Mesabi Range in the United States neared exhaustion, costs for processing iron ore increased, thereby making scrap more attractive as a raw material, given the predominance of the open hearth method for producing steel. Subsequently pelletizing was developed, which enabled economic upgrading of low-grade iron ores (35–40 percent) to high-grade ores (65–68 percent). This tended to shift the relative use back toward iron ore.

Traditionally the technology for processing junked vehicles involved cutting and compressing a stripped and burned-out hulk into chunks of impure "No. 2" scrap. With the open hearth technology for producing steel, about 70 percent of the charge could be relatively impure scrap. With the advent and growing use of the basic oxygen furnace (BOF) for producing steel—a less expensive production process than the open hearth—the use of scrap tended to decline because the maximum scrap charge to the BOF is about 40 percent. By 1970 BOF steel production exceeded open hearth steel production in the United States.

Around 1960 a technological development for processing obsolete steel scrap was introduced—the shredder. Whole automobile bodies are chopped into small pieces, enabling removal of a higher proportion of the impurities and producing a secondary raw material of better quality than produced by the strip-and-burn method. A shift in relative use toward the secondary material has tended to result.

Technological developments can affect, not only the type of secondary material which can be used in a production activity, but also the quantity and amount of NPOs generated in that activity. Continuous casting, only recently beginning to be used in the United States steel industry, reduces scrap generated internally in a steel mill. In conventional steel production, scrap is generated in ingot and slab trimming and in rolling operations in an amount up to 30 percent of the steel poured. Continuous casting cuts this generation to 10 percent or less. Because the BOF operates on a low scrap charge, it is desirable to minimize internal scrap generation. Thus the BOF and continuous casting tend to reduce the relative amount of scrap used.

While these various technological developments were taking place, changes were occurring also in the product output specifications for automobiles in terms of the component materials. As indicated above, the value of a secondary material is a function of the quality of the material which can be produced from it, as well as the cost of processing. But the quality depends, in turn, on the original quality of the secondary material. The more impurities in scrap steel, the lower its value. With respect to automobiles, the trend has been ever upward in the content of nonferrous materials. The average 1970 model United States car contained about 100 pounds of zinc, 75 pounds of aluminum, 38 pounds of copper, and about 100 pounds of plastics. The last was above five times the amount used in 1960; the trend has been upward since 1970 and probably will continue as pressure increases for lighter-weight automobiles. Increased impurities in the secondary material increase the cost of processing and/or decrease the quality of the output and hence the value as a raw material.

SOME ISSUES

Given the foregoing definitions and facts of life, some issues relating to the economic dimensions of recycling can be suggested. Many of these are addressed in one or more of the following chapters. No order of importance is implied by the order of identification of the issues.

1. Product output specifications are an important determinant of the extent of recycling—that is, the yield strength of steel, the octane rating of automotive fuel, the brightness of a paper product. In some cases, such as the latter, the specification relates solely to aesthetics and not to function. If a paper towel of GEB brightness value 80–82 is desired, the maximum percentage of furnish* which can consist of No. 1 Mixed paper stock would be 25 percent. If a brightness of only about 25 is acceptable, all other specifications remaining the same, the furnish can be comprised of 100 percent No. 1 Mixed. On the other hand, for given product output specifications, the characeristics of secondary materials will limit or even preclude their use as raw materials. To the extent that material *content* specifications are used instead of *performance* specifications, use of secondary materials may in some cases be inhibited. Changing product specifications, including increasing durability, can—but do not always—reduce the total materials and energy throughput in a society.

One other aspect of product output specification and the related "end uses" merits more explicit attention than usually is given to it. That is the "sacrificial" uses of materials—end-uses which result in wide dispersion (as in vaporization) or in combining with other elements to make separation infeasible without large inputs of energy and other materials. Recycling of such materials is essentially impossible, so that the larger the component of sacrificial uses in final demand, the larger is the absolute drain on resources.

2. For a given final demand in a society, recycling policies should be developed in a "total systems" context, encompassing all possible flow paths of materials and energy to produce a given product or set of products, including the residuals discharges and their environmental consequences at each point in the system. Figure 1–5 exemplifies the total system for steel. The optimum combination of secondary

---

* *Furnish* refers to the input to the paper machine in a paper mill.

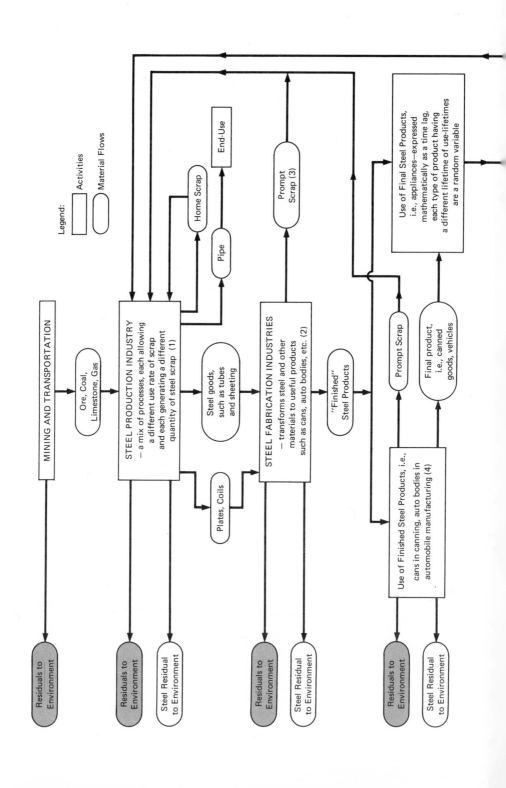

Legend:

☐ Activities

⬭ Material Flows

MINING AND TRANSPORTATION

Ore, Coal, Limestone, Gas

STEEL PRODUCTION INDUSTRY
— a mix of processes, each allowing a different use rate of scrap and each generating a different quantity of steel scrap (1)

Steel goods, such as tubes and sheeting

Plates, Coils

Home Scrap

Pipe

End-Use

STEEL FABRICATION INDUSTRIES
— transforms steel and other materials to useful products such as cans, auto bodies, etc. (2)

Prompt Scrap (3)

"Finished" Steel Products

Prompt Scrap

Use of Finished Steel Products, i.e., cans in canning, auto bodies in automobile manufacturing (4)

Final product, i.e., canned goods, vehicles

Use of Final Steel Products, i.e., appliances—expressed mathematically as a time lag, each type of product having a different lifetime of use-lifetimes are a random variable

Residuals to Environment

Residuals to Environment

Steel Residual to Environment

Residuals to Environment

Steel Residual to Environment

Residuals to Environment

Steel Residual to Environment

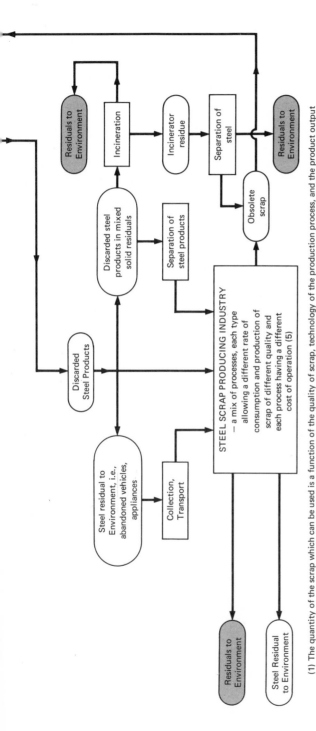

(1) The quantity of the scrap which can be used is a function of the quality of scrap, technology of the production process, and the product output characteristics, i.e., reinforcing bars, special strength steels, alloy steels, etc. Similarly, the quantity of scrap—and residuals—generated is function of the same variables.

(2) For some products fabrication may take place at the same location as steel production, i.e., pipe, re-inforcing bars.

(3) The quantity of scrap generated is a function of the technology of fabrication and product output specifications. The extent of use of the scrap generated is probably a function of size of operation, location, and transport costs.

(4) Where the "finished steel product" is an intermediate product, i.e., steel cans, the manufacture of the cans may take place at the same location as the "use of the finished steel product", i.e., cans in canning.

(5) The "steel scrap producing industry" logically should include the collection and handling of its raw material, as well as the production and transport of its output. The two segments may be undertaken by the same firm or by different firms. For example, collection/transport of used steel cans may be done by a dealer, the processing (grinding, melting) to produce the raw material for steel production, by the steel production firm, at the location of steel production.

Figure 1—5 Simplified flow diagram of steel supply system showing the major recycle loops and primary materials is not likely to be achevied by separate decisions at the plant and firm level unless the externalities at each point in the system can be adequately reflected in factor prices faced by each unit in the system.

3. The contention is often made that the prices of secondary materials fluctuate more than the prices of virgin materials. To what extent is this the case, and, if so, for what reasons? The prices of *all* raw materials fluctuate in response to variations in demand associated with fluctuations in economic conditions. If fluctuations in prices are greater for secondary than for primary materials, one contributing factor may well be the different structures of the so-called primary and secondary industries. In the United States the former, particularly with respect to metals, tends toward oligopoly—dominated by a few firms—in contrast to the many small firms that comprise each secondary materials industry. In addition, many of the firms in the primary sector are vertically integrated, with virgin raw materials through fabrication of final products under one ownership, often including exploration capacity and transport facilities. Another factor may be that certain types of secondary materials are used primarily in the production of a single raw product for a single use. For example, certain types of secondary materials are predominantly used in making roofing felt for housing construction. When the housing construction industry slumps, demand for—and hence the price of—those secondary materials fall. Price fluctuations for othr types of paper stock, such as tab cards, envelope clippings, and the like, do not exhibit much fluctuation.

4. Competition is presumed to exist between secondary and virgin materials. Two types of "competition" can be identified. One type occurs when it is possible to make the identical product with either raw material, for example, where the equivalent furnish to a paper machine—for the production of a particular paper product—can be produced using either secondary or virgin material. The relevant comparison is at that *point* in the "system," including the costs of all processing and residuals management up to that point, *not* the relative prices of found wood or round wood chips and paper stock. Even the comparison at that point is likely to be incomplete. Location of production in relation to the source of raw material inputs

and in relation to the market, as well as possible differences in scale, will affect the economics of the alternative systems.*

The second type of competition exists where substitutable but not identical products are produced. For example, some packaging materials produced from secondary material are of slightly lower quality in terms of appearance, brightness, and printability. If this slightly lower quality is accompanied by a sufficient price differential, in comparison with packaging produced from virgin material, additional use may be stimulated.

A better specification of the points in the system where competition occurs and the characteristics of that competition is crucial to a better understanding of the economic dimensions of recycling.

5. Limitations imposed on the use of the natural environment for disposal of residuals has important implications for recycling. The assumption has often been made that increased recycling—increased use of secondary materials relative to virgin materials—is "environmentally desirable." This assumption is not necessarily valid. Essentially all secondary materials require some processing: the insulation must be stripped from copper wire; dirt, adhesives, staples removed from used paper products. This processing results in the generation of residuals. Whether or not these residuals are more or less environmentally damaging than the residuals generated in the processing of a virgin material, and whether or not the costs of managing those residuals to mitigate any adverse impacts on the environment are less or more, depends on the particular situation.

For example, if 100 percent paper stock is used to make a paper product, in contrast to softwood using the kraft process, the former results in the generation of relatively few gaseous residuals—the amounts depending on the quality of fuel used to produce process steam—but substantially more dissolved and suspended solids than does the kraft process. Whether or not the gaseous residuals generated in the kraft process are more damaging or are more costly to modify than the residuals generated in processing the paper stock to produce the same product depends on the particular situation. Nevertheless, in a significant number of situations, increasing the limitations on the

---

* Mills producing paper products from virgin material generally tend to be significantly larger than those producing paper products from secondary materials.

use of the environment for disposal of residuals—whether by effluent standards or effluent charges—will stimulate increased recycling.

6. The significant increase in energy prices throughout the world since 1973 also has had, and will continue to have, important implications for recycling, both directly and indirectly. This is particularly true for energy-intensive activities such as production of aluminum and bleached paper products. The fact that much less energy is required to produce a ton of aluminum from some secondary aluminum materials than from virgin ore (bauxite) has been one—albeit not the only—major stimulus to the recycling programs by various companies in the United States. Because bleaching cellulose fibers is an energy-intensive process, the increased cost of energy has stimulated a reduction in the brightness specification of some paper products, such as industrial paper towels and toweling. Such a change not only reduces energy use per unit of product but also means that more secondary materials can be used in the manufacture of such products. The fact that a returnable beverage container system would require less total energy than a nonreturnable system has been one of the arguments used in United States attempts, both successful and unsuccessful, to pass legislation to ban or require significant deposits on nonreturnable beverage containers.

In general, increased energy prices will increase material/energy recovery and by-product production in manufacturing activities and increased use of secondary materials.

7. The factors which affect the movement of secondary materials in international trade are essentially no different than those affecting primary materials. The factors listed in Table 1–1 are relevant to both international and national contexts. However, there is one additional factor, namely export *supplies,* and import-competing *supplies* of secondary materials are a function of *past* production of goods (and imports), unlike primary materials.

CONCLUDING COMMENT

Recycling cannot be analyzed adequately, nor rational policies with respect to it developed without a clear understanding of the multiplicity of factors that affect the extent of recycling as they relate to different materials/energy and to different economic activities. It is particularly important to recognize that: (1) policies not specifically directed toward recycling can have important effects on recycling, such as tax and "pollution control" policies; and that (2) changes in input prices, such as energy, crude petroleum, and services can have major impacts on recycling. The impacts can induce more or less recycling, or can make recycling more or less physically and economically feasible. For example, the increase in price of crude petroleum, and the concomitant increase in price of lubricating oil, has stimulated a substantial increase in recovery and re-use of used lubricating oil from rolling operations in steel mills. The increased price of lubricating oil for vehicles, coupled with the increased price of lubrication in service stations and garages, has stimulated increased "do-it-yourself" oil changes by vehicle owners. That practice disperses the generation of used oil and makes recycling more difficult.

PART I

Economic Dimensions of
Materials Scarcity

CHAPTER 2

Secondary Materials and Economic Growth: Needs and Measures for a Comprehensive Policy

Bernd Wolbeck

The problem of secondary materials management in principle affects nearly all fields of economic activity. Secondary materials occur as residuals, by-products, or end products in the production, distribution, or consumption of commodities. To the extent that appropriate materials are being fed back into the production-consumption cycle for economic reasons—which is being done today to a high degree—they do not represent a central problem of public concern either in view of the protection of the environment or under economic aspects. Increased attention in technical and policy discussions is, rather, focused on that part of materials to which no economic value is attributed for the time being and which, therefore, has to be disposed of as "waste."

A secondary materials policy will not meet the actual problem requirements if it confines itself solely to the aspects of "recycling." Indeed, the relevant consideration should include all those processes that have a bearing on the generation, utilization, and disposal of primary and secondary materials. Only if this comprehensive approach to the problem is made will it be possible to avoid inadequate coordination of individual measures, the occurrence of undesirable problem shifting, as well as economic misallocations of public and private initiatives (e.g., investments).

THE ENVIRONMENTAL PROBLEM ASSOCIATED WITH SECONDARY MATERIALS

Increased production and consumption of commodities have in the past resulted in ever-growing quantities of wastes. At the same time, due to new production techniques and changing consumer attitudes, a substantial change has taken place in the composition of the substances concerned. For the member countries of the European Communities alone, the EC Commission at present assumes the annual amount of unused secondary materials in the order of more than 1.5 billion tons.

A direct consequence of this development is the occurrence of bottlenecks in the disposal of wastes as well as considerable financial expenditure on the part of public authorities and industry for the solution of their waste problems. In the Federal Republic of Germany alone, approximately DM 4 billion are spent for waste disposal every year.

A particular threat to the environment is caused by hazardous industrial wastes, with their high concentrations of pollutants. Methods needed for a proper treatment and monitoring are either insufficiently available or inadequately applied. Moreover, this situation is influenced by more stringent laws on air and water pollution control, which inevitably result in new accumulations of pollutants. As in the case of radioactive waste, increasing reluctance of the public is directed against the environmentally necessary establishment of treatment and disposal plants for the residues concerned. This trend strongly justifies the demand that the quantities of residues and wastes no longer utilized should be reduced further or at least should not be allowed to increase without effective control.

ASPECTS RELATING TO RAW MATERIALS

The recycling of secondary materials is gaining importance with a view to the supply of raw materials. For the time being, this development is due to an increase in the prices of raw materials largely contingent upon political factors and increasing costs for exploitation rather than to a elementary scarcity of raw materials. In this connection, new efforts are emerging at the international level, aimed at subjecting the trade in raw materials to dirigistic rules, a trend giving reason to anticipate a further increase in the price of raw materials.

Already the use of secondary raw materials is of very great importance. In the Federal Republic of Germany, for example, statistics
show that production residuals at a rate of up to 80 percent are
being partly utilized by the plastics industry, while paper mills are
using waste paper at an average rate of about 45 percent. In the
case of lead and copper, approximately 45 percent of the demand is
covered by scrap. The high potential of wastes produced by consumers has so far remained largely unused. This is to be regarded as a
point of special concern for future recycling efforts.

Not least because of the worldwide interdependence in the economic field, a policy relating to the utilization of secondary materials
should be carefully oriented toward the initial situation in regard to
supply with primary raw materials. According to the rules of supply
and demand, international conditions of the primary raw materials
sector also influence the markets for secondary raw materials. Despite
this influence, however, it is to be noted that the policy concerning
secondary materials is much more nationally oriented than is the case
for primary raw materials. This fact is especially noticed, for example,
in the Federal Republic of Germany, being the third largest raw
material consumer in the Western world and dependent to a particular extent on imports. An important political element should be
seen in the high degree of national independence regarding the secondary raw materials policy—that is, self-sufficiency.

ENERGY ASPECTS

The "recycling of wastes" is nearly always linked to the question of
energy balance. This effect, which is directly apparent for energy
recovery from wastes, likewise applies to the recovery of materials.

Comparison between energy use for the extraction and processing
of primary raw materials, and energy use connected with appropriate
processing of wastes, provides an important criterion in assessing the
value of recycling. Considering that energy use and its adverse effects
on the environment (e.g., air pollution) are correlated factors, it is
also possible simultaneously to make an ecologic assessment in addition to the economic evaluation.

Energy consumption and residue generation in processing materials is dependent on the "state of dispersion" of the system under
consideration.

For instance, it decreases to the extent to which the purity and concentration of raw material resources or the homogeneity of the wastes increase. Studies undertaken in the field of recycling often reveal a trend in the direction of energy conservation as compared with the use of virgin raw materials, including exploitation. Reference may here be made, by way of example, to corresponding comparisons in respect to aluminum, copper, scrap steel, glass, or paper. In some cases the differences are considerable, up to factor 10. On the other hand, energy consumption may also constitute a limiting factor for recycling, for example, if one considers the processing of highly mixed wastes with low concentration of valuable materials.

AIMS

With regard to the twin objectives "resource conservation" and "protection of the environment," the policy for secondary materials management is directed at the following aims: (1) reduction of no longer utilizable materials (wastes) at the production and consumer levels by reducing wastes generated in the production process, applying environmentally sound production techniques (reduction of air and water pollution), extending the life of products, and increasing the re-use of products; (2) substitution of scarce for less scarce raw materials in the production process (while retaining the purpose for which the product is to be used); (3) increased utilization of wastes by recycling during the production process (recovery of materials), recovery of the energy content of wastes and feedback into biological cycles; and (4) environmentally sound disposal of wastes. These objectives are not to be regarded as separate and isolated tasks. Rather they should be tackled in a joint approach, taking into account the materials concerned. Thus, for example, increased recycling of wastes does not replace efforts made in the direction of a direct saving of raw material but only complements such efforts for reasons of raw material management and environmental policy.

The direct reduction of consumption of materials by producers and consumers must be considered as the most urgent challenge both on a medium and long-term basis. This is shown, for example, by the following comparison:

In the European Common Market the recycling rate for copper at present amounts to an average of about 40 percent of the copper scrap available. If it were raised to 100 percent, this would defer the critical point of time (exhaustion of known resources) by 3 years, given an annual growth rate of consumption in the order of 4.6 percent and an average life span of 22 years for the products concerned. On the other hand, lowering the rate of consumption to 0 percent, with the same recycling rates of 40 and 100 percent respectively (life span of 22 years), would defer the critical point of time by 59 and 195 years respectively. This leads to the following conclusion: curtailment of absolute consumption and appropriate application of raw–material-saving technologies have a much more positive effect on the conservation of raw material resources than recycling.

Disposal, in turn, often provides an *economically* and *ecologically* reasonable solution of the problem in those cases where appropriate materials, being "dispersed" in terms of time and location or having been put to multiple uses, occur as a mixture of most varied substances and materials.

BASIC PRINCIPLES: THE WASTE MANAGEMENT PROGRAM OF THE FEDERAL REPUBLIC OF GERMANY

In the framework of the private market economy system, economic processes such as those taking place in the field of secondary materials management are in first place subject to decision of producers, distributors, and consumers. In the light of this principle, governments and public authorities have to concentrate on supporting measures and the provision of guiding principles and information in order to direct the efforts of these groups toward the politically desired objectives.

Having this in mind, the German Federal Government presented at the end of 1975 a comprehensive waste management program. Some two hundred experts from relevant fields of industry and business, science and public administration took part in its preparation. This preparatory work provided a realistic basis for the appraisal of the current situation, and simultaneously led to a closer cooperation between those concerned.

In its program the Federal Government basically rejected the idea of special conditions for secondary materials vis-à-vis other sectors of the economy, as in the form of subsidies. Apart from the fact that any treatment of this kind would involve a variety of unresolved and often unresolvable problems of delimitation on account of the close connection of secondary materials management with other economic activities, the Federal Government feels that such a special treatment would in principle be undesirable in the light of political considerations. Secondary materials management is to constitute an integrated partial domain of the economic system as a whole.

As far as support by the State is concerned, the Federal Government considers that the following priority measures will be necessary: (1) improvement of statistics as well as development of forecasting models; (2) education of producers and consumers; (3) promotion of the basic and further training of specialized manpower; (4) promotion of research and development projects as well as demonstration plants; (5) improvement of conditions for the marketing of secondary materials by eliminating discriminatory policies with regard to recycling products and by establishing quality criteria; (6) financial aid in particular cases (i.e., tax releases); (7) improvement of the organization of secondary materials management; and (8) further development of legislation on waste management (e.g., separate collection of materials, prohibition of certain production techniques).

In addition, the program includes a variety of individual measures and recommendations for as many as ten major types of wastes. It may already be stated that this program has greatly enhanced the political awareness toward the existing problems and has equally provided a strong incentive for many public and private initiatives.

PROBLEMS

Information and Distribution

The collection, evaluation, and provision of relevant information on wastes are essential prerequisites for any systematic planning of recycling.

As regards the establishment and further development of relations between producers and users of such materials, adequate knowledge of the type, quantity, and place of production of the materials and the factors influencing their generation is of utmost importance, together with possibilities for their use and marketing. Information of this kind can be made available, for example, in the form of periodic publications such as waste exchanges, through the medium of circulars and meetings of specialized associations, by advanced training courses, or by the establishment of information systems with inquiry facilities.

Practical solutions regarding the use of secondary materials require much more detailed information than those relating to disposal. Apart from technical data, organizational and economic issues are of equal interest, the latter frequently being sensitive to regional and even local needs. With rising demands on the substance of the information, the difficulties in making the information available increase. Often adequate knowledge on the composition of wastes, for example, does not exist even at the factory level, where these wastes are generated.

Moreover, available information is often retained for reasons of economic competition or for fear of public reaction—for example, in the case of wastes with harmful effects on the environment. Among other efforts, improved training and advice will be needed, as well as more open-mindedness and closer cooperation within the sectors of economy concerned.

The distribution of secondary materials in terms of location and time is a decisive factor in determining the economic efficiency of recycling outside the plant. As a consequence of this distribution, the transport routes in particular have repercussions on costs and on sufficient utilization of capacity of recycling plants. Where the sources of secondary materials are scattered, as in the case of metal surface treatment or consumer wastes, new possibilities of recycling often can only be put into practice if the multiplex interests of individual plants are coordinated so as to achieve what may be called "recycling in a combined system." Increased recycling more and more calls for giving up a philosophy based on the concerns of individual plants.

Collection of secondary materials—the rate of secondary materials in the production process

Even in discussions among experts, the impression is often given that increased recycling of secondary materials primarily depends on the raising of collection and reprocessing rates—that is, the degree to which such materials are separately collected or sorted for onward processing. Not neglecting the importance of this factor, it must be emphasized that this view does not meet the real problems. The most important factor for recycling is the rate of utilization of secondary materials in the production of appropriate products. Recycling is predominantly a problem of demand. The rate of use—for example, the proportion of waste materials related to the total amount of raw materials used—is determined by the manufacturing technology, product design, and price situation. This dependence shows little variability, at least in the short-term range. Recycling of secondary materials is closely linked to the total production. Consequently, for example, changes in the demand for steel mostly entail an analogous response on the scrap market; a decline in the consumption of paper generally results in a corresponding decrease in the demand for waste paper.

Taking into account that product design and product requirements are connected, expanded utilization of secondary materials will decisively depend on the following three conditions: (1) development of new production techniques; (2) development of new products and marketing potentials; and (3) change of requirements on products, frequently in the sense of reducing certain quality requirements. This dependence makes evident that research and development have to be considered as focal tasks in the field of waste management.

Whereas the development of new production techniques or products in many cases is a long-term objective, the reduction of certain quality requirements can be achieved at relatively short notice. Products with and without waste content are frequently offered together on the market and are often designed to be used for the same purpose.

RECYLING DESIGN

Recycling design is concentrating on the following tasks: (1) designing of products with a view to facilitating their recycling after use, and (2) designing and developing new products with the aim of increasing the portion of secondary materials (prior to use) in the products. Both tasks tend to raise—as the determining factor for recycling—the rate of utilization of secondary materials in the production process which is depending on technical and economic requirements.

"Recycling design" is subject to a very different set of factors and questions. For example, new developments in the field of research are playing an important role, as do consumer attitudes. On the basis of a considerable know-how already available, it will be necessary, not only to promote new means of recycling by adequate product design, but also to recall former patterns that are no longer used. In this connection, there is no need to emphasize that there exists a high degree of dependence on the type of material under consideration.

In view of the readjustments which are aimed at in the field of secondary raw materials management, the systematic treatment of the set of questions connected with "recycling design" must be regarded as an important task. Only in this way will it be possible to render things transparent for decision makers, not least in the political sphere. Of particular importance is the demand for binding or recognized assessment and quality criteria for the economic and environmental "usefulness" of recycling. Their quantification is of special necessity if the instrument of cost-benefit analysis is to be usefully applied in this field. Recycling is not an end in itself but must be *economically* and *ecologically* defensible.

In many areas there is still a substantial shortfall in research and information which permit a reliable assessment of the relevant facts. However, they are indispensable prerequisites if standardization committees and other bodies are to consider in the future the interests of secondary materials management in formulating their regulation. In this connection, it is important to note that the purposes for which products are designed should have priority over obvious effects. As it is, secondary raw materials are not always offered in a pure form.

Consumer Behavior

The consumer has an important role to play in regard to the future development of secondary materials management. Among other things, it will depend on his behavior, for example, whether the use of short-lived one-way commodities will continue to increase. Consumer demand will also determine the marketing prospects of a recycled product. Furthermore, the success of the separate collection of residual materials will depend to a considerable extent on the cooperation of individual citizens. This might be accomplished for example, by buying particularly durable products, by giving preference to returnable instead of one-way containers, or by using certain paper products with a higher content of waste paper. In many cases a price benefit is linked to such behavior.

Secondary raw materials and products manufactured from such materials still have the reputation of inferiority among a large part of the population. Here a basic change of thinking must be encouraged. At present, products that can be manufactured from secondary materials often do not meet existing standards or use-specifications, although the qualities of such products may well be sufficient for the intended purpose. The elimination of prejudice and impediments to recycling should become an important task for consumer associations and public authorities. As practiced in the Federal Republic of Germany, government can set a good example in this regard through its own policy of awarding contracts.

POLITICAL ASPECTS

Developments and needs in the field of secondary materials are not only subject to purely technical aspects. On the contrary, a strong influence on the part of political parameters is making itself felt to a decisive extent.

Economic growth, with the ensuing increase in production and consumption, will remain an indispensable political element in the near future. Recent experience with economic recession has made this quite obvious. The demand for conservation of resources must be related to this fact. Employment policies, international trade relations and agreements, as well as technical and economic adjustment processes—to mention only a few factors—make it politically difficult to enforce any radical short-term changes in production and consumption structures as would be required by a "consistent" secondary materials policy. The compromise between short-term economic policy and long-term safeguarding of resources is not yet defined as clearly as is frequently supposed and implied in statements on public policy.

A greater share of services in economic growth as well as technological progress might at least temporarily spare the politician the trouble of having serious problems with raw materials supply in his country. The resultant time for reflection, however, will not relieve him from the duty to take early action to economize in the consumption of raw materials. What he fails to do today will cost him dearly tomorrow.

CHAPTER 3

Scarcity of Basic Materials and Fuels: Assessment and Implications

M. H. Govett and G. J. S. Govett

The title of this chapter—with its emphasis on scarcity—was no doubt chosen by the organizers of this symposium to express a certain point of view about resource supply and demand. The word *scarcity* implies a shortage in terms of physical supply relative to demand. Politicians and economists are generally most concerned with demand; scientists (especially geologists) are concerned with supply. Unfortunately, in much of the debate about the adequacy of world mineral supplies to meet projected demand, the views of the economists and the politicians have dominated; we hope to redress the imbalance somewhat in this chapter.

This chapter deals exclusively with primary mineral supplies. To the geologist the supply of minerals was essentially fixed by geological processes millions of years ago (with the exception of the manganese-oxide nodules on the sea floor which may provide an important future source of minerals). There are fairly reliable data on the chemical composition of the earth's crust and on the abundance of elements that occur as economically important minerals. These data do not, however, tell us very much about the present or the future *availability* of the materials man is using up at an ever-increasing rate, since only a small portion of the total amount of an element in the earth's crust is economically mineable under given technological conditions at a given time.

Scarcity is relative—relative to future demand, and, most importantly, relative to such factors as exploration success, mining techniques, processing technology, and world mineral prices. The most serious problem in assessing future resource adequacy is in estimating possible mineral supplies; this chapter will, therefore, concentrate on a consideration of the availability of primary supplies of minerals to meet whatever the future demand may be. The first section will deal briefly with demand forecasts; the second section will discuss the geological and technological constraints of mineral supply in some detail; the third section will assess the adequacy of mineral supplies within the geological and technical constraints; and a final section will deal briefly with the political realities of assuring the world adequate mineral supplies.

ECONOMIC REALITIES

The Rate of Growth of World Mineral Demand

World population, on present projections, will probably exceed six billion by the year 2000—barring a global catastrophe or the remote possibility that mankind will come to its senses and take the drastic steps necessary to limit the birth rate. At the present rate of growth of world demand, the amount of metal consumed in the next thirty years could equal the total amount consumed in recorded history (Lovering, 1969).

If per capita world mineral consumption did not increase at all in the next thirty years—a most unlikely assumption—population growth alone would result in a doubling of current world mineral consumption by the year 2000. At a realistic rate of increase in world mineral consumption—4 percent annually—production would have to double in eighteen years and increase fourfold in thirty-six years; an exponential increase of this magnitude is very likely unless drastic steps are taken (Govett and Govett, in press; Lovering, 1969). The most extreme models show that if United States consumption remained at 1970 levels, while the less developed countries increased their per capita consumption to current United States levels in the next three decades, annual world mineral production by the year 2000 would have to increase thirty times (see Govett and Govett, 1972).

Debate about exponential growth, forecasting techniques, and the reliability of resource estimates has filled many volumes; it is, in our view, largely futile (Govett and Govett, 1976a). Future demand will depend on such a wide range of social, political, and economic factors—the rate of economic growth in the developing countries, the ability of mineral producers to form cartels or otherwise restrict production, the rate of worldwide inflation and the resulting dislocations, the economic prosperity of the industrialized countries, development in the communist countries—that precise forecasts in the near future are difficult and forecasts beyond the year 2000 are little more than exercises in computer programming.

Nevertheless, demand projections are widely used as a framework for discussion (e.g., Landsberg, 1964; U.S. Bureau of Mines, 1970; Meadows et al., 1972; Malenbaum et al., 1973; U.S. National Commission on Materials Policy, 1973). Table 3–1 summarizes one of

TABLE 3–1

GROWTH RATE (PERCENT PER YEAR) OF WORLD PRIMARY DEMAND FOR MINERALS TO THE YEAR 2000—HIGH AND LOW FORECASTS BY THE U.S. BUREAU OF MINES (1970)

	High forecast (%)	Low forecast (%)
World		
Energy	5.2	3.3
Ferrous metals	3.4	2.3
Nonferrous metals	7.0	4.6
Nonmetallic minerals	5.1	3.8
All minerals	5.5	3.6
United States		
Energy	5.2	2.7
Ferrous metals	3.5	2.4
Nonferrous metals	7.3	5.1
Nonmetallic minerals	4.9	3.5
All minerals	5.5	3.4
Rest of the World		
Energy	5.3	3.6
Ferrous metals	3.3	2.2
Nonferrous metals	6.9	4.5
Nonmetallic minerals	5.1	3.8
All minerals	5.5	3.7

SOURCE: United States Bureau of Mines.

the most widely quoted forecasts, that of the U.S. Bureau of Mines (1970), which is based on contingency (technological) forecasts for 88 minerals. The method used involved "predicting and simulating alternative futures based on contingencies assumed for technological, economic, social, environmental, and other relevant influences" (p. 9).

The implication of the high projections in Table 3–1 is that world mineral demand will double in less than fourteen years. World demand for nonferrous metals (which make up one-sixth of the total value of world mineral production) could easily double in ten years; hence the concern that we will voice in the next section about the urgent need to develop new exploration and extraction and processing technology. The lower rate of growth forecast for the ferrous metals, while it may be realistic for the United States due to anticipated increases in efficiency in the iron and steel industry and the substitution of other materials, may not be realistic for the developing and the communist countries. The worldwide increase in per capita steel consumption in the period 1957–1967 was 44 percent, which was four times the increase in the United States during the period; in Japan there was a 270 percent increase during the same ten years (Cottrell, 1974). The energy demand projections for countries other than the United States may also be too low, as will be discussed below.

Geographic Distribution of World Mineral Consumption

In the next thirty years most countries are expected to have higher rates of growth in mineral consumption than the United States. By the year 2000 the United States may account for only one-quarter of total world demand, a sharp decrease from its share in the 1950s. Figure 3–1 illustrates the trend for a number of important minerals, and Table 3–2 illustrates the expected changes in the pattern of world consumption. Petroleum and copper (necessary for energy and electrical transmission) and phosphorous (essential for agriculture) show the highest rates of increase in countries other than the United States. In contrast, demand for metals such as tungsten and vanadium (used in high-technology industry) is expected to increase relatively more in the United States. The high ratio of demand for uranium in both the United States and the rest of the world reflects the opinion that nuclear power will become a major energy source by the year 2000,

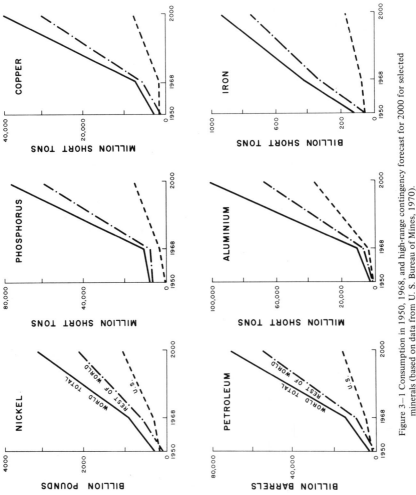

Figure 3–1 Consumption in 1950, 1968, and high-range contingency forecast for 2000 for selected minerals (based on data from U. S. Bureau of Mines, 1970).

TABLE 3–2

RATIO OF MINERAL DEMAND IN 1968 TO THE HIGH CONTINGENCY FORECAST
MINERAL DEMAND IN 2000 BASED ON PROJECTIONS OF
THE U.S. BUREAU OF MINES (1970)

Mineral	United States	Rest of the World
Uranium	29.1	24.8
Aluminium	9.5	10.6
Vanadium	6.5	3.6
Tungsten	5.7	2.4
Petroleum	3.3	5.6
Lead	3.1	2.1
Zinc	2.8	2.8
Phosphorus	2.8	7.8
Iron ore	2.1	2.2
Tin	1.7	2.1
Copper	1.3	6.1

SOURCE: Adapted from Govett and Govett, in press.

although it now accounts for less than 2 percent of total world energy (United Nations, 1973).

Recent evidence indicates that in spite of the "energy crisis" of 1973, energy demand in the developing countries is continuing to grow at rates considerably in excess of 5 percent. While most of the less developed countries may not reach Japan's recent rates of growth (between 1961 and 1971, Japan's per capita energy consumption increased by 148 percent), the potential for increase in per capita consumption is enormous in a large number of countries. Between 1961 and 1971, per capita energy consumption grew by more than 100 percent in a number of the larger developing countries including Iran, Sudan, Ghana, and Thailand; in Chile, Brazil, the Philippines, and Nigeria it grew by more than 50 percent (United Nations, 1973, 1974). In 1971 the United States consumed 11,241 million metric tons coal equivalent per capita; among the main developing countries only Iran, Chile, Mexico, and Venezuela consumed more than 1,000 metric tons per capita (in spite of Japan's phenomenal growth rate, in 1971 it consumed only 3,267 million metric tons) (United Nations, 1973). Darmstadter (1972) forecast an annual rate of growth over the next three decades of 7.3 percent in Latin America,

7.2 percent in noncommunist Asia, and 8.8 percent in communist
Asia. These rates are considerably in excess of the U.S. Bureau of
Mines (1970) forecasts, and if realistic, are indeed alarming.

Geographic Distribution of World Mineral Supplies

Five developed countries—the United States, the Soviet Union,
Canada, Australia, and South Africa—produce the bulk of the world's
economically important minerals with the exception of cobalt, tin,
tungsten, and bauxite.* These five countries produce more than 50
percent of the molybdenum, vanadium, titanium, nickel, phosphate,
manganese, iron ore, potash, lead, zinc, chromium, silver, and
uranium, and more than 40 percent of the copper and petroleum.
They currently hold more than one-half of the world's reserves of
these minerals with the exception of copper, nickel, and phosphate
(see M. H. Govett, 1975, 1976). The historical reasons for this
pattern of production and reserve-holding are not hard to find: all
these countries have had major exploration programs in the past few
decades, all are large and geologically favorable areas, and all
(except South Africa) are geographically diverse.

In the next few decades these countries will probably continue to
be the main suppliers of most conventional primary metals and fuels.
Even if there are large expenditures on exploration and development
in Latin America, Asia, and Africa—the relatively less well-explored
parts of the world—the possibilities of important discoveries in new,
presently unknown districts are limited. According to the U.S. Geological Survey resource appraisals (Brobst and Pratt, 1973), future
discoveries of conventional types and grades of deposits of the industrially important minerals in new, unknown districts will probably be
limited to copper, chromium, nickel, phosphate, and titanium. The
future of world mineral production will depend to a very large extent
on continued and intensified exploration in presently known districts
and, as we shall see, on the development of techniques to exploit
currently nonconventional or very low-grade sources of minerals.

-----

* Twenty minerals make up more than 90 percent of total world mineral
production: tin, tungsten, nickel, aluminium, copper, phosphate, titanium, lead,
iron, silver, zinc, manganese, potash, molybdenum, uranium, vanadium, the
platinum group of metals, and petroleum.

GEOLOGICAL AND TECHNICAL CONSTRAINTS
Abundance and Availability

Statements such as that by Boyd (1973) to the effect that the world's total resources are "large enough to stagger the imagination" and the suggestion by Brown (1954) and others that mankind could, if necessary, glean minerals from the leanest ores and even mine whole rock for its constituents, have led a number of writers to take a very optimistic view of the "potential" wealth of minerals in the world (see Govett and Govett, 1974). The abundance of elements in the earth's crust is frequently cited as proof that, in the long run, there can be no resource shortage. While conceptually it would be possible to mine whole rock—100 tons of average igneous rock contains 8 tons of aluminum, 5 tons of iron, 1,200 pounds of titanium, 70 pounds of chromium, 30 pounds of vanadium, 20 pounds of copper, and 4 pounds of lead—the technical problems, the enormous quantities of energy required, and the environmental consequences of treating billions of tons of rock argue against it as a practical possibility. Thus, while conceptually the earth's resources are enormous, a geographic concentration of elements in the earth's crust which make it economic to mine the ore is an abnormal and rare geological event; economically mineable supplies of minerals are limited by the form in which they occur, by the places where they are concentrated, and by man's ability to find them, mine them, and process them.

The earth's crust—which makes up less than 0.4 percent of the total mass of the earth—is the source of all the metals, nonmetallic minerals, and fuels used by man; the continental crust, which makes up only 0.29 percent of the earth's mass, is the primary source of minerals (Vokes, 1976). Only the upper 3.5 km of the continental crust are accessible (although some oil wells reach greater depths); thus, only the outer one-tenth of the crust is of concern in a discussion of mineral resources (Dunham, 1974).

Fig. 3–2 illustrates the gross chemical composition of the continental crust; the one percent at the top of the diagram represents the trace elements that are industrially important. Fig. 3–3 classifies some of the most important elements into categories of relative abundance. Fig. 3–4 shows the relationship between average crustal abundance of the elements and the minimum concentration that can be economically mined today for eleven minerals; in the case of the more abundant elements—iron and aluminium—the minimum concentration needed

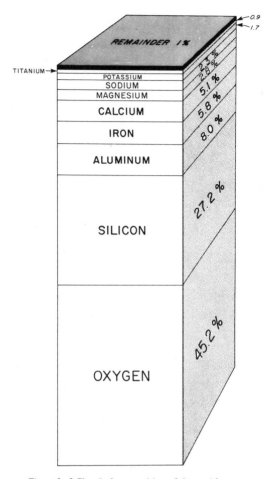

Figure 3–2 Chemical composition of the earth's crust.

is small; for elements such as chromium it is as high as 3,000 and for tin it is 5,000.

To be "available" to man, an element must not only be concentrated above its crustal abundance, it must also occur in a chemical combination that is amenable to extraction and separation from other unwanted (gangue) minerals. For example, aluminium, although very abundant, is unfortunately found primarily in minerals such as feldspars and in clay minerals from which it is very difficult to extract economically; most of the aluminium produced today comes from bauxite—from which it can be easily extracted.

While the availability of elements is, therefore, not necessarily

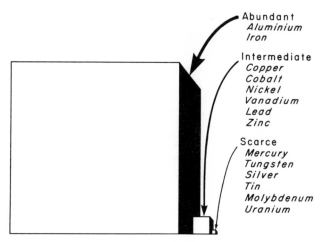

Figure 3–3 Schematic illustration of relative crustal abundance of some industrially important elements.

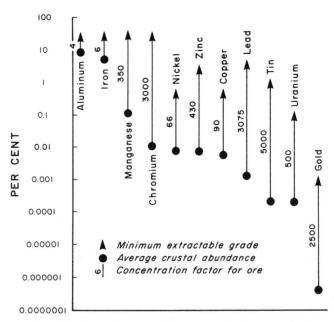

Figure 3–4 Average abundance in the earth's crust and minimum concentration that can be mined of some industrially important minerals (Reproduced from G. J. S . Govett, in press; originally published in *Journal of Royal Australian Chemical Institute*).

proportional to their abundance, recent studies (McKelvey, 1960; Sekine, 1963; Ovchinnikov, 1971; Govett and Govett, 1972, 1976; Erickson, 1973) have shown a fairly close linear relationship between crustal abundance of the elements and supplies of a number of minerals. In Fig. 3–5, world reserves are plotted against abundance in the continental crust; the correlation for all except three of the metals (aluminium, cobalt, and vanadium) is close, and the spread is remarkably narrow (expressed by $R = 6.8A \times 10^5$ to $A \times 10^7$, where R = reserves in tons and A = abundance in the continental crust in parts per million). The closeness of the correlation suggests that the inclusion of undiscovered deposits would bring total resources of the metals considered to $R = A \times 10^7$. In Fig. 3–6, the correlation between production and abundance has about the same spread. Cobalt, aluminium, and especially vanadium again fall outside the main correlation belt and are underproduced relative to their abundance; this could explain why reserves of these three metals in Fig. 3–5 also fall below the line. The fundamental reason for this discrepancy lies in the high crustal abundance of aluminium, largely in a form that is not presently recoverable, and the fact that cobalt and vanadium are produced largely as by-products of other metals. Lead, copper, tin,

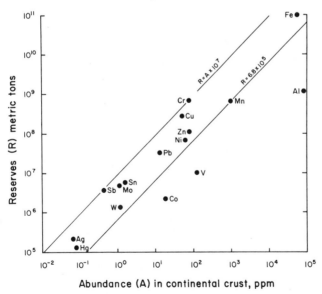

Figure 3–5 Relation between world reserves and abundance of elements in the continental crust for 16 common elements (reproduced with permission from Govett and Govett, 1976b).

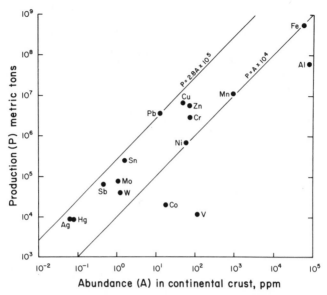

Figure 3–6 Relation between world annual production and element abundance in the continental crust for 16 common metals (reproduced with permission from Govett and Govett, 1976b).

antimony, silver, and mercury are being produced at the upper limit of the abundance relation.

These correlations do not indicate the upper limit of resources; they do, however, indicate that considerable additional supplies of metals in the lower range of the relation should be found and exploited. Also, those elements that fall below the limits of the linear relationship could be exploited in greater amounts if new extraction and processing techniques were developed.

Aside from the concentration of an element and the form in which it occurs, the *geographic* concentration of an element—and the discovery of the districts in which it is concentrated—is of the utmost importance in determining availability. Some regions are abundantly supplied with ores—nickel in Canada and Australia, tin in Southeast Asia, antimony and tungsten in China, iron and gold in the world's ancient shield areas. Identification and location of metallogenic provinces—as the districts where a given element is concentrated are commonly known—have become the subject of intensive study. More than one-half of the "first-order" copper mines discovered in the past thirty years in the United States have occurred within a well-defined metallogenic subprovince (Noble, 1974); Flawn (1966) has justifiably described tin as an "Asiatic metal." Information on metal-logenic provinces for a large number of elements was used in the U.S. Geological Survey resource appraisals (Brobst and Pratt, 1973).

While theoretically the seas and oceans seem to provide vast mineral resources, in terms of technology in the foreseeable future the abundance of the elements in the oceans is deceptive. There are 1.4×10^9 cu km of seawater; each cubic kilometer holds some 40 million tons of dissolved solids, and some seventy-seven elements have been identified; however, only twelve constituents are present in concentrations greater than one part per million (Wang and McKelvey, 1976). The availability of these (and other elements) is severely limited; only four elements are currently economically recoverable in any quantity—sodium and chlorine (in the form of salt), bromine, and magnesium. Metalliferous muds and brines offer a potentially better source of minerals, but exploitation of the heavy metals that are highly concentrated (such as iron, manganese, zinc, lead, copper, gold, and silver) will depend on the development of a technology to handle corrosive materials at great depths and at considerable distances from shore.

The main exploitable resources of the deep ocean basins are the manganese-oxide nodules that contain large concentrations of manganese, iron, nickel, copper, and cobalt. Fleming (1973) cites estimates of 2.4×10^9 tons of copper and cobalt, 3.6×10^9 tons of nickel, and 96×10^9 tons of manganese in the nodules. Wang and McKelvey (1976) have estimated that by 1980 one mining operation alone could supply 2.0 percent of the world demand for manganese, 7.9 percent of the cobalt, 1.3 percent of the nickel, and 0.13 percent of the copper. Late in 1976 it was reported that two United States companies have each spent between $25 and $35 million on research and development programs off the coast of Georgia and on the floor of the Pacific Ocean and are preparing to enter preproduction development (*CIM Reporter,* 1976).

Prospects for mining the energy fuels from the continental shelves, slopes, rises, and small ocean basins are good. Currently 18 percent of world gas and oil production is from off-shore areas, and this percentage is expected to increase (Wang and McKelvey, 1976). On the other hand, extraction of nonfuel minerals, which now account for only about 2 percent of total world production, will probably not be a significant factor in world mineral supplies for some time to come because of extraction and processing costs.

Fossil fuels presently account for more than 95 percent of total world energy consumption; opinions on their adequacy to meet future demand are as diverse as the opinions on the potential of nuclear energy and the exotic sources of energy (solar, geothermal, tidal, wind). Data on the abundance of coal indicate that there are enormous supplies. However, there is no consensus on the abundance of petroleum and natural gas in the earth's crust. As McCulloh (1973) has said: "Who can say what the undiscovered resources of petroleum and natural gas are of the world? . . . Our techniques for identifying hydrocarbon traps, or even those areas that especially favor hydrocarbon accumulation, are very imperfect" (pp. 487–89). Fisher (1975) has optimistically concluded that fossil fuels will continue to be available in adequate amounts in the future, which is in direct contrast with the views of Hubbert (1969, 1973), who believes that the age of fossil fuels is nearly over, and that world petroleum production will have peaked by 1990 or 2000.

Whatever actual supplies of fossil fuels may be, the factors that influence the availability of the metals will also be operative in the case of the energy fuels—especially extraction and processing technology. The tar sands and the oil shales, potentially a major source of petroleum (see Thomas, 1976), can only be exploited if a cheap method of extraction is developed; world coal resources can only be recovered if an environmentally acceptable means can be found to mine and use the coal.

Mineral Exploration and Development

It is only after the discovery of a mineral concentration that we can speak of a mineral deposit—and a mineral deposit may not prove to be economically mineable. "It is difficult to convey to someone who is not a geologist the magnitude of the problem of finding a mineral deposit, even in a favourable region. To find near-surface deposits beneath the cover of glacial debris and the endless coniferous forests of Canada or beneath twenty metres of lateritic soil in tropical Africa is an awe-inspiring task. To expect to be able to find a deposit in such circumstances, and especially to find one located hundreds of metres below bedrock surfaces, implies an extraordinary faith in exploration methods" (Govett and Govett, 1976a, p. 4).

Future exploration in the well-prospected areas of the world will be especially difficult. Fig. 3–7 illustrates (for Canada) the decreasing probability of finding a new mine compared with the cost of finding it over the past twenty years; the same trend is apparent in the United States. There seems little likelihood of the situation improving since mineral deposits with surface expressions in the well-prospected parts of the world are becoming fewer; in much of the world ever-deeper deposits will have to be found at increasing cost. The need to develop new techniques—geochemical and geophysical—to detect "blind" and deeply buried deposits is urgent, especially since a lead

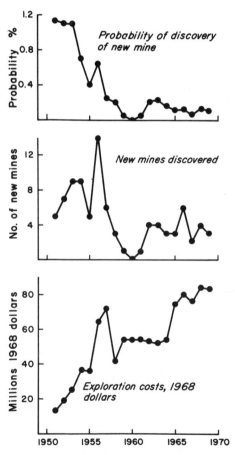

Figure 3–7 Probability of discovery of new mines, new mines discovered, and exploration costs in Canada (reproduced with permission from G. J. S. Govett, 1976).

time of about ten years between the decision to explore and the actual opening of a mine (assuming an exploration success) is common; lead times for research into new techniques can be much longer (see G. J. S. Govett, 1976).

Once a deposit has been discovered, considerable investigation is required to determine whether the element or elements of interest can be economically mined. A deposit only becomes an orebody if the grade is sufficiently high relative to the prevailing price of the ore and there are sufficient reserves to warrant mine development work. Deposits with 13 percent copper were ores in 1700; in 1900 copper grading 5 to 2.5 percent was mined; a few years ago ores with less than 0.4 percent copper were mineable, but this is no longer true at today's copper prices due the recent escalation of capital and energy costs (J. A. Coppe, personal communication).

There is a great deal of debate on the magnitude by which a decrease in mineable grade will increase the supply of a mineral. For many minerals the relationship between a change in grade and a change in reserves is not arithmetic; a decrease of one-half in mineable grade may result in an increase in reserves by a factor much greater than two (see Lasky, 1950; Lovering, 1969; Singer et al., 1975). However, it can not be concluded that reserves of *all* minerals will increase geometrically with a decrease in grade; it depends upon the particular mineral concerned. Furthermore, the lower the grade of the ore the higher the extraction and processing costs may be— particularly energy costs per kilo of metal recovered. Indeed, the energy requirements to extract metal from ore show a catastrophic exponential increase as ore grade decreases (Roberts, 1974; Page and Creasy, 1975). For example, in the case of copper, a reduction of ore grade from 2.0 to 1.0 percent requires only about a 30 percent increase in energy required to extract the copper; a decrease from the current acceptable 0.5 percent to 0.25 percent copper would require an increase in energy of 100 to 200 percent (Chapman, 1974).

ADEQUACY OF WORLD MINERAL SUPPLIES IN THE FUTURE

Reserves and Resources

The concept of reserves—which has been avoided as much as possible up to this point—has led to a great deal of confusion and misunderstanding among writers on the subject of mineral supplies. Figures for reserves of a mine are estimated by mining companies for their own use; development work each year is generally aimed at proving adequate ore to replace that extracted during the year so that a fairly constant reserve—normally fifteen to twenty years at current mining rates—is maintained (see McAllister, 1976). Unfortunately, until recently a compilation of individual mining company reserves estimates (of varying degrees of reliability) has been the main source of information available to national and international authorities to use as a basis of supply calculations.

On a regional, national, or international basis reserves are defined as "known deposits from which minerals can be extracted profitably under present economic conditions and with existing technology" (Govett and Govett, 1976b, p. 16; see also Blondel and Lasky, 1956; McKelvey, 1972; Brobst and Pratt, 1973). As such, they are never static, changing as price, technology, exploration and development work take place. For example, between 1947 and 1974, estimates of world chrome reserves increased sevenfold, estimates of iron ore reserves increased tenfold, and tin reserves actually decreased (M. H. Govett, 1975). A doubling of the price of copper would make it possible to quadruple output from existing mines (Cottrell, 1974), and uranium reserves could increase by several orders of magnitude with price increases adequate to allow mining and extraction of low-grade or difficult deposits (Fig. 3–8).

Resources, on the other hand, are the total amount of an element, both known and unknown, down to some defined grade that is higher than crustal abundance but lower than the currently mineable grade. Therefore, resources are fixed, although they cannot be quantified. Fig. 3–9 schematically illustrates the relationship between reserves and resources, emphasizing the importance of changes in grade, technology, and exploration success.

Until the publication of the U.S. Geological Survey resource appraisals (Brobst and Pratt, 1973) there were no reliable internationally comparable data for known resources of industrially important minerals. Thus, in a recent paper (Govett and Govett, 1972) we presented calculations of the years of supply remaining of a number of important minerals given current rates of growth of demand, assuming that estimated reserves were increased five times (Meadows et al., 1972, made similar calculations). These data are shown in summary in Table 3–3 and should be regarded as only indicating or-

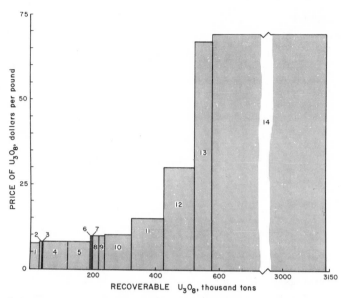

Figure 3–8 Availability of uranium at different price levels (from McAllister, 1976; redrawn with permission from C. L. Bieniewski,F. H. Persse, and E. F. Brauch, 1971, Availability of uranium at various prices from resources in the United States. U. S. Bureau of Mines Information Circular 8501, 92 pp.). 1 = copper leach solutions; 2 = uranium-vanadium ore; 3 = uraniferous lignite ore; 4 = other uranium ore mineable by open pit; 5 = other uranium ore mineable by underground methods; 6 = uranium-vanadium deposits; 7 = uraniferous lignite deposits; 8 = other uranium deposits mineable by open pit; 9 = other uranium deposits mineable by underground methods; 10 = wet-process phosphoric acid; 11 and 12 = high-cost conventional deposits; 13 = Florida phosphate rock leached zone; 14 = Chattanooga shale.

ders of magnitude. The reason for making the calculations (and for including them here) was to show that even with a fivefold increase in reserves, the supply of a number of the minerals would not increase by very much relative to the size of the demand projections.

Resource Estimates

The postulated fivefold increase in reserves in Table 3–3 can now be viewed in the light of the U.S. Geological Survey's resource appraisals. These present estimates of various categories of resources, based on assessing "geologic availability," which "requires basic knowledge of the geology, mineralogy, and geochemistry of that material, the geologic environments in which it occurs, and its concentration in those environments. The technology of exploration, mining, beneficiation, recovery, and use is founded upon this information" (Brobst and Pratt, 1973, pp. 5–6).

The three categories of resource estimates are "identified," "hypo-

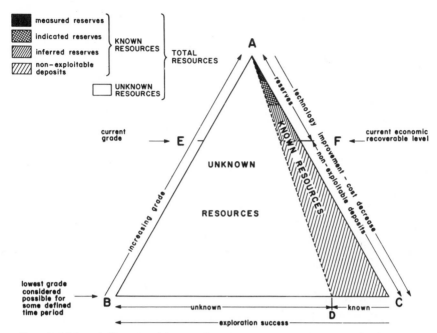

Figure 3–9 Schematic illustration of dynamic relation between reserves and resources (after Govett and Govett, 1974; redrawn with permission of *Resources Policy*, vol. 1, p. 53.).

TABLE 3–3

CALCULATED YEARS SUPPLY REMAINING OF SOME METALS BASED ON 1968–1970 RESERVES AND DEMAND PROJECTIONS TO THE YEAR 2000

	Years Supply			
	1968–1970 Reserves		1968–1970 Reserves × 5	
Metal	High Demand	Low Demand	High Demand	Low Demand
Tin	16	26	55	121
Zinc	16	20	51	66
Copper	21	25	56	70
Lead	21	28	66	96
Tungsten	24	30	73	84
Molybdenum	30	37	78	96
Titanium	31	57	81	142
Nickel	54	74	124	171

SOURCE: Adapted from Govett and Govett, 1972.

thetical," and "speculative"—defined respectively as "specific bodies of mineral-bearing rocks whose existence and location are known"; "undiscovered resources that we may still reasonably expect to find in *known districts*"; and "undiscovered resources that may exist elsewhere" (pp. 3–4). For a number of minerals (the volume includes seventy mineral groups) the ratio of reserves to identified resources is unexpectedly small; among fifteen industrially important minerals, only in the case of lead, zinc, and petroleum is it greater than five (see Govett and Govett, 1976b). If the estimates of hypothetical and speculative resources are added to identified resources, the ratios are relatively high, particularly for aluminium, iron, chromium, and vanadium; on the other hand, tht ratio of hypothetical to speculative resources is relatively low, reflecting the belief that, in many cases, regions that have a significant discovery potential are already largely known. It is only when nonconventional sources are included (as in the case of metals from the sea-floor nodules) that the speculative resource estimates are very high.

On Fig. 3–10 (a, b), estimates of reserves and identified resources are compared with the U.S. Bureau of Mines cumulative high-range demand forecasts for the period 1968–2000 for a number of minerals. Identified resources were used because the data are more complete and reliable as an indicator of supply in the next three decades than the other resource estimates. Data for aluminium, vanadium, iron, nickel, manganese, cobalt, coal, and phosphate are not plotted since both reserves and resources are estimated to be very large, although these estimates are based on optimistic assumptions about technical progress in extraction and processing of ores and on energy costs remaining relatively low. For example, it is expected that the large lateritic nickel deposits in Australia, Indonesia, and Colombia will be exploited and that the sea-floor nodules will provide an increasing source of nickel; this latter assumption now seems reasonable (see *CIM Reporter,* 1976).

As would be expected, the reserve data in Fig. 3–10 (a, b) show shortages of the same metals as Table 3–3—tin, zinc, copper, lead, tungsten, and molybdenum—and in addition indicate shortages of petroleum, mercury, and silver (which were not included in the 1972 study). When the cumulative demand forecasts are compared with identified resources, only three of the minerals offer serious problems —copper, tin, and uranium.

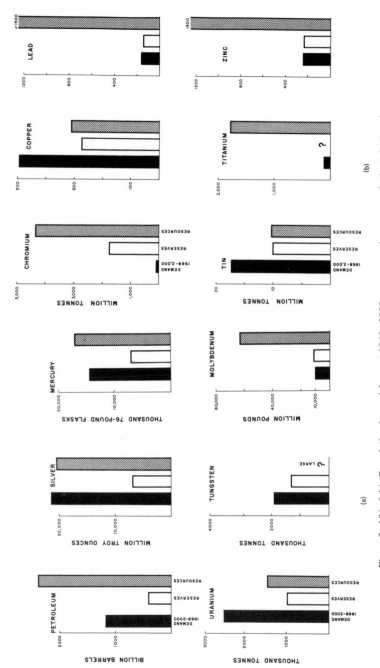

Figure 3–10(a & b). Cumulative demand forecast 1968–2000, reserves, and resources of selected minerals (data from U. S. Bureau of Mines, 1970; Brobst and Pratt, 1973; and Govett and Govett, 1976b).

In the case of copper, the resource estimates seem conservative; Cox et al. (1973) have not included the copper in the ocean sediments and sea-floor nodules and have excluded some very low-grade deposits. A recent study by the Commodities Research Unit (see *Northern Miner,* 1976), predicts a below-trend growth in consumption until 1985, which would ease the pressure on reserves. On the other hand, the exploration slowdown for base metals and the effect of low world prices and environmental protection measures—plus the increasing costs per kilo mined due to rising energy costs—could reinforce the seriousness of the long-run situation, especially since it is calculated that a price of over one dollar a pound would be necessary for the development of new low-grade deposits.

Although tin resources are clearly inadequate, this is not viewed as a serious problem. Substitutes (aluminium, plastics, tin-free steel) are available, secondary materials can provide a large source of the metals, and the current loss of tin during processing could be reduced.

The low uranium resource estimate is based on the opinion of Finch et al. (1973) that the technical problems of extraction of uranium from known deposits are either unsolved or costly, that a great deal of material can only be recovered as a by-product, and that the environmental problems of recovery are severe. Davies (1972) stated that the discovery rate in the 1980s would have to increase threefold to meet demand; Bowie (1976) is pessimistic about meeting predicted demand to 1990; Derry (1974) has voiced grave concern about the long lead-times in uranium exploration. *World Mining* (1976) summed up the situation as follows: "experts around the world took turns at analyzing the supply/demand position and were practically unanimous in forecasting shortfalls in supply in the United States by 1978 and in the balance of the Western World by 1981" (p. 86).

The U.S. Geological Survey estimates for the other minerals in Fig. 3–10 (a, b) indicate adequate supplies based on new sources of both low-grade and high-grade ore. Enormous submarginal resources of lead have been recognized in the sea-floor nodules; there are still high-grade zinc deposits to be discovered, and substantial subeconomic zinc deposits are known in Europe and North America. Tungsten resources in China and Southeast Asia are considered to be large. The high estimates of molybdenum resources may be too optimistic unless the problems of strip mining can be overcome.

The results of all the resource appraisals assume that deposits that are not now recoverable will become economically workable in the future. As Brobst and Pratt (1973) have pointed out: "the resource estimates . . . are indeed estimates, not measurements; and they present an optimistic outlook for many commodities *only in the context that they represent a potential, not a reality*" (p. 2, authors' italics). Whether the potential will become a reality depends on *current* exploration and research and development, and on society's willingness and ability to pay the increasingly high costs—both monetary and environmental—that will be a consequence of mining ever lower grade and nonconventional deposits.

Energy as a Special Case

Fig. 3–10 (a, b) shows a relatively promising situation for petroleum, although there is no real concensus on the adequacy of petroleum supplies for the future. The U.S. Bureau of Mines (1970) cumulative world demand high forecast for 1968–2000 was 1.2×10^{12} barrels; estimates of remaining years of supply of petroleum range from a low of 17 years to a high of 100 years, and remaining supplies of conventional petroleum have been estimated at a low of 1.8×10^{12} barrels to as high as 2.5×10^{12} barrels—according to Hubbert (1973), 2.0×10^{12} barrels is an acceptable estimate.

Coal resources (not included in Fig. 3–10 (a, b)) are probably sufficient for centuries—if the technical problems of processing and extraction can be solved. Identified resources of coal are estimated at 8.6×10^{12} tons; hypothetical resources add another 6.6×10^{12} tons, and there are an additional 15.3×10^{12} tons of speculative resources (Averitt, 1973). However, outside of the Southern Hemisphere and Eastern Europe, coal currently supplies only about one-quarter of world energy demand, and its use has been declining for the last few decades.

Nuclear power now accounts for approximately 2 percent of total world energy produced; its future, which until recently seemed bright, now seems to be in doubt, and the International Atomic Energy Agency projections that nuclear energy would provide 6 percent of the world's energy by 1980 and 20 percent by 2000 seem too optimistic (Darmstadter, 1972, 1974). Reactors are extremely costly to build, and the waste disposal problems are serious; in the short-term the supply of uranium, as noted above, could be a limiting factor.

Those who argue that the coming era of cheap nuclear power based on the breeder reactor will solve any problem of resource inadequacy forget that while the cost of fuel and the demand on uranium stocks will be low with the breeder reactor, the capital investment required for power plants, power transmission, waste disposal, and other environmental protection measures will be high. Observers like Cottrell (1974) have pointed out that the high cost of energy—including nuclear energy—may ultimately prove to be the one factor that can reduce the present high rate of growth of world energy consumption.

POLITICAL REALITIES

While the use of global figures is justified to appraise world resource adequacy, the problem of "shortage" is primarily viewed as a national problem. In the United States the National Commission on Materials Policy (1973) concluded that the United States will have a serious supply problem for those minerals that are currently imported if the political climate worsens. The United States currently imports more than 90 percent of its chromium, cobalt, manganese, nickel, platinum metals, and tin and more than one-half of another dozen important minerals including aluminium, titanium, zinc, and mercury. When cumulative demand in the United States forecast to the year 2000 is compared with United States "identified resources," there are serious problems for chromium and mercury, and possible problems for cobalt, natural gas, platinum metals, silver, nickel, copper, and tungsten. In Canada a recent study showed that among the main metals there is a forecast shortfall in both domestic and export supplies of copper, zinc, lead, molybdenum, and uranium (Martin et al., 1976). Britain hopefully will be able to meet her energy needs from North Sea oil and gas, as will Norway, but the rest of Western Europe will remain largely dependent on Middle East oil imports. Uranium exploration is currently a matter of high priority in Canada and the United States, but for the other metals and energy fuels there seems to be little concerted action to increase exploration or to develop new technologies for extraction and processing.

In two of the most important mineral-producing countries—Canada and Australia—the trend in exploration has been down (Fig. 3–11). Exploration costs are mounting; governments are unwilling to spend

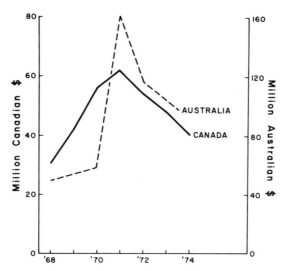

Figure 3–11 Total mineral exploration expenditures 1968–1974
in Canada and Australia (after Derry, 1974).

money on research and development; investment in the mining industry is deterred in a number of Western countries by negative government fiscal measures; the less developed countries are unwilling
to allow foreign investment in mining and, at the same time, lack the
domestic means to undertake the technically complicated production
and marketing arrangements necessary in the mining industry.

Since the "energy crisis" of 1973 many nations of the world have
become aware of their vulnerability to cartels or other forms of mineral
production restriction. While the danger of OPEC-type action for
most minerals is fortunately limited—both by the inability of the
producers to get together and stay together and by the availability of
substitutes or secondary sources for minerals such as copper and
aluminium (the prime candidates today for cartels)—there is nevertheless a very real danger that the Western countries may have to
face short-term economic dislocations. Potentially more serious is the
possibility that the developing countries of Asia and Africa—affected
by worldwide inflation and rising energy costs—may no longer be
willing to subsist at their present levels of poverty. The evidence is
mounting that there may have to be an urgent reappraisal of the
industrialized countries' attitudes toward their use of mineral resources.

Of even more immediate concern is the inability of the developed and developing countries to agree on the jurisdiction over the ocean's resources. The Fifth Law of the Sea Conference ended in September 1976 without agreement, in spite of the pressing need to find a formula for exploiting the sea-floor nodules. The ownership of, and the benefits from, the ocean's resources may well prove to be one of the most critical issues of this decade.

CONCLUSIONS

Given present projections, a "reserve" crisis of differing magnitudes for different minerals is probable in the next few decades. Among the minerals considered here, the situation with regard to copper, lead, zinc, tungsten, molybdenum, tin, uranium, and petroleum could be critical unless immediate steps are taken; in the longer run, assuming increased exploration and improvements in extraction and processing technology, the minerals that could pose serious problems are limited to copper, tin, and uranium.

The probability of continuing to use petroleum and natural gas as primary energy sources for more than a decade are not good. There is time to avoid a new energy "crisis" and to save the fossil fuels for use as raw materials for industrial production by developing new sources of power and by conservation measures. The solution of the energy problem is critical: given adequate energy "most other necessary materials can be got or recycled. Without adequate energy, the outlook is bleak indeed" (Dunham, 1974, p. 13).

Whether the forecasts of mineral consumption and supply cited here are correct or not, there is no question that we are dealing with a high and continuing rate of growth of world demand—the doubling period may be eighteen years (4 percent per annum) or ten years (7 percent per annum); the problem is one of recognizing in time that in a world of finite resources exponential growth cannot continue unchecked. The fundamental causes of the continuing pressure on mineral resources are population growth, the developing countries' determination to break out of the vicious cycle of poverty, and the continuing high rates of economic growth insisted upon by the industrialized countries. It appears to be unrealistic to expect an early reversal of these trends. Although this implies an impending shortage of minerals, we must conclude that there need be no general scarcity of primary materials *if* steps are taken to develop new exploration techniques for blind and deeply buried mineral deposits, to encourage and finance exploration in the less well-prospected parts of the world, to develop nuclear power in a manner acceptable to the environmentalists, to undertake major research and development programs for methods of exploiting currently nonconventional sources of metals and energy, and to solve the political problems of the jurisdiction over the oceans and the sea floor.

BIBLIOGRAPHY

Averitt, J., 1973. Coal. *In* D. A. Brobst and W. P. Pratt (eds.), *United States mineral resources.* pp. 133–42. Washington: U.S. Government Printing Office.

Blondel, F., and Lasky, S. G., 1956. Mineral reserves and mineral resources. *Economic Geology* 51:686–97.

Bowie, S. H. U., 1976. Whither uranium? *Transactions,* Institution of Mining and Metallurgy 85:B163–169.

Boyd, J., 1973. Minerals and how we use them. In E. N. Cameron (ed.), *The mineral position of the United States, 1975–2000,* pp. 1–8, Madison: University of Wisconsin Press.

Brobst, D. A., and Pratt, W. P. (eds.), 1973. *United States mineral resources.* Washington: U.S. Government Printing Office. 722 pp.

Brown, H., 1954. *The challenge of man's future.* New York: Viking. 290 pp.

Chapman, P. F., 1974. Energy costs of producing copper and aluminium from primary and secondary sources. In *Proceedings of the Conference on the Conservation of Materials, Harwell,* pp. 125–36. Oxfordshire: Harwell.

CIM Reporter, 1976. Vol. 2, no. 8, p. 1.

Cottrell, Sir. A., 1974. The age of scarcity? *Transactions,* Institution of Mining and Metallurgy 83:A25–29.

Cox, D. P., Schmidt, R. G., Vine, J. D., Kirkemo, H., Tourtelot, E. B., and Fleisher, M., 1973. Copper. In D. A. Brobst and W. P. Pratt (eds.), *United States mineral resources,* pp. 163–90. Washington: U.S. Government Printing Office.

Darmstadter, J., 1972. Energy. In R. G. Ridker (ed.), *Population, resources and the environment,* pp. 103–49. Washington: U.S. Government Printing Office.

Darmstadter, J., 1974. *Energy in the world economy.* Baltimore: Johns Hopkins Press.

Davis, M., 1972. Uranium supply and demand. In S. H. U. Bowie, M. Davis, and D. Ostle (ed.), *Uranium prospecting handbook,* pp. 17–32. London: Institution of Mining and Metallurgy.

Derry, D. R., 1974. World mineral resource adequacy. In *Proceedings of the 10th Commonwealth Mining and Metallurgical Congress,* pp. 147–63. Ottawa, Canada.

Dunham, Sir. K., 1974. Non-renewable mineral resources. *Resources Policy* 1:3–13.

Erickson, R. L., 1973. Crustal abundance of elements, and mineral reserves and resources. In D. A. Brobst and W. P. Pratt (eds.) *United States mineral resources*, pp. 21–26. Washington: U.S. Government Printing Office.

Finch, W. I., Butler, A. P., Armstrong, F. C., and Weissenborn, A. E., 1973. Uranium. In D. A. Brobst and W. P. Pratt, *United States mineral resources*, pp. 456–67. Washington: U.S. Government Printing Office.

Fisher, J. C., 1975. Energy crisis in perspective. In L. C. Ruedisili and M. W. Firebaugh (eds.), *Perspectives on energy*, pp. 41–49. New York: Oxford University Press.

Flawn, P. T., 1966. *Mineral resources*. Chicago: Rand McNally. 406 pp.

Fleming, M. G., 1973. Man and minerals—A viable contract. *Transactions, Institution of Mining and Metallurgy* 82:A29–39.

Govett, G. J. S., in press. Exploration geochemistry—A challenge for the chemist. *Journal of the Royal Australian Chemical Institute.*

——, 1976. The development of geochemical methods and techniques. In G. J. S. Govett and M. H. Govett (eds.), *World mineral supplies— Assessment and perspective,* pp. 343–76. Amsterdam: Elsevier.

—— and Govett, M. H., 1972. Mineral resource supplies and the limits of economic growth. *Earth-Science Reviews* 8:275–90.

—— and Govett, M. H., 1974. The concept and measurement of mineral reserves and resources. *Resources Policy* 1:46–55.

—— and Govett, M. H. (eds.), 1976a. *World mineral supplies—Assessment and perspective.* Amsterdam: Elsevier. 472 pp.

—— and Govett, M. H., 1976b. Defining and measuring world mineral supplies. In G. J. S. Govett and M. H. Govett (eds.), *World mineral supplies—Assessment and perspective,* pp. 13–36. Amsterdam: Elsevier.

Govett, M. H., 1975. The geographic concentration of world mineral supplies. Resources Policy 1:357–370.

——, 1976. Geographic concentration of world mineral supplies, production, and consumption. In G. J. S. Govett and M. H. Govett (eds.), *World mineral supplies—Assessment and perspective,* pp. 99–145. Amsterdam: Elsevier.

—— and Govett, G. J. S., in press. The problems of energy and mineral resources. In F. R. Siegel (ed.), *Review of research on modern problems in geochemistry* (Paris: UNESCO).

Hubbert, M. K., 1969. "Energy resources." In Committee on Resources and Man, *Resources and Man.* San Francisco: W. H. Freeman, Pp. 157–242.

——, 1973. Survey of world energy resources. *CIM Bulletin* 66:37–53.

Landsberg, H. H., 1964. *Natural resources for U.S. growth.* Baltimore: Johns Hopkins Press. 257 pp.

Lasky, S. G., 1950. How tonnage-grade relations help predict ore reserves. *Engineering Mining Journal* 151:81–85.

Lovering, T. S., 1969. Mineral resources from the land. In Committee on Resources and Man, *Resources and Man*, pp. 109–34. San Francisco: W. H. Freeman.

Malenbaum, W., Cichowski, C., and Mirzabagheri, F., 1973. *Material requirements in the United States and abroad in the year 2000*. University Park: University of Pennsylvania. 30 pp.

Martin, H. L., Cranstone, D. A., and Zwartendyk, J., 1976. Metal mining in Canada to the Year 2000. In G. J. S. Govett and M. H. Govett, *The Canadian minerals industry, resources policy* 2:11–24.

McAllister, A. L. 1976. Price, technology, and ore reserves. In G. J. S. Govett and M. H. Govett (eds.), *World mineral supplies—Assessment and perspective*, pp. 37–63. Amsterdam: Elsevier.

McCulloh, T. H., 1973. Oil and gas. In D. A. Brobst and W. P. Pratt (eds.), *United States mineral resources*, pp. 477–96. Washington: U.S. Government Printing Office.

McKelvey, V. E., 1960. Relation of reserves of the elements to their crustal abundance. *American Journal of Science* 258A:234–41.

———, 1972. Mineral resource estimates and public policy. *American Scientist* 60:32–40.

Meadows, D. H., Meadows, D. L., Randers, J., and Behrens, W. W. III, 1972. *The limits to growth*. New York: Universe Books. 205 pp.

Noble, J. A., 1974. Metal provinces and metal finding in the western United States. *Mineralia Deposita* 9:1–25.

Northern Miner, 1976. 2 September, pp. 1, 10.

Organization for Economic Cooperation and Development, 1973: *Oil: The present situation and future prospects*. Paris. 293 pp.

———, 1974. *Energy prospects to 1985*. 2 vols. Paris.

Ovchinnikov, L. N., 1971. Estimates of world reserves of metals in terrestial deposits. *Doklady Akad. Nauk USSR*, v. 196 (AGI Translation, 200–203).

Page, N. J., and Creasy, S. C., 1975. Ore grade, metal production, and energy. *Journal of Research of the U.S. Geological Survey* 3(1):9–13.

Pratt, W. P. and Brobst, D. A., 1974. Mineral resources: Potentials and problems. U.S. Geological Survey Circular 698. 20 pp.

Roberts, F., 1974. Energy consumption in the production of materials. *Metals and Materials* 8:167–73.

Sekine, Y., 1963. On the concept of concentration of ore-forming elements and the relationship of their frequency in the earth's crust. *International Geological Review* 5:505–15.

Singer, D. A., Cox, D. D., and Drew, D. J., 1975. Grade and tonnage relationship among copper deposits. U.S. Geological Survey Professional Paper 907A, pp. A1–11.

Thomas, T. M., 1976. Future world energy demand and supply. In G. J. S. Govett and M. H. Govett (eds.), *World mineral supplies—Assessment and perspective*, pp. 185–219. Amsterdam: Elsevier.

United Nations, 1973. *The growth of world industry*. New York.

———, 1974. *The growth of world industry*. New York.

U.S. Bureau of Mines, 1970. *Mineral facts and problems.* Washington: U.S. Government Printing Office. 1,291 pp.

U.S. National Commission on Materials Policy, 1973. *Material needs and the environment today and tomorrow.* Washington: U.S. Government Printing Office.

Vokes, F. M., 1976. The abundance and availability of mineral resources. In G. J. S. Govett and M. H. Govett (eds.), *World mineral supplies— Assessment and perspective,* pp. 65–97. Amsterdam: Elsevier.

Wang, F. F. H. and McKelvey, V. E., 1976. Marine mineral resources. In G. J. S. Govett and M. H. Govett (eds.), *World mineral supplies— Assessment and perspective,* pp. 221–86. Amsterdam: Elsevier.

World Mining, 1976. *Yearbook, catalog survey, and directory,* p. 86.

CHAPTER 4

Intertemporal and International Aspects of Virgin Materials Taxes

Talbot Page *

Much of the economic policy analysis of recycling and the use of the resource base has been from a neoclassical point of view. The theoretical part of this chapter follows in the neoclassical tradition, but develops a policy perspective which departs from the usual one. In the first part of this chapter, I discuss a number of the equity and efficiency considerations which may well be useful in developing public policy toward the use of the resource base—for recycling, materials use and conservation, durability, depletion, the development of substitutes, and the treatment of material wastes. In the second, more speculative part of the chapter, I discuss some of the possible international ramifications of these policy considerations.

INTERTEMPORAL SEQUENTIAL ECONOMIES

It appears that there are two strands of neoclassicism underlying resource economics. At the heart of resource economics is the question of the proper intertemporal allocation of resources. Here the basic approach has been to define the intertemporal analog to the Walrasian market. Goods and depletable natural resources at different times are treated as different commodities; future prices are interpreted as pres-

* I wish to thank Mark Sharefkin for many helpful suggestions.

ent values of future deliveries; and each person is given a utility function, evaluated once, for all time. Sometimes for convenience it is assumed that all people who will ever live are alive and present in this giant intertemporal Walrasian market. Alternatively, it is assumed that we in the present know the utility functions of those to be born in the future, and hence can calculate their demands conditional on future prices—which of course depend upon and in turn guide our present consumption and investment decisions. In any case, this intertemporal version of the static Walrasian market is a one-shot market. There is just one (instantaneous) tatonnement process which not only determines once and for all the allocation of goods and depletable natural resources in the present but also determines an allocation plan for the future.[1] From this first strand comes the intertemporal version of the fundamental theorem of welfare economics: A perfect market is Pareto optimal intertemporally as well as intratemporally.

The second strand underlying traditional thinking about resource economics comes from growth theory. Here the procedure is to write down a single aggregate utility function for the whole economy. The function is "instantaneous" and separable in time. A single fixed discount rate is chosen, and the present value of the intertemporal utility stream is maximized subject to the intertemporal production constraints. A bridging theorem states that a competitive equilibrium can be modeled in terms of the maximization of an aggregate social welfare function.[2]

The kind of intertemporal policy prescription that emerges from these strands of neoclassical treatment of the depletable natural resource base is what one would expect from a purely static analysis. The competitive market solution being optimal, most recommendations have to do with correcting market inefficiencies—elimination of percentage depletion allowances and other implicit subsidies to virgin material industries, disposal taxes on solid waste or other correction of the market system's failure to include disposal costs in product price, and substitution of marginal cost pricing for demand pricing in the areas of transportation and energy. Each of these recommendations helps recycling of waste materials. But in the neoclassical view recycling is not a good in itself. There should be no special subsidy for recycling and there should be no special conservation measures, such as virgin material taxes (severance taxes), unless some special inefficiency can be identified for which such measures would be a remedy.

The attention is focused to such an extent on efficiency that it is often forgotten that there is inherently nothing very strong about it. Each intertemporal distribution of resource endowments and hence market power is likely to have its own Pareto optimal equilibrium. With the control of the depletable natural resource base highly skewed in the actual intertemporal economy (all to the present), it is possible that the actual market intertemporal allocation could be Pareto optimal but intertemporally inequitable. This possibility is admitted by the neoclassicists but given scarce attention. In such a case the remedy is the analog of the remedy in the intratemporal static case—lump sum transfers of wealth. To avoid inefficiency in transfer it is suggested that the transfer should be a general one and not a specific resource. Hence the recommendation to use monetary policy to affect the general rate of savings and investment.[3]

In the Walrasian static market, lump-sum transfers are assumed possible from any agent to any other. In the actual intertemporal market, the feasibility of transfer is much more constrained. By tax and expenditure policy it is possible to shift resource control from some in the present generation to others in the present generation, thus indirectly affecting the use and control of the resource base over time. Monetary policy is available to affect the savings rate. Manipulation of the savings rate at time t affects the transfer of resources from generation t to generation $t + 1$. But is it hard to see how a direct transfer could be made by tax and monetary policy alone to affect, say, a transfer from generation t to generation $t + 10$. With many potential transfers infeasible, it may not be possible to guarantee that all intertemporally efficient allocations can be supported by competitive prices.

While this last point does not appear to have been made in the literature, the infeasibility of many lump-sum transfers is unlikely to be taken as a serious problem in the real world. In the neoclassical tradition it is generally accepted that things are getting better—if there are intertemporal inequities involved, they have to do with the impossibility of transferring more well-being from the future to the present. This optimism concerning use of the depletable natural resource base is based partly on the decline in the Barnett-Morse index of scarcity,[4] real prices of natural resource commodities, and partly on concepts of elasticity of capital for resources in aggregative production functions. As to the Barnett-Morse scarcity index, Georgescu-Roegen replies that it tells us what we already know— in an age of bonanza, the index will go down. He asks what will happen in the next fifty or one hundred years and reasonably asserts that this is not dictated by what happened in the last hundred years. Use of the concept of the aggregate elasticity of substitution has been criticized on several grounds: (1) the assumed aggregate production function may not be derivable from the underlying individual production functions—the capital aggregation problem as well as a resource aggregation problem; and (2) the assumed aggregate production functions, and hence the underlying individual ones, do not obey the laws of mass balance, physical and energy entropy, and other physical constraints.[5]

The important observation about neoclassical optimism of the equities in the use of the depletable natural resource base—that if anything the future is going to get too much of the resource base and us too little—is that this optimism is based not on deductive analysis of market behavior but upon faith. Where the faith is strong, analytical justification seems superfluous. In the use of this resource base there are two principal ways that the inequities may go the other way, with the present imposing burdens upon the future. As we physically deplete the resource base, we impose a risk burden upon the future, a risk burden that we will not develop alternative technology and substitutes in a timely fashion. Second, as we transform the resource base into products for our own use, we create wastes, some of which are long-lived, far longer than the capital instruments which we consider a benefit for the future and a recompense for the resource depletion. How the equities go appears at least an open question.

INEFFICIENCY IN SEQUENTIAL TRANSFER

In the analysis of the intertemporal use of the resource base, surprisingly little attention has been focused upon the actual sequential nature of markets. In the real world, of course, there is no one-shot Walrasian market whose allocation plan is good for all time. Instead there is a new market and a new market solution in each period. As noted, because of the sequential nature of actual intertemporal markets, most trades between agents are blocked. Only those living at the same time and participating in the same market can trade; and as a practical matter, only transfers from one generation to the same or the next generation are possible. As might be expected, the infeasibility of voluntary trade and transfer can lead to inefficiency in the intertemporal use of the resource base. Samuelson has considered the sequential nature of markets and showed one type of intertemporal inefficiency associated with them.[6]

However, sequential markets can be intertemporally inefficient in another way, besides the one described by Samuelson and others. Consider the following simple example of a sequential economy. The present generation is a single agent which enjoys utility from its own consumption and contemplation of future generation's consumption. The present generation has an ordinal utility function ranking its own and future consumption. The present generation is strongly altruistic in the sense that zero consumption for any future generation is associated with infinite negative utility. Zero present consumption is also associated with infinite negative utility. However, the present generation is not completely selfless—at equal levels of consumption between present and future, the present weighs present consumption more heavily. The two sources of utility are specified by

$$U^1(c_1, c_2, \ldots) = \ln(c_1) + \alpha\ln[\min(c_2, c_3, \ldots, c_t, \ldots)]$$

where $U^1 =$ generation 1's utility function
$c_i =$ generation 1's consumption
$\alpha =$ measure of altruism, $0 < \alpha < 1$.

As in the actual world economy, the present generation (generation 1) is the owner and controller of the entire world depletable natural resource base R_1. Generation 1 can directly consume the resource base. What generation 1 does not consume is willy nilly the inheritance of generation 2, and eventually other future generations, depending on generation 2 and other generations' use of the resource base as well. The resource base is assumed to be productive. What the present generation does not consume grows by a factor g for the benefit of the following generation. The intertemporal resource constraint is

$$R_{t+1} = g(R_t - c_t) \qquad \text{for } t \geq 1$$

Following in the neoclassical tradition of resource economics, generation 1 maximizes (1) subject to (2). The problem is simplified because generation 1 is what might be called suggestively but incorrectly a "Rawlsian for the future." [7] Resources will be thrown away in utility terms unless there is a steady state from generation 2 on. For such a steady state we have

$$R_{t+1} = g(R_t - c_t) = R_t \qquad t \geq 2$$

or

$$c_t = R_t(g - 1)/g \qquad t \geq 2$$

Thus generation 1's problem is simplified to be the maximization of

$$\ln(c_1) + \alpha\ln[(g - 1)R_1 - (g - 1)c_1] \qquad \text{over } c_1$$

This is easily solved for the optimal consumption-allocation plan

$$c_1 = R_1/(\alpha + 1)$$
$$c_t = (g - 1)R_1 - (g - 1)c_1$$

To show an actual plan, suppose $\alpha = \frac{1}{2}$ and $g = 2$; then $c_1 = (\frac{2}{3})R_1$ and $c_t = (\frac{1}{3})R$. Generation 1's optimal plan is to consume $\frac{2}{3}$ of the resource base and set aside $\frac{1}{3}$ of it, which is enough to sustain perpetual future consumption of $(\frac{1}{3})R_1$—see Figure 4–1.

The customary practice in the neoclassical tradition is to stop at this point, tacitly assuming that future generations will follow generation 1's optimal plan. The model is indeed simple. With only one agent alive at each point in time, there is no scope for voluntary trade. One would expect that for this model of voluntary transfer, the "optimal" plan chosen by generation 1 should at least be Pareto

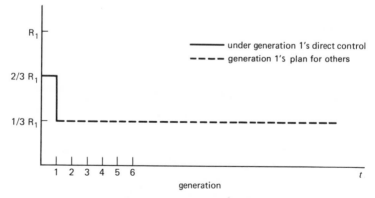

Figure 4–1 Generation 1's optimal plan

optimal. The plan is indeed Pareto optimal—there is no way to better another generation without hurting generation 1—as long as we can expect the plan to be followed. But why would the future wish to follow generation 1's plan? It makes sense to investigate the matter a little further.

The next period brings a new actor with its own utility function. For simplicity and a kind of justice through symmetry, let us assume that generation 2 has the same ordinal utility function as generation 1. Further, let us assume that generation 2 plays by the same rules as generation 1. Generation 1 did not docilely follow a plan laid down by a previous generation, so neither will generation 2. Like generation 1, generation 2 defines its own optimal plan by maximizing its utility function subject to its own resource constraint. Generation 1 defined its optimal plan on the tacit assumption that future generations would follow it. By now this assumption, which may be called "myopic maximization," is clearly inappropriate, but it is nevertheless useful to trace out what happens if generation 2 naïvely and myopically plays by the same rules governing generation 1's behavior. So we suppose that generation 2 also defines its optimal plan on the tacit assumption that future generations will follow it. Generation 2 maximizes

$$\ln (c_2) + \alpha \ln[(g - 1)R_2 - (g - 1)c_2] \qquad \text{over } c_2$$

subject to

$$R_{t+1} = g(R_t - c_t) \qquad t \geq 2$$

Again the maximization is straightforward and generation 2's optimal plan is so shown in Figure 4–2. Clearly "optimal" depends upon the eye of the beholder. We can easily guess the pattern if each succeeding generation is like generation 1. This means that all generations are presumed to have the same utility function and follow the same procedure as generation 1 in defining their respective optimal allocation plans. A naïve myopia which assumes that the future will follow the present's "optimal" plan leads to a quite different actual consumption path, which asymptotically approaches zero (Figure 4–3). We can easily compute the utility stream associated with this implied sequentially chosen path. It is minus infinity for each generation. Any plan which provides at least finite subsistence for each

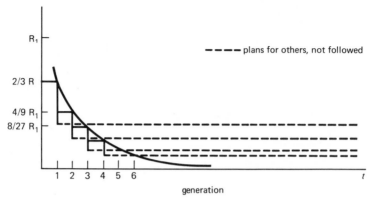

Figure 4—2 Sequential result of naïve myopia

generation Pareto dominates that achieved by selfish and myopic maximization by each generation in its turn.

In this simple model the market solution of sequential maximization is the worst possible stream of utility for all time. The fundamental reason for such market failure is the infeasibility of trade between generations. Presumably if all generations could meet together as in the giant Walrasian intertemporal market, they could unaminously agree that implied sequential system of transfers was inefficient and presumably they could swap conditional transfers to a point of intertemporal efficiency. The question is sometimes rhetorically posed, "What can the future do for me?" The answer is simple, it can wreck your plans—as many parents have no doubt found out. In an intertemporal Walrasian market where the future and present

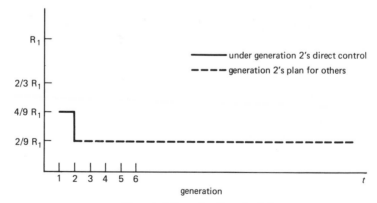

Figure 4–3 Generation 2's optimal plan

could meet and bargain face to face, the future would have bargaining power as long as there is altruism. If representatives from all generations were in a Rawlsian original position in which each generation was unaware of its temporal position, symmetry might suggest that there would be a unaminous agreement to jump into a steady state with respect to the depletable natural resource base from the first period, a solution which would also be Pareto optimal.

ENLARGING THE PERSPECTIVE

The above example breaks with what appears to be the consensus neoclassical tradition of resource economics in several ways: First, it suggests that maximization of the present generation's welfare on the tacit assumption that the future will follow the present's optimal plan (myopic maximization) stops the analysis too short. The intertemporal resource management problem is really a problem of intertemporal social choice. This observation is often obscured when only the present generation's choice is considered, and implicitly the intertemporal social choice problem is "solved" by casting the present generation as the intertemporal dictator.

Second, in the model there is no reason why the present generation cannot look ahead to see where the rules of the game are leading. Presumably the present would reject myopic maximization and would like to strike a bargain with the future saying "I will be a little more conservative in the use of the resource base if you will too." Not being able to deal directly with later generations, the present might see the value in developing institutions, such as common law, which reach across generations and which might increase the intertemporal management of the resource base. Such a role for intertemporal institutions does not have much of a place in the neoclassical tradition.

Third, the conventional assumption in neoclassical theory that time preference is characterized by fixed, geometric discount factors is not made in the example. As Strotz has shown, when time preference is not characterized by an unchanging discount rate there will be an "intertemporal tussle." [8] Strotz thought that people commonly did not have fixed geometric discount factors, and that the intertemporal tussle was a common problem. Certainly it is too much to ask to have a fixed discount rate, unchanged for all time. And it seems that this assumption is one of convenience rather than of reality. Strotz's model is one of an individual's behavior. A single individual evaluates his utility function at different times of his life and comes out with inconsistent results. There being just one individual, there is no inefficiency. In our example, each agent evaluates his utility function only once so that there is no individual inconsistency, and the Strotz "intertemporal tussle" is ruled out, at the individual level.[9] But the same problem re-emerges at the intergenerational level, this time causing inefficiency. The purpose of the example is to suggest that the intertemporal depletable natural resource problem should be viewed as an intertemporal *social choice* problem. This is most easily done when there is an intertemporal conflict of choice. In a Rawlsian setting, one out of time where there are no sunk costs, time preference characterized by fixed discount rates toward the future but declining weight for the past also leads to intertemporal conflict.[10]

Fourth, the usual neoclassical perspective on resource economics is one of optimism in markets—the market solution is "optimal" so there is no need to do anything except improve markets. When it is pointed out that optimal means Pareto optimal, monetary policy is chosen as the appropriate instrument for a generalized (lump sum) transfer of wealth from one generation to the next, sufficient for purpose of equity and the intertemporal redistribution of market power. The above model, simple as it is, suggests that the transition from the giant intertemporal Walrasian market to sequential economies is neither automatic nor to be taken for granted. In the model, voluntary self-maximization does not imply Pareto optimality and neither monetary policy nor tax and expenditure policy will correct the inefficiency. While in this model there is simply no role for either, it suggests that more elaborate models can be constructed, with overlapping generations and many agents each period, where it would also not be possible to correct intertemporal inefficiency by monetary, tax, and expenditure policies.

Finally, the above example may serve to make us a little more skeptical in our faith of what markets can be expected to do, in an intertemporal setting. As mentioned at the beginning, much of the neoclassical analysis and policy perspective concerning the depletable natural resource base comes from an analogy of intertemporal and intratemporal markets. The example is meant to illustrate that there is indeed an analogy between intratemporal social choice and intertemporal social choice, but that care must be taken to distinguish what is different between the two time perspectives. Unlike the intra-temporal setting, in the intertemporal one most of the potential trades are blocked. Moreover, the endowment of resource control is highly skewed, and its intertemporal distribution depends upon conditional interactions between the intergenerational players. In the intertemporal setting, preservation of the natural resource base depends upon altruism, a precautionary saving for one's own old age, and the physical inability of the present controllers of the resource base to destroy it in their lifetime. In making the analogy between the inter-temporal and the intratemporal, it is important to realize that the last two factors may not play the same role in the two time per-spectives—especially the last one, which is entirely missing from the usual intratemporal discussion. Yet in the real world the last factor has changed greatly in recent decades. Until the last century, it was physically impossible to change the world's known depletable natural resource base significantly in the case of a few years. No matter what the plans and desires of each present generation, the depletable natural resource base was passed on to the succeeding generation in much the same form as the preceding generation found it. Now, with vast changes in population and in the power of technology, this time restraint has disappeared.

No one doubts the existence of forward markets, however im-perfect they are in the real world. But forward markets do not mean that the future will be "taken care of" optimally from the point of view of all generations. Our example shows that what is optimal from the point of view of the present generation's market is not necessarily optimal—or even livable—from the vantage point of another gen-eration. There is indeed an analogy between intertemporal social choice and intratemporal social choice, but to use the analogy we must note the differences in the two time perspectives. Having done so, we may be a little less quick in our reliance in the standard policy prescriptions, drawn from the intratemporal case, in their application to chosen intertemporal policy goals.

MAINTAINING THE RESOURCE BASE
AS A MATTER OF EQUITY

In the depletable natural resource area, an intertemporal equity goal emerges if we view the resource base as jointly belonging to all generations. One definition of intertemporal equity is to preserve the resource base intact from generation to generation. It may be argued that this equity goal is too narrow, and that the present should be allowed to trade off depletion of the natural resource base against increases in the man-made capital stock. However, the market does not make this trade-off. The costs of depletion depend upon the impact of present and future technology to renew the resource base. If today's technology is not keeping up with today's depletion, it becomes very uncertain what the costs of depletion really are, depending as they would upon future "fixes." But if today's technology keeps up with depletion in the sense of preventing the costs of materials production from rising, then in an important sense there are no costs of depletion.[11] When the resource base is not being renewed, the costs of depletion imposed upon the future are largely in the nature of a risk burden. This being so, there is no certain way of defining equitable compensation to the future in the form of capital or other "gifts." Thus it may be more practicable to stay with the narrower concept of intertemporal equity in the use of the resource base— equity as maintaining the resource base intact over time, in an aggregate sense that allows one resource to substitute for another.

In discussions of intratemporal equity, it is often suggested that equity does not require equal utility among people, but equal opportunity and endowment of resources. In the intertemporal case, the idea of trading off a little more depletion against a little more capital may be prompted by an idea of equal *welfare* across time. The idea of preserving the depletable natural resource base directly stems from the goal of preserving the *means* or opportunity of future well-being with a high degree of certainty. The latter may be a more attractive concept of intertemporal equity in concept, as well as a more operational one in practice. If our goal of equity in the use of the natural resource base arises from a concept of intertemporal joint ownership of the resource base, it may make sense to focus some policy instrument upon the management of that resource base itself.

Elsewhere I have discussed the role of the severance tax, which slows down the rates of depletion and increases the pay-off to substitutes, as a policy instrument to preserve the resource base intertemporally.[12] The above discussion is meant to suggest that the severance tax,[13] which at first glance seems incompatible with the market neutrality emerging from the neoclassical perspective, is by no means to be discarded lightly. Intertemporal considerations provide a rationale for policy instruments beyond those casually borrowed from static theory. If we wish to increase the probability that the services available to society from the depletable natural resource base thirty years from now will be in no worse condition than now, we may want to eliminate percentage depletion allowances on virgin resource extraction and institute 20 percent severance taxes—in effect change the sign on the present system of depletion allowance. As in the usual neoclassical perspective, once the policy instruments are set for the equity goals, the market is encouraged to work within the resulting context.

INTERNATIONAL ASPECTS OF VIRGIN MATERIALS TAXES

Although the above discussion suggests a role for severance taxes that goes beyond the customary neoclassical reliance in market neutrality, it does not tell us how high they should be. Perhaps the intertemporally fair severance tax should be zero. Development of appropriate levels for severance taxes depends in large part on the empirical judgment of geologists and other physical scientists. The impression one gets from Brobst and Govett—who talk about extraordinary efforts in planning and suggest increased stress on the competence of our institutions—is that an increased incentive for materials conservation would be considered prudent by at least some of the geologists.[14]

Severance taxes for the promotion of intertemporal equity is a countercyclical idea, and one often contrary to traditional practice. In the past, when there has been the threat of scarcity of some natural resource, the political temptation has been to subsidize that scarce resource in the hope of keeping its nominal price constant for consumers. The idea here is to meet anticipated scarcity with higher nominal prices to consumers in order to maintain the real costs of resource production over time.

Today, the idea of preserving the resource base almost necessarily means considering the resource base in a worldwide sense. Moreover, the problem of the world depletable natural resource base is the other half of the world population problem. What is important is the resource base per person. As the population doubles, the effective resource base halves.

It is often suggested that the conservationist's idea of treating the resource base on a *sustainable yield* basis is a kind of luxury good. People in wealthy countries can afford to think of the continued well-being of future generations, while people in developing countries are forced to think of present survival. There is some irony in this perspective, since the best examples—in fact, the *only* examples—of treating the depletable natural resource base on a sustainable yield basis come from traditional societies. Moreover, some developing countries relying heavily on a single depletable resource are taking active policy measures to stretch out the resource until substitute sources of productivity are developed. Nonetheless, there may be something in the view that wealthy countries are more interested in policy measures furthering intergenerational equity than poorer countries.

If so, we might expect whatever impetus there is, or will be, toward a system of virgin materials taxes to start in the developed countries. In the United States the traditional approach, which has been to subsidize virgin material production, has indeed come under increasing criticism. National depletion allowances have been lowered slightly, and severance taxes at the state level, which used to be negligible, are rising dramatically. Although some of this turnaround undoubtedly reflects growing concern with the depletion of the natural resource base, there are clearly other factors such as the state's increased realization of opportunities to "export" its tax base through severance taxes. In response to the scarcity imposed by the oil crisis, President Ford proposed—and for a time enforced—tariffs in order to promote energy conservation. It appears the European countries have been politically far more successful in imposing taxes to promote conservation in response to the energy crisis.

A frequently cited fact is that the United States consumes an enormous share of the world's natural resources on a per capita basis. Suppose the United States took seriously the goal of intertemporal equity, what could be done? It is quite possible that the step of "changing the sign on the depletion allowances" would be nearly costless to the present generation. Existing inefficiencies in the treatment of virgin material industries provide a certain slack, so that swapping existing subsidies for actively conservationist policies might impose little or no net burden on the present, except for the immediate transition costs associated with change itself. Once severance taxes for the purpose of intertemporal conservation were imposed on resources extracted inside the United States, it would be logical to impose corresponding tariffs on imported virgin materials. We might expect that domestic extractive companies and labor unions would demand it for parochial reasons, and at the same time such a move would in effect "export" the conservation incentive.

Countries exporting virgin materials to the United States, many of them developing nations, would oppose such conservation tariffs. They could nevertheless be imposed unilaterally, although there is in this case the opportunity of mutually advantageous trade. To spread the conservation incentive further, the United States might offer to withdraw the tariff if the resource-exporting country were to impose equivalent severance taxes, not only on the material exported to the United States, but to all countries. Since underdeveloped countries have for years tried to increase the export prices of raw materials, presumably they would welcome a material-consuming country's switch from opposition to assistance in their endeavor.

How other resource-consuming countries would react to these developments is another matter entirely. On the one hand they could try to undermine unilaterally instigated system of worldwide severance taxes by negotiating rebates—perhaps clandestine ones to avoid the exporting countries' loss of United States tariff forgiveness. On the other hand, people in other developed countries may have much the same value system as in the United States. With high incomes also, people in other developed countries may wish to promote, rather than undermine, policy to renew and preserve the resource base. Moreover, there could be some direct advantages for other developed countries to go along with worldwide severance taxes. As we have seen in the case of oil, heavy import dependence on raw materials implies political vulnerability. If this vulnerability could be lessened through moderately higher virgin material prices, with the long-run adjustments of greater internal recycling of secondary materials, longer product durability, and higher service intensity per unit material consumed, then there might be some reason to support a worldwide system of severance taxes —especially if the developed countries participated in their establishment and had a voice in their control.

If the developed countries' goal is a narrow one focusing on a greater degree of independence from virgin material imports, a system of tariffs would be of greater direct benefit to them than severance taxes in the exporting countries. This is too narrow a view of the matter, however. The developed countries as a whole have given significant aid to the developing ones, and in fact one of the forms of this aid has been special preferential trade arrangements. It is a happenstance of geology that many of the developed countries are have-not countries with respect to the world's depletable natural resource base, while many developing countries are richly endowed with one or more of these resources. Encouragement of developing countries' severance taxes in place of developed countries' tariffs may be viewed as another form of development assistance.

This form of foreign aid could be of substantial benefit to the developing countries. One of their strongest needs is to diversify their economies, reducing their heavy dependence on raw material exports. The present system of escalating tariffs makes the process of diversification difficult, especially when developed countries have accentuated the effective tariff differentials by special exemptions of tariffs on virgin materials. The move toward severance taxes would act like a reversal in the tariff rate structure, with direct transfers of income to the developing countries. By changing the terms of trade between manufactured goods and raw materials, diversification would be encouraged.

It has often been argued that increased world trade increases world stability. However, the exponential growth in world consumption of virgin material cannot continue for very long. The growing scramble for virgin materials, with fewer sellers and more buyers, may lead into a kind of new mercantilism and increased world instability. A slowdown in this process through a system of worldwide severance taxes might provide a breathing space, and in the long run a greater worldwide stability. Thus, worldwide severance taxes might promote world stability for several reasons: (1) as a measure to help close the wealth gap between rich and poor countries; (2) as an incentive for diversification in developing countries; (3) as mitigation from the mercantilist scramble among developed countries; and (4) as a shift from the present politics of confrontation toward cooperation.

Unfortunately the coincidence between intertemporal and intratemporal equity goals, and other goals, is not complete. Several of the resource-rich countries are no longer poor countries. The obvious examples are some of the OPEC countries. It is not likely that developed countries would wish to further increase the wealth of these countries by additional increases in what is effectively the severance tax on oil—developed countries might be better off with increased tariffs on imported oil, as an increased conservation measure, however. More serious as an intratemporal equity matter is the plight of relatively resource-poor developing countries. For an explicit example, though perhaps not the most appropriate example, we may choose India. The immediate result of a worldwide system of severance taxes could be to make India substantially worse off.

It is in the spirit of the neoclassical perspective to suggest that this intratemporal equity problem, stemming in part from an intratemporally skewed distribution of the depletable natural resource base, could be handled by giving the resource-poor, developing countries claims on new resources. The newest resource augmentation is the ocean floor. Already it is sometimes called the "common heritage of mankind," and it is sometimes suggested that the benefits of its exploitation could be disproportionately allocated to the resource-poor developing countries. Such an arrangement may be a solution to some of the difficulties arising from the intratemporal distribution of the depletable natural resource base which are likely to be exacerbated by attempts to promote intertemporal equity. But the solution seems a little too simple, a little too much like a *deus ex machina*. It is reminiscent of articles written in the 1960s on the chronically high unemployment rate among blacks in the United States. The neoclassical advice was that there existed no need for painful structural changes in the economy—the solution was growth. With everyone better off, special unemployment problems will take care of themselves. In the last fifteen years we in the United States have learned the hard way not to rely on growth as the solution to social, structural problems. In the same way, the solution to the world's resource problems will not always come painlessly from outside the system in a Pareto-dominating way. Eventually there is the necessity of balancing the internal dynamics of population and resources in terms of their limitations.

Although it seems clear that the recent increases in energy prices have made India worse off, it is not clear that the previous low energy prices, over the past twenty years, favored India's long-term development. In the case of oil, the present increased prices result from cartel successes and not from scarcity. Still they give us a preview of what can happen when a resource becomes scarce, as energy-related materials may indeed become scarce in the next few decades. If there is to be a genuine scarcity, it may be better to anticipate it early with gradually increasing prices rather than later with sharply increased prices. India, over the past twenty years has become increasingly dependent on energy imports. When imported energy was much cheaper, until the early 1970s, India made a heavy commitment in an energy-intensive form of the green revolution. Delicate but high-yielding grains were introduced at the price of greater dependence on pesticides, chemical fertilizers, and water. It is quite possible that India would be better off now if oil prices had begun to increase earlier and more gradually. In that case India might now have a sturdier form of the green revolution, with somewhat less delicate and high-yielding grains with lower dependence on imported energy and a greater tolerance of climate fluctuations as well. Not just for India but for the development prospects of the world as a whole, we would not have to consider such profoundly depressing concepts as the one of "triage" if we had managed the resource base and population growth on a sustainable yield basis all along.

NOTES

1. E. Malinvaud, "The Analogy Between Atemporal and Intertemporal Theories of Resource Allocation," *Review of Economic Studies* 28 (June 1961): 143–46.

2. Harold Hotelling, "The Economics of Exhaustive Resources," *Journal of Political Economy* 39 (April 1931):137–75; Kenneth Arrow and Mordecai Kurz, *Public Investment, The Rate of Return and Optimal Policy* (Baltimore, Md., Johns Hopkins University Press for Resources for Future, 1970), p. 11; Tjalling Koopmans, "Some Observations on 'Optimal' Economic Growth and Exhaustible Resources," Cowles Foundation Discussion Paper no. 356, March 28, 1973, p. 3; Richard Gordon, "A Reinterpretation of the Pure Theory of Exhaustion," *Journal of Political Economy* 75 (No. 3, June 1967):277; Vernon Smith, "An Optimistic Theory of Exhaustible Resources," California Institute of Technology Social Science Working Paper no. 39 (April 1974), p. 3; Oscar Burt and Ronald Cummings, "Production and Investment in Natural Resource Industries," *American Economic Review* 60 (1970):579; C. G. Plourde, "Exploitation of Common-Property Replenishable Natural Resources," *Western Economic Journal* (No. 3, September 1971):256; and Neil Vousden, "Basic Theoretical Issues of Resource Depletion," *Journal of Economic Theory* 6 (April 1973):126–43.

3. Joseph Stiglitz, "A Neoclassical Analysis of the Economics of Natural Resources," paper presented at the Conference on Scarcity, RFF, October 17–18, 1976.

4. Barnett and Morse constructed price indices for four resource composites: agriculture, minerals, fishing, and forestry. They then compared each index with the general price level as a test of scarcity. For price data over the period of 1870–1957 they found only timber to show a real price increase. Harold Barnett and Chandler Morse, *Scarcity and Growth,* Johns Hopkins Press for Resources for the Future, Baltimore, Md., pp. 209–16.

5. Conference on Scarcity, comments by Georgescu-Roegen, Schulz, and Daly.

6. Paul Samuelson, "An Exact Consumption-Loan Model of Interest with or without the Social Contrivance of Money," *JPE* 66 (December 1958): 467–82. See also David Starrett, "On Golden Rules, the Biological Theory of Interest, and Competitive Inefficiency," *JPE* 80(2) [March–April 1972]: 276–91.

7. Rawls did not recommend his (intratemporal) maximin criterion in the intertemporal case. For the intertemporal case, Rawls recommended a golden rule of saving effort, whereby the present generation makes a saving effort for the next generation equal to what it would have liked the previous generation to have made for it.

8. Robert Strotz, "Myopia and Inconsistency in Dynamic Utility Maximization," *Review of Economic Studies* 23 (1955–56):165–80.

9. Samuelson avoids the problem of intertemporal inconsistency by his footnote 3; Samuelson, "Consumption-Loan Model," p. 469.

10. I tried to show this in "Equitable Use of the Resource Base," *Environment and Planning,* forthcoming.

11. This statement is a little loose. It may be possible to run through a geological inheritance in a century or so. During this time, resource prices may fall to later rise with later burdens upon the future. This may in fact be an accurate description of the actual world economy and thus the time scale for the concept of an "intact" resource base is an important consideration.

12. Talbot Page, *Conservation and Economic Efficiency,* Johns Hopkins University Press for Resources for the Future, forthcoming.

13. Or other policy instruments affecting the intertemporal maintenance of the resource base.

14. Donald A. Brobst, "The Systems Approach to the Analysis of Resource Scarcity," paper presented at the Conference on Scarcity, RFF, Oct. 17–18, 1976; also M. H. Govett and G. J. S. Govett, "Scarcity of Basic Materials and Fuels: Assessment and Implications," in this volume.

CHAPTER 5

Pollution Charges: The Practical Issues

Fred Lee Smith, Jr.*

It can be said that no environmental issue has been so well studied as pollution charges. The great American pollution paradox is that no serious economic study has concluded that discharge fees should not be a major tool of public policy, whereas no serious environmental measure has included them.[1]

INTRODUCTION

The problems of pollution can be viewed either as a violation of a social norm—the transgression of some specific rule of moral/ethical behavior—or, alternatively, as a failure of those responsible for pollution to reimburse society for the costs their activities entail. That is, pollution can be viewed either as a moral or as a market problem. The former view leads those concerned with pollution to favor explicit, stringent restrictions on activities that generate pollution, that is, increased reliance on standards and regulations. This approach has traditionally been advocated by the legal profession and by environmental activists. To these groups, pollution is a criminal activity to be legislated out of existence.

* The views expressed in this paper are those of the author and do not necessarily reflect those of the Environmental Protection Agency.

Although there is an important role for this approach, relying solely on regulation creates a number of difficulties. A large body of theoretical literature and a smaller but developing applied literature indicate that regulations are unlikely in practice to prove an effective way of reducing pollution.[2] In brief, the argument is that our society relies heavily on private market choices. These private choices are affected by the economic incentives or lack of incentives associated with various production or consumption decisions. Generally, the private decision maker will experience the costs of any pollution control, whereas the benefits of reduced pollution will be enjoyed by others. Regulations may constrain the amount of pollution that can be produced, but will not change the economics of pollution control as viewed by the polluter.* Since the economic incentive structure is left intact, self-interest will continue to dictate that the firm make only a minimum effort to control pollution. Since self-policing cannot be relied upon, continued centralized enforcement and a heavy reliance on the court systems are essential. Finally, since regulations fail to make pollution control economically valuable, there is little incentive for technological or managerial innovation in the area of pollution reduction and control.[3]

An alternative approach views excessive pollution as the natural outcome of a situation in which polluters lack incentives to consider the costs associated with their activities. This view leads to efforts to estimate these costs and to charge the polluter accordingly. This concept of charging a fee for the use of environmental resources or to pay for pollution control is not new.[4] As noted in the epigraph, economists have long recommended economic disincentives as a way of reducing pollution. The intent of this paper is to review the problems encountered in actually implementing such an approach.

There is a value in either view of pollution. Indeed, a strong moral tone is necessary to overcome social inertia. No environmental legislation would have been enacted had there not been enthusiastic committed citizens dedicated to a cleaner world. Kenneth Boulding, the American economist, has pointed out that it was the abolitionists fired with moral indignation—not the economists concerned with

---

* Regulations also tend toward increasing complexity over time as more special cases are incorporated into the rules, require detailed knowledge concerning the operations being regulated, and are difficult to adjust to account for dynamic changes in the industry being regulated.

market efficiency—that led the fight to abolish slavery. My point is that, whereas this moral view may well be necessary to induce social intervention to alleviate pollution, this may well prove a very inefficient way of actually reducing pollution. In the remainder of this paper, I return again and again to this theme. My objective is to show that charges are compatible with the visceral reaction against waste and pollution and, moreover, promise to actually reduce the problem.

"TAXES" VERSUS "CHARGES"

The reader will note that throughout this paper the term *charge* is used instead of the term *tax* to refer to pollution charge proposal. This use of terms is deliberate and a brief digression is justified to explain why.

The dictionary defines a tax as any compulsory contribution levied by government. Nonetheless, the term *tax* has increasingly been used to apply only to revenue-raising measures. The etymology is instructive.[5]

In 1480, the term *tax* was used in Caxton's *English Chronicles* in a way that clearly emphasized this revenue-raising connotation:

King Johan . . . [imposed] . . . a huge tax throughout all englond.

However, Hume in 1752 pointed out the incentive value of taxes in a quote taken from his *Essays and Treatises:*

A tax on German linen encourages home manufacture.

And this point was further clarified in an 1840 article on taxation in the *Encyclopaedia Britannica:*

A tax may be either direct or indirect. It is said to be direct when it is taken directly from capital or wealth; and indirect when it is taken by requiring [a fee to be paid] for the liberty; to use certain articles or to exercise certain privileges.

Thus, on historical grounds, the use of the term *tax* to signify a fee paid for the use of resources is completely justifiable. However, the unavoidable revenue-raising connotation of a tax makes it advisable henceforth to use the term *charge* when referring to fees collected for the use of environmental resources.*

WASTE DISPOSAL CHARGES

Let me now discuss the work of the Office of Solid Wastes of the U.S. Environmental Protection Agency over the last several years on one specific pollution charge. This charge would be a fee collected from a product manufacturer to cover the eventual costs of the collection and disposal of that product when it becomes waste.[6] Our (Environmental Protection Agency) analysis and evaluation of this concept have required that we address most issues that arise in exploring any charge strategy. Moreover, many of the tools that we have developed will be useful in examining other pollution charge strategies.[7]

In this chapter I first describe the rationale, evolution, and problems encountered in developing the waste disposal charge concept. I then describe our efforts to answer these objections and several general

---

* In a private conversation, William Irwin of the Environmental Law Institute has suggested another reason for making a distinction between the two terms. Irwin has pointed out that in the evolution of Federal powers in the United States, the taxing power specified in the Constitution was first used to restrict or restrain activities viewed as socially undesirable. Later this same effect was achieved by the extension of the commerce powers of the Constitution via direct regulation.

For example (see Lee [1975]), the Federal tax power was once used to restrict the white phosphorus match industry, which created a serious occupational health hazard. (A tax approach was felt more suitable than a regulatory approach, since in some cases only intrastate commerce was involved.) Today, society is attempting to ensure occupational safety via regulations justified under the now broadly defined commerce powers of the Constitution.

Irwin points out that the shift from achieving social objectives via the taxing power to that of relying on the commerce power has meant that the body of legal decisions regarding the use of fees based on the taxing power for social regulatory purposes is less well-developed than is the comparable body of law dealing with regulatory charges based on the commerce clause of the Federal Constitution. For these reasons, Irwin argues that to rely on a regulatory tax rather than a commerce-based regulatory charge approach might generate legal issues that would require extensive court rulings to resolve. This possibility may well exist and any effort to enact either a tax or a charge should consider this issue.

findings that emerge from our work. Our experience demonstrates that the difficulties associated with charge strategies, while significant, are not insurmountable. I conclude this chapter with a brief discussion of some trends that should improve the likelihood of charge approaches receiving more serious consideration in the future.

EPA first began to evaluate waste disposal charges the way most United States agencies become involved with issue: The United States Congress passed the Resource Recovery Act of 1970 requiring that EPA evaluate a charge on products that enter municipal solid waste. The three major characteristics of such a charge (based on the hearings leading to this Act and on subsequent proposals) are

- A charge on consumer products and packaging roughly equal to the costs of managing the solid wastes associated with these items.
- A reduction in the charge levied on any products covered by the proposal for use of secondary materials.
- Provision for redistributing all or most of the revenues obtained to local governments for solid waste management purposes.

From 1969 onward, a number of such bills have been introduced in one or both houses of the United States Congress.[8]

Congress, in introducing such legislation, recognized that the decisions to produce and consume products entering municipal waste involve downstream costs that are not considered by these producers and consumers. Typically, the costs of collection and disposal are paid out of general revenues. And even when solid waste fees are paid directly by the household, they are typically paid in fixed monthly amounts that do not vary with the amount of solid waste generated.

This failure to price solid waste management services based on the amount of wastes generated results in both economic inefficiencies and inequities. First, the decisions by a producer to employ a specific technology or by a consumer to purchase a specific product are made without considering the implications of such decisions on the amount of resulting solid waste. That is, no incentives exist for the producer or consumer to consider whether the wastes associated with a product are excessive. The lack of incentives results both in an underdevelopment of resource-conserving technology (for example—products designed to use less material or to be re-used, or improved recycling processes) and in an under-utilization of whatever conservation technologies already exist. The economic signals that would induce these developments are lacking.*

The second result is that, rather than having the costs of solid waste management paid by those responsible for generating these wastes, costs are paid by the public at large. This shifting of costs to the general public is inequitable and in direct conflict with the polluter-pays-principle.[9] Moreover, in aggregate, these "shifted costs" are substantial. In 1975, it is estimated that the United States spent well over two billion dollars for solid waste management, with some estimates ranging as high as six billion dollars. Often, these costs are paid from local property taxes—straining the tax base of the local community.†

DIFFICULTIES ENCOUNTERED

Waste disposal charges were first proposed in the United States Congress in 1969; yet no action was taken. The reasons for this lack of success are important inasmuch as the arguments raised against a solid waste charge are typical of those likely to be raised against any pollution charge strategy. Opponents presented the following arguments:

- "Charges create a license to pollute."
- "Charges would be passed on to the consumer—producers wouldn't reduce their wastes."
- "Charges are regressive."
- "A charge program would be a bureaucratic nightmare."

Similar arguments have been raised to oppose every charge strategy introduced in the environmental area to date (see, for example, Lumb [1971]).

---

* To explain this concept of external costs to noneconomists, we found it useful to compare two systems for supplying milk to the household—a returnable and a one-way system. We then reviewed the cost considerations that might lead a dairy to switch to a throwaway system. It becomes immediately apparent that in this decision the costs of collecting and disposing of the discarded containers are not considered by the dairyman, because they are not borne by him.

† One device we found useful to explain the problem of paying costs collectively was to develop the analogy of a shared lunch. Given this example, people immediately grasp that when everyone pays equally regardless of his contribution to total costs, incentives to keep costs low are minimal.

To address these objections, a series of in-house, contract, and grant policy evaluation studies were conducted. Presentations were also made on the subject to public interest, environmental, and business groups, and other governmental agencies. These meetings were most useful in pointing out areas where the original charge concept needed refinement and in developing less-theoretic, more comprehensible arguments for a charge approach. Our conclusions and some of the methodological approaches developed to address these objections are discussed below.

The "License to Pollute" Argument

The moral/ethical issue of eliminating pollution by laws rather than rationing it via prices was raised in our encounters with environmental groups. There is appreciable sentiment for bans and restrictions to reduce waste directly rather than relying on increased costs to achieve this same result.[10] Foes of "overpackaging" are not readily reconciled to the view that solid waste should be viewed as an economic problem—a failure of the responsible parties to pay the associated social costs—rather than as a moral failing of big business.

This argument is difficult to address since it reflects the wish that pollution could simply be eliminated rather than controlled and that those who pollute are in some sense wrongdoers who should repent. The reflection of Pogo on this topic—"We have met the enemy and he is us!"—is not always understood.

The strongest arguments we developed on this topic are those discussed below and outlined here. First, we developed the material balance argument to explain how some pollution is inevitable. Second, we discussed the implications of current regulatory programs, so that people realize that the choice is between granting polluters the right freely to create some level of pollution or requiring that they pay a fee for this privilege.

The desire to ban rather than to reduce pollution is normal. Unfortunately, the nature of pollution renders this concept infeasible. Pollution is simply the unwanted energy and material residues of production and consumption activities; and the laws of energy and material conservation ensure that any production or consumption activities will involve unwanted by-products. Of course, it is possible to modify the physical form in which pollutants occur. An air pollutant, such as sulfur dioxide, can be converted to sludge. And this process may well reduce the damages associated with that pollutant; nonetheless, the tonnage of materials remains constant. Thus, pollution control should be viewed as the process of comparing the relative costs and benefits of alternative pollutants and determining which mix would minimize the overall damage to the environment. A materials flow approach forces attention on this issue rather than on the unattainable goal of eliminating all pollution.

Current environmental management policies do not face this issue squarely. In practice, firms and municipalities are granted permits which permit, in total, large amounts of pollution to be discharged. These permits are often rationalized by assuming that pollution below some "threshold" level is harmless or more explicitly in recognition that some level of pollution can be assimilated by the environment without causing serious environmental harm. In either case, this regulatory approach grants a "free license to pollute" up to this threshold level.

The "Industry Will Not Respond" Argument

Despite the fact that Americans live in a market economy, read Horatio Alger stories in their daily papers, and endure long speeches extolling the virtues of the free market system—very few understand how the market system works. In particular, there is remarkably little understanding of what problems may arise in a market or how a market responds to cost changes. Two basic approaches were adopted to address this problem. First, we developed a more coherent explanation as to why the market system was failing to provide proper waste reduction incentives. (The example cited earlier of the shift from the returnable to the one-way milk container was a very successful way of communicating the concept of external costs.) At the same time, we developed a series of examples of the type changes that might be expected were a charge imposed. A series of analytic studies to estimate quantitatively the effects of various charge levels were conducted simultaneously.

There is no magic way to persuade people that the market works. Demand and supply curves are rarely persuasive to a lay audience. We found examples and analogies most useful. For example, almost everyone realizes that higher labor costs induce firms to invest in labor-saving equipment. As a result of the energy crisis, most of us are also aware that higher energy costs have stimulated many energy-saving innovations. The next step is to persuade people that there is nothing unique about labor and energy—pollution charges will have a similar effect on pollution-reducing innovations.

Specific examples of possible impacts of a solid waste disposal charge were described: an improvement in the relative economics of re-usable as opposed to throw-away containers, a stabilization and increase in the prices obtained for secondary materials (since a firm could reduce its charge bill by using more recovered material), an increased likelihood that firms would consider solid waste problems in designing their products, and a way of providing revenues for cities to finance resource recovery efforts. Such examples proved useful in aiding an audience to understand the range of responses to solid waste charges.

We also noted that, whether a firm passes along a pollution charge or not, it still has an incentive to reduce its charge bill (just as is the case for energy and labor). For example, were a waste disposal charge in effect, then virgin newsprint producers would likely raise their prices. A newsprint producer relying on secondary fiber would be free either to raise his prices to the same extent to improve his profitability—since his charges would be less—or not to raise his prices, which would improve his market share position. In either case, the relative profitability of the less wasteful recycling mill has increased and its share of newsprint production (and hence recycling) can be expected to improve.

To obtain quantitative estimates of these impacts, analytic studies were carried out on producer and consumer responses to a waste charge. That is, how would the industry respond to higher costs of virgin materials and how would the consumer respond as these costs are passed along? The analysis took the following form: the effected industries were analyzed, the technological substitution possibilities were explored, and the short- and long-run responses of supply and demand to price changes were estimated.

Our quantitative analysis assumed the following basic charge: a charge on most paper products and nonpaper packaging material (comprising over 80 percent of the product portion of municipal waste in the United States); the charge to be twenty-six dollars per ton for paper and other flexible packaging and one-half cent per rigid container; the charge to be collected at the bulk manufacturing or fabrication stage of production; a full rebate to be allowed for the use of secondary materials; and a phase-in period of ten years over which the charge would be introduced.

Our analysis indicated that a charge proposal of this type would substantially increase the level of recycling. The preliminary nature of these findings suggest that one should be extremely cautious in relying on the exact numerical results; however, it appears that recycling increases would be on the order of 20 to 30 percent of all major materials now in the municipal waste stream. Adequate models do not exist to evaluate the total waste reduction effect of a charge proposal; however, the effects resulting only from the price-induced demand shifts suggest that material use would fall by about 3 percent below projected levels.

The increased price of most consumer products under a charge scheme, even assuming all costs are passed along, does not appear to be large. For most retail products, the increases are estimated at less than one-half of one percent of current product prices. The overall impact of a waste disposal charge on the Consumer Price Index compiled by the Bureau of Labor Statistics and used as a measure of inflation would be barely perceptible—an increase on the order of two-tenths of one percent.

The state of the art of applied economic analysis is not all that one would wish; nor has a similar detailed analysis been carried out for other pollution charges. However, tools do exist, and much applied economic work has already been published. The impacts of selected pollution taxes, including sulfur taxes and BOD effluent fees, have been estimated quantitatively (see Bingham [1974, 1976], and Meta Systems, Inc. [1975]). Moreover, industry studies funded by EPA to estimate the costs of our various air and water pollution control programs may also be useful in analyzing various charge approaches. Thus, the ability to estimate the impacts and likely effectiveness of a charge approach does not appear to be a major factor hindering a greater use of charge mechanisms in environmental management.[11]

The "Regressive" Argument

The third issue—the extent to which a charge approach is perceived as creating a greater burden on lower income groups than would a regulatory approach—is an important one in a society concerned with distributional equity. Some individuals have argued that environmental issues have become a white-collar, suburban concern and shy away from any suggestion that improving the environment may involve any expense to the poor.

As part of the evaluation of product charges, EPA has developed methods whereby the financial implications of a charge strategy can be expressed in terms of the additional costs that the average family in each income group would experience. It was found that a waste disposal charge would require a typical family in the lowest income decile to spend an additional $7 per year to purchase the goods and services it now consumes. The comparable figure for the wealthiest families is $60 per year. This is "regressive." The $7 is a higher percentage of the income of the poorest families than is $60 of the richest families. More importantly, however, it is obvious that the total impact is relatively small even for a poor family.[12]

The methodology developed for analyzing waste disposal charges may also be used to understand the distributional impacts of other pollution charge proposals. It should be noted that distributional studies of regulatory programs indicate that they, too, are regressive (see, for example, Dorfman [1973]). Thus, even if a charge strategy proves regressive, it may be less so than the regulatory alternative. In addition, any initial regressive impact of a charge strategy can be reduced by using the charge revenues collected to fund various programs which help the poor. For example, returning charge-derived revenues to local governments would result either in reduced taxes or upgraded services. In either case, any initial regressive effect would be reduced. Moreover, the environmental benefits of reduced wastes may accrue to the poor preferentially, since the poor are less able to relocate to avoid areas of low environmental quality.

The "Administrative Nightmare" Argument

The fourth issue addressed was that of determining the costs of administering a waste disposal charge program. To examine this issue, the comparative costs of administering several federal excise tax* programs were examined.[13] This approach was taken since a waste charge would be similar to an excise tax, and would be very similar to a specific excise tax, which is an excise based on some physical property of the product. The waste disposal charge would involve

---

* An excise tax is a tax levied on a selected product or activity, as distinct from a tax levied on total sales or income.

collecting from the producer of those products entering municipal solid waste a fee based on the volume or weight of the product adjusted for its secondary material content.

This comparative analysis of existing excise tax programs was very instructive. One finding was that, whether a pollution charge or an excise tax program is being considered, a series of regulatory refinements involving a degree of arbitrariness and judgment are necessary. Our review considered the tax collected on the alcohol content of beverages sold for consumption. This creates a monitoring problem because the alcoholic content in a given volume of beverage is not immediately apparent. Moreover, a series of regulatory rulings were necessary to develop a workable alcohol tax program. For example, how were high-alcohol content patent medicines to be treated? Were brandied fruits or rum-filled chocolates to be taxed? Based on such a comparison, it is clear that the many arbitrary choices that will be encountered in implementing pollution charges are neither unique nor irresolvable. Similar problems have been faced—and solved—in implementing excise taxes of comparable complexity.

Our analysis also attempted to determine the direct administrative costs of selected excise tax programs. The result indicate that such costs are less than 1 percent of total tax collections. Comparing the complexity of the tax programs evaluated with that of proposed pollution taxes reveals no reason for expecting higher administrative costs in this latter case. A major reason, of course, is that existing federal tax programs would be used to collect a pollution charge. In most cases, pollution charges would require only a few additional entries on the standard corporate tax return.[14]

One other point is that to some extent a tax or charge approach is self-enforcing. For example, a small producer may avoid paying taxes —just as he may avoid installing pollution control equipment. However, under a tax approach his liability increases during the evasion period; whereas, under a regulatory approach, any delay in installing a piece of equipment results in a direct financial gain to the firm.*

---

* Note that if an evading firm grows to a scale where their activities become important, then their evasion is likely to be known and reported by those competing firms who do pay their taxes. Indeed, since the tax code grants a "finder's fee" to those who assist the IRS in catching tax evaders, the tax mechanism may prove a very effective control strategy.

THE NEED TO SPECIFY A CONCRETE PROPOSAL

One major point that has emerged from our experience with solid waste charges is that little progress on implementing a charge approach is possible as long as the discussion remains at a conceptual level. Agreement in principle is all too likely to collapse when the details of a specific proposal are revealed. And this process of translating an idea into actual legislation takes considerable time and effort. (As noted, this refinement and specification of the waste disposal charge has continued over six years.) A familiarity with an existing regulations dealing with that pollutant is necessary, and then a detailed design compatible with and supplementing the ongoing program must be developed.

Moreover, any charge strategy will involve a number of alternative design options. The pros and cons of each alternative design should be resolved, if possible, before entering the political arena. The evolution of the sulfur tax proposed during the 1970s is instructive. Many issues arose during design process: the charge level could be based on an estimate of the damage produced or on the costs of control. The tax might be uniform across the nation or vary among regions. The charge might be restricted to sulfur-content fuels or be expanded to include other sources of atmospheric sulfur. A charge might be based only on the sulfur content of emissions or might vary depending on the form in which the sulfur is emitted. Monitoring might or might not be included as an integral aspect of the program. The charge might be introduced at once or be phased in gradually over some period of time. Small emitters might or might not be exempted from the charge. Finally, the charge revenues might or might not be used for a specific purpose.

It is possible, I believe, to arrive at a reasonable resolution of each of these various design questions. But this should be done in advance after analysis and evaluation. The implications of the specific choice in each of these areas are not always easy to understand. And time for analysis is rarely possible in the turmoil of a legislative session.

This discussion provides a good point to indicate the major problem hindering the progress of pollution charge approaches. That is the lack of any group responsible for designing, evaluating, and implementing alternative pollution charge strategies.* This vacuum becomes particularly evident whenever a specific policy in this area is attempted. An ad hoc group is hastily assembled, a crude proposal developed and floated up, and then the team is disbanded while the ill-designed proposal collapses.

STILL OTHER PROBLEMS

In developing a charge approach, one must confront several other obstacles. These include the problem of developing an understanding of a new idea and various special political problems. Nothing is less likely to receive serious consideration than a new idea or approach. And charge strategies until recently were considered a novel idea. Any specific charge approach will need to be considered publicly far in advance of the time it can realistically be expected to be enacted into law.

Waste disposal charges do have a long history. As noted earlier, the concept was first discussed in Congress in 1969 by Leonard Wegman. In 1972, Senators Proxmire and Nelson introduced legislation along these lines; again in 1974 Senators Philip Hart and Frank Moss re-introduced the measure and, at that time, hearings were held on the concept. More recently, in the 94th Congress, a charge measure was introduced first in a draft House Commerce Committee bill, then in draft legislation circulated within the Senate Finance Committee, and finally in a bill on which hearings were held in the Senate Public Works Committee. Waste disposal charges are thus not a new idea.

Although Congressional discussions on other specific pollution charges is less widespread, there is a large and growing discussion of this strategy. A recent bibliography (Smith, 1977) on applied charge approaches lists several hundred articles, hearings, research reports, and statements of support or opposition dealing with various pollution charge concepts. As a result of this rapidly expanding

---

* Some groups have attempted to fill this gap—the Environmental Law Institute, the Environmental Group of the Organization for Economic Cooperation and Development (OECD) and (until its disbandment in 1974) the Washington Environmental Research Center of EPA—but none have enjoyed both the organizational responsibility for policy implementation and the level of funding necessary to carry out this role.

literature, the idea of charging for pollution emissions rather than relying solely on a regulatory approach is becoming increasingly familiar to those who deal with environmental issues.

Another obstacle involves the unique political advantages the current regulatory program provides Congress. Current environmental programs leave almost all difficult issues with the regulatory agency, EPA. From the viewpoint of the politician, the situation is ideal. If EPA follows the letter of the law, and in so doing necessitates very large expenditures on the part of some industrial sector or geographic region, then the legislator can lambast EPA for bureaucratic inflexibility—for failing to take account of the real economic costs and dislocations involved. If EPA is flexible, then the legislator can criticize the Agency for watering down the clear environmental goals expressed so eloquently by Congress.*

In this area, there has been little change. One can only hope that legislative bodies will become more concerned with the effectiveness of legislation rather than with its symbolic purity.

FAVORABLE TRENDS

To conclude, there are two areas where trends seem to indicate a more favorable climate for charge approaches: (1) the growing concern over where to obtain the revenues to meet the increasing costs of environmental control, and (2) the growing interest in regulatory reform.

Where should the revenues be obtained to meet environmental control costs? For solid wastes, this funding problem has become important with the passage of the Resource Recovery and Conservation Act of 1976 (Public Law 94–580). This law requires that states, local communities, and private waste management groups upgrade current solid waste management facilities. The total costs to achieve this have not been estimated but clearly will be substantial. Local governments, in particular, may find it difficult to rely on traditional sources of funds to cover these increased solid waste service costs.

---

* The legislative system in the United States is somewhat unique, since agency heads are not members of the legislative body. Thus, criticisms by legislators need not involve intraparty conflicts. To what extent a parliamentary system is subject to similar effects is unclear.

Charge approaches with rebates for local governments are likely to receive increasing support for this reason.

Obtaining adequate revenues are even more difficult for air and water pollution control, where the total costs are massive. It seems unlikely that enough general tax revenues will be diverted to fund the national cleanup program. Thus, charge strategies may receive more favorable consideration as a logically defensible way of raising revenues for pollution control purposes.

Various options have been suggested for using the revenues collected under a pollution charge scheme. Proposals have included the use of these funds to reduce national or local taxes; to reimburse those who suffer pollution damages; to finance pollution control expenditures; or to provide funding to local governments. Designs which use the charge-derived revenues in such ways are likely to prove far more politically viable. In any event, the increasing competition for general tax dollars will almost certainly require that environmental programs place greater reliance on user fees.

The second trend—the growing interest in reducing the role of direct regulation as a way of addressing social issues—raises both a threat and an opportunity. EPA is one of the largest federal regulatory agencies, and the growing negative view of regulation does threaten the broad political support now enjoyed by the agency. Regulations are perceived as cumbersome, unwieldy, ineffective, subject to co-option, and as placing an unreasonable burden on the court system. The regulatory reform movement represents a general reaction against central governmental controls.

The positive side is that regulatory reform offers an opportunity to shift to more efficient social policies to ensure social goals.* Current environmental strategies tend to ignore cost or efficiency considerations, and place almost total reliance on the coercive powers of the courts (see Alexander [1976]). Cost effectiveness—one of the major benefits of a charge approach—becomes increasingly important at higher levels of treatment, since control costs rapidly increase. Thus, regulatory reform offers an opportunity to modify existing environmental policies and a new forum in which to argue the strengths of a market-based approach.

---

* Charles Schultze in the Fall 1976 Godkin Lectures discussed this theme at length. See Schultze (1977).

CONCLUSION

To summarize, the United States experience on solid waste disposal charges has been a valuable demonstration that progress in advancing pollution charges is feasible. The analytic procedures used to evaluate waste charges will be useful in assessing other charge approaches. Moreover, effective answers have been developed to many of the practical problems that must be faced whenever a charge strategy is considered. Finally, trends favorable to charge strategies have been identified. I hope that others will review what we have done and will benefit from it. I believe our work on waste disposal charges has advanced the prospects of other pollution charge strategies.

NOTES

1. Excerpt taken from the introduction of *Economic Analysis of Environmental Problems* edited by Edwin S. Mills, November 1975, New York.

2. A bibliography on the pollution charge issue citing several hundred articles is available from the author. A selected bibliography follows these notes.

3. The inefficiency of regulatory approaches has been discussed extensively; see, for example, Kneese and Schultze (1975) and Schultze (1977).

4. A review of various charging concepts is included in Irwin and Liroff (1974).

5. All citations are from the *Oxford English Dictionary,* 1971, Compact Edition.

6. For a more detailed description of this work, the reader should review the *Third and Fourth Reports to Congress on Resource Recovery and Waste Reduction,* U.S. EPA.

7. The work reported on in this paper deals exclusively with solid waste management issues in the United States. Nonetheless, this experience is, I believe, more generally applicable. Where exceptions appear relevant, I have so indicated in a footnote.

8. The concept was first discussed in the Senate hearings that led to the Resource Recovery Act of 1970. See Wegman (1970).

9. This principle requires that all pollution control costs be borne directly by the polluter. Subsidies are specifically precluded. See OECD (1975).

10. Several bills restricting "excessive" packaging have been introduced in Congress over the last several years. The State of Minnesota has passed legislation requiring that any new type of packaging receive prior approval by the Minnesota Pollution Control Agency. This is discussed in our *Fourth Report to Congress,* now in preparation.

11. The major problem is that the translation of a general charge approach

into a specific proposal takes considerable staff and funds. Over the last three years virtually no effort has been devoted to this work.

12. This analysis is being carried out by the Research Triangle Institute. A final report on this work is expected by fall 1977.

13. Richard Slitor (1976).

14. Morris (1976). Note especially Appendix B: "Evolution of the Sulfur Oxides Tax."

BIBLIOGRAPHY

Alexander, T. An agenda for the new administration III; If we persist on the present regulatory paths, costs will outweigh benefits and, oddly enough, the environment may get dirtier. *Fortune,* 94(5):129–31, 230, 232, 234.

Anderson, F. R. Environmental charges; Economic, technical, legal and political aspects. [Washington: National Academy of Engineering, Committee on Public Engineering Policy], July 1975. 241 pp. (Draft report)

Bingham, T. H. [Research Triangle Institute]. Allocative and distributive effects of alternative air quality attainment policies; final report. Washington: U.S. Environmental Protection Agency, Implementation Research Division, October 1974. 119 pp. (Unpublished report.)

——— [Research Triangle Institute]. *Cost-effectiveness of a uniform national sulfur emissions tax; final report.* Washington: U.S. Environmental Protection Agency, Feb. 1974. 203 pp. (Distributed by National Technical Information Service, Sprinfield, Va., as PB–236 586).

——— [Research Triangle Institute]. *An evaluation of the effectiveness and costs of regulatory and fiscal policy instruments on product packaging.* Environmental Protection Publication SW–74c. Washington: U.S. Environmental Protection Agency, 1974. 301 pp.

Cannon, D. W. A pollution tax won't help control pollution. Remarks of Daniel W. Cannon, Director of Environmental Affairs, National Association of Manufacturers, before the Environmental Study Conference, U.S. Congress, Washington, D.C., May 26, 1976. P. 6.

Carson, W. D., Jr. A uniform charge on emissions in an urban air basin. [Sacramento], California Air Resource Board [n.d.]. 22 pp. (Draft report)

Cell, D. C. Aircraft noise policy: The role of the airports; A statement submitted to FAA and EPA. [Mount Vernon] Iowa: Cornell College, Jan. 17, 1977, 12 pp.

Chapman, Duane. A sulfur emission tax and the electric utility industry. *Energy systems policy* 1 (Fall 1974):1–30.

Citizens' Advisory Committee on Environmental Quality. *A new look at recycling waste paper; Report on a Conference, May 11, 1976.* Washington: U.S. Government Printing Office, 1976. 88 pp.

Committee for Economic Development, Research and Policy Committee. *More effective programs for a cleaner environment; A statement on national policy.* New York, April, 1974. 85 pp.

DeLucia, R. J. [Meta Systems, Inc.]. *An evaluation of marketable effluent permit systems; Final report.* Washington: U.S. Environmental Protection Agency, Office of Research and Development, September 1974. 363 pp. (Distributed by National Technical Information Service, Springfield, Va., as PB–239 418.)

Diamond, H. L. Two modest proposals. Keynote address presented at meeting, National Association of Recycling Industries, New York City, Oct. 7, 1976. 5 pp.

Dorfman, N. S., and Snow, A. [Public Interest Economics Center]. *Who bears the cost of pollution control? The impact on the distribution of income of financing federally required pollution control.* Washington: Council on Environmental Quality and U.S. Environmental Protection Agency, Aug. 15, 1973. 120 pp. (Distributed by National Technical Information Service, Springfield, Va., as PB–226 447.)

Freeman, A. M., III, and Haveman, R. H. Residuals charges for pollution control: A policy evaluation. *Science,* 177 (4045): 322–29, July 28, 1972.

Gaba, J. M. Regulation of municipal solid waste through taxation; The New York Recycling Incentive Tax. *Columbia Journal of Environmental Law* 1(2) (Spring 1975):312–30.

Hart, G. Keynote address. Presented at 5th Annual Solid Waste Conference, University of Tennessee, Nashville, Jan. 19–21, 1976. 13 pp.

Irwin, W. A., and Liroff, R. A. [Environmental Law Institute] *Economic disincentives for pollution control: Legal, political and administrative dimensions.* Washington: U.S. Environmental Protection Agency, July 1974. 257 pp. (Distributed by National Technical Information Service, Springfield, Va., as PB–239–40.)

Johnson, R. W. and Brown, G. M., Jr. Comprehensive management and effluent charge systems in European water management. Presented at International Conference on Water Law and Administration, AIDA II, Caracas, Venezuela, Feb. 8–14, 1976. 31 pp.

Kneese, A. V., and Schultze, C. L. *Pollution, prices and public policy.* Washington: Brookings Institution, 1975. 125 pp.

Lane, Lee. New opportunities for pollution taxes. *Tax Notes,* 3 (49): 13–21, Dec. 8, 1975.

Lee, R. A. *A history of regulatory taxation.* [Lexington] University Press of Kentucky [1973]. 222 pp.

Lumb, H. C. *Economic incentives for pollution control.* Testimony on behalf of National Association of Manufacturers presented by H. C. Lumb, Vice-President, Corporate Relations and Public Affairs, Republic Steel Corporation, before the Subcommittee on Priorities and Economy in Government, Joint Economic Committee, Congress of the United States, July 19, 1971. 17 pp.

Meta Systems, Inc. *Effluent charges: Is the price right?* Washington: U.S. Environmental Protection Agency, September 1973. 135 pp., app.

Mills, E. X., and White, L. J. *Government policies toward automotive emis-*

sions control. Princeton: Princeton University, Economics Department [1976]. 84 pp.

Morris, S. E. Office of Management and Budget and Office of Tax Analysis. Environmental regulation: The desirability of a tax/incentives approach. [29 pp.] (Memorandum from S. E. Morris to Domestic Council Review Group.)

New York (State), Legislature. *An act to amend the tax law, by adding thereto provisions enabling any city with a population of one million or more to impose taxes to promote the recycling of containers and reduce the cost of solid waste disposal to such city.* 1971. 6 pp.

Organization for Economic Cooperation and Development. *Pollution charges; An assessment.* Paris.

Pearce, D. *Economic instruments and the control of waste lubrication oil.* AEU/ENV/75.3. Paris: Organization for Economic Cooperation and Development, June 25, 1975. 30 pp.

Pearce, D. W., and Sharp, C. Charging for noise. Ad Hoc Group on Noise Abatement Policies working paper no. 1. Paris: Organization for Economic Cooperation and Development, Environment Directorate, Feb. 23, 1976. 41 pp. (ENV/N76.100)

Report on the Tax Policy Advisory Committee to the Council on Environmental Quality. Washington: U.S. Government Printing Office, 1973. 49 pp.

Schultze, C. L. The public use of private incentives. Oct. 5, 1976. [132 pp.] (Author's rough draft; material used for the Godkin Lectures, December 1976.)

Slitor, R. E. *Administrative aspects of a dedicated manufacturers' excise tax on solid waste creating products; Final report.* Washington: U.S. Environmental Protection Agency, Resource Recovery Division. (In preparation)

Smith, Fred Lee. Bibliography on pollution charges and related issues. [Draft] December 1976.

Suurland, J. A. Noise charges in the Netherlands. Ad Hoc Group on Noise Abatement Policies working paper no. 2. ENV/N/76.102. Paris: Organization for Economic Cooperation and Development, Environment Directorate, Apr. 2, 1976. 46 pp.

Tunderman, D. W. Economic enforcement tools for pollution control: The Connecticut plan. Presented at the Environmental Study Conference Briefing; Tax and Fee Approaches to Pollution Control [Washington], May 26, 1976. 21 pp.

Urban Systems Research & Engineering, Inc. *The distribution of water pollution control costs; Final report.* Washington: National Commission on Water Quality, March 1976. 2 vols.

U.S. Congress, Joint Economic Committee. *Economic analysis and the efficiency of government; Hearings before the Subcommittee on Priorities and Economy in Government,* 92nd Cong., 1st session; ot. 6. Economic incentives to control pollution, July 12 and 19, 1971. Washington: U.S. Government Printing Office, 1971. Pp. 1,185–1,308.

U.S. Congress, Senate. *A bill to establish a program to provide assistance to local governments for solid waste disposal programs.* S. 3874, 94th Cong., 2d sess. [Washington: U.S. Government Printing Office], Oct. 1, 1976. 18 pp.

U.S. Congress, Senate. *Solid Waste Source Reduction and Recycling Incentives Act of 1973.* S. 1879, 93d Cong., 1st sess. [Washington: U.S. Government Printing Office], May 23, 1973. 40 pp.

U.S. Congress, Senate, Office of the Legislative Counsel. *A bill to amend the Internal Revenue Code of 1954 to impose a manufacturers' excise tax on the sale of rigid containers for consumer goods and on the sale of flexible packaging and packaging paper used in consumer goods,* 94th Cong., 2d sess. 5 pp. (Senator Haskell) Transmitted to Undersecretary Charles Walker on Jan. 26, 1976.

U.S. Environmental Protection Agency, Office of Solid Waste Management Programs. *Resource recovery and waste reduction; Third report to Congress.* Environmental Protection Publication SW–161. Washington: U.S. Government Printing Office, 1975. 96 pp.

U.S. Environmental Protection Agency, Office of Solid Waste. *Resource recovery and waste reduction; Fourth report to Congress.* [In preparation]

Wegman, L. S. Statement of Leonard S. Wegman, Leonard S. Wegman Co., Inc., New York. In U.S. Congress, Senate, Committee on Public Works. *Resource Recovery Act of 1969* (pt. 3). *Hearings before the Subcommittee on Air and Water Pollution,* 91st Cong., 2d sess., on S. 2005, Feb. 20, 23–25, 1970. Washington: U.S. Government Printing Office, 1970. Pp. 1,854–1,866.

Wilson, D. G., and Chen, P. W. [Massachusetts Institute of Technology]. *An analysis of emission charges as a method of reducing sulfur pollution.* Upton, N.Y.: Brookhaven National Laboratory, Biological and Environmental Assessment Group, September 1975. 95 pp.

PART II

Recycling:
Problems and Alternatives

CHAPTER 6

Municipal Waste: Economic Aspects of Technological Alternatives

Joan Wilcox *

Recent years have seen an upsurge in concern for the environment. This has led to increasing pressure both for measures to reduce the generation of waste and to encourage greater re-use, recycling, and reclamation of waste.

Several waste disposal techniques, most with recycling possibilities, have been developed. This paper considers a number of them and assesses the conditions under which they are likely to be financially viable. There follows a short discussion of the extent to which financial criteria may lead to investment decisions inappropriate from the point of view of society as a whole. The last section presents some conclusions.

Inevitably, this paper draws heavily on United States literature, particularly the excellent Environmental Protection Agency publications. This is supplemented by United Kingdom experience and En-

* Helpful comments on this paper have been received with gratitude from a number of my colleagues. Special thanks are due to the engineers who have been unstinting in their help ever since I became involved in the economics of waste management. Naturally, any views expressed in this note are my sole responsibility; they do not necessarily reflect the views either of the Department of the Environment or of the Economics Directorate.

glish data.† Some caution should be exercised in interpreting the data. Certainly the English cost data, and probably the American data, relate to historic accounting costs, which are hardly a reliable guide to the present situation. Accordingly, where possible, investment cost data relating to 1974/75 have been used to supplement average historic cost data and to give a clearer idea of current costs.

It is possible to draw general conclusions from these data on the relative resource costs and benefits of different disposal methods. However, costs can vary widely with local conditions. Labor, fuel, and transport costs differ considerably within countries, even more so between countries. Site preparation costs are extremely site specific, land costs only marginally less so. Thus, the general conclusions reached here cannot replace a full evaluation of available options when investment decisions are to be made. The emphasis, as always, should be on opportunity cost. For example, in considering an incineration scheme, it is not the absolute cost that is relevant, but the difference between it and the cost of some other alternative, usually bulk transport and landfill. It is important also to use discounted cash flow techniques, especially for projects which will affect site life and thus subsequent investment. This is the procedure recommended to waste disposal authorities in England by the Department of the Environment (United Kingdom Department of the Environment [1976]).

CONTROLLED LANDFILL

Although landfill is the final step in all waste treatment, it is by far the cheapest and most widespread method of waste disposal. It thus merits first place in the discussion.

In the past, uncontrolled dumping of household waste led to odors, fire risk, littered paper, and a problem with rodents. In addition, careless site selection risked water pollution. To reduce these problems, controlled landfill was introduced into the United Kingdom fifty years ago. Although it is still not uniformly practiced, the eventual implementation of the Control of Pollution Act 1974 should remedy this. This contrasts with the United States, where uncontrolled dumps predominate.

Controlled landfill involves the deposit and compaction of waste in

---

† The United Kingdom data presented in this paper relate to England unless otherwise indicated.

shallow layers with the exposed surfaces covered daily with soil or other suitable inert material. Providing that sites are chosen with care, this goes a long way to ensure that the externalities associated with landfill constitute nuisance rather than long-term or permanent degradation of the environment. Landfill or unprocessed waste does mean that potentially recyclable materials are lost, probably irretrievably. On the other hand, derelict land can be restored to use after landfill. The benefits to society as a whole of such reclamation schemes can be considerable, providing of course that the land reclaimed is truly derelict, and its reclamation does not upset the ecological balance.

The cost of a landfill operation consists of the initial investment in land, site works and plant, and the operating costs. Following the conventions used in *Decision Makers Guide in Solid Waste Management* (United States Environmental Protection Agency [1976]), the main items of initial investment are

1. Land
2. Planning and Engineering
   a. Site investigation
   b. Design, plans specification
   c. Permit application
3. Site Development
   a. Land development
   b. Access roads
   c. Fencing, signs
4. Facilities
   a. Administration
   b. Equipment maintenance
   c. Sanitary facilities, utilities
   d. Weight scales
5. Equipment—tractors, etc.

It is difficult to present meaningful cost data since costs, particularly for site development, vary so much with local circumstances. This is demonstrated in Table 6–1 (reproduced from United States Environmental Protection Agency [1976]), which gives initial investment costs for three controlled landfill sites in the United States. The site lives appear to be, respectively, 15 years, 5 years, and 28 years. English data is presented in Table 6–2, where the sites lives are 5, 5,

TABLE 6–1

INITIAL COST OF THREE SANITARY LANDFILLS, 1975

Item	Site 1 (50 tons/day) Cost Total ($ thousands)	Per ton ($)	Site 2 (150 tons/day) Cost Total ($ thousands)	Per ton ($)	Site 3 (300 tons/day) Cost Total ($ thousands)	Per ton ($)
Planning and design	20	0.10	16	0.07	130	0.06
Site development	10	.05	1	—	624*	0.30
Facilities	52†	.26‡	7‡	.03	241	0.12
Equipment	329	1.64	226	1.02	1,033	0.50
TOTAL	411	2.05	250	1.12	2,028	0.98

SOURCE: United States Environmental Protection Agency (1976).
* Includes 3-mile paved road.
† Includes fencing.
‡ No fencing.

and 25 years respectively. In both tables, the site development costs vary widely, and are unrelated to size. On the other hand there is, predictably, evidence of scale economies associated with equipment costs. The lack of a similar relationship in the case of facilities almost certainly indicates differences in standards.

Again following the *Decision Makers Guide in Solid Waste Management* (United States Environmental Protection Agency [1976]), the main categories of operating costs are

1. Personnel
2. Equipment
   a. Operating expenses
   b. Maintenance and repair
   c. Rental, depreciation, or amortization
3. Cover material—material and haul costs
4. Administration overheads
5. Miscellaneous tools, utilities, insurance, maintenance of roads, fences, facilities, drainage features.

In the United Kingdom, the cost of a unit of labor and equipment

Joan Wilcox

INITIAL COSTS FOR THREE CONTROLLED LANDFILLS OF DIFFERENT
CAPACITIES, 1975

	Site 1 (90 tons per day) (117,000 tons total capacity)		Site 2 (150 tons per day) (195,000 tons total capacity)		Site 3 (700 tons per day) (4,550,000 tons total capacity)	
	Cost		Cost		Cost	
	Total (£ thou- sands)	Per Ton (£)	Total (£ thou- sands)	Per Ton (£)	Total (£ thou- sands)	Per Ton (£)
Planning and design *						
Site development	20	0.17	81	0.42	67	0.015
Facilities	5	0.04	34	0.17	5	0.001
Equipment †	35	0.30	35	0.18	96	0.021
TOTAL	60	0.51	150	0.77	168	0.037

SOURCE: United Kingdom Department of the Environment informal survey of
waste disposal authorities.
* Not available.
† Equipment cost was calculated on the basis of a 5-year replacement cycle
and then related to total site capacity.

tends to be fairly uniform but disposal cost per ton* can vary with
the method and efficiency of operation. On the other hand, unit
costs of cover material and leasing rights tend to vary quite widely,
regardless of efficiency. The most recent English cost data available,
relating to 1974–75 (United Kingdom Department of the Environment and Society of County Treasurers [1975]), indicate that the
average disposal cost for household waste, including capital charges
but excluding transport, was £0.92 a ton, within a range of £0.33
to £3.04 per ton. (This relates only to waste transported in collection
vehicles, about 87 percent of household waste.)

The average cost of landfill including transport is likely to increase
sharply in real terms as landfill standards rise and as sites close to
centers of population become increasingly scarce. These costs can be
reduced by seeking cheaper methods of transport, extending site life,

---

* Most of the United Kingdom data relate to tons while the United States
data relates to short tons: (2,000 lb.) 1 ton = 1.1 short tons.

or by resale of various of the constituents of waste. Bulk transport can reduce haulage costs and extend site life. Shredding or baling can extend site life. The introduction of any of them will provide an opportunity for extraction of resalable materials. These options are considered in the following three sections.

BULK TRANSPORT

Collection vehicles can be driven to a transfer station and the waste transferred to faster bulk transporters. Some compaction is achieved, and a full load can be ensured. This can, under certain conditions, prove cheaper than delivery to the disposal site direct by collection vehicle. By switching to use of bulk transporters, savings can be made in the numbers of collection vehicles used, and reduction in their mileage. These savings have to be set against the high initial investment costs (a United Kingdom Department of the Environment engineering estimate for a 250 ton per day operation is up to £1,000,000 [1975 prices]), the transfer station operating cost and the bulk transport cost.

Work done by Mason (1975), updated to 1975 prices, provides a breakdown of the estimated costs of bulk transfer based on a variety of sources, reproduced in Table 6–3. These figures are corroborated by English 1974/75 transfer plus haul costs, displayed in Table 6–4 (United Kingdom Department of the Environment, Society of County Treasurers [1975]).

TABLE 6–3

ESTIMATED COSTS OF BULK TRANSFER*

	Autumn 1973		Spring 1975	
	Cost per ton (£)	%	Cost per ton (£)	%
Transfer	0.44	24	0.60	24
Bulk transport	1.42	76	1.85	76
Total	1.86		2.45	

SOURCE: S. Mason (1975).
* Assuming transport by road a distance of 20 miles to landfill site and transfer station operation at 4,000 hours per annum with some degree of compaction. Capital costs have been amortized at 10% for 1973 and 12% for 1975.

Joan Wilcox 111

TABLE 6–4

U.K. Transfer Station Operation Plus Haul Costs
(Including Capital Charges) 1974/75

Waste Disposal Authority	Average Haul (round trip in miles)	Cost Per Ton (£)
1	17.0	2.75
2	6.0	1.67
3	22.0	2.64
4	12.0	2.58
	7.0	
5	9.0	2.73
	7.0	
6	9.5	4.35
7	5.0	2.48
8	7.5	2.51

Source: United Kingdom Department of the Environment and Society of County Treasurers (1975).

Clearly, per ton costs will vary not only with length of haul but with average speed. Taking this into account, Mason (1974) estimated a relationship, based on 1973/74 prices, between total disposal cost and distance to landfill. This is reproduced in Figure 6–1. Bulk transfer by rail is cheaper than by road over longer distances and environmentally less damaging. However, the use of rail transport is heavily constrained by the necessity for appropriate links, and is rarely used in the United Kingdom. As will be seen from later sections, at least in England, bulk transport over considerable distances followed by landfill compares favorably with other waste disposal options.

VOLUME REDUCTION PROCESSES

Shredding

Shredding is a volume reduction process in which solid waste is shredded into relatively homogeneous material. It is usually a necessary preliminary process to methods of disposal such as composting, pyrolysis, and, in some instances, incineration. Shredding may also be used prior to landfill, sometimes enabling the use of sites unsuitable

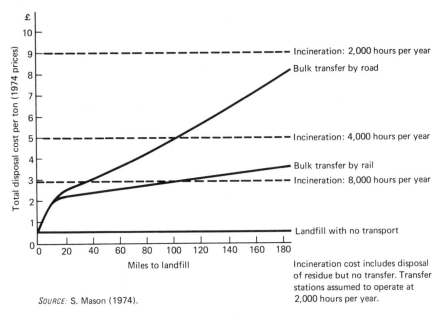

SOURCE: S. Mason (1974).

Figure 6–1 Cost of bulk transport and landfill

for untreated waste. Site management is easier, as shredded waste is more easily controlled in landfill than untreated waste, reduces fire risk, is less attractive to rodents and insects, and less offensive visually during the landfill operations.

There are potential cost advantages with shredding. Because of the volume reduction, site life is increased; and, since settlement is more uniform, the land can be brought back into use earlier. This can be important where replacement sites are expensive or very distant, or where the value of the reclaimed land is very high. The depth of cover material required is less than for untreated landfill, which may be important if cover material is being transported long distances. Furthermore, shredded waste is more easily compacted, which some-times results in lower transport costs. The most important cost ad-vantage, as with any waste handling operation, is the possibility of extraction for resale of ferrous metal. However, similar landfill standards can be achieved, given sufficient care, with untreated waste. Unless required by the planning consent, therefore, shredding should be used only if it is the cheapest way of meeting the required stan-dards. The cost advantages must be set against the operating costs and the initial investment costs, which are likely to be high unless part of an already existing transfer station. In England the average 1974/75 cost of shredding was £3.54 per ton excluding the cost of landfill itself (United Kingdom Department of the Environment and Society of County Treasurers [1975]), more than three times the average landfill cost. In the United States, costs per ton (1974 prices) ranging between $8.60 and $10.66 have been reported (United States Environmental Protection Agency [1976]). It seems unlikely, therefore, that shredding can be justified on that basis. It is generally accepted that shredding is uneconomic at throughputs below 150 tons a day, or if run below design capacity.

Baling
In this system, untreated waste is compressed in a hydraulically operated machine into bales each weighing about 1 ton. Self-sustaining bales (i.e., bales unsecured by wire) can be formed at pressures of 3,000 pounds per square inch although increased stability of the bales is achieved with higher pressures. Shredded waste can be formed into stable bales of similar density by lower pressures; they need to be bound with baling wires but probably expand less than self-sustaining bales and are less likely to disintegrate during transfer.

Baling is only in the experimental stage in the United Kingdom, and no cost data are available. In the United States, 1975 costs of $6.38 and $9.20 a ton respectively are reported for the pilot plants at Saint Paul and San Diego (United States Environmental Protection Agency [1976]). The United States experience indicates that a baler operating at 80 percent or better of design capacity is economically competitive with shredding or small scale incineration at throughputs of over 400 tons per day. The Environmental Protection Agency recommends that cities with less than this minimum tonnage should examine the prospects of a joint venture with neighboring communities before abandoning the baling concept. This implies that, even when quite high haulage costs are incurred, high density baling can still be worthwhile.

Incineration Without Energy Recovery
Incineration of untreated waste can reduce the weight by between one-half and two-thirds and the volume by 90 percent, at the same time providing an opportunity to extract resalable material. There remains the solid residue to be landfilled, but landfill costs will clearly be much

reduced. There are externalities associated with incineration plants. Some of the more obvious problems associated with landfill operations are largely avoided, but this gain is offset by the emission, which can never be entirely eliminated, of gases and grit into the air.

The initial investment costs are high. Most recent United Kingdom incinerators have been 20 ton per hour plants, and have cost about £4,000,000 each (1975 prices), £200,000 per hourly capacity installed. Similarly, the operating costs are high, mainly because of the number of skilled operators required. The evidence on economics of scale is not entirely compatible, as Figure 6–2 shows, but there is a clear indication that there are significant economies of scale up to 500 tons per day operation. In England, the 1974/75 average incineration costs of those authorities with no energy generating incinerators, including capital charges but excluding landfill of residue, was £5.11 per ton (United Kingdom Department of the Environment and Society of County Treasurers [1975]).

The initial investment costs constitute about 75 percent of the total incineration cost. It is, therefore, most important that the plant is operated at as near to full capacity as is possible, on a 24-hour basis. Figure 6–1 compares the cost of bulk transfer and landfill with incineration at various levels of efficiency (1974 United Kingdom

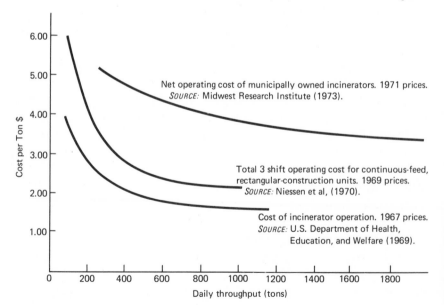

Figure 6–2 Economies of scale in incineration

prices). It shows that even when an incinerator is operating efficiently, bulk transport to landfill sites up to 100 miles away can be cheaper; if the incinerator is running below capacity, it simply cannot compare.

The discussion so far has centered on processes essentially aimed at volume reduction and resulting lower total disposal costs. Whether any of these results in a reduction in net present cost depends on the cost, including transport costs, of both existing and replacement landfills, and, often crucially, the opportunities for extraction and resale of ferrous metals. In some instances, this may mean that even a quite small throughput justifies some form of volume reduction. However, given the existence of economies of scale in all three processes, it will usually only pay for tonnages of over 150 per day for shredding, 400 for baling, and 600 a day for incineration.

The next part of the chapter concentrates on processes with potential for energy generation and materials recovery.

ENERGY GENERATING PROCESSES

Incineration With Energy Recovery

Only six incinerators in the United Kingdom incorporate significant energy recovery. The capital cost is higher, in 1975 prices £250,000 per ton of hourly capacity installed, and it can be difficult to obtain markets to justify the extra cost. The Edmonton incinerator in London is the best documented (P. K. Patrick [1975]). It serves an area of about 1¼ million population and processed 370,000 tons of waste in the twelve months from April 1974, an average of more than 1,000 tons per day. The total cost of the plant, including all major modifications to the boilers, was approximately £13,500,000, spread over several years. The gross expenditure in 1974/75, including capital charges, was £2,900,000. Some 162 million units of electricity were produced, of which 135 million units were sold. Income from the sale of electricity, baled ferrous metal, and furnace ash amounted to £788,000. The net expenditure was £2,160,000, £5.72 per ton.

On the basis of a £50,000 difference per hourly ton of capacity between conventional incinerators and those producing energy, the extra capital cost is probably justified in the Edmonton case. However, since the efficiency of converting solid waste to power is low, it is only likely to be true in plants like Edmonton, which are very large and operate twenty-four hours a day, seven days a week, and have a guaranteed market for their energy. In any event, it is still more expensive than even quite distant landfill.

Waste as a Fuel

Where there is landfill available, incineration, even with power generation, is not competitive. However, recent years have seen an upsurge of interest in the use of the combustible fraction of waste as a supplementary fuel in existing boilers.

A project at Saint Louis in the United States is possibly the most advanced scheme of this kind at present. Waste is shredded and separated by air classification into the light combustible fraction (about 80 percent of the input by weight) and the heavy fraction (mostly metals, glass, stones, etc.). This light fraction of shredded waste is utilized in a power station, where it is fed pneumatically to a modified-suspension-fired boiler and accounts for around 15 percent of the boiler feedstock, the balance being pulverized coal.

The cost of the facility was about $3 million in 1971 (United States Environmental Protection Agency [1975]). Gross operating and maintenance costs for the City and Union Electric Company, based on operating experience from July 1972 to November 1974, were $5.90 per ton of solid waste processed and $8.50 per ton of solid waste fuel burned respectively. During this time, however, the facilities operated at only about 30 percent of design capacity. More intensive capacity utilization is necessary for viability. It is not yet clear that this will be possible. Judgment on the Saint Louis project must, therefore, be deferred.

In any event, at least in the United Kingdom, any scheme to provide supplementary fuel for power stations requires very large-scale production of waste. An approach with more promise for the United Kingdom is the use of shredded waste in industrial boiler plants using chain grate stokers. A full-scale sorting plant is being constructed in Newcastle by the Tyne and Wear Waste Disposal Authority, partly financed by the Department of the Environment. It will sort 300 tons a day of household waste. The ferrous content will be extracted for resale and the light combustible fraction shredded for use as a supplementary fuel.

In assessing the financial viability of this scheme, the criterion is not whether a profit is made, but whether the net present cost of the scheme is less than available alternatives. In this case, the alternatives considered were landfill via collection vehicles, incineration and landfill via bulk transporters. The net present cost of the sorting scheme, on very conservative assumptions about the resale value of the supplementary fuel and ferrous scrap and the required modifications to existing boiler plant, was lower than that of the cheapest alternative, landfill via bulk transport.

It must be stressed that this project is not yet under way; this conclusion should be regarded as provisional. However, it is hoped that this research project will demonstrate that waste can be processed continuously and used successfully as fuel with only minor modifications to existing boilers.

As mentioned earlier, there are economies of scale associated with both transfer stations and shredding plants. It is also important that markets exist for the supplementary fuel. This means it is probable that daily throughputs of less than 250 tons a day will not prove viable unless there are absolutely no landfill sites available.

A rather different approach is being adopted in the West Midlands, where Imperial Metal Industries are taking, as a fuel supplement, up to 60,000 tons of untreated household waste a year, on a five-year contract. Imperial Metal Industries will extract the ferrous content for resale and use the remainder, shredded, as fuel. This is still in the experimental stages, and no disclosure of anticipated savings has been made. However, Imperial Metal Industries is convinced "that they are the kind of returns you would willingly invest £¼m on" (*Surveyor* [1976]).

Another experimental but promising scheme is a process developed by Associated Portland Cement Manufacturers, Ltd. (D. Knights [1976]). Shredded household waste, the ferrous content extracted, will take the place of a proportion of the coal normally used to fire the kiln in cement manufacture. The quality of the cement is not affected. There are two particular advantages of this new process. First, the acid gases normally produced when incinerating waste are neutralized by the alkaline materials used for the manufacture of cement. Second, although it is necessary to strike the correct balance between the lime and other constituents, with waste becoming part of the cement clinker, there is no residual ash disposal problem.

The viability of the process is determined by fuel costs, the calorific

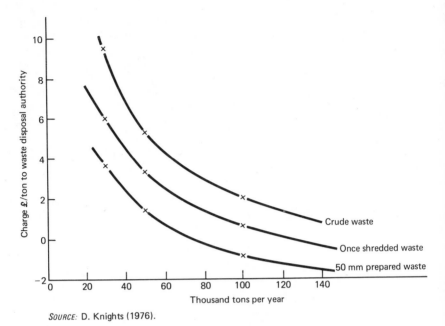

SOURCE: D. Knights (1976).

Figure 6–3 Relationship between charge (£/T) to local authority and refuse tons/annum

value of the waste, which varies regionally and seasonally, the quantity of waste that can be absorbed, and the capital and operating costs of the plant required. On the basis of the proposed charges to local authorities, shown in Figure 6–3, it seems unlikely that this will ever be attractive to waste disposal authorities that have suitable landfill sites available for untreated waste. However, waste disposal authorities whose only alternative is landfill considerably more distant than the cement works or who are required by planning consents to shred waste may well find this an attractive proposition. The scheme is as yet experimental, but an operational unit is expected to come into production early in 1977.

Pyrolysis

The principle of pyrolysis applied to the disposal of solid waste is that shredded waste is heated around 800°C, in the absence of air or in an oxygen-deficient atmosphere. The intense heating causes the organic matter to decompose physically and chemically rather than burn. The products of pyrolysing solid waste are gas, liquid, and char. The gas given off during the process has a high calorific value and can be used to sustain the process, with any balance, if worthwhile, stored for other uses. The liquid is mostly oil and water. Where the primary consideration is volume reduction, pyrolysis of solid waste may prove environmentally more attractive than incineration and, on the basis of early estimates, no more costly. Unfortunately, pyrolysis plants have not yet proved operationally successful, so that these cost estimates cannot be viewed with confidence. In any event, the use of waste as supplementary fuel, although not yet proven, is based on known and relatively simple technology, and is likely to prove more than competitive with pyrolysis.

Acid Hydrolysis Process

Acid hydrolysis of cellulose is a process for producing ethanol from domestic waste. The waste is pulverized, cans and other ferrous objects magnetically separated, and the lighter mainly cellulosic fraction removed by a special pulper or dry separation using air blast and a baffle or "zigzag" separator. Plastics and fine particles may be removed, and the lighter cellulosic fraction is then fed to the continuous reactor for hydrolysis.

Dr. A. Porteous (1976) has prepared cost estimates for an acid hydrolysis plant processing 250 tons of waste a day, reproduced in Table 6–5. *On the basis of these cost estimates,* acid hydrolysis would

TABLE 6–5

ECONOMIC ANALYSIS FOR A 250 TONS REFUSE/DAY ACID HYDROLYSIS PLANT
£10,000/TON OF DAILY CAPACITY

	40% Paper Content Cost (£)	60% Paper Content Cost (£)
Plant cost	2,500,000	2,500,000
Fixed charges at 20%	500,000	500,000
Wages	60,000	60,000
Energy and materials	185,000	179,000
BOD reduction	71,500	180,000
Residue refuse disposal charges (at £2/ton)	108,000	76,000
Total Annual Cost	914,000	923,000
Ethanol revenue at £100/ton	816,000	1,290,000
Profit per ton of refuse	−1.07	4.00

SOURCE: Dr. A. Porteous (1976).

appear to compare favorably with incineration but not with bulk transport to landfill or the use of waste as a fuel, unless the paper content is well over 40 percent. This is not likely to be the case, since the average paper content of United Kingdom waste is about 30 percent, and of United States waste about 33 percent (see United States Environmental Protection Agency [1976]). Further, it must be emphasized that no pilot plants for acid hydrolysis yet exist, so that it is difficult to draw any firm conclusions as to its merits relative to incineration.

MICROBIAL AND CHEMICAL CONVERSION OF WASTE

Some basic research has been carried out into the biological processes for converting organic waste into useful products. The waste includes household, forestry, farm, food, and other industrial waste and sewage sludge. The products include single-cell protein, methane, and alcohol. Considerable pretreatment by separation, sizing, and screening is usually necessary, and there are residues and effluent produced which require disposal.

The processes have many variants but basically involve either direct feeding of the waste to animals, or microbial-based processes such as fermentation and anaerobic digestion. Research into microbial and chemical conversion of waste is still in the early stage, and it is not yet possible to say whether or not they will be viable methods of waste disposal.

MATERIALS RECOVERY

Materials Recovery at the Collection Stage

It is possible to recover materials from household waste either at the collection or disposal stages. In November 1974 almost half of the collection authorities in England and Wales were running permanent schemes to encourage the collection at source of mixed waste paper, and a further 10 percent had temporary schemes.

The main factors determining financial viability are the type of collection scheme, the system of payments it is possible to negotiate with the work force, the scale of operations, minimum uptake, and the resale value. Unfortunately, the latter fluctuates violently, and is a major disincentive to both local authorities and voluntary organizations. Significantly, an unpublished survey by the Department of the Environment suggests that in England and Wales the more profitable schemes are, on average, the schemes collecting larger weights of paper.

Materials Recovery at the Disposal Stage

It is usually not practicable to recover more than one or two items at the collection stage. However, a number of methods have been proposed for sorting waste that has previously been subjected to size reduction. These include screening, density separation as used in the Saint Louis scheme, magnetic extraction, and optical separation. For the most part, these processes have not been technically successful when applied to solid waste, with the profitable exception of magnetic extraction. In any event, it is unlikely that the extra expenditure associated with such processes would have been justified by the income from the materials recovered.

Rather more ambitious are total recycling schemes, recovering material either from raw unprocessed waste or the residual material remaining after thermal treatment. An example of the latter is a process developed by the United States Bureau of Mines. It uses a series of shredding, screening, grinding, and magnetic separation procedures to produce metallic iron concentrates, nonferrous metal composites, glass fractions, and fine carbonaceous ash tailings. Examples of materials recovery from untreated waste are the Black-Clawson Hydrasposal/Fiberclaim demonstration plant at Franklin, Ohio, which uses a wet process system for recovering paper pulp, steel, glass, aluminium, and ash, and the Warren Spring Laboratory, Stevenage, England, sorting plant, which recovers paper and board, ferrous metal and glass.

None of these systems is in widespread use, so it is difficult to assess their cost, their reliability, or the existence of stable markets for the recovered material. However, the Midwest Research Institute (1973) made 1971 estimates of a materials recovery process consistent with wet and dry separation process, although not tied to any one system. The conclusion was that, except for tonnages over 600 per day, materials recovery processes did not compete with distant landfill; incineration with residue recovery could not compete at all.

As for the United Kingdom, an operational development of the Warren Spring Laboratory is to be set up in Doncaster, England, but as yet no data are available.

NONFINANCIAL COSTS AND BENEFITS

The discussion so far has concentrated on the financial aspects of a number of waste disposal technologies. However, there is pressure from some quarters to ignore financial viability when assessing waste disposal options. Although rarely explicit, this is an acknowledgment that market forces are not always the best guide of what is best for society as a whole.

There are a number of market imperfections that could result in too low a level of re-use, recycling, and reclamation of waste. Lack of full information about available technologies is one such market imperfection, but it can be remedied. The Environmental Protection Agency has made a considerable contribution in this direction in the United States. The Department of the Environment has made similar efforts in England and Wales. Another problem is the existence of externalities in waste collection and disposal techniques, which could lead to a bias against environmentally less damaging techniques. This bias can in part be offset by standards to control some of the adverse impact of these processes. Differing valuations of the future relative to the present may result in a lack of concern to conserve nonrenewable resources, manifested by market prices for energy or metals too low to encourage recycling. On the other hand, monopoly in resource ownership could result in market prices being too high. Problems can also be caused by the existence of particular taxes or regulations imposed for reasons other than to make private and social costs coincide, or an overvalued currency. The former can bias manufacturers in favor of virgin rather than recycled inputs. An overvalued currency can result, for example, in recycled wood pulp comparing unfavorably with imported virgin wood pulp.

The instruments appropriate to improving the workings of particular markets relevant to recycling and reclamation vary according to the market and the obstacles to its smooth running. Most can only be taken at a national level, some at international level. A municipality evaluating a range of waste management options may well go beyond the financial aspects and consider the relative external effects of different options. However, it cannot reasonably be expected to consider the impact, for example, on the balance of payments or the world's stock of nonrenewable resources. Central government action of one sort or another is required to ensure that private or local decisions do not militate against the overall welfare of society.

Action to readjust an inappropriate tax structure, impose higher operating standards, or institute schemes to provide insulation against highly fluctuating markets is in principle easy to take. Such action, if not already taken, is being considered in many countries. This may affect the earlier conclusions on financial viability, more in some countries than in others. That is not important if proper evaluations are being made in each case, since market prices will now be an appropriate guide.

What is important is whether there are other sources of divergence between social and private costs which cannot easily be assessed and thus corrected, and which may alter the project ranking achieved using financial criteria.

Even with the imposition of operating standards, some waste disposal methods are more environmentally damaging than others. In the absence of any well-defined methodology for evaluating environmental damage, it is reassuring to observe that the financially most attractive waste disposal options appear to be the least damaging environmentally. In the United Kingdom, landfill is the cheapest acceptable method of disposal, and remains so even when the more serious problems of public health or water pollution that can be associated with landfill are avoided by proper site selection, development, and operation. Of the thermal reduction and heat recovery processes, all of which cause some measure of air pollution in addition to the usual problems of nuisance, possibly the least polluting are pyrolysis and the use of the combustible fraction of waste as a supplementary fuel. As has been seen, although still in the development stage, the latter is, after short-distance landfill, potentially the most viable financially. There seems, therefore, no strong reason to worry about the divergence between private and social costs arising from externalities.

A more serious problem is that market forces are unlikely to take into account the effect on future generations of the depletion of nonrenewable resources. Most of the constituents of household waste cannot be considered to be depletable resources. However, metals, some 9 percent by weight of household waste in Britain (United Kingdom

Department of the Environment [1971]) are clearly nonrenewable resources. It is also arguable that since fossil fuels are nonrenewable, waste disposal processes which generate usable energy should be valued very much more highly than market prices suggest.

In this case, the equivalence in ranking by private and social costs is not as evident. Landfill of untreated waste does prevent the re-trieval of metal except at the collection stage. However, it is increas-ingly the case that waste is transferred to bulk transporters, shredded, and so forth. This gives an opportunity to extract the metal content. Indeed, the income from sale of ferrous scrap is often the deciding factor in the investment decision.

Landfill of waste also precludes its use for energy generation. This highlights the real problem in evaluating waste disposal processes. It can be argued that market prices undervalue energy, although the argument has less force than for metals. It can also be argued that market prices undervalue the benefits of the reclamation, for public use, of derelict land. It is not obvious where the divergence between social and private cost is greater. Given the present state of the art, the final judgment must lie with the decisions taker.

CONCLUSIONS

It must be emphasized again that local circumstances vary widely. A complete evaluation of available waste disposal options must pre-cede any investment decision. However, it is possible to draw some general conclusions.

In choosing between waste disposal options, it is important to be aware that the costs of inefficient or unreliable operation can be very high. Waste is generated on a regular basis and all sorts of problems, usually costly to remedy, can arise if there is any serious delay in processing it. Clearly, the more complicated the process, the greater the chance of breakdown. Other things being equal, then, tried and tested processes are usually to be preferred. Many waste handling processes have relatively high capital costs. If they are to be viable, they must be run efficiently and to full capacity. It is also sensible to take any opportunity for metal extraction. This can be very profitable since the incremental cost is usually small compared with the revenue generated. This depends, of course, on the existence of a market, vitally important in any scheme to recycled waste.

Joan Wilcox
125

The evidence from both the United States and the United Kingdom indicates that high-standard controlled landfill of waste, even when transported over long distances, remains the cheapest acceptable waste disposal method. Its main drawback is that landfill of untreated waste precludes metal extraction, although the increasing use of pretreatment processes is remedying this. It is also true that a chance for energy generation is lost, although there is the compensation of derelict land reclamation, important in a densely populated country like the United Kingdom.

Although continuing widespread mineral extraction in the United Kingdom ensures no shortage of landfill sites in most areas, this is not always the case in other countries. The best-established but far more expensive alternative to landfill is incineration.

However, there are processes being developed which also allow ferrous extraction and energy generation, and which should prove cheaper than incineration. Of these, the most promising is the use of the combustible fraction of waste as a supplementary fuel in existing boilers, a process based on known and tested technology. If it fulfills its early promise, this should prove financially competitive even with landfill in urban areas. Not only is it probably less environmentally damaging than incineration and the use of conventional fuels, it also has the added advantage of reducing the depletion of nonrenewable resources.

Financial criteria are not always the best guide in choosing between different waste management options. However, many of the market imperfections associated with waste disposal are susceptible to correction, and indeed in many cases have already been corrected. The most intractable are externalities and the depletion of nonrenewable resources. It is not the purpose of this paper to argue the extent to which market prices undervalue the benefits of recycling waste. However, it seems likely that, in many if not most cases, financial criteria will provide the ranking of waste management options most appropriate for society as a whole.

BIBLIOGRAPHY

Knights, D. 1976. *Domestic refuse disposal via cement kilns.* Symposium on Associated Portland Cement Manufacturers and Waste Disposal in the United Kingdom, 2 June.
Mason, S. 1974. *The economics of solid waste disposal: A cost comparison*

between bulk transfer and incineration. Redland Purle/ISCOL Conference, London, May.

————, 1975. Bulk transfer of refuse to landfill—An analysis of costs involved, *Environmental Pollution Management,* July/August.

Midwest Research Institute, 1973. *Resource recovery, the state of technology.* Prepared for the United States Council on Environmental Quality, February.

Niessen, W. R., 1970. *Systems study of air pollution from municipal incineration.* Prepared by Arthur D. Little, Inc., for the United States Department of Health, Education, and Welfare.

Patrick, P. K., 1975. *Operational experience in energy recovery through incineration,* Public Health Engineering Department, Greater London Council.

Porteous, Dr. A. 1976. Economic comparison of large scale energy recovery refuse recycling methods. *Resources Policy,* December.

Surveyor, 1976. Refuse: Watts in it for industry. 30 February.

United Kingdom Department of the Environment, 1971. *Refuse disposal: Report of the Working Party on refuse disposal,* Her Majesty's Stationery Office, London.

United Kingdom Department of the Environment, 1976. *Reclamation, treatment and disposal of waste; an evaluation of available options,* Waste Management Paper No. 1, Her Majesty's Stationery Office, London.

United Kingdom Department of the Environment and the Society of County Treasurers, 1975. *Waste disposal enquiry.* London.

United States Environmental Protection Agency, 1975. *Third report to Congress: Resource recovery and waste reduction.* Washington, D.C.

United States Environmental Protection Agency, 1976. *Decision makers guide in solid waste management.* Washington, D.C.

United States Department of Health, Education, and Welfare, 1969. *Master plan for solid waste collection and disposal in parish metropolitan area of New Orleans.* United States Public Health Service, Washington, D.C.

CHAPTER 7

Consumer Product Life Extension in the Context of Materials and Energy Flows

W. David Conn *

It is nothing new to hear consumers complaining that so-called durable products such as automobiles and household appliances, "are not made to last long enough." However, a subject that has long been an issue in consumer affairs is now receiving attention from a different angle, as a result of our growing awareness of problems of resource depletion and environmental damage. Product life extension (PLE) is being suggested as a possible means of conserving natural resources, reducing environmental impacts, and providing a check on the ever-increasing costs of waste management.[1] Stated simply, it is thought that by making products last longer, both the generation of discards and the demand for replacements can be reduced.

In its intent, PLE is an example of "waste reduction" (i.e., the prevention of waste at its source). Other examples of waste reduction include the development and use of products requiring less material per unit of product (for example, smaller automobiles, thinner-walled containers, etc.), the substitution of re-usable products for single-use

* The author wishes to thank Thomas E. Smith for assisting in a preliminary study of the product lifetime issue, sponsored by the Academic Senate of the University of California, Los Angeles. Donald M. McAllister, David W. Pearce, and Blair T. Bower kindly provided comments on earlier drafts of this paper.

"disposable" products, and an increase in the number of times that items are re-used (for example, re-usable plates and cutlery, refillable beverage containers, etc.), and a reduction in the number of units of product consumed per household per year (for example, fewer automobiles per family).

It may be noted that waste reduction complements resource recovery as a means of conserving natural resources and reducing the flows of materials and energy requiring disposal to the physical environment; the former seeks to reduce the rate at which materials and energy *enter* the waste stream, while the latter seeks to recover and re-use resources *after* they have become wastes.

The potential contribution of PLE as a method of waste reduction is still largely unexplored. To place it in perspective, the U.S. Environmental Protection Agency (1975) has made some simple calculations to estimate the possible impact of PLE applied to passenger car tires and automobiles in the United States. Based on figures reported by Westerman (1974), one calculation indicates that if all original equipment tires purchased after 1978 were to last for 100,000 miles, and if all tire replacements were to be retreaded 100,000 mile tires that would last for an additional 27,000 miles, then tire consumption (and ultimate waste) would be reduced by 143 million tires per year by 1990; this would represent an annual saving of 23 million barrels of oil, 1.75 million tons of rubber, and 525 million pounds of carbon black, with accompanying reductions in the environmental impacts associated with the production of these materials. However, a 100,000 mile tire is not yet available although its development is thought feasible in the foreseeable future.

Turning now to cars, if all of those sold in 1980 were to last for twelve years (instead of about ten as at present in the United States), then by 1990 (assuming a steady state situation), new car sales would be expected to decrease by about 20 percent from a predicted level of about 14,300,000 units to 11,500,000 units. Annual resource/waste savings throughout all phases of the automobile life cycle would amount to about 6,700,000 tons, composed of 5,500,000 tons of steel, 151,000 tons of aluminum, and 142,000 tons of zinc.

As mentioned above, these estimates are based on very simple calculations and therefore must be treated with caution. For example, it is important to realize that the resource savings quoted for the automobiles would not correspond directly to savings in virgin materials since the calculations do not distinguish between material inputs from secondary as opposed to virgin sources. The situation would be complicated by the fact that the reduction in waste generation would also reduce the amount of secondary material potentially available for recycling.

Even if the only concern is the magnitude of the flow through the system (regardless of its source), there are other complications that make prediction of the impact of PLE extremely difficult. These are the subject of a theoretical discussion later in this chapter. However, before proceeding to that discussion, I shall briefly review the existing policy-relevant literature in the field and outline some of the factors that affect product lifetimes, suggesting the kinds of policies that might be used to influence them.

EXISTING KNOWLEDGE REGARDING PRODUCT LIFETIMES

Two recent searches of the existing literature have revealed rather little on the subject of product lifetimes that policy makers are likely to find really useful (Butlin, 1976; Smith and Conn, 1976). On the theoretical side, there are contributions to the economics literature that both consider the nature of durable goods (portraying them as goods that provide services over an extended period of time) and develop models to explain the supply of and (to a lesser extent) the demand for this category of goods.[2] A major focus of the discussions is the question of whether a monopolistic or a competitive industry is likely to produce the more durable products. However, the models used are highly abstract, containing restrictive and generally unrealistic assumptions. Only occasionally (e.g., in the dissertation by Avinger, 1968) are there insights into broader aspects of the durability issue that may be of greater interest to policy makers.

On the applied side, the list of useful contributions identified by the two searches is also short. It includes: (1) a survey of possible sources for obtaining data on product lifetimes and a brief discussion of possible mechanisms for influencing them (Teknekron, 1973); (2) procedures for empirically measuring lifetimes (Chapman, 1975; Smith, undated); (3) calculations of life expectancy for certain products based on the actuarial analysis of survey results (Pennock and Jaeger, 1964; Ruffin and Tippett, 1975); (4) data on the life-

130   CONSUMER PRODUCT LIFE EXTENSION

cycle costs of selected major household appliances and information on
the productivity of the associated repair/maintenance industries, with
implications drawn regarding products lifetimes (Massachusetts Institute of Technology, 1974; Flanagan and Lund, 1976); (5) empirical information on the demand for certain durable products, with
estimates of demand elasticities (Harberger, 1960); (6) discussions
regarding lifetimes of electric-light bulbs (Avinger, 1968; Prais,
1974); and (7) a study that attempts to define the most economically
efficient durability of automobile tires (Westerman, 1974).

In addition, there have been several contributions on the subject of
automobile lifetimes. Automobiles are an obvious target for study in
this regard, owing to the availability of data on registration and, for
some countries, periodic testing; furthermore, there are very significant materials and energy flows associated with their life cycles.
The roles of durability, model styling, changes in models, and model
proliferation in the automobile industry are discussed by White
(1971), who presents data for the United States market, as does
Frain (1970). The most comprehensive presentation yet on United
States data, based on figures compiled by R. L. Polk and Company,
is given by Parks (1976). A comparison of changes in the median
lifetimes of cars in four countries over the past decade or so is provided by Hundy (1976); his data suggest that lifetimes have decreased
in the United Kingdom and West Germany while at the same time
they have increased in Sweden and the United States (no explanation
is offered). Elsewhere in his paper, Hundy examines different ways
of improving the physical durability of automobiles, concluding that
an increase of about 3 years in the median life of a car in the United
Kingdom could be achieved for an increase of about £40 (under
$70) in the selling price. Based on a set of postulated assumptions
regarding annual mileage, operating costs, and so forth, he estimates
that an owner would have to retain a car for about 6 years (instead
of the usual 2–4 years as at present) to make the extra expense
worthwhile. Hundy's finding can be compared with that of a recent
German study [3] which has shown that the use of higher quality
materials required to double the life expectancy of a car (to 20 years
or more) would cause a cost increase of approximately 30 percent.

There is reason to hope that our knowledge on the subject of
product lifetimes will grow in the next few years as a result of a new
interest being taken by international agencies such as the Organization

for Economic Co-operation and Development (OECD) and the Commission of the European Communities (CEC), national agencies in many countries including the United States, Canada, the Netherlands, Norway, France, and West Germany, and by researchers in universities and other institutions. In the United States, for example, the National Science Foundation (NSF) is currently sponsoring a project examining warranties, service contracts, and life-cycle costs in their application to major consumer durable products,[4] and has recently funded a new study[5] that will specifically seek to identify the principal factors affecting product lifetimes. In the next section, I provide some preliminary thoughts on the factors likely to be important in this regard and outline some possible implications for policy formulation.

FACTORS AFFECTING PRODUCT LIFETIMES

Without waiting for more information on the subject to become available, some legislators have already begun to press for legislation to influence product lifetimes. For example, a draft of an act that was circulated in the U.S. House of Representatives early in 1975 contained a proposal for the establishment of product standards that would take into account, among other things, a product's durability. Two bills * introduced during the same session of Congress would have required that durable consumer products be labeled as to their expected product life. The possibility of requiring minimum warranty periods on durable products has also been widely discussed.

It seems that the intention behind all of these proposed measures is to encourage manufacturers to make their products physically more durable. The encouragement would come either via direct regulation or via indirect market pressure (on the assumption that consumers, if better informed, would tend to favor longer-lived products when making purchases). However, it is by no means certain that the physical durability "built in" by the manufacturer is in practice the primary or even a major determinant of a product's lifetime. The latter is likely to be influenced by a wide variety of factors, some of which fall under the manufacturer's control but others do not. Actions of the consumers, the distributive trades, the repair/maintenance

---

* H.R. 876 and H.R. 5540, introduced in the 94th Congress.

industries, and second-hand dealers must not be overlooked. Furthermore, these actions are likely to vary according to the general economic climate prevailing at any given time.

Examples of some of the factors over which the manufacturers generally have control are

- The technical design of the product (affecting its potential reliability, its repairability, and its potential ultimate lifetime).
- The degree of quality control and testing.
- The marketing strategy (advertising, stylistic obsolescence, provision of information to consumers about projected durability, etc.).
- The availability and pricing of spare parts.

On the other hand, the consumers have control over

- Their decision to purchase (which is likely to be influenced by the range and prices of available new and used products, the availability and accuracy of information about these products, 'anticipated changes in the consumers' needs, the availability and cost of credit, etc.).
- Their treatment of the product in use (whether it is heavily or lightly used, whether it is treated roughly, whether it is regularly maintained, etc.).
- Their decision to repair or discard (which is likely to depend on the availability and cost of trustworthy repair services, spare parts, etc.).
- Their use of a second-hand market (which is likely to depend on the availability of an appropriate market, the transaction costs involved, etc., as well as on the costs associated with alternative methods of disposal).

It is very important that policy makers have an understanding of these and other relevant factors before proceeding with efforts to influence product lifetimes, for otherwise their actions might be misdirected. It is hoped that the findings of the new NSF study, together with those of other similar studies, will provide specific guidance to policy makers in this regard.

For example, if the investigation of decisions by consumers to dispose of their products reveals that physical durability (or the lack of it) is a key factor, then policies designed to make these products intrinsically more durable (e.g., by implementing product standards) would deserve further attention. On the other hand, if it is found that in practice products are likely to be discarded before they reach the technical limits of their durability, there would be little point in persuading manufacturers to make possibly very expensive changes in their existing processes in order to produce more durable goods. If an inability to obtain spare parts and/or qualified repair services is found to be a key factor in consumers' disposal decisions, then various means of ensuring the greater availability of these parts and services (e.g., by requirements imposed on manufacturers) should be explored. If repair costs appear to represent a key factor, then the basis for these costs should be examined to determine if they can be reduced (e.g., by requiring/encouraging manufacturers to make products more intrinsically repairable).

If stylistic obsolescence is found to be a key factor, then policies designed to encourage consumers (e.g., by educative means) to exercise restraint in changing models for the sake of style and/or to discourage manufacturers from proliferating styles might be explored. This would obviously be a sensitive area for public policy in view of the problems of infringing on market freedoms that many hold to be fundamental. Furthermore, the situation would be complicated by the difficulty of distinguishing stylistic changes from technological "improvements." If technological obsolescence proves to be a key factor, this would also pose a major problem for public policy, since technological innovation has generally been considered advantageous for society; however, a careful weighing of the *full* benefits and costs (including the costs of resource depletion, environmental impacts, etc.) might reveal that some innovations are not worthwhile.

PRODUCT LIFE EXTENSION AND MATERIALS/ENERGY FLOW [6]

As I mentioned in the introduction, product life extension is being proposed as a method of waste reduction, on the assumption that it would reduce the flow of materials and energy through the economic system. However, it is important to realize that this assumption cannot be taken for granted; in fact, as I shall show in the following analysis, the relationship between product lifetime and materials flow * is by no means straightforward.

---

* To make my presentation less cumbersome, I use the term *materials flow* to describe the flow of both materials and energy.

The Flow Associated with a Single Unit of Product

I shall first consider the *magnitude* of the materials flow associated with the production, use, and disposal of a single unit of product.* If the lifetime of the unit is extended, this flow *may* increase in absolute quantity, depending on the means employed to achieve the extension: for example, more material may be used to manufacture a product with greater physical durability (e.g., steel may be plated with zinc to resist corrosion, or thicker material may be used to strengthen areas of potential weakness, etc.).† On the other hand, if the product is simply retained in service when it would otherwise have been replaced for stylistic reasons by a newer model, then no additional material is likely to be needed. However, whether the *annual rate* of flow increases or decreases depends on the ratio M/L where M is the total amount of material used to produce, operate, maintain, repair, and dispose of the product, and L is the product lifetime.

The Flow Associated with All Units of a Product

I shall now consider the flow associated with all units of a given product. Smith (1973) has analyzed a steady state situation, in which consumers maintain a stock of the product, with the rate of addition to the stock (purchase) equaling the rate of subtraction (disposal). He suggests that there are two possible extreme adjustments that consumers might make to an increase in the product's average lifetime. On the one hand, they might maintain their current rates of purchase and disposal while allowing their stock to increase; on the other hand, they might maintain their stock at its current level and reduce their rates of purchase and disposal. Smith comments that in practice the outcome will lie somewhere between the two

---

* Of course, the *nature* of the flow (i.e., the particular materials/energy forms involved and their associated impacts on the environment) is also of concern; I shall return to this point in a later section.

† It is conceivable (although perhaps unlikely) that more material would be used in extending a product's lifetime by repeatedly replacing parts than would be used in simply replacing the whole product. This possibility raises a question that is not addressed in this paper but is particularly important in planning empirical studies, namely, how should product lifetime be defined for measurement purposes? If virtually all of the parts in a product are replaced, is the lifetime of that product being extended, or is a "new" product being produced with some used parts?

extremes, and that it is not possible to say a priori how much a given extension of product lifetime will reduce the rates of production and disposal without having "specific knowledge of behavioral adjustment processes relating to stock-holding decisions on the part of consumers."

One factor that Smith does not consider explicitly is the effect of the lifetime extension on the price to consumers for the services provided by the product. Other things being equal, one would expect that this price would determine whether and by how much the consumers adjust their stocks.* At least in principle, the price will depend both on the life-cycle costs and the lifetime of the product. If life-cycle costs remain unchanged but the lifetime increases, the price will decrease. However, it is perhaps more likely that life-cycle costs will increase: for example, the initial purchase price may increase if the product is designed to be physically more durable, the product may cost more to operate (e.g., if it is heavier), and/or it may cost more for maintenance and repair to keep the product longer in service. On the other hand, a decrease in life-cycle costs is also possible: for example, in re-designing the product to increase its durability, greater efficiency in operation and/or greater reliability could also be achieved.

Because of the wide range of possible outcomes, the net effect on the price of the product's services cannot be predicted a priori. Furthermore, in practice, there are other complications in predicting the behavior of consumers, for in determining the quantity of services demanded they may discount or ignore altogether the later costs in the product's life cycle (even if these costs are known, which may not be a realistic assumption). Their purchases may also be significantly constrained by a lack of credit availability.

Without becoming enmeshed in the complications, it is sufficient to say that if there is an increase in the price of the product's services, consumers are likely to reduce their stock, while if there is a drop in this price, the consumers' stock is likely to grow. For some products, particularly large appliances such as washing machines and refriger-

---

* The price may also affect the consumers' intensity of use of the product, a factor which is assumed constant in this analysis. In practice, intensity of use may well be a variable: for example, a consumer who faces the higher price of driving a more durable but heavier (and less fuel-efficient) automobile might travel by public transit more frequently. Of course, if he does so, his automobile might last even longer.

ators, the price elasticity may be small due to indivisibilities in consumer demand; in other words, an individual household would not normally be expected to purchase two washing machines simultaneously, even if the price drops significantly. Even for products of this kind, however, unless there is 100 percent saturation of the market, there are likely to be marginal consumers whose purchasing decisions will be sensitive to price. In addition, there are many products (including, for example, radios and televisions) for which demand is less likely to be indivisible and which would therefore be expected to show a greater price elasticity. Thus, depending on the elasticity actually exhibited, there seems to be no reason why Smith's two "extremes" should necessarily hold; indeed, it is possible to envisage situations in which *both* the stock and the purchases necessary to sustain it are greater after an extension of product lifetime, as well as situations in which they are both less.

A numerical illustration may help to clarify this point. Suppose that a particular appliance has a two-year lifetime and that the stock held by consumers in steady state is 90. The number of appliances purchased each year (which is also the number discarded) equals 45. Now suppose that the product's lifetime is increased to three years, without any change in the life-cycle costs. This would be equivalent to a reduction in the price paid by consumers for the services of the appliance, and (depending on the demand elasticity), consumers might react by increasing their stock to 150. As a result, annual purchases would also rise, to 50. Alternatively, the extension in lifetime might cause an increase in life-cycle costs that is sufficient to raise the price of the product's services. Consumers might react by reducing their stock to 60, with an annual purchase rate of 20.

It is significant that, even if it were possible to predict the effect of an extension in product lifetime on the consumers' stock and purchase rate, this would not necessarily tell us how the annual flow of *materials* would be affected. To predict this, we would also need to know of any changes in the quantity M, which was discussed earlier. It is quite possible that the stock and purchase rate would both *decrease*, while the rate of flow of materials would simultaneously *increase*. For example, in the illustration given above of the appliance whose lifetime is extended from two to three years, the extension might be achieved only by doubling the amount of material used in the product's manufacture. This could cause an increase in life-cycle costs which could in turn cause consumers to reduce both their stock and their purchase rate.

The Flow Associated with Systemwide Adjustments

To make matters worse (from the viewpoint of one who wishes to achieve a reduction in materials flow), it must be realized that the discussion so far has failed to take into account the effect that a change associated with a single product will have on the rest of the economic system. If there is a change in the price to consumers for the services provided by one product, then some re-allocation of expenditures among all products would be expected. For example, if the extension of a particular product's lifetime results in a net saving to consumers, they are likely to spend more on other products. How this will affect the overall materials flow will obviously depend on the quantity and nature of the other products involved. The possibility exists that the reduction (if any) in flow associated with the product whose lifetime is extended would be more than offset by an increase in flow due to greater consumption elsewhere in the economy.

As an illustration, consider what might happen if a product is given a longer life by having it exchanged in a second-hand market and subsequently re-used, instead of being discarded by the first owner (and sent to landfill). The effect on the overall materials flow would be determined by (1) how the first owner spends his extra income (the net proceeds from the sale plus any saving in disposal cost), and (2) the adjustment in expenditure that is made by the purchaser. If the latter would otherwise have purchased the product new, then the flow associated with the product itself would decrease, but this reduction might be at least partially offset due to the fact that other goods could be bought with the money saved (presumably) on the second-hand purchase. On the other hand, if the purchaser would not otherwise have purchased the product at all, then the effect on the flow would depend on what he would have bought instead.

The Product Lifetime/Materials Flow Relationship: Summing Up

Enough has already been said in this section to demonstrate that the relationship between product lifetime and materials flow is extremely complicated. There are, moreover, some additional complications that have not as yet been considered. For example, as product life-times grow longer, the advantages to be gained from technical inno-vations—which may reduce the amount of material (M) in the asso-ciated flow—will be realized more slowly (since the older, more material-intensive products will remain longer in service before being replaced).

It is evident, therefore, that product life extension per se will not necessarily reduce the overall materials flow; indeed, it is impossible to say for certain a priori what the effect on this flow will be. Further-more, I have said nothing so far about the *nature* (as opposed to the magnitude) of the flow. It may be that even if the flow's magnitude is reduced, the types of materials needed to make a particular product more durable would be considered more important to conserve than the materials used in the original, less durable version. In addition, the new materials might have a more significant impact on the en-vironment; for example, if zinc is used as a coating to extend the lifetime of steel, there is likely to be an increase in the amount of cadmium (which is known to be a toxic pollutant) entering human bodies from zinc refinery dusts.

PRODUCT LIFE EXTENSION AND ECONOMIC WELFARE

So far in this paper I have been concerned with product life exten-sion as a means of reducing materials flow; I have not considered its impact on economic welfare. Although professional economists have attempted to develop more sophisticated ways of measuring economic welfare based on the notion of consumer surplus, there is little doubt that most policy makers are still greatly influenced by conventional macroeconomic indicators that simply register the market value of the flow of goods and services through the economy. Measured in this way, economic welfare will often be found to *decrease* rather than increase with a reduction in materials flow. Conversely, an in-crease in materials flow (which I have hitherto implied to be undesir-able) may be associated with an increase in economic welfare. This last situation could arise, for example, when extending the life of a product causes a drop in the price paid by consumers for its ser-vices; the consumers would then be better off (on economic grounds), but if they spend their extra income on additional products, they could cause an increase in overall materials flow.

Policy makers should realize, however, that economic welfare as conventionally measured may not coincide precisely with their perception of social welfare. One reason is that (as is now generally agreed) market values frequently fail to reflect many of the factors that affect the well-being of society. Costs such as resource depletion and environmental pollution, for example, commonly remain external to economic accounting since, under existing property rights, private individuals and firms are not required to take into account the full consequences of their actions. If these costs were internalized, an increase in materials flow might no longer produce an increase in economic welfare.

Another reason for not necessarily basing decisions on changes in economic welfare as conventionally measured is that the criterion underlying the operation of the market system is not regarded by everyone as appropriate for guiding public policy. There is nothing "inherently correct" about employing the Pareto criterion, and many people are disturbed by the fact that its use almost invariably implies acceptance of the existing distribution of wealth. In view of the huge inequities in the current ownership of materials (worldwide), this consideration is particularly relevant in developing and assessing materials-related policies.

CONCLUSIONS

Product life extension is actively being considered as a possible means of reducing materials flow for the purpose of conserving natural resources, reducing environmental impacts, and lowering the costs of waste disposal. Unfortunately, we currently have inadequate knowledge both of the kinds of policies that are most likely to achieve product life extension and of the relationship between product lifetime and materials flow. I have attempted to show in this paper that the considerations involved are extraordinarily complicated.

Policy makers who are primarily concerned with materials flow reduction should be aware of the fact that by simply extending the lifetimes of one or more products, they may not achieve their objective; indeed, their efforts may even prove counterproductive. Not only will this problem arise when the incremental use of materials to increase a product's lifetime is greater than the savings realized from delaying that product's replacement, it may also result from consumers adjusting their expenditure patterns so that additional products are purchased.

It is evident that policies must be designed very carefully if they are to maximize the likelihood of a reduction in overall materials flow. For example, one approach might be to tax away any extra income that consumers gain as a result of an increase in product lifetime, to prevent them from spending it on other products. Of course, the government would have to ensure that the proceeds from such a tax would not be used in a manner which itself causes an increase in materials flow.

It is impossible to provide more concrete guidance to policy makers until additional information becomes available. My own feeling, admittedly based more on intuition than on hard data at this time, is that the product lifetime issue is an important one for those concerned with resource and environmental problems to explore. I tend to agree with those who argue that these problems will be solved in the long term only by a fundamental re-shaping of our present materialistic life styles, and I suspect that by attempting to influence product lifetimes, we may be taking a first step toward making the kinds of changes that resource shortages and environmental disruption will ultimately force upon us.

NOTES

1. See, for example, U.S. Environmental Protection Agency (1974, 1975), Wahl (1976), Conn (1976 a, b).

2. See, for example, Avinger (1968), Diewart (1974), Douglas and Goldman (1969), Kamien and Schwartz (1974), Kleinman and Ophir (1966), Levhari and Srinivasan (1969), Martin (1962), Miller (1961), Parks (1974), Ramm (1974), Schmalensee (1970), Sieper and Swan (1973), Su (1975), Swan (1970 a, b; 1971).

3. Cited at the Seminar on the Principles and Creation of Non-Waste Technology and Production, U.N. Economic Commission for Europe, Paris, 1976.

4. This project, entitled "Consumer Durables: Warranties, Service Contracts and Alternatives," is being conducted by the Massachusetts Institute of Technology, Center for Policy Alternatives.

5. This project, to be conducted by me, is entitled "Factors Affecting Product Lifetime: A Study in Support of Policy Development for Waste Reduction." It will involve a consumer survey, data collection from manu-

facturers and trade associations, and an investigation of second-hand markets.
6. In this section I reiterate and expand on some of the observations made by Randers (1971).

BIBLIOGRAPHY

Avinger, Robert L., Jr. 1968. The economics of durability. Unpublished Ph.D. dissertation, Duke University.

Butlin, John 1976. *The economics of product life—A critical bibliography.* Prepared for Environment Directorate, Organization for Economic Co-operation and Development, Paris.

Chapman, P. F. 1975. Models for estimating the potential supply of secondary materials. Mimeographed. Economic Group, Waste Management Advisory Council, London.

Conn, W. David (ed.) 1976a. *Proposed policies for waste reduction in California.* Source Reduction and Packaging Policy Committee, California State Solid Waste Management Board, Sacramento.

———— 1976b. *Waste reduction—Issues and policies.* Presented at 11 International Symposium on New Problems of Advanced Societies, HWWA-Institut fur Wirtschaftsforschung, Hamburg (also forthcoming in *Resources Policy*).

Diewart, W. E. 1974. Intertemporal consumer theory and the demand for durables. *Econometrica,* vol. 42, May.

Douglas, A. J., and Goldman, S. M. 1969. Monopolistic behavior in a market for durable goods. *Journal of Political Economy,* vol. 77, January–February.

Flanagan, W. F., and Lund, R. T. 1976. *Factors controlling longer product life: The case for consumer durables.* Prepared for the Office of Technology Assessment, Washington, D.C.

Frain, Kevin F. 1970. Problems in the disposal of solid waste from durable goods. in A. J. Van Tassel (ed.), *Environmental side effects of rising industrial output.* Heath Lexington Books, D. C. Heath and Co., Lexington, Mass.

Harberger, Arnold C. (ed.) 1960. *The demand for durable goods.* University of Chicago Press, Chicago.

Hundy, B. B. 1976. The durability of automobiles. *Resources Policy,* vol. 2, September.

Kamien, Morton J., and Schwartz, Nancy L. 1974. Product durability under monopoly and competition. *Econometrica,* vol. 42, March.

Kleinman, E. and Ophir, T. 1966. The durability of durable goods. *Review of Economic Studies,* vol. 33, April.

Levhari, David, and Srinivasan, T. N. 1969. Durability of consumption goods: competition versus monopoly. *American Economic Review,* vol. 59, March.

Martin, David D. 1962. Monopoly power and the durability of durable goods. *Southern Economic Journal,* vol. 28, January.

Massachusetts Institute of Technology, Center for Policy Alternatives, with Charles Stark Draper Laboratory, Inc., 1974. *The productivity of servicing consumer durable products.* Massachusetts Institute of Technology, Cambridge.

Miller, H. Laurence, Jr. 1961. On the theory of demand for consumer durables. *Southern Economic Journal,* vol. 28, April.

Parks, Richard W. 1974. The demand and supply of durable goods and durability. *American Economic Review,* vol. 64, March.

———. 1976. The determinants of scrapping rates for post-war vintage automobiles. Mimeographed. University of Washington, Seattle.

Pennock, Jean L., and Jaeger, Carol M. 1964. Household service life of durable goods. *Journal of Home Economics,* vol. 56, January.

Prais, S. J. 1974. The electric light monopoly and the life of electric lamps. *Journal of Industrial Economics,* vol. 23, December.

Ramm, Wolfhard 1974. On the durability of capital goods under imperfect market conditions. *American Economic Review,* vol. 64, September.

Randers, J. 1971. *The dynamics of solid waste generation.* Club of Rome Project on the Predicament of Mankind, System Dynamics Group, Alfred P. Sloan School of Management, Massachusetts Institute of Technology, Cambridge, Mass.

Ruffin, Marilyn Doss, and Tippett, Katherine S. 1975. Service-life expectancy of household appliances: New estimates from the USDA. *Home Economics Research Journal,* vol. 3, March.

Schmalensee, Richard 1970. Regulation and the durability of goods. *Bell Journal of Economics and Management Science,* vol. 1, Spring.

Sieper, E., and Swan, P. L. 1973. Monopoly and competition in the market for durable goods. *Review of Economic Studies,* vol. 40, July.

Smith, Frank A. 1973. *Product design modifications for resource recovery, source reduction, or solid waste management purposes,* Section entitled "Economic Durability of Products," Mimeographed (largely reproduced as Appendix B of *Second Report to Congress, Resource Recovery and Source Reduction,* U.S. Environmental Protection Agency, 1974).

Smith, R. J. undated. Medium term forecasts reassessed: IV Domestic appliances, *National Institute Economic Review.*

Smith, Thomas E. and Conn, W. David. 1976. *Product durability: Economics and related aspects—An annotated bibliography.* Discussion Paper no. 74, School of Architecture and Urban Planning, University of California, Los Angeles.

Su, Teddy T. 1975. Durability of consumption goods reconsidered. *American Economic Review,* vol. 65, March.

Swan, Peter L. 1970a. Market structure and technological progress: The influence of monopoly on product innovation. *Quarterly Journal of Economics,* vol. 84, November.

———. 1970b. Durability of consumption goods. *American Economic Review,* vol. 60, December.

————. 1971. The durability of goods and regulation of monopoly. *Bell Journal of Economics and Management Science,* vol. 2, Spring.

Teknekron, Inc. 1973. Factors influencing product durability, summary in *Resource conservation, resource recovery, and solid waste disposal* (Studies prepared for the Committee on Public Works, U.S. Senate, by the Environmental Policy Division, Congressional Research Service, Library of Congress, Washington, D.C., Serial No. 92–12).

U.S. Environmental Protection Agency 1974. *Second report to Congress— Resource recovery and source reduction* (Environmental Protection Publication SW–122, Office of Solid Waste Management Programs, Washington, D.C.).

————. 1975. *Third report to Congress—Resource recovery and waste reduction* (Environmental Protection Publication SW–161, Office of Solid Waste Management Programs, Washington, D.C.).

Wahl, D. 1975. *Reduce—Targets, means, and impacts of source reduction* (Publication no. 576, League of Women Voters, Washington, D.C.).

Westerman, Robert R. 1974. The management of waste passenger car tires (Unpublished Ph.D. dissertation, University of Pennsylvania).

White, Lawrence J. 1971. *The automobile industry since 1945,* chapter 12, "Product Behavior: Durability, Styling Models and Model Proliferation" (Harvard University Press, Cambridge, Mass.).

CHAPTER 8

Allocative and Distributive Effects of a Disposal Charge on Product Packaging

Tayler H. Bingham *

INTRODUCTION

Packaging can provide consumers and retailers with a wide variety of services in addition to the traditional services of pre-unitization and protection. For example, it may provide a vehicle for communicating the proper use of a product. It may be easy to store, stack, price-mark, open, reseal, or discard. In providing these services, packaging may reduce the out-of-pocket and/or time costs to consumers of selecting and using the product. It may also reduce the quantity and price risks associated with the purchase and use of a product. And it may increase the size, price variety, and availability of products.†

Over the last several years, however, there has been increasing concern over some of the less desirable impacts that packaging may have on society. For example, of the 135 million tons of "postcon-

* This research was supported by contracts 68–01–0791 and 68–01–2981 with the Environmental Protection Agency. Appreciation is extended to other members who participated in these contracts and in particular to Allen K. Miedema for his helpful insights and criticisms. Also, the comments of the symposium participants have been helpful and are appreciated.

† The above attributes of packaging were, in part, summarized from *The Role of Packaging in the U.S. Economy*, Arthur D. Little, Inc. (1966).

Tayler H. Bingham

TABLE 8–1

MATERIAL FLOW ESTIMATES OF DISPOSED POSTCONSUMER SOLID WASTE, 1973

Material	Product category tons, as generated		
	Containers, Packaging	Other Products	Total
Paper	23.3	20.9	44.2
Glass	12.1	1.1	13.2
Metals	6.5	6.0	12.5
Ferrous	5.6	5.4	11.0
Aluminum	0.8	0.2	1.0
Other nonferrous	0.1	0.3	0.4
Plastics	3.1	1.9	5.0
Rubber and leather	trivial	3.6	3.6
Textiles	trivial	1.9	1.9
Wood	1.9	3.0	4.9
Total nonfood product waste	46.9	38.5	85.4
Food waste			22.4
Yard waste			25.0
Miscellaneous inorganics			1.9
Total			134.8

SOURCE: Adapted from Table 1 in U.S. Environmental Protection Agency, *Third Report to Congress: Resource Recovery and Waste Reduction,* Washington: U.S. Government Printing Office, 1975.

sumer" ‡ solid wastes discarded in 1973, 35 percent (47 million tons) consisted of packaging (Table 8–1). At a national average of $26 per ton, the collection and disposal of these packaging wastes cost society $1.2 billion. In addition, packaging is commonly littered— imposing disamenities and additional collection costs on society. For example, based on a roadside survey, about 36 percent of littered items are packages or containers (Table 8–2).

The concern over packaging is manifested in several ways. Most notably, there is concern over beverage containers. Currently, at the state level alone, 140 laws are being considered for action in 36

‡ "Postconsumer" solid wastes include only those discarded by the final consumer; these include refuse material collected from household and business establishments. Other solid wastes from mining, agricultural, and industrial processing and from construction, street sweeping, and sewage sludge—though markedly greater in volume—are not included in this total (see U.S. EPA, 1975, p. 10).

TABLE 8–2

Estimated Number of Littered Items, 1968

Item	Frequency (items per mile per month)
Packaging items	
Paper packages and containers	150
Plastic packages and containers	34
Glass bottles and jars	77
Steel and aluminum cans	213
Nonpackaging items	
Paper items	626
Plastic items	42
Other items	167
Total	1309

Source: Research Triangle Institute, *National Study of the Composition of Roadside Litter* for Keep America Beautiful, Inc., New York, New York, 1969, p. A–01.

states (see *Beverage Industry*, 1976, p. 1). On a broader basis, taxation and the direct regulation of packaging have both been proposed at the national and state levels. In May of 1976, hearings were held in the U.S. Senate to examine the potential of imposing disposal charges on the items entering the municipal solid waste stream. This policy would impose the estimated solid waste management costs of a product on producers, and hence give consumers and producers an incentive to reduce the generation of solid wastes.

This paper provides an initial analysis of the possible impacts such a charge would have on consumer product packaging wastes, resource use, and consumers. In developing this analysis we assume that the area under the demand curve for a packaged consumer product represents the maximum aggregate value of the product to society. Similarly, the area under the supply curves for packaged products and solid waste management services is assumed to represent the opportunity costs of these products and services to society.

DISPOSAL CHARGE CONCEPT

Under certain conditions, prices established in competitive markets convey all the information necessary to producers and consumers so that resources are allocated in such a way that economic welfare is maximized. However, when discarded products enter the solid waste stream and when bills for solid waste services are not based on the amount of discarded material, resource allocation may not be optimal (Miedema, 1976).

As an example, consider a hypothetical packaged good (Figure 8–1). The supply curve for the packaged good is S_p; the demand curve D_p. In the absence of unit pricing of solid waste management services, consumers have no incentive to consider the costs of these services to society. Hence they purchase Q^0 units of the packaged product per unit time at a price of P^0 per unit. However, the true costs to society of the product are not only the area OFQ^0 in Figure 1 but also the solid waste collection and disposal costs incurred when the package is discarded.

Suppose that solid waste services are produced under conditions of constant costs and that there is a fixed technical relationship between the packaged product and these services. Then the supply function for solid waste management services can also be shown on Figure 8–1 as S_w. Thus the total social costs of Q^0 units of the packaged product are $OFQ^0 + OBGQ^0$. The total value of the benefits to

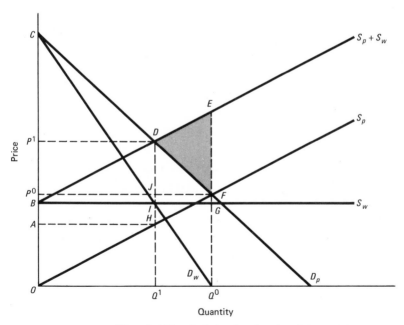

Figure 8–1 Hypothetical packaged good market

consumers of Q^0 is $OCFQ^0$. Although the demand curve for solid waste management services may not be revealed in the absence of unit pricing of these services, it can be regarded as a joint demand for the packaged product. Hence, it can be constructed by comparing the difference between what consumers are willing to pay, D_p, for alternative quantities of the packaged product, and what they would have to pay, S_p; that is, by computing the vertical distance between D_p and S_p (Friedman, 1962, pp. 148–59). The resulting demand curve for solid waste management services is shown as D_w in Figure 8–1.

It is clear in Figure 8–1 that the convention of lump-sum pricing of solid waste management services results in too much of the packaged product being consumed. The purpose of a disposal charge is to internalize these costs, S_w, by assessing producers the solid waste management costs their products incur.

One important issue to be considered is the potential social benefit of such a policy. In estimating the benefits of a disposal charge, we are concerned not only with the net aggregate amount of benefits regardless to whom they accrue (allocative efficiency) but also the interpersonal distribution of the benefits and costs of the policy (distributional equity). A policy is efficient in an allocative sense if it produces benefits in excess of its costs. In this case the potential exists to make everyone better off than before, if costless redistribution of the gains is possible, and still have resources available to apply to other wants. However, the equity of any particular distribution of incomes is a matter of social values. Hence we are concerned here only with the development of estimates of the distributional implications of a disposal charge. Both issues are examined below with the aid of Figure 8–1.

Efficient pricing of resources requires that the value of the marginal unit to consumers be equated to the value of that unit to society. In Figure 8–1 the output of the packaged good associated with that price, P^1, is Q^1.

From the quantity axis perspective, as we move from Q^0 to Q^1 resources are released from the production and disposal of the product in the amount Q^1DEQ^0. However, the reduction in the equilibrium quantity of the product reduces the total benefits conferred on consumers by the amount Q^1DFQ^0. Thus the net impact on society is to increase allocative welfare by the difference between the change in costs and benefits or by the triangle DEF.

The distributional implications of the disposal charge can be examined by looking at the impact of the charge on the product price. Although the entire value of Q^0 units of the packaged good to consumers is $OCFQ^0$ they enjoy a surplus, P^0CF, above their expenditures OP^0FQ^0. Similarly, producers enjoy a surplus, or rent, on Q^0 in excess of the resource costs of OFQ^0. The amount of this producers' surplus is OP^0F.

However, as prices are increased from P^0 to P^1, consumers' surplus is reduced by amount, P^0P^1DF. (This amount can be defined as the maximum consumers would have been willing to pay to avoid the price increase of P^0P^1. It consists of the extra outlays, P^0P^1DJ, for the remaining quantities, plus the forfeited surplus, JDF, on the quantities no longer purchased). Similarly, producers lose AP^0FH. (This area can be subdivided into the losses on the remaining quantity, AP^0JH, plus the losses on the quantities no longer purchased, HJF). The losses in consumers' real income are transmitted via higher product prices; the losses in producers' real income via smaller returns.

The total loss to consumers and producers is AP^1DFH. However, of this amount, AP^1DH represents transfers to government. And, $HDEF$ is saved in solid waste management services. Thus, DEF is the net benefit of a disposal charge.

Although the above example has been couched in terms of the packaged good, Miedema (1976) and others (Smith [1974], Summers [1973]) argue that the charge should only be applied to the virgin material content of packaging and not to packaging produced from recycled or re-used materials or products. Below we outline an empirical model for estimating the costs and benefits of a disposal charge of $26 per ton applied to the virgin material content of product packaging.*

---

* Many other packaging tax bases besides weight have been proposed. Most commonly mentioned are "disposability," biodegradability," and "recycling potential." Most of these bases are, at best, difficult to define and measure; many suffer from a lack of agreement over their desirability. For example, is it desirable that solid waste degrade, or would it be better to remain in its discarded form to be "mined" at a future time?

ANALYTICAL MODEL

Packaging may be considered as one of the factor inputs in the production of consumer goods. For this analysis the producer is assumed to combine packaging and all other inputs in fixed proportions. However, within packaging, 9 materials have been identified (4 flexible packaging materials: paper, plastic, steel closures, and aluminum; and 5 rigid packaging materials: paper boxes and containers, plastic bottles, glass bottles and jars, steel cans, and aluminum cans). Consumer expenditures were disaggregated into 30 products most of which are food or household goods. Estimates of the use of each packaging material, measured both in weight and dollars, for each product were developed from a variety of trade and government sources for the 1958–70 period.

From the above described data set estimates of the own-price and cross-price elasticities of demand for packaging were developed. These estimates permit direct estimation of the change in the use of packaging by material type as the relative price of packaging materials are changed with the disposal charge. A set of nine coefficients was used to convert the weight-based charge to a share-of-price value.

Since the disposal charge as analyzed here would only apply to the virgin material content of packaging, it was also necessary to examine the opportunities of substituting recycled for virgin inputs to the production of paper, plastics, glass, steel, and aluminum packaging materials. Unfortunately, the lack of data required a very simple approach. A "supply" function for recycled paper and steel was developed, based on operating cost data for a recycling pilot plant. For the other materials, a single supply price was chosen based on trade estimates.

A "demand" function for each recycled material was developed using data on the spatial distribution of production facilities for the subject materials and the cost of the resources for which the recycled material would substitute. Technological limits to the use of recycled materials were identified from the literature.

ALLOCATIVE EFFECTS

In the analytical model outlined above, the packaged good was assumed to be produced under conditions of constant returns to scale. The package-material producer combines recycled and the virgin inputs, which have the charge applied to them, to produce the material at the least cost per unit, subject to technological restrictions on the use of recycled inputs. The consumer goods producer chooses among the alternative materials, also minimizing per unit costs. Unless the recycled materials are perfect substitutes for virgin inputs, the final price of the packaged good increases.

All allocative effects can be measured in the final markets for packaged consumer products and solid waste management services. In the packaged consumer products market the price increase of P^0P^1 results in a loss in consumers' surplus of area $A + B + C$ in Figure 8–2. This area can be empirically approximated over small movements along a demand curve as

$$E_j = \left(\frac{dP_j}{P_j}\right)\left(1 - \frac{1}{2}\eta_j\frac{dP_j}{P_j}\right)$$

where E_j = expenditures on product j
$\quad\quad P_j$ = price of consumer product j
$\quad\quad \eta_j$ = price elasticity of demand for product j

The area A represents the forfeited losses in consumers' surplus due to the reduction in quantity demanded and can be approximated as $\frac{1}{2}dQdP$. The remaining loss in consumers' surplus consists of the charge payments shifted forward to consumers, say B, and the increase in the unit production costs, say C. Under the assumption of constant costs, all charge payments, which are the product of the weight of the virgin material content of packaging and the disposal charge ($26 per ton), are shifted forward to consumers. The increase in unit production costs is a result of the charge-induced substitution of recycled for virgin inputs to package material production. Prior to the imposition of the charge, producers were employing a least-cost mix of factors, for a given output; thus recycled inputs can only be further substituted for virgin inputs at a higher unit cost of production—unless recycled and virgin inputs were perfect substitutes. Although consumers lose area B (the charge payments), they can potentially gain it back (minus transactions costs *) through a reduction in income or other taxes or through the increased provision of government services. Therefore, the net loss in consumers' surplus— cost to society of a disposal charge—is $A + C$. The estimated total reductions in consumer surplus are $573 million annually. Of this

---

* *Transactions costs* are the cost of administering a policy.

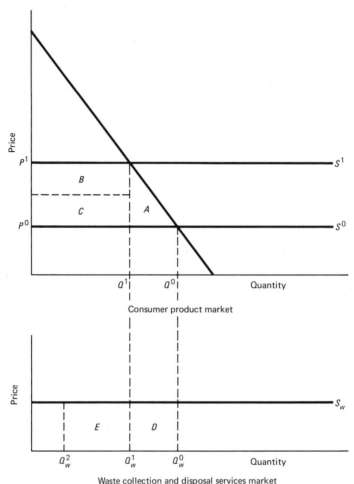

Figure 8–2 Final product and services markets

total, $507 million represents the charge payments; thus the net reduction in consumers' surplus is $66 million.

The estimated benefits to society are the reduced solid waste costs due to the reduced generation of packaging solid wastes and to the increased recycling of postconsumer wastes. These are illustrated in the lower panel of Figure 8–2. The reduction in demand for the packaged product (Q^0Q^1) results in a reduction in solid waste generation of $Q_w^0Q_w^1$ (the waste reduction effect). Further, because the charge is only applied to the virgin material content of packaging, there is an increased demand for recycled inputs. These are repre-

Tayler H. Bingham

TABLE 8-3

REDUCTIONS IN SOLID WASTES (1970 RATES)

	Thousands of Tons Annually
Waste reduction effect	426
Waste recovery effect	6,210
Total	6,636

sented in the lower panel of Figure 8—2 as distance $Q_w^1 Q_w^2$ (the waste recovery effect). The numerical estimates for this analysis are shown in Table 8-3. Valuing these reductions in solid waste generation and increases in recycling at \$26 per ton, the savings in solid waste management costs are \$173 million annually (area $D = \$11$ million, area $E = \$161$ million).

The estimated total costs and benefits of a disposal charge applied to packaged consumer goods are summarized in Table 8-4. Subtracting the costs (minus transfers) from the benefits leaves a net allocative gain to society of the disposal charge of \$107 million annually.

Based on the assumptions stated above and the preliminary numerical estimates developed here, it would appear that on an efficiency criterion alone a disposal charge on product packaging is justified—providing it can be administered for less than \$107 million annually. We next turn to the equity criterion.

TABLE 8-4

COSTS AND BENEFITS OF A PRODUCT CHARGE ON PACKAGING
(1970 RATES)

	Millions of U.S. Dollars Annually
Costs	
Gross reduction in consumers' surplus	573
Transfers	
Charge revenues	507
Benefits	
Reductions in solid waste management costs	173
Net social gain	107

DISTRIBUTIVE EFFECTS

Although the above analysis appears to indicate the desirability of a product charge on efficiency grounds, as Shultz (1974) has observed:

> anyone who has spent some time around the political world knows that things are not that simple. The key word there is really equity. So I think that the question we're really dealing with is this: Can we do the things that will give us the efficiency we need in our system, that will give us real growth, that will allow us to exercise the necessary discipline, and can we do all these things in a way that is consistent with the demand of the political process for equity? *

The incidence of the costs of a product disposal charge on packaging will be either on the stockholders of the firm that would be affected by the charge through lower profits and/or on consumers through higher prices for packaged products. No attempt is made here to estimate the incidence of the charge on stockholders. However, estimates in the decline in consumers' real income have been developed.

To develop estimates of the impact of increases in consumer product prices on consumers by income group, estimates of consumer spending on packaged products by income group were needed. Preliminary Bureau of Labor Statistics expenditure estimates for fifty product categories and ten income classes were matched to the thirty packaged consumer products. A unique set of nineteen products were identified. The complete matrix with the projected product price increases is shown in Table 8–5. The estimates were developed for decile groupings of families—the first income class includes the lowest 10 percent of families in terms of income, the second class the next lowest 10 percent, and so forth. Estimates of the weighted average price increase for each income group were developed by multiplying the product price increase by the share of income spent on each product by each income group and summed for each income group. The results were then multiplied by the average income for the group to develop an estimate of the loss in real income for the average family in each group under the assumption that product demand was perfectly inelastic.

---

* An alternative view, not under discussion here, is that equity issues per se are not so much of interest to the politicians as is the maximization of their political support. For example, see Lindstrom (1959).

TABLE 8-5

SHARE OF EXPENDITURES ON PACKAGED PRODUCTS BY INCOME LEVEL, 1972

PCE Category	Level of annual family income before taxes, 1967 dollars										Percent change in price due to disposal charge
	Under 1,444	1,444– 2,617	2,618– 3,850	3,851– 5,312	5,313– 6,737	6,738– 8,084	8,085– 9,663	9,664– 11,703	11,704– 14,995	Over 14,995	
Cereals, flour, and macaroni	.0259	.0126	.0084	.0079	.0061	.0047	.0047	.0040	.0035	.0024	.107
Baked goods	.0585	.0304	.0225	.0200	.0180	.0156	.0146	.0129	.0123	.0087	.186
Fresh and cured meat	.1794	.0920	.0796	.0633	.0542	.0499	.0480	.0442	.0399	.0281	.153
Fresh and cured poultry	.0339	.0174	.0133	.0093	.0085	.0067	.0068	.0058	.0051	.0042	.140
Fresh and cured fish and seafood	.0179	.0103	.0080	.0062	.0052	.0047	.0044	.0036	.0034	.0032	.140
Dairy products	.1130	.0577	.0424	.0369	.0327	.0281	.0260	.0229	.0209	.0150	.206
Produce	.0738	.0320	.0230	.0173	.0144	.0125	.0137	.0114	.0108	.0082	.161
Frozen foods	.0193	.0098	.0072	.0062	.0052	.0046	.0042	.0037	.0036	.0024	.195
Canned foods	.0285	.0145	.0107	.0092	.0078	.0069	.0063	.0055	.0052	.0036	1.189
Candy and chewing gum	.0187	.0108	.0083	.0067	.0060	.0054	.0052	.0045	.0039	.0031	.220
Other foods	.0638	.0320	.0260	.0228	.0207	.0186	.0165	.0145	.0127	.0091	.511
Soft drinks and prepared beverages	.0525	.0282	.0204	.0173	.0159	.0135	.0133	.0107	.0101	.0068	3.174
Pet foods	.0066	.0032	.0028	.0025	.0023	.0021	.0019	.0016	.0015	.0010	.637
Distilled spirits, wine, and beer	.0039	.0077	.0093	.0112	.0107	.0112	.0110	.0113	.0098	.0088	1.527
Tobacco products	.0124	.0163	.0169	.0157	.0144	.0126	.0114	.0079	.0079	.0048	.064
Health aids	.0302	.0137	.0111	.0095	.0079	.0058	.0058	.0051	.0034	.0043	.786
Beauty aids	.0285	.0145	.0111	.0112	.0098	.0090	.0079	.0076	.0070	.0047	1.618
Household supplies	.0543	.0300	.0211	.0180	.0158	.0134	.0144	.0125	.0119	.0085	1.215
Other general merchandise	.9698	.8182	.6487	.5956	.5687	.5474	.5262	.4991	.4504	.3839	.053
Total	1.7909	1.2513	.9908	.8868	.8243	.7727	.7423	.6888	.6233	.5108	

SOURCE: Developed from preliminary U.S. Department of Labor, Bureau of Labor Statistics, data from the 1972–73 Consumer Expenditure Survey.

TABLE 8–6

DISTRIBUTION OF THE COST OF A PRODUCT CHARGE ON PACKAGING
BY INCOME CLASS
(1970 RATES, 1967 DOLLARS)

Family Income * (dollars per year)		Reduction in Real Income	
Class	Average	Percent	Dollars per family annually
< 1,444	716	.5228	3.74
1,444–2,617	2,013	.2984	6.01
2,618–3,850	3,248	.2304	7.48
3,851–5,312	4,560	.2058	9.38
5,313–6,737	5,961	.1860	11.09
6,738–8,084	7,390	.1667	12.32
8,085–9,663	8,843	.1612	14.25
9,664–11,703	10,672	.1438	15.35
11,704–14,995	13,202	.1313	17.33
> 14,995	21,950	.0993	21.80

* Based on number of families reporting, 88.3 percent of universe (U.S. Department of Labor, 1975). The 1972 income was deflated to 1967 dollars using the implicit price deflator for personal consumption expenditures.

Two measures are developed of the distributive effect of the charge on consumers: (1) the reduction in real family income expressed as a percent of income and (2) the dollar magnitude of the reduction in real income per family.

As shown in Table 8–6, measured on a share of income basis, the charge tends to be regressive. Families falling in the lowest decile would experience reductions in their real income of 0.5 percent. For families in the highest decile, the reduction would be 0.1 percent. On the other hand, on an absolute basis the families in the highest decile would be experiencing dollar reductions about six times those of families in the lowest decile.

However, the estimated revenue from a product charge would be $507 million annually. In addition, $173 million would be saved due to the reduction in solid waste generation and the increases in recycling projected with the charge. Thus government could offset the loss in consumers' real incomes, through lower taxes or revenue sharing for example, and still have $107 million annually remaining to administer the charge.

BIBLIOGRAPHY

Beverage Industry. New York, N.Y., June 18, 1976, p. 1.

Bingham, Tayler H. *An evaluation of the effectiveness and costs of regulatory and fiscal policy instruments on product packaging.* Final Report prepared by Research Triangle Institute for Environmental Protection Agency, Contract No. 68–01–0791, March 1974.

Friedman, Milton. *Price theory: A provisional text.* Chicago: Aldine Publishing Co., 1962.

Griliches, Zvi. Research costs and social returns: Hybrid corn and related innovations. *Journal of Political Economy,* vol. 66, No. 5, 1958, pp. 419–31.

Harberger, Arnold C. Three basic postulates for applied welfare economics: An interpretive essay. *Journal of Economic Literature,* vol. 9, No. 3, 1971, pp. 785–97.

Lindstrom, Charles E. The science of muddling through. *Public Administration Review,* 79, 1959.

Little, Arthur D., Inc. *The role of packaging in the U.S. economy.* Report to the American Foundation for Management Research, Inc., 1966.

Miedema, Allen K. *The case for virgin material charges: A theoretical and empirical evaluation in the paper industry.* Draft Final Report prepared by Research Triangle Institute for Environmental Protection Agency, Contract No. 68–01–3267, January 1976.

Research Triangle Institute. *National study of the composition of roadside litter.* Prepared for Keep America Beautiful, Inc., New York, N.Y., 1969, p. A–01.

Shultz, George P. Economic efficiency vs. political reality. *New York Times,* Dec. 15, 1974, sec. F, p. 14.

Smith, Fred L. Jr. The disposal charge concept. Unpublished paper, U.S. Environmental Protection Agency, November 1974.

Summers, Wallen M. Externalities of paper and paperboard. Unpublished dissertation, Harvard University, 1973.

Tullock, G. Excess Benefit. *Water Resources Research,* vol. 3, no. 2, 1967, pp. 643–44.

U.S. Department of Labor, Bureau of Labor Statistics. *1972–73 Consumer expenditure survey,* Washington: U.S. Government Printing Office.

———. *News,* Washington: U.S. Government Printing Office, May 15, 1975, Table 1.

U.S. Environmental Protection Agency. *Third report to Congress: Resource recovery and waste reduction,* Washington: U.S. Government Printing Office, 1975, Table 1.

U.S. Senate, 94th Congress, 2nd Session. *To consider the effects of product disposal charges on municipal waste recovery and reuse.* Hearing before the Panel on Materials Policy of the Subcommittee on Environmental Pollution of the Committee on Public Works (Serial no. 94–H42), May 20, 1976.

CHAPTER 9

Recycling Policy: Basic Economic Issues

Robert C. Anderson

The interest of governmental policy makers in stimulating the recovery of waste materials is underscored by the numerous options which have received serious consideration recently. At least a dozen different bills containing significant components related to resource recovery and recycling have been introduced in recent sessions of the United States Congress. On a more informal level, other related policy options have been reviewed by the Environmental Protection Agency, the Department of the Interior, the Department of the Treasury, the Congressional Research Service, and others. Policies which have been considered in Congress and elsewhere have never been examined thoroughly with respect to their attainment of social objectives. It is often implicitly assumed that recycling is good and that more re-cycling would be even better. Because recycling requires the use of scarce capital and labor inputs, augmenting present levels of recycling normally requires sacrifices in the production of other goods and services. The central question I wish to examine here is whether or not the free market, unfettered by further governmental controls, will provide the correct amount of recycling services. For a variety of reasons, one is led to the conclusion that competitive markets pro-vide insufficient recycling services. The appropriate role for govern-ments in correcting this deficiency is then examined.

158

The recovery of waste materials is but one component of overall material use patterns. For over one hundred years, economists have debated the issue of how rapidly society should deplete its nonrenewable resources and harvest its renewable resources. The issue still rages on, making it unlikely that one can state confidently that one has determined the "correct" policy for use of natural resources. Nonetheless, under a reasonable set of assumptions concerning resource use, one can indicate instances where markets fail to provide what society would otherwise desire, instances where governmental intervention in the market can improve the allocation of resources.

The perspective chosen for the analysis of recycling policy is that of maximizing the present value of social welfare. In general, this implies that future values will be discounted; that the welfare of future members of society is of less importance than the welfare of existing members of society. A narrow definition of welfare is used, the total value of market and nonmarket goods and services produced in the economy. All issues of how the goods and services are to be distributed among members of society are ignored. Under the very restrictive assumptions that there are no uncertainties, no externalities, and no taxes, Hotelling has shown that a competitive resource market would allocate resources intertemporally to maximize the present value of profits and in so doing would also maximize the social value of the resource. When the assumptions are relaxed to reflect real world considerations, the conclusion no longer holds. Existing markets may fail to develop resources and recycle scrap materials in manners consistent with the maximization of social welfare.

MATERIALS FLOWS

This section presents a general schematic representation of primary and secondary materials flows within the economy as a foundation for the discussion of sources of market failure. The aim is twofold. First, this approach clarifies the determinants of demand and supply and the inputs and outputs of production processes at various stages of the flow of materials. Second, it provides a convenient summary of the sources of market failure and is suggestive of the correct policy prescriptions to rectify the market failures.

All production processes can be placed into one of six broadly defined categories. What may be termed a secondary materials sector comprises three of these categories. Production processes in this sector transform secondary material inputs into intermediate and final products. The other three categories constitute the primary materials sector. This sector includes all other production processes, both those which use only virgin material inputs and those which handle some mix of virgin and secondary materials.

The secondary materials sector consists of collection, processing, and manufacturing activities. Collection includes such related activities as dismantling obsolete products, sorting, cleaning, and consolidating scrap material into forms which are convenient for handling. Generally these activities alter only the physical properties of secondary materials. Processing activities involve both physical and chemical alteration as scrap inputs are transformed into outputs of purer and more uniform quality. Manufacturing operations combine materials into a variety of intermediate and final consumption goods. The principal activities of the primary sector may be analyzed analogously.

Two additional processes, important in the overall characterization of materials flows, are the activities of consumption and disposal. Final outputs of primary and secondary processing and manufacturing become items of consumption and investment. When these items cease to provide useful service, they enter one of three streams: goods which are collected for recycling, items collected for disposal, and discarded items which are not collected.

Figure 9–1 depicts the flow of materials through the primary and secondary materials sectors, on to consumption and, finally, disposal. The pathways indicated on the diagram, while not comprehensive of every material flow in the economy, do represent all of the important flows. At this point it is convenient to review each of the activities in Figure 9–1. The principal inputs, outputs, and functions of each activity will be examined for sources of market failure.

Primary Extraction

Primary extraction uses virgin natural resources as inputs to produce items suitable for further chemical and physical processing. Typical activities in primary extraction include mineral exploration, removal of minerals from the ground, and timber harvesting. Outputs of the primary extraction sector include natural resources suitable for further processing such as mineral ores and cut timber, as well as undesirable by-products such as air and water pollution and disruption of scenic natural environments. In addition to externalities which create a divergence between the private and social cost of virgin material production, a wide variety of other forces may create biases in the prices of virgin materials as they leave the extractive sector.

The extractive sector is subject to an unusually large number of taxes and tax deductions including depletion allowances, expensing of exploration and development outlays, capital gains treatment of profits on standing timber, bonus bidding for mineral lease rights, production royalty payments, and severance taxes, as well as ordinary sales, income, and property taxes. Some of these taxes and tax subsidies are easily incorporated into an economic model of production from a mineral deposit. For example, Sweeney and Peterson have shown that lump-sum and pure profits taxes would not distort production decisions, and hence would have no effect on market prices. Included in this category of taxes would be bonus bids and ideal income taxes. Among those forces which accelerate production and lead to lower virgin material prices are capital gains treatment on standing timber, mineral depletion deductions, and expensing of exploration and development (though the latter has not been analytically demonstrated in the literature). When property taxes are based on the value of minerals remaining in the ground, they too can accelerate production and lead to lower prices. Forces which serve to slow the price of virgin resource extraction include royalty payments and severance taxes.

Because the concentration of ownership in many of the extractive industries is quite high, the impacts of monopolistic forces on the rate of resource development should be considered. Hotelling investigated this point and concluded that monopolies would tend to hold resources off the market, leading to higher prices for virgin resources in the near term. Subsequent investigation by Sweeney and Lewis have revealed that monopolists do not always maximize the present value of profits by holding resources off the market. To date no one has attempted to evaluate the net impact of imperfect competition, or whether the demand conditions discussed by Sweeney and Lewis are important in the real world.

Uncertainty in the extractive sector is another force which may bias virgin material prices. At least three important instances of uncertainty in the extractive sector are discussed in the literature: uncertain tenure of resource ownership, uncertain price (demand) expectations, and

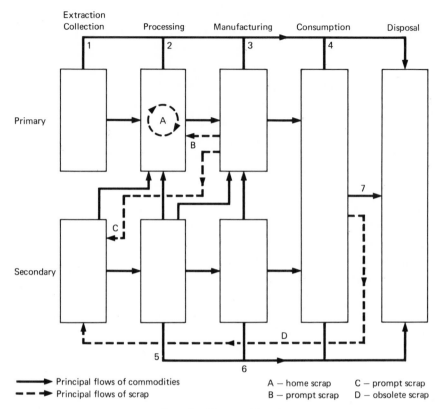

Figure 9–1 The materials cycle

uncertainty over future technology and factor costs. Assuming that natural resource owners are risk averse, each source of uncertainty should, other things equal, create incentives to accelerate the rate of production.

Primary Processing

The primary processing sector receives as inputs the metal ores, cut timber, and so forth from the primary extractive sector and high-grade scrap from secondary material collectors and from the primary manufacturing sector. Using such techniques as smelting and refining for metal ores and debarking, sawing, chipping, and the like for timber, the primary processing sector prepares natural resource products for manufacturing. Principal sources of a divergence between private and social costs of production occur when effluents are discharged into the environment. Federal statutes such as the National Environmental Policy Act, the Federal Water Pollution Control Act, and the Clean Air Act have reduced significantly the magnitude of this externality for most processing operations, leaving an unknown divergence between private and social costs. The primary sector is the principal source of home scrap, nearly all of which is recycled by primary processors. Little or no home scrap is discharged into the environment.

Primary Manufacturing

Inputs to primary manufacturing originate in primary processing and in the secondary processing and manufacturing sectors. In the primary manufacturing sector, the various inputs are fabricated into items for final consumption. Significant quantities of prompt, industrial scrap are produced in these manufacturing operations. Much of the prompt scrap is shipped back to the primary processing sector to be used as an input in the processing operations. Other portions of the prompt scrap are received by secondary material dealers as inputs to their operations.

Secondary Collection

Scrap dealers obtain their inputs from the primary manufacturing sector and as items of final consumption which have served their useful lives are discarded. In the primary manufacturing sector, typical sources of prompt scrap include metal turnings, shavings, trimmings, and paper trimmings. Typical activities of the scrap collectors include sorting, baling, and compacting. Some scrap materials which need only be collected, and perhaps physically altered, move directly to primary production processes. Generally this material is of high quality to start with, most likely originating as home or prompt scrap. It must be clean and its chemical composition known with a great degree of certainty. Most scrap materials become acceptable as inputs to primary materials processing operations only after they have received somewhat more extensive treatment. These materials go from scrap dealers to secondary processors before being shipped to primary processors.

Secondary Processing

Some secondary processing activities closely parallel related operations in the primary processing sector. For example, the secondary lead industry uses smelting and refining processes which are essentially identical to those used for primary lead. In other cases the activities of the secondary processors are largely unrelated to those of the primary sector. Wastepaper, particularly used newsprint, typically must be de-inked and repulped before it can be accepted as an input in the manufacture of items for final consumption.

Much of the scrap which enters secondary materials processing facilities is converted into intermediate products which compete directly with virgin-based products at the manufacturing stage. Lead from secondary smelters and refiners is indistinguishable from primary lead. Both products enter as inputs to the same manufacturing operations. Some scrap copper is smelted and refined into secondary grades that are identical to grades of primary copper. In the case of steel, the secondary processors are electric furnaces to produce high-alloy grades of steel which substitute to a much more limited degree with the products of primary steel producers.

Although statistics on the relative amounts of pollution created by secondary processors could not be obtained, it is known that some secondary operations produce particularly noxious effluents. Wastepaper de-inking and secondary lead smelting are two such examples.

Secondary Manufacturing

Some of the better examples of secondary manufacturing operations are the aluminum, iron, brass, and bronze foundry industries. They are characterized as secondary manufacturing because all or nearly all material inputs are produced from scrap. Most of the outputs of these industries are intermediate goods, such as engine blocks and bearings, which are used as components in a wide variety of final outputs. Some materials are manufactured directly into items for final consumption. One of the best examples of this flow is paper made entirely of recycled fiber.

Consumption and Disposal

For our purposes the most interesting feature of consumption activities is the process through which used consumption goods are discarded. As Wertz shows, consumers have three choices of disposal: littering, municipal waste collection, and delivery to scrap dealers. Of the three choices, only delivery to scrap dealers does not involve externalities. Littering involves large social costs which are not borne by those doing the littering.

Most consumers have free use of municipal waste collection systems. This creates a divergence between private costs of waste disposal, which are zero, and social costs of waste disposal, most of which are reflected in municipal budgets for waste collection, incineration, landfill, and the like. Some social costs such as air and water pollution from waste processing activities are not reflected in municipal cost calculations.

MARKET FAILURES

The schematic review of materials flows has revealed several instances in which goods are not priced at their full social cost of production. This section will attempt to provide a reasonably comprehensive enumeration of such possible market failures, and their likely impact on recycling. The discussion will follow the same sequence chosen for the review of materials flows.

Primary Extraction

Primary extractive operations are taxed at significantly lower rates than is general manufacturing. Percent depletion, expensing of exploration and development, and capital gains treatment on standing timber far outweigh the effects of severance taxes and royalty payments, resulting in effective tax rates in mining and timber management which are significantly lower than the average effective rates for all industrial operations.* Because capital flows in the economy are equilibrated when the after tax rate of return to investment is the same in every industry (after allowance for differences in risk), differential tax treatment of investment results in unequal rates of return before taxation. As Harberger has shown, this is an inefficiency in

---

* A random sampling of income tax returns for calendar year 1973 revealed the following:

Industry	Number of Firms	Average Effective Tax Rate
Forest Products	10	40.7%
Pulp and Paper	9	40.6%
Mining	12	25.5%
Manufacturing	15	45.9%

SOURCE: R. C. Anderson and R. D. Spiegelman, *The Impact of the Federal Tax Code on Resource Recovery*, U.S. Environmental Protection Agency, 1975.

the allocation of factors of production. Societal returns from investment could be increased by shifting investment funds from the lightly taxed extractive sector to the more heavily taxed areas of general manufacturing. It has been argued that the special tax treatment of the extractive sector results in unfair competition between primary and secondary materials and leads to less than optimal levels of resource recovery. While not disputing the point that tax deductions in primary industries do tend to inhibit recycling, Harberger would argue that societal welfare is enhanced by equal treatment of investment in all activities. Rather than extend income tax subsidies to secondary industries, the government should raise the tax burden of the extractive sector to the level which prevails in ordinary manufacturing operations.

Uncertainties are inherent in the search for and development of mineral resources. To the extent that these uncertainties result in premature resource extraction, virgin material prices may be biased downward. While this point has not been investigated thoroughly, it appears that when reduction of the uncertainty is infeasible, government-imposed severance taxes and royalty payments for primary producers can correct the distortions which would otherwise exist. Subsidies to scrap collectors would not be desirable in that such subsidies would further the distortions which exist between the price of natural resource based raw materials and other factor inputs. Too many materials (both virgin and recycled) would be used relative to the use of capital and labor inputs. Again, Harberger would argue that social welfare would be enhanced by raising the price of virgin materials.

Primary Processing and Primary Manufacturing

A source of market failure which cuts across primary extraction, processing, and manufacturing is the production of environmental externalities in the form of air and water pollution and the disruption of natural environments. All of these externalities represent instances in which the social costs of an activity exceed the private costs. It has not been the practice in the United States to impose effluent taxes on those creating environmental externalities. Rather, Congress has opted for systems of direct controls and effluent standards. Although some gains of economic efficiency may be sacrificed through a standards system of control, a standards system may have the advantage over effluent taxes in terms of political acceptability.

Our interest here is not in the design of optimal systems for the control of environmental externalities, but rather in whether or not externalities in primary production ever offer an argument for subsidization of secondary producers. On efficiency grounds (the attainment of Pareto optimality), the answer is negative. The literature on externalities (e.g., Baumol and Oates, Holtermann) suggests that Pareto optimality can be achieved through a set of corrective taxes. Ideally the externality should be taxed directly, but where that is impossible, Pareto optimality can be achieved by a set of taxes imposed on all of the other inputs and outputs of the agent creating the externality. A subsidy to recyclers might reduce primary demand, but it would not correct the divergence between private and social costs in primary production.

Secondary Collection, Secondary Processing, and Secondary Manufacturing

The review of activities in the secondary materials sector suggest only one important source of market failure. This is the production of air and water pollution in secondary smelting and refining and wastepaper de-inking. As in the case of primary production, considerations of economic efficiency would dictate that charges be levied on the production of effluents equal in magnitude to the divergence between private and social costs of production.

Consumption and Disposal

The failure to charge for municipal waste collection creates a divergence between private and social costs of waste disposal. Because this effectively is a subsidy for materials which flow from consumption to disposal, it biases the flow of waste materials away from recovery by secondary material dealers. Were consumers charged for their use of waste disposal services, more of them would be inclined to haul recoverable wastes to scrap dealers. As it is, consumers find it cheaper to dispose of these materials through the municipal waste collection system. Charges for incremental use of municipal waste collection and disposal services have one important drawback; they would provide greater incentives to litter, thereby stimulating use of the other form of free disposal. Because littering involves large social costs, policies which encourage littering should be discouraged.

Two suggestions for public policy to correct the market failure attributable to free municipal waste collection services are direct subsidies for recycling and mandatory deposits on all recyclable materials. Mandatory deposits on all beverage containers are required by state statutes in Oregon, Michigan, Vermont, South Dakota, and Maine. Whether or not deposits on recyclable materials achieve economic efficiency in material consumption and disposal is an unanswered question. In a frictionless world, deposits would correct the source of market failure. In practice, a system of deposits may impose significant transactions costs on those using recyclable materials.

Subsidies for recyclers, in principle, also correct the source of market failure attributable to free disposal by households. The maximum subsidy which could be justified on efficiency grounds would equal the full social costs of postconsumer waste disposal. Although such a subsidy would appear to have solved the problem of market failure, it would have some rather serious problems of implementation and enforcement. In the United States, at least, primary manufacturing operations which are the source of prompt, industrial scrap must pay for any disposal services which they use. Therefore, any subsidy for postconsumer waste recycling must not be applicable to industrial scrap. In practice, it may be difficult to distinguish between some sources of scrap. A subsidy on only one class of scrap would create a powerful incentive for scrap dealers to make it appear that some of their industrial scrap was really postconsumer scrap. The problem of distinguishing sources of scrap for purposes of subsidization should be addressed in recycling legislation. The problem is complex and difficult, and a solution will not be proposed here.

A final argument for federal intervention in materials markets is that information flows through the price system from consumers back to manufacturers, and processors may be far from perfect. Fred Smith has argued that consumer desires, especially in the area of packaging design, may never be transmitted back to those who design packaging materials. Smith has proposed that product charges be levied on materials used in processing or manufacturing operations in order to encourage less wasteful use of raw materials. This appears to be, in part, another mechanism for correcting virgin material prices to reflect their full social costs of production. By exempting recycled materials from the charge, such a system would also serve to stimulate recycling. Therefore the product charge would be, in part, also a device for correcting a portion of the market failure attributable to free disposal.

RECENT LEGISLATIVE ACTIVITY IN THE UNITED STATES

In recent years there has been an active interest in federal policies to stimulate the recovery of scrap and waste materials. In the 94th Congress at least eight bills were introduced which contained specific provisions to encourage greater recycling. In addition to legislative proposals, a number of existing statutes have a direct bearing on recycling. Five major thrusts of this activity have developed.

One such threat is the attempt to prohibit labeling requirements which discriminate against recycled materials. Section 383 of the recently enacted "Energy Policy and Conservation Act" accomplished this goal for waste oil. This section reads in part: "No rule or order of the Federal Trade Commission may require any container of recycled oil to also bear a label containing any term, phrase, or description which connotes less than substantial equivalency of such recycled oil with new oil."

A second major thrust has been the analysis of railroad freight rates for evidence of discrimination in favor of virgin over recycled materials. Several recent studies (see Albrecht for further references) have shown that virgin materials incur somewhat lower charges per ton mile traveled. To establish conclusively that discrimination exists, one must compare charges as well as costs incurred by the railroads. One component of the "Railroad Revitalization and Regulatory Reform Act of 1976" directs the Interstate Commerce Commission to perform a comprehensive study of railroad costs and charges for different classes of materials.

A third area of Congressional interest is in assisting states to develop plans for solid waste reduction and energy and resource recovery. Senate Bills 2150 and 1474, which were introduced in the 94th Congress, are examples of this interest. In a related vein, House Bill 1045 would provide for loan guarantees for facilities which generate energy from solid waste, and House Bill 1046 would grant tax deductions for similar activities.

Another area of Congressional activity has been stimulated by research at the Environmental Protection Agency on the merits of incorporating disposal fees in the manufacturing cost of consumer goods. Section 306 of the proposed "Solid Waste Utilization Act of 1975" contained such a provision. Several recent bills have proposed a national system of beverage container deposits which would be levied at the consumer level. An example is Senate Bill 613.

The final area of Congressional interest in recycling policy is the use of the tax code to subsidize recycling activities. House Bill 148 would grant to scrap processors depletion deductions which are very nearly the same as the deductions obtained by those who extract virgin materials. House Bill 148 would apply to all scrap recovered and would not differentiate according to source. House Bill 10612 would offer similar deductions, but only to that portion of scrap recovered which exceeded 75 percent of a base figure. The design of House Bill 10612 may eliminate some of the problems of subsidizing industrial scrap recovery which are present in House Bill 148. Another House Bill, number 7974, would grant to purchasers of recyclable materials a tax credit which could be earned only when applied to the cost of building a recycling facility. Yet another variant on this theme is House Bill 9467, which would grant a direct credit against income tax liabilities equal to $10 for every ton of postconsumer wastepaper which is collected and processed into commercially marketable materials.

CONCLUSIONS

Of all of the arguments for a revision of existing policy with respect to materials use, three key areas appear to deserve attention. First, the subsidies to virgin material production should be eliminated. Second, divergences between private and social costs in all stages of activity in both the primary and secondary sectors should be corrected by suitably designed effluent taxes or regulations. Third, the market failure attributable to free disposal of postconsumer wastes should be corrected.

The legislation recently considered by Congress does not focus on these basic problems. Removal of tax subsidies to any industry has proved difficult in the past. The power of the extractive sector and the long history of privileged tax status both suggest that lawmakers may be reluctant to tackle such a strong adversary. It would be much more expedient politically to give further subsidies to recyclers. Yet, as we have seen, such subsidies would not improve aggregate social welfare. Rectifying the problem of free waste disposal for consumers is a problem which can be solved at other than the national level. Simply charging consumers for the full social costs of disposal would correct the market failure (and create new incentives for recycling), but such an initiative must originate at the local level of government. The difficulty of designing appropriate recycling subsidies to correct this source of market failure may preclude an active role for the federal government in the solution of this problem. Although most of the legislation which has been proposed in Congress has not been subjected to a careful economic analysis, some of the subsidy proposals have. Elsewhere Richard Spiegelman and I have reported findings that subsidies such as in House Bills 148 and 10612 would cost the Treasury several times the value of the scrap which would be recovered. Furthermore, the magnitude of the subsidy would be many times as large as needed to correct the market failure attributable to free disposal. Such subsidy programs should be rejected until they can be redesigned to produce more acceptable results.

BIBLIOGRAPHY

Albrecht, O. A. Shipping wastes to useful places. *Environmental Science and Technology* 10 (May 1976):440–42.

Anderson, R. C. Tax incentives for the recovery of secondary lead. *Resource Recovery and Conservation,* forthcoming, 1977.

———— and Spiegelman, R. D. Tax policy and secondary material use. *Journal of Environmental Economics and Management,* forthcoming, 1977.

Baumol, W. J. and Oates, W. E. *The theory of environmental policy.* Prentice-Hall, 1975.

Harberger, A. C. Efficiency effects of taxes on income from capital. In *Effects of the corporate income tax* (Kryzaniak, ed.) Detroit, 1966.

Holtermann, S. Alternative tax systems to correct for externalities and the efficiency of paying compensation, *Economica,* February 1976, pp. 1–16.

Hotelling, H. The economics of exhaustible resources. *Journal of Political Economy,* 1931, pp. 37–175.

Lewis, T. Monopoly exploitation of an exhaustible resource. *Journal of Environmental Economics and Management,* October 1976, pp. 198–204.

Page, T. *Conservation and economic efficiency,* Johns Hopkins, 1977.

Peterson, F. M. A variational model of mining and exploration. Unpublished, April, 1973.

Smith, F. The disposal charge concept. Unpublished, September 1974.

Sweeney, J. Economics of depletable resources: Market forces and intertemporal bias. *Review of Economic Studies,* forthcoming.

Wertz, K. Economic factors influencing households' production of refuse. *Journal of Environmental Economics and Management,* April 1976, pp. 263–72.

CHAPTER 10

Recycling Policy:
An International Perspective

Robin Bidwell

Action to promote recycling* is often only one part of a more general government program designed to encourage the rational use of resources and to reduce waste.† The specific objectives for such a program may include one or a combination of the following: reduction in the costs, environmental hazard, or nuisance associated with the collection, treatment or disposal of household and industrial wastes; the desire to minimize the use of primary materials and to reduce reliance on imported resources. It is the emphasis placed on any one or a combination of these objectives that will at least in part determine the priorities and the type of measures that are selected.

The object of this chapter is to examine the action that may be taken by governments to promote recycling. In particular, the paper

---

* *Recycling* is used as a generic term to include *reclamation* (the recovery of materials and discarded products from waste), *re-use* (the reclaimed product is used again for a similar purpose), *materials' recycling* (the reclaimed material is used to produce more of a similar material), and *by-product generation* (the reclaimed materials and products are used for a different purpose).

† Recycling is only one of a number of measures that may be employed to achieve the twin objectives of resource conservation and waste management: other methods include product controls (e.g., the redesign of products to extend the product life or to minimize the use of certain resources), specific waste disposal measures, etc.

considers the reasons why a government may decide such action is
necessary, the type of action that may be taken, and the development
of an integrated recycling program. It should be noted that this paper
does not set out to provide a comprehensive review of current recycling policies; rather it aims to identify the alternative approaches
taking into account current practice. To this end, examples are given
of the policy and measures adopted in selected countries.

THE RATIONALE FOR ACTION

One can do little more than speculate on the reasons for the development of the recycling policies of individual governments; although published material and discussions with relevant officials
provide some guidance.* It is likely that *reduction in the use of
resources,* particularly in the context of the increasing cost of imports, has probably provided a major impetus for some if not all of
the European government recycling programs. Loss of potential raw
materials is specifically identified in the paper setting out the United
Kingdom government's views on recycling (Cmnd 5727, HMSO,
Sept. 1974); and it is recognized by the French government both in
their recent report (Ministère de la Qualité de la Vie, 1974) and
as an objective for setting up their Raw Materials Commission
(France, 1975), one of whose aims is to reduce raw material use
through recycling. In Sweden, an important factor in the program to
encourage waste paper recycling has been the need to avoid a short-
fall in the raw material for paper products, since this is one of the
country's most important exports (Sweden, 1975). The Netherlands,
in an unpublished note on recycling policy, observes that one reason
for encouraging recycling is the reduction in the consumption of
energy associated with the use of recycled material as compared with
primary ores. They also note the need to reduce dependence on
imports of raw materials and to overcome problems of treatment and
disposal brought about by an increasing quantity of waste.

The need to reduce the quantity of waste requiring disposal is
perhaps the other main objective of government programs; prior to
the post-1973 increase in resource costs, it was perhaps the most
important. So the German Federal Government in their 1975 Waste

* The sources of unpublished information provided by government officials
have not been identified in this paper.

Disposal Program, note (see par. 1, Berlin, 1975) that, while in 1971 they were concerned primarily with "problems of systematic waste disposal," now the cost in manpower and resources of providing disposal services, the need to protect the environment, and the dependence of the country on imported raw material supplies are identified as three main reasons for action: the program proposes that such action should not be confined to systematic waste disposal but rather should "strive for a reduction in the amount of, and increased utilization of waste." In the United States, the primary objective may perhaps still focus on reducing the total quantity of waste requiring disposal and minimizing the litter problem. In 1970, the President, in a message to Congress proposing, inter alia, an extension of the Solid Waste Disposal Act, suggested the need to redirect research so as "to place greater emphasis on techniques for recycling materials and on development and use of packaging in other materials which will degrade after use." The message also noted that existing packaging methods, with an emphasis on "non-returnable bottles and cartons" had created an increasing volume of waste and refuse; and the traditional method of dealing with the problem was to continue spending money on collection and disposal of wastes which "amounts to a public subsidy of waste pollution" (C.Q. Almanac, 1970).

The aims of *preventing environmental damage and reducing litter* usually receive a mention in recycling-waste reduction programs, for example, in the United Kingdom government's "War on Waste" (HMSO, 1974) and the French "La Lutte Contre le Gaspillage," (Ministère de la Qualité de la Vie, 1974). These aims tend to be of importance in the case of specific recycling programs such as the recycling of waste oils (to minimize pollution) and controls over packaging materials. In the United States, litter reduction appears to have been the primary objective of the Oregon legislation to control beverage containers (see U.S. EPA, 1973); although it is of interest to note that similar regulations in Sweden were brought in primarily to help finance a freeze on the prices of certain food products (I. Olson, 1975).

In Europe, there are the wider trade implications. In their draft resolution for a Community Action Program on the Environment (1977–81), the Commission of the European Communities include as a reason for pursuing an active antiwaste policy, the need "to contribute to the harmonious development of the economic activities entrusted to it by the EEC Treaty" (European Communities, 6/76). The resolution points out that such development cannot avoid the negative impacts of the increase in the cost of raw materials, of dependence of the Community and the Member States on external sources of supply and, in the long run, of the foreseeable depletion and resulting predictable rise in the cost of certain materials; and that it will be necessary to obviate distortions to competition and obstacles to trade which would inevitably occur if measures are taken to deal with waste solely at national level. The resolution also notes the need to reduce pollution arising from the accumulation and processing of waste.

MEASURES TO PROMOTE RECYCLING

Measures designed to encourage further recycling need to take into account the reasons why the resources are not at present recovered. The fundamental obstacle may be that it is just not sufficiently financially advantageous for the parties involved; that is, the waste handlers and secondary material merchants and users. But there may also be other obstacles that act as a disincentive to further recycling and which may partially determine the overall economic feasibility. In discussing the obstacles and possible recycling action below, a distinction has been made between obstacles to *demand* for the recycled materials and obstacles to *supply;* this is not a rigid distinction but, as discussed later, it is of importance when considering the development of a recycling program.

Demand for Recycled Materials

The demand for the recycled material may be limited in a number of ways. First, there may be *market obstacles.* There may, for example, be a belief that the secondary material is inferior and an unsatisfactory substitute for a certain primary material; this belief may be based on sound technical grounds, but equally it may derive from an attitude of the secondary material user or final consumer. Examples of the latter include a preference for bleached paper and clear uncolored glass. Alternatively, specifications may be prepared that exclude the use of secondary materials that would perform technically as well as their virgin counterparts. For example, certain of the International Wool Secretariat standards are based upon the requirement that no recycled fiber should be incorporated in the material *; and in the case of tires, remolds showed they perform as well as their virgin counterparts for those uses where the vehicle is not to be driven at high speeds. Measures may be taken to prevent unnecessary discrimination against secondary materials—or products incorporating the secondary material. For example, the French waste law prohibits the discrimination against the presence of recovered materials and products which satisfy regulations and standards; it also prohibits any publicity based on the absence of recovered materials (Art. 18, 19, France, 1975). Such regulations may be supported by further regulations laying down quality specifications for secondary materials and products—in France, the Raw Materials Commission is working with the French Standards Organization (AFNOR) and the International Standards Organization, investigating whether primary materials in specifications can be replaced by secondary materials.

There may be *technical* (practical) obstacles to the demand for secondary materials. For example, it may prove difficult (and costly) to clean and upgrade a particular material to a quality acceptable to potential users. Where it is clear that the main obstacle to demand for a specific recycled material is a technical problem, R & D may be subsidized by the government. Problems of this type that have received attention include investigation into methods of de-inking and upgrading waste paper, and de-tinning; and research into new uses for materials that are difficult to recycle or re-use. Examples of the latter include the search for new uses of cullet and the development of building materials from pulverized fuel ash and from refuse residues. Much of the R & D work of this type has been undertaken in the private sector; government-sponsored R & D has concentrated more on the supply problems of initial reclamation and materials separation (discussed later).

The demand for recycled materials may also be limited because potential users may not have *adequate information* on the availability and use of suitable secondary materials. In this case, the government may assist in the setting up of information centers where data on

---

* Neither the Woolmark nor the Woolblendmark (the certification trademark of the International Wool Secretariat) allow for fibers from postconsumer textiles to be included in the material.

arisings and the use of secondary materials may be held. In Europe, there are a number of publicly sponsored waste material exchanges: for example, in the United Kingdom, in Scandinavia, and in the Netherlands.*

Finally, overall demand may be stimulated by action *encouraging the use of secondary materials in products* or stimulating the re-use of products through regulations or fiscal incentives. In France, for example, the Raw Materials Commission has stated that it is actively considering ways of increasing the use of recycled materials in products and under Title V (Act 17) of the law relating to the elimination of wastes and recovery of materials, the government can fix a minimum proportion of recoverable materials, or components to be used in the manufacture of products or product categories (France, 1975). In Germany, France, and Italy, taxation favors the use of re-processed oils as compared with primary oils. Demand for certain specific products may be stimulated by *government purchasing (procurement) policies*: that is, the requirement that certain products or materials purchased by public authorities should incorporate some proportion of secondary material. This proportion may be fixed as part of a procurement specification. In Denmark, the government has plans to specify proportions of recycled fiber to be contained in supplies of paper procured for the public sector. This is also under consideration as part of a national resource recovery program in the Netherlands, where the government is currently examining the possibilities of specifying proportions of secondary materials in goods procured for the public sector. In Germany there are plans to revise the conditions of certain state contracts to include, where appropriate, a requirement that goods supplied should incorporate secondary materials. The status of procurement programs in the United States is reviewed in the Second Report to Congress (see USEPA, 1974). The General Services Administration requires that paper procured should include certain proportions of recycled fiber from postconsumer waste as well as from industrial sources: these proportions are established taking into account the performance required, the supply of secondary material, and product price. The Department of the Army has a policy of tire retreading for automobiles and trucks.

---

* The Nordic Organization for Waste Exchange, the United Kingdom Materials Waste Exchange, the Dutch Center for Wastes Exchange.

The Supply of Secondary Materials

The supply of secondary materials may be limited in the first place because *waste producers and waste handlers may not be prepared to separate out secondary materials* and make these available. Fluctuations in the price for secondary materials may be seen as an important reason why waste producers and waste handlers often view recovery with something less than enthusiasm. Two methods have been considered for stabilizing prices in the secondary materials market: these include the financing of stocks of secondary materials during times of low demand ("stockpiling") and the use of long-term contracts where both the reclaimer and user agree a price and organize their operations over a fixed period during which little or no account is taken of the prevailing market prices. Excess stocks schemes for paper to reduce the effects of peaks and troughs in demand have been implemented in Norway, France, and Japan. Proposals for paper stockpiling have also been considered but not implemented in the Netherlands, United Kingdom, and Belgium. In Germany the possibility of standard contract conditions for the supply of secondary materials by local authorities is being examined. Regulations may be designed specifically to ensure that there is an adequate supply of secondary materials. In Sweden, under the 1975 Act (Sweden, 1975) householders may be required to separate out newspapers and magazines from their refuse and keep these separately for removal by the local authorities (or their own agents); it is envisaged by the government that by 1980 separate collection will be in force in all areas of the country where it is a practical proposition and where there is justification for it, probably only the major urban areas. The Swedish Minister for Agriculture and Environment noted (see BIR, 1975) that the measure was taken to avoid timber shortages and save energy; that industrialists within the paper industry in Sweden were prepared to make the investment in increased waste-paper processing plants, but that they had laid it down as a condition of such expansion that the supply of waste paper should be guaranteed. In Italy, there is legislation (Law no. 366, 1941) that requires communities with a population of over 50,000 to segregate refuse for the purpose of recovery; this regulation is not currently enforced although there is a suggestion that it may be revived.

Fiscal incentives may be used to promote recovery and make the material available for recycling. Under recent Swedish legislation (see *SFS, 1975*) an owner, before he can de-register his car (and cease paying a car tax), must be issued a certificate from an authorized person (e.g., a vehicle-breaking company) confirming that the vehicle has been received for scrapping. Every car manufactured or imported into Sweden from 1976 will bear an additional charge of 250 Swedish crowns; the car owner will receive a premium of 300 Swedish crowns when the car is de-registered. In Germany, the Waste Oil Law (*Waste Oil Law, 1975*) provides for the payment of a subsidy if the waste oil is collected and used in an approved manner. In France, the Waste Disposal and Recovery Law (France, 1975) enables the authorities to require that waste disposal methods should, where possible, allow for material and energy recovery (Art. 15).

Measures may be taken *to ensure the return of products that can be re-used* and that might otherwise be discarded as waste: in practice, this means containers made of glass, metal and, to a lesser extent, plastic. In Sweden, there is a tax at the point of manufacture on all beverage containers whose contents are more than 0.2 liters and less than 3 liters. In Norway, there is a tax on one-way containers and the deposit on recoverable containers is fixed by law (Norway, 1974). In the United States, a number of states are considering, or have taken, action to encourage the re-use of containers. These include Oregon, whose "Bottle Bill" was passed by the state legislature in July 1971 and became effective on 1 October 1972. The purpose of the legislation was to control litter (see USEPA, 1973) and it required that a two-cent deposit should be levied on all standard bottles that were refillable by more than one bottler; and a five-cent deposit for all other containers, such as nonstandard bottles (for example, bottles with trademarks). The EPA has proposed guidelines for beverage containers; in particular, the guidelines require that carbonated beverages sold in federal establishments should be sold in returnable beverage containers on which there would be a deposit of at least five cents (see Federal Register, 1975). The Commission of the European Communities and the OECD (through the Waste Management Policy Group) are both examining questions of container re-use.

The availability of secondary materials may also be limited by *technical difficulties in recovering and separating materials* (particularly from mixed wastes and from multimaterial discarded products). Where technical problems arise from product characteristics, these may be controlled by government regulation. A number of European governments have the power to require that specific products are changed to facilitate their recovery or disposal. In France, under Title V, Article 16 of the Waste Law (see France, 1975), the Council of State is able to regulate, by decree, methods of using certain materials, components, or energy so as to facilitate subsequent recovery. In Germany, while there is no legislation, the Government has noted (see Berlin, 1975) that some products contain different mixtures of materials whose recovery is difficult and expensive, and it is therefore necessary that waste management measures should start at the product design stage; to this end a degree of standardization may be required. In the Netherlands, the government, through the proposed Waste Materials Bill (see Netherlands, 1975), would be able to regulate or prohibit the manufacture or sale of certain goods which, because of their nature, composition, weight, or volume are difficult to recover.

Where there are recovery problems to be overcome, the government may make available *finance for research and development programs*. In the United States, the Solid Waste Disposal Act (U.S., 1965) of 1965 established the National Solid Waste Research and Development Program and provided state and local governments with technical and financial aid. The 1970 Resource Recovery Act (U.S., 1970) directed attention specifically to resource recovery. It allows for grants by public agencies for resource recovery demonstration plants or construction of innovative waste disposal facilities. The federal share of demonstration grants is set at 75 percent; the federal share of construction grants at 50 percent if the project serves only a single municipality and 75 percent in other cases. Finance has been made available for research into resource recovery systems by most European countries. France has investigated separate collection systems (Ministère de l'industrie et de la Recherche, 1975); Germany, the United Kingdom and the Netherlands have financed the development of resource recovery systems (Krauss-Maffei, Warren Springs Laboratory, and TNO plants respectively), and Denmark also makes grants available on an ad hoc basis. Grants may also be made available to waste handlers (usually local authorities) for recycling plants; for example, investment grants are available in Belgium (up to 60 percent of construction costs available to municipalities for waste treatment and recovery plants), and grants are available in Germany for plants designed to reclaim energy from waste.

In addition to subsidies and grants to industry of this type, loans may be made available on special terms for recycling projects. In Sweden, the Board of Technical Development provides a form of loan to industry for environmental technological developments. If the project is successful, the borrowed money is repaid at 1 percent over the Swedish bank rate; if unsuccessful, no repayment is made. At a more general level, there are also facilities provided through the Swedish Investment Bank which enables the company to borrow the funds necessary to take a project from the research and development stage to a commercial full-scale operation; the borrower pays a risk premium so that if a project is successful, about 25 percent over and above the amount borrowed is repaid (a commercial interest rate is charged). Again, if the project is unsuccessful, there is no requirement to repay.

At the European level, there is a Raw Materials subcommittee of the European Communities Scientific and Technical Research Committee (CREST). Its principal tasks include the assessment of existing and planned EEC R & D activities relating to secondary materials and, where desirable, to suggest areas where joint or concerted action would be desirable.

Measures may also be taken to provide collection and disposal authorities with *information on recovery methods*. In France the government plans to set up through the newly created Agence Nationale pour la Recuperation et l'Elimination des Dechets (see France, 1976) an information service for local authorities and others engaged in recycling: it has already produced and circulated a booklet on separate collection (see Ministère de la Qualité de la Vie, 1976). In the United Kingdom, the government, through the Department of the Environment and the Waste Management Advisory Council, has provided local authorities with advice on waste paper recovery (HMSO, 1976) and on other recycling decisions. Other government information services and waste material exchanges have already been mentioned in the context of demand; these, of course, also assist suppliers to find a market.

Finally, measures may be required to overcome *specific economic factors* that may be seen as being a disincentive to further reclamation. It will be appreciated that the financial benefit to be derived from recycling a material will depend partly on the saving in the cost that would otherwise have been incurred in waste treatment and disposal; in cases where the necessary measures to protect the environment are not being taken, the cost of disposal to the producer will be low, reducing the incentive to reclaim. There will, therefore, be a consequential social cost to the community. There has been a trend in recent years, certainly in Europe, the United States, and Japan, toward more stringent controls over treatment and disposal of effluents and solid waste and such measures have undoubtedly provided some impetus for increased recycling. However, in the case of postconsumer wastes, the product designer and manufacturer have no incentive to take account of the eventual problems and costs of disposal. As mentioned, France, Germany, and the Netherlands are considering direct product controls to facilitate recovery; an alternative, currently under study in the United States (and, it is planned, to be studied by the OECD) is a tax on the product to take account of the eventual disposal cost. There may also be other specific disincentives that have developed in individual countries that may require adjustment: one example is the possible discrimination of freight rates against the transport of scrap materials in the United States (U.S. EPA, 1974, Chap. 7).

DEVELOPMENT OF THE RECYCLING PROGRAM

Priorities for Action

The priorities for action are likely to be determined by the government's overall rationale in establishing a recycling program and also by the existing status of resource recovery. Programs primarily designed to reduce the amount of postconsumer waste requiring disposal are likely to concentrate on packaging materials: this is the case, for example, in Germany and it is one of the objectives of the solid waste program of the Ministry for the Quality of Life in France. But programs designed to reduce dependence on imports may select other priorities: the French Raw Materials Commission is looking at plastics, copper, textiles, phosphates, and the energy and paper aspects of packaging. In the United Kingdom, priority is to be given to "encouraging reclamation which can be shown to be economic" (Kruse, 1976); this is likely to result particularly in encouraging further reclamation of ferrous and nonferrous metals. In Sweden, where the

economy is dependent on ferrous metal and paper exports, action has
been directed toward recovering waste paper and cars.

Selection of Measures
In order to bring about the necessary action to promote recycling, a
government has a choice between intervention of some type (through
regulations or fiscal means) and encouraging voluntary action. In
some cases, an incentive for voluntary action may be the knowledge
that the government is actively considering intervention. For example,
in Denmark and Germany the packaging industry is voluntarily restricting one-way containers and promoting the recycling of containers; in each country the government has powers to regulate
packaging under existing legislation (see Denmark At. no. 293, 1971
and Germany, Abfallbeseitigungsesetz, 1972).

The criteria for determining what form of measure to introduce to
achieve the program's objectives will include the need to bring about
the requisite changes efficiently, cheaply (in terms of the cost of their
administration), and with the minimum of unwanted side effects.

In discussions of possible action to promote recovery, a distinction
was made between actions to increase the demand for secondary
materials and actions to increase the supply. It was noted that this
is by no means a rigid distinction; certain actions (such as the provision of information centers) should stimulate both. It is, however, an
important distinction to bear in mind in the development of a recycling program. Taking action solely to encourage supply of the
material, for example, by requiring that waste paper should be separately collected, is likely to depress the price and may result in some
of the waste paper finding no market at all. If action were taken to
stimulate only demand, there could also be the danger of shortages
and disproportionately high prices in the short term. However, it may
be that it is on actions to stimulate demand that the emphasis should
lie, thereby providing the incentive for waste producers and handlers
to find a way to increase supply. The converse (that is, that increased supply will lead to an increase in the use of secondary materials) may not always be the case.

Two examples where intervention has been designed primarily to
assist to secure or stabilize the supply of waste paper are the stockpiling schemes and encouraging separate selection from householders.
In Norway, the Department of Environmental Protection provides

low-interest loans to finance the industry's stockpiling operations; while it is too early to judge the long-term success of the scheme, the immediate results are that the industry has built up considerable stocks and there have been no efforts to divert the waste paper to uses other than the traditional "low grade" corrugated and other packaging uses. In Sweden, as noted, regulations requiring the separate collection of paper have been proposed, and, as an immediate result, large stocks of waste paper have been built up; however, industry has agreed to increase de-inking capacity so that the waste paper can be used for a wider range of products (see BIR, 1975).

The point that must be stressed is, therefore, that unless *demand* for the recovered materials can be increased, action to improve supply will not result in an overall increase in recycling activity; the only exceptions are the metals which can be readily substituted for the high-value virgin materials. Actions to encourage demand have been discussed. They include measures to prevent discrimination against secondary materials; fiscal measures to tax virgin materials and subsidize recovered materials; and government procurement policies. The latter may not create a significant new market demand; however, it is argued that in the United States action on procurement policies at the federal level can be of general assistance in laying down guidelines: on the technical and economic limitations of recycled material use in various products, on criteria for selecting materials and products to be considered for use in products and on present and future sources of secondary materials (see USEPA, 1974). The tax-subsidy approach is used in West Germany, where a levy on all taxed lubricating oil goes into a fund which subsidizes the collection and recycling (or incineration) of waste oil (see *Waste Oil Law, 1969*).

In addition to the need for the supply and demand measures to be integrated, it is necessary to establish that the individual measures will have the desired result with the minimum of unwanted side effects. In the case of the Swedish returnable container scheme discussed above, Olson, Head of the Swedish Environmental Protection Board, has commented (1975) that the main effects of the tax have been to increase the number of containers above or below the limit set by the legislation and to bring about some shift from the use of non-returnable containers. There has perhaps been some decrease in litter, but there is doubt as to whether this results from the tax or the associated publicity; and it has been calculated that there has been a very small reduction in the quantity of solid waste produced per year (of the order of 1.0 kg per person per year) and in the amount of energy consumed (reduction of about 0.01 percent). Industry has argued that the scheme has conferred few, if any, environmental or economic benefits and, has resulted in some unemployment (see Olsen [1975] and PLM [1975]). A more recent report on whether or not to increase the container tax (Stockholm, 1976) has argued that while this may not induce the required consumer behavior, it will raise money to help in antilitter campaigns.

The problem of potential distortions and dislocations warrants careful examination, and the potential dangers may even act as a deterrent. It was, for example, noted in the First Report to Congress on Resources Recovery and Source Reduction (see Act No. 293, 1971) that "additional Federal incentives for recycling are not considered desirable at this time. Studies to date indicate that the effectiveness of specific incentive mechanisms that can be formulated is extremely difficult to predict. New tax incentives may well distort the economics of resource utilization much as preferential treatment of virgin materials distorts them today."

Concern over unwanted side effects may be one of the main reasons why up until now there have been few fundamental government measures * to promote recycling. In Europe and the United States these are limited to fiscal incentives to encourage waste oil recycling (Germany, France, Italy), the reclamation of cars (Sweden) the stockpiling of paper (Norway and France), the use of returnable containers (Sweden and the United States), and regulations to encourage the separate collection of waste paper (Sweden and some United States cities). A number of countries (Germany, France, Italy, and Netherlands) have existing or planned legislation under which specific action could be taken. Existing government action has centered primarily on research (both technical and economic) and the provision of information. In Germany, the UBA (Umweltbundesamt) has a research program covering the recycling (and overall reduction) of postconsumer waste and the program includes investigation into the possibilities for private and public financing of waste handling facilities; the ecological and socioeconomic consequences of using non-

---

* That is, intervention where the primary result has been to increase recycling. More stringent controls over waste treatment and disposal also will have this effect.

returnable plastic bottles; the consequences of raising waste collection and disposal charges to promote recovery and of providing government price support for the collection of waste materials. Priority is also to be given to establishing a centralized data bank on technical and economic aspects of recycling and on the provision of information to public and private bodies. In France, a program of investigation into resource reduction and recycling is currently being carried out within the Ministry of the Quality of Life; as mentioned, the new Agency (see France, 1976) will have responsibility for co-ordinating research and providing an information service. In the United States, the principal EPA activities (as reported in the Reports to Congress) have included the provision of financial aid on recovery systems, studies on the economics of recycling and recycling incentives; and the preparation of guidelines on container re-use (see *Federal Register, 1975*). The Commission of the European Communities, in its draft resolution for a new Environment Programme (see p. 38, European Communities, 6/76) also plans further studies: these include plans to study ways and means of making the market for secondary raw materials more stable; to consider what measures the authorities could take to improve, by means of public procurement contracts, outlets for certain secondary materials; to arouse public awareness of, and encourage co-operation with, actions launched; to study means of improving the flow of information to industrialists on supply and demand for waste; to carry out optimization studies and cost benefit analyses as a means of arriving at a more accurate assessment of the types of processing to be used for waste; and to consider which research and development sectors require support and co-ordination at community level. The Commission also plans (see p. 37, European Communities, 6/76) measures to encourage and improve recycling and re-use operations.

Co-ordination

Finally, there is the need for a co-ordinating body, in particular where there are a number of government departments and organizations with an interest in different aspects of recycling. For example, in France the ministries with an interest in recycling include the Ministry for the Quality of Life, the Ministry of the Interior (in charge of solid waste treatment plants in the municipalities), the Ministry of Agriculture (as for Ministry of Interior but for rural communities), the Ministry for Industry and Research (resources and their economics from an industrial viewpoint), the Ministry of Equipment, and so forth. Policy on recycling is currently co-ordinated by the Ministry for the Quality of Life; although there is some overlap with the Raw Materials Commission (under the Ministry for Industry and Research). In May 1976 the Agence Nationale pour la Recuperation et l'Elimination des Dechets was set up. It is not yet fully established, but it will be responsible for co-ordinating recycling action, centralizing data on waste, promoting and organizing research and development; and proposing methods for encouraging recycling (see France, 1976). In the United Kingdom a Waste Management Advisory Council (WMAC) was set up by the Secretary of State for the Environment and the Secretary of State for Industry in December 1974; its terms of reference require it, inter alia, to keep under review the development of waste management policies, to give particular consideration to resource recovery, the technical, economic, administrative, and legal problems involved; and to "consider the program of research and development" (see par. 1, HMSO, 1976). In late 1976, a director of the National Anti-Waste program was appointed within the Department of Industry to give the council "a keener cutting edge" (see *Municipal Engineering,* 1976). The co-ordinating role may be given to an individual government department. In Germany, the primary responsibility rests with the Ministry for the Interior; the Ministry is advised by the Federal Environment Agency (Umweltbundesamt or "UBA"). In the United States, the Environmental Protection Agency (EPA) has the responsibility for studying resource recovery and the reduction of solid waste at source. Within the EPA, the Office of Solid Waste Management Programs and the office for Research and Development are responsible for resource recovery from solid waste.

At the European level, a co-ordinating body, the Committee on Waste Management, has been established by the Commission of the European Communities (see European Communities, 1976) based on a proposal by the Environment and Consumer Protection Service. The Committee will consist of two members from each of the Member States and two from the Commission. Its terms of reference include the requirement that it should supply the commission with an opinion on matters relating to the formulation of a policy for waste management and on the different technical, economic, administrative, and legal measures which could prevent the production of wastes or ensure their re-use, recycling, or disposal (see Article 2(a)(b), European Communities, 1976).

CONCLUSIONS

The rising cost of raw materials and more stringent environmental protection standards have probably provided added impetus to government recycling programs where policy objectives may have been to reduce the quantity of waste and the associated problems and costs. The main obstacle to further recycling is often that it is not at present sufficiently financially advantageous for the parties concerned to reclaim, process, and use material from waste. But there tend also to be specific obstacles which partly determine the overall economics of recycling. These obstacles may be of a primary technical nature, or they may result from a shortage of adequate information on reclamation and use of secondary material; they may also result from the attitudes of industry and the consumer who may have evolved preferences for primary materials and may not be prepared or organized to accept secondary materials.

In order to overcome the obstacles and promote recycling a government may "oil the wheels" of the system or it may take more fundamental action. Action in the former category includes providing finance for technical developments, establishing information centers, encouraging industry, and arousing public interest. More fundamental action involves government regulations and fiscal incentives to encourage and increase the reclamation and re-use of products and materials that would otherwise be disposed of as waste. In developing a program, it is essential to take account of the need to stimulate demand as well as encourage the reclamation of the material.

At present, much of the government action in Europe and North America is designed to "oil the wheels." There are, however, some specific measures in Europe and North America governing container re-use, waste oils, waste paper, and car recovery; four European governments (France, Netherlands, Germany, Denmark) have passed or are planning to pass legislation that provides them with the power to take more fundamental action; and in the United States, consideration is being given in particular to further container re-use regulations and product charges. In both Europe and North America, research is being undertaken into how more fundamental measures designed to reduce waste and conserve resources may be introduced without bringing about unwanted side effects.

BIBLIOGRAPHY

BIR, 1975. S. Lundkvist, Swedish Minister of Agriculture and Environment, in an address delivered to the General Assembly of the BIR in Stockholm on 14th May 1975.

Berlin, 1975 "Waste Disposal Programme of the Federal German Government." (Translation of Abfallwirtschaftsprogramm der Bundesregierung).

COA, 1970 *Congressional Quarterly Almanac* 1970 (p. 514). "Solid Waste: Bill Stresses Recovery and Recycling."

European Communities Supplement, 6/76 "A Continuation and Implementation of a European Community Policy and Action Programme on the Environment." Draft resolution of the Council presented by the Commission on 24th March 1976.

European Communities, 1976. Commission decision of 21 April 1976, setting up a Committee on Waste Management. *Official Journal* of the European Communities L115/73, May 1976.

France: Decree No. 75–200, of 23rd April, 1975.

France: Loi No. 75/633: Elimination des Déchets et Récupération des Matériaux. 15th July 1975.

France: Decree No. 76/473 of 25th May 1976. Agence Nationale pour la Récupération et l'Elimination des Déchets.

Federal Register, 1975—Guidelines for Beverage Containers, first published 13 November 1975 in *Register*.

Germany: *Waste Oil Law, 1969,* State Law Gazette 1, page 89.

Germany: *Abfallbeseitigungsgesetz, June 1972.* Par. 14.

HMSO, 1975: *War on Waste, A Policy for Reclamation,* Cmnd 5727, HMSO, London, September 1974.

HMSO, 1976: Waste Management Advisory Councils, *First Report.*

HMSO, 1976: Waste Management Advisory Council, *Report on Waste Paper Collection by Local Authorities.*

Italy: *Law No. 366,* March 1941.

Italy: *Act No. 293,* 9 June 1971.

Kruse, E. P. "Waste Management Policies with Particular Reference to the Reclamation of Materials," paper given at the 103rd Annual Conference of the Institution of Municipal Engineers. June 1976.

Ministère de la Qualité de la Vie, Paris, 1974: "La Lutte Contre le Gaspillage." Groupe interministeriel d'evaluation de l'environnement. For French recycling policy, see also Les Déchets Solides, Propositions pour une Politique. Rapport du groupe d'études sur l'élimination des résidues solides.

Ministère de L'industrie et de la Recherche. October 1975: "Evaluation des Techniques de Collecte Sélective des Ordures Ménagères d'après les

Expériences Françaises." Bureau des Recherches Géologiques et Minières, Ministere de L'Industrie et de la Recherche.

Ministère de la Qualité de la Vie, 1976: "La Collecte Sélective des Ordures Ménagères: Questions & Résponses." Secretariat d'Etat à l'Environment.

Municipal Engineering, January 1976: Quote by the Director reported in Waste Management Report, page 77.

Netherlands: Bill No. 13364, 1975 (expected to be passed by May 1977).

Olson, I: "Duty on Beverage Containers in Sweden," UNECE Conference on Solid Waste, ENV/SEM3/R2/COM2, 1975.

Oslo: Law No. 35 14th June 1974. "Provisional Law on Deposits for Packaging for Beer, Mineral Wastes and Soft Drinks."

Stockholm 1976: SOU 1976:35. "Dryckes förpackningar och miljö." Betänkande av Utredningen om kostnaderna för miljövarden. (Packaging)

Sweden: PLM, June 1975: Taxes on Beverages and Beverage Containers in Sweden.

Sweden: SFS 1975: 495: "Förordning om statligt stöd till avfallsbehandling." (Waste Disposal Regulations).

Sweden: SFS 1975: 343: Bilksrotningflag (Car recovery regulations).

USEPA 1974: "Second Report to Congress on Resource Recovery and Source Reduction." US Environmental Protection Agency, 1974.

USEPA, 1973: (SW–10). "Oregon's Bottle Bill—The first six months."

USEPA, 1974: "First Report to Congress on Resource Recovery and Source Reduction."

CHAPTER 11

International Markets
for Secondary Materials

Rüdiger Pethig *

When in recent years, with increasing consciousness of environmental
disruption, economists investigated causes and consequences of pollution, its close relationship to the economics of natural resources
became evident. In fact, both issues are interdependent in a way that
was adequately illustrated by the well-known paradigm of the earth
as a spaceship: pollution and resource depletion are joint plagues
which inevitably accelerate each other. Among the various policy
proposals for environmental management and basic materials management there is one that promises to fight simultaneously and successfully the battle against both pollution and materials depletion.
It is the device of recycling, by which we understand the recovery and
re-use of basic materials from the stream of waste products (secondary
materials) that is generated by the economic activities of production
and consumption.

In the context of resource economics, recycling has an obvious
international dimension for two major reasons. First, the worldwide
reserves of many "virgin" materials are declining rapidly, and some
may be exhausted in a few decades from now. Recycling, then,

---

* This chapter presents in simplified form the findings of the study on international economic dimensions of recycling. The more formal discussion is
contained in the appendix to this volume.

has the effect of economizing the world's global reserves of basic material. Second, these reserves are distributed extremely unevenly between countries, so that for many countries the recycling issue has received great attention as a means of reducing the dependence on (uncertain) foreign supply.

In contrast, the international aspects of recycling within the context of the economics of pollution (environmental economics in the narrow sense) do not appear to be so evident.

There is already a broad body of literature analyzing the relevance of recycling for the enforcement of national environmental objectives. Also, various international dimensions of environmental management have already been studied and clarified. But it seems that, with the exception of a recent paper of I. Walter (1975), there is no investigation on the conceptual level of the impact of "comparative advantages of recycling" on environmental and basic materials management.

As is well known from Yates (1959), the bulk of trade in the real world is in intermediate products. In addition, Walter (1975) showed convincingly that a nonnegligible part of trade consists of waste products or secondary materials which typically are intermediate products. Hence it is natural and important to ask (1) what are the determinants of this empirical pattern of trade, (2) how does trade in secondary materials affect the national and the overall rates of recycling, and (3) what is the relationship between international markets for secondary materials and national environmental management programs.

The purpose of the present paper is to approach these questions on a conceptual level making use of and integrating recent developments in both the theory of international trade with pure intermediate goods and the theory of environmental management by price and standard systems. To the best of our knowledge there is no general equilibrium model in the literature of a closed economy that allows us to analyze, explicitly and rigorously, recycling and (national) markets for secondary material. Hence a substantial part of the paper must be devoted to the development of such a model, which will then enable us to derive trade and policy implications.

For the benefit of those readers who are more interested in the (policy oriented) results of the model than in its technical details, the paper is organized as follows: in the first part, the general structure of the model is sketched and the main results are reported and discussed in a nonformal way, whereas in the major second part the model is defined and handled rigorously. The second part is not merely an appendix to (or a collection of proofs from) the first one but can be read as a self-contained paper by those familiar with this area of economic theory. On the other hand, the first part may be best characterized as a detailed summarizing survey and economic interpretation of the second part. In this summary, some statements are unprecise since we purposely left out detailed references to the formal model and minor (technical) qualifications.

The presentation should not be started without a warning. Although recycling is a complex issue, in order to keep the model manageable we have to use some simplifications the removal of which may change results significantly. One of these neglected problems is that recycling itself may generate waste products with severe polluting impacts (see Pearce [1974]). Further problems and limitations of the approach taken here are discussed in the concluding section.

THE CLOSED ECONOMY

We consider an economy that produces two (private) consumption goods with two inputs: labor and basic material. The production technology is such that, along with the consumption goods, a by-product (secondary material) is generated. This by-product is assumed to be useless for consumption; it may be either discharged into the environment or used as an input in the production of basic material (recycled).

The basic material industry has two options: it may either produce basic material with labor as the only input (virgin material technology), or it may combine labor and secondary material to recover basic material from secondary material (recycling technology). For simplicity we assume that virgin and recycled materials are homogeneous goods.* It is possible that the basic materials industry does not demand all secondary material generated. Then the excess supply

---

* Such an assumption seems to be adequate in the cases of copper and oil, for example. But different (usually low) qualities of reclaimed material as well as different grades of secondary material are also important empirical cases. B. Bower pointed out in the discussion that he expects the results of the model to change significantly with such heterogeneity assumptions being taken into account.

of secondary material is released into the environment, thus lowering the environmental quality and affecting the consumers' well-being (preference satisfaction).

Figure 11–1 illustrates these relationships and interdependencies. It demonstrates that basic material is a pure intermediate good: It is an input as well as an output but no consumption good. If recycling takes place, the same is true for the secondary material although it need not be completely recycled. Note that in Figure 11–1 some interdependencies are suppressed, in particular additional arrows from boxes 5, 6, and 8 to box 7, and from box 9 to all other boxes. There is, of course, evidence for the relevance of these interdependencies,[1] but they will be ignored here to keep the analysis manageable.

The secondary material generated in (and supplied by) the consumption good industries need not be completely recycled. Suppose the demand of the recycling sector for secondary material falls short of the supply; that is, there is an aggregate excess supply of secondary

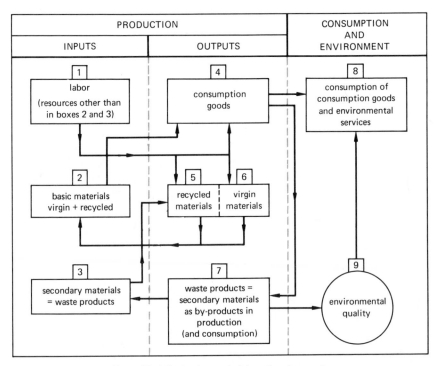

Figure 11–1 Production, materials, and environment

material. Then this excess supply is discharged into the environment, causing environmental deterioration which may be measured by a decline of a suitable index of environmental quality (compare the arrow from box 7 to box 9 in Figure 11–1). Finally, the consumer's well-being not only depends on their consumption of the consumption goods (box 4) but also on the prevailing environmental quality (box 9).

In such an economy we distinguish two different kinds of equilibria: a so-called laissez-faire equilibrium and an equilibrium relative to an environmental price and standard system. The former equilibrium implies a set of nonnegative prices, at which markets are cleared. If the price for secondary material is positive, supply equals demand for secondary material, and no environmental disruption occurs. If, however, its price is zero, secondary material may be in aggregate excess supply, implying that the index of environmental quality is below its maximum. In such a case the society may want to improve the environmental quality above its laissez-faire level. A given target level of environmental quality which is assumed to be established (and may be changed) by some decision process is implemented by levying an effluent tax (charge) on the secondary material. Such an effluent tax appears as a negative price in the associated price and standard equilibrium.

Figure 11–2 illustrates this situation by showing the trade-off between the feasible supply of consumption goods and the "supply" of environmental quality. Suppose the point H indicates the allocation assigned to the laissez-faire equilibrium. Then, roughly speaking, an improvement of the environmental quality is only possible at the cost of a reduced provision of consumption goods. The equilibria for alternative environmental quality standards may be represented by points on the line $HKLM$ on the production possibility frontier in Figure 11–2.

Figure 11–2 does not extend to the case that, in laissez-faire equilibrium, secondary material is a scarce intermediate good as is the basic material. To illustrate such a situation, the production possibility set in Figure 11–2 must be replaced by a set for which the plane ABC coincides with the plane $OD'E'$.

So far we indicated the (potential) link between the generation of secondary material and the environmental problem. The link between secondary material and the resource management question is built by

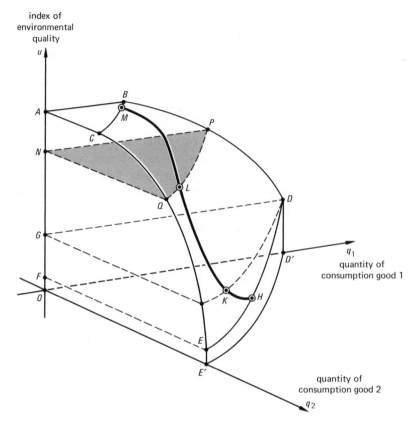

Figure 11–2 Environment-production trade-off model

the rate of recycling, defined as the ratio of basic material produced in the recycling industry and the total amount of basic material produced, that is, the sum of the output of the virgin material production and the recycling industry.

Note that in laissez-faire equilibrium the rate of recycling can attain any value in the closed interval between zero and one, depending on the recycling technology available and the productivity of the virgin material production. We say that the virgin material production dominates the recycling technology if a given output of basic material cannot be produced by the recycling industry with some secondary material and at most as much labor as is necessary to produce this amount of basic material in the virgin material sector.

The comparative static results for the closed economy which will be of major interest for the discussion of trade in secondary material can be summarized as follows:

1. Suppose that secondary material is a scarce pure intermediate product in the initial (laissez-faire) equilibrium. Then, if under some qualifications the endowment of labor increases,

   • the relative price of secondary material (expressed in units of labor *or* basic material) increases, and
   • the rate of recycling decreases or remains one.

2. Suppose that the economy implemented an environmental price and standard system with a nonzero effluent tax in its initial equilibrium.

   (a) Then, if under some qualifications the endowment of labor increases, the relative effluent tax increases in absolute value and the rate of recycling increases or remains one.

   (b) Then, if under some qualifications the environmental quality standard is raised, the relative effluent tax increases in absolute value (unless some exceptional demand conditions occur) and the rate of recycling increases or remains one.

It is easily acceptable that with increasing labor force the price of labor declines relative to that of secondary material if its price is positive. But on economic grounds it does not seem to be obvious that the scarcity of (a positively priced) secondary material increases relative to that of basic material in a growing economy (or, roughly speaking, with an increasing degree of industrialization).

An important aspect of this result is that if secondary material is completely recycled, there is no danger that this by-product will eventually contribute to pollution as long as labor is nondecreasing. On the other hand, the corresponding result for the case of a nonzero emission tax should clearly be expected, since in order to maintain a given environmental quality standard in a growing economy the relative emission tax must be raised in absolute value.

The economic intuition is also confirmed by the result that under some qualifications the relative emission tax must be the higher in absolute terms, the higher the environmental quality standard is chosen. But the sufficient conditions for this result are also interesting and economically straightforward. Suppose that the production of good 1 is relatively environmental intensive; then the qualification for the mentioned result is that the demand for good 1 must not decrease too much when the environmental quality increases. Since if with growing environmental quality there is a sufficiently strong demand shift away from the environment intensive good, a higher environmental quality may well be compatible with a lower relative emission tax.

It can be shown that the rate of recycling is a monotonically decreasing function of the relative price of secondary material. A necessary condition for zero changes in the rate of recycling in response to exogenous shocks is that in the initial equilibrium the recycling rate is equal to one or zero. If the virgin material technology does not dominate the recycling technology, then the recycling rate is already equal to one in laissez-faire equilibrium and a fortiori in a price and standard equilibrium. Since this case appears to be exceptional in the real world, the model leads us to conclude that, for many material resources, the virgin material technology dominates the recycling technology where high collection and transportation costs in the recycling industry may be a (or the) major explanation for this dominance.

It is often argued that a low degree of market organization and information as well as high costs of collection and transportation are typical features of many secondary material markets. Such market imperfections can be considered by assuming that the purchase of secondary material by the recycling sector requires labor input. One would expect an incentive for recycling if the market organization is improved; that is, if the labor requirements are reduced parametrically. However, for a reasonably large class of relevant economies the formal model does not support the plausible argument that a reduction in collection and transportation costs and so forth increases the rate of recycling. Moreover, if we interpret this reduction as a subsidy (in labor units) per unit of secondary material used in the recycling industry, it might be possible that recycling is not stimulated in our model.

TRADE IMPLICATIONS

Our model contains five commodities that can potentially be traded. If, however, trade in more than two goods is introduced, the well-known problem of indeterminacy may arise.[2] Since we are interested here in international markets for secondary material, we avoid these difficulties by restricting the subsequent analysis to trade in basic and secondary material only. The following results refer to the so-called two-country case where the equilibrium prices on the international market for secondary material are determined endogenously.

1. Trade in secondary and basic material takes place between two countries if their pretrade relative prices for these products are different. Regardless of the sign of these prices, the pattern of trade follows the comparative advantage, that is, a country exports secondary material if in this country the price ratio between secondary material (or the emission tax not in absolute value) and basic material is lower than in the other country. Moreover, the equilibrium world market price ratio lies strictly between the countries' pretrade price ratios unless the pretrade price ratio is zero in one country.

2. Trade in secondary material (i.e., export or import) is welfare increasing for each individual country not only when secondary material commands a positive price but also when it is a (negatively priced) detrimental waste product, provided that in the latter case the respective trading country enforces an environmental price and standard system with a binding emission standard before trade. So far Melvin's (1969) possibility of gainless trade does not extend to the present model.

3. The gains from trade can be interpreted as reducing the net cost of domestic environmental control [3] in the following sense: in an economy with a single consumption good, let the quantity of this good consumed be q, q' and q'' under environmental laissez faire (q), under a binding emission standard $\bar{e} > 0$ in autarchy (q') and after trade (q''), respectively. We may expect that $q > q'' > q'$. Then the pretrade net cost defined as the opportunity cost in terms of consumption foregone is measured by $q - q'$ and the reduction of this cost due to trade is $q'' - q'$.[4] Observe that whenever a country gains from trade, its net cost of environmental management is reduced whether it exports or imports secondary material.

4. A country has a comparative advantage for secondary material relative to the other country, if

- secondary material is scarce under environmental laissez faire and ceteris paribus its initial endowment of labor (secondary material) is smaller (larger) and

- an emission tax is levied on secondary material and ceteris paribus its initial endowment of labor is larger or its emission standard is more restrictive than in the other country.

5. Consider a country that enforces a price and standard scheme before trade. If this country has a comparative advantage for secondary material, its environmental quality may increase above the standard chosen. Alternatively while this country can always choose a tighter domestic environmental quality target, the converse is not true: the lower bound for its environmental quality in trading equilibrium is not determined domestically.

6. Suppose on the other hand that a country has a comparative disadvantage for secondary material under environmental laissez faire (which implies that the other country implements an emission tax). Then trade leads to environmental deterioration in this country which may be so severe that the country suffers a welfare loss from trade. More realistically, trade will probably force this country to introduce environmental management if its trading partner has already done so.

7. Consider a country that has a comparative advantage for secondary material when this commodity is positively priced. Then after trade as compared with the pretrade situation

- the relative price of secondary material increases;
- the price of the consumption good which is produced with the greater gross secondary material intensity decreases relative to the price of the other consumption good; [5]
- the gross secondary material intensity decreases in the sector with the smaller gross secondary material intensity and decreases (increases) in the other sector, if and only if its gross generation of secondary material per unit of output is negative (positive);
- the recycling rate decreases except that it may keep the value of one or zero if initially it was at this level.

8. Consider a country that has a comparative advantage for secondary material when an emission tax is levied on this product. [6] Then after trade as compared with the pretrade situation

- the relative price of secondary material increases (it may decline in absolute terms);
- the price of the consumption good being produced with the greater gross secondary material intensity increases relative to the price of the other consumption good;

- the gross secondary material intensity increases in the sector with the greater gross secondary material intensity and increases (decreases) in the other sector if and only if its gross generation of secondary material per unit of output is positive (negative);
- the recycling rate decreases except that it possibly retains the value one (zero) if it was already one (zero) before trade.

9. The last statement of the two preceding paragraphs has an important implication: if one country is small so that it has (almost) no influence on the world market prices of basic and secondary material and if the price of basic material is ceteris paribus raised by an autonomous OPEC-style action of the other country, then our model predicts that the recycling rate increases in the small country. This conclusion is not (generally) incompatible with that of Walter (1974, p. 23), according to whom such an OPEC-style action "will substantially increase price incentives for recycling. . . ." It says, however, that if the volume of recycled basic material should increase, then the domestic production of virgin material will increase by a smaller percentage or decrease.

10. The structural changes in the secondary material importing country can be deduced analogous to those listed in the two preceding paragraphs 7 and 8, where we have to take special care of the case described in paragraph 6. Of particular interest is that the recycling rates in the secondary material exporting and importing countries vary adversely.[7] Therefore, a priori the world recycling rate may either increase or decrease. Our model does not confirm the plausible conjecture that the overall (absolute) quantity of basic material reclaimed from secondary material increases after trade.

11. I. Walter (1975, p. 52n) argues that the principal trade-policy issue relating to the secondary materials sector is export control. In terms of our model, an export embargo means that the two countries move from the trading equilibrium back to their respective autarchic equilibria. First, it is obvious that both countries' welfare declines. But if the exporting country's objective and motivation for an export embargo had been the increase of its recycling rate, it does in fact reach this goal (as can be seen from paragraphs 7 and 8). This result seems to be opposite to Walter's (1974, p. 53) suggestion.

The preceding discussion calls for a final remark on trade in secondary materials and its relation to domestic environmental management. It is obvious that international markets for secondary material have no impact on the issue of environmental management if in both countries the pretrade prices for secondary material are positive. This is no longer true if the autarchic price of secondary material is positive in one country and zero in the other since in this case the zero-price country is able to export (part of) its excess supply of secondary material that otherwise may have polluted its environment. We have also a close relationship between trade and environmental management if the autarchic price of secondary material is positive in no country and in at least one country is negative. But there are good reasons to argue that the conceptional discussion of such trade situations is purely academic and completely irrelevant for practical policy recommendations. One major reason appears to be that environmental price and standard systems as discussed in this paper will presumably not play any significant role in controlling internationally tradeable waste products in the near future.

We agree on this view and do not intend to overstress this issue of trading "bads." But the economist concerned with allocative efficiency may be allowed one defending argument: Even if no large-scale emission tax systems will be implemented on the basis of which trade may take place, we know that many countries are in the process of formulating and enforcing detailed environmental quality targets. For this purpose various kinds of possibly inefficient nontax policy instruments may be applied. But in any case the waste products being involved in such controls will have negative shadow prices, and thus allocative efficiency raises the question of comparative advantage and trade: it is conceivable that a country exports a nonpriced detrimental waste product, pays for its export with a scarce (hence positively priced) commodity and that after these "one-way" transactions both countries are better off.

CONCLUDING REMARKS

We shall conclude by briefly discussing three major issues that arise from the preceding presentation. First, we did not exhaust the analytical capacity of the model presented here; that is, there are many more economically interesting questions with respect to international markets for materials that can principally be discussed within the model. Second, even though our model may describe a typical structure of recycling, environmental management, and trade in secondary materials, it certainly cannot capture all revelant features of these extremely complex issues. Several of these aspects that are neglected or not satisfactorily treated in our model can be included and analyzed by modifying some of the assumptions used. But—and this is the third point to be made—there are limitations inherent in the approach taken here that prevent us from studying some other important problems related to the international markets of secondary materials.

Let us recall that trade implications have been studied only for the case that no commodities except basic and secondary materials are traded. But the model can, of course, also be used to investigate trade between any other pair of commodities (or more generally, each subset of at least two commodities). For example, the problem of trade between the two consumption goods—only without the aspect of recycling—has already been analyzed in the literature, in particular by H. Siebert (1974, 1976, I), I. Walter (1974), and R. Pethig (1976, II). Using the present model to study this issue will presumably yield qualitatively similar results as the model in Pethig (1976, II), so that we expect to obtain modified statements of the Heckscher-Ohlin Theorem(s) and the Factor Price Equalization Theorem.

Furthermore, one will find in this case, as well as for any other trading configuration, that trade has an important impact on recycling and that changes in the restrictiveness of domestic environmental controls do not only affect the volume and (possibly) the direction of trade but also the rates of recycling. Another neglected aspect of the model is the boundary solutions, which may well constitute empirically significant cases. It seems particularly worthwhile to study the model under the assumptions that $Q_s^i < 0$ everywhere on D_Q^i and $M_s > 0$ everywhere on D_M and to investigate the impact of the signs and amounts of the various elasticities of substitution (in production), in particular that of σ_m which has tacitly been assumed to be nonzero (see notation in the Appendix).

As to the second topic, there is a long list of modifications in assumptions and in the structure of the model that appear necessary to investigate some important international recycling issues. Let us only mention a few of them:

- Recycling generates waste, that may be even "more polluting than the disposal of 'virgin' waste . . ." (Pearce [1974, p. 91]).

- Pollution may affect the production technologies.
- Virgin basic material and the output of the recycling industry may not be homogeneous products.
- The ɓasic material may not only be a produceable production input (pure intermediate product) but a consumption good as well (Walter [1975, pp. 15–22]).
- International transactions costs tend to reduce favorable trade opportunities.
- Intercountry differences in the virgin material and in the recycling industries may be major explanations for comparative advantages.
- The virgin material industry may be subject to decreasing efficiency, and there may be technical progress in the recycling industry.

Finally, some severe limitations of our model are due to its static nature. Intertemporal aspects are decisive in environmental as well as in natural resources management. Pollutants accumulate over time and may lead to irreversible environmental damage that cannot be adequately accounted for by a myopic cost-benefit comparison (as is done by the use of an atemporal welfare function (see Pearce [1976]). Equally restrictive is the static view in materials management for the correct determination of the rate of exploitation of both renewable and nonrenewable resources. Hence, whenever future generations are significantly affected, they must have a voice in the political decision process. Another dynamic though typically short-run problem is that of unstability and volatility of (international) markets for secondary materials (see I. Walter [1974] and D. Pearce and R. Grace [1976]) that demands quite a different framework of analysis and hence is beyond the scope of this paper.

NOTES

1. The importance of the arrow from box 5 to box 7 is stressed by Pearce (1974, p. 96); that from box 8 to box 7 is analyzed in Mäler (1974) and Pethig (1976, III). For the arrow from box 9 to box 4 see L. E. Ruff (1972), Tietenberg (1973), Siebert (1975), and Pethig (1977).

2. See, for example, Batra (1973, p. 192).

3. This point is stressed by I. Walter (1974, pp. 15, 22, 55, 58). It is not made quite clear, however, how the cost of environmental control and its reduction via trade in secondary materials are defined.

4. This measure of environmental control cost will generally be meaningless when more than one consumption good is involved. But it is possible for any

number of goods to determine the theoretically exact "cost index" on a welfare economic basis along the lines suggested in Pethig (1977).

5. This statement presupposes that there is no reversal of the gross secondary material intensity ranking, since the change from autarchy to trading equilibrium is not local. Observe also that no statements about changes of (the structure of) production in the consumption good industries can be made, since these changes depend on the volume of trade that can be interpreted as nonmarginal changes in the economy's endowments of secondary and basic material.

6. Suppose that each country has implemented a price and standard system. In this case, comparative advantages are completely determined (i.e., created, destroyed, or reversed) by the relative restrictiveness of domestic emission targets. For similar comparative advantage reversals in a different context, see also Pethig (1976, II).

7. While Walter (1974, p. 58) concludes that the incentive to recycle increases in countries exporting secondary materials and decreasing them in importing countries, we reached the opposite result in terms of recycling *rates*.

BIBLIOGRAPHY

Batra, R. N. *Studies in the pure theory of international trade*. London: Macmillan & Co., 1973.

———— and Casas, F. R. Intermediate products and the pure theory of international trade: A neo-Heckscher-Ohlin framework. *American Economic Review* 63 (1973):297–311.

Baumol, W. J., and Oates, W. E. The use of standards and pricing for the protection of the environment. *Swedish Journal of Economics* 73 (1971): 42–52.

Intrilligator, M. D. *Mathematical optimization and economic theory*. Englewood Cliffs, N.J.: Prentice-Hall, 1971.

Jones, R. W. The structure of simple general equilibrium models. *Journal of Political Economy* 73 (1965):557–72.

Mäler, K. G. *Environmental economics: A theoretical inquiry*. Baltimore: Johns Hopkins University Press, 1974.

Melvin, J. R. Intermediate goods, the production possibility curve, and gains from trade. *Quarterly Journal of Economics* 83 (1969):141–51.

Moeseke, P. van. Constrained maximization and efficient allocation. In P. van Moeseke (ed.), *Mathematical programs for activity analysis*. Amsterdam: North Holland, 1974, 9–22.

Pearce, D. Fiscal incentives and the economics of waste recycling: Problems and limitations. In *Institute for Fiscal Studies Conference on Fiscal Policy and the Environment, IFS*, London (1974), 83–105.

————. The limits of cost-benefit-analysis as a guide to environmental policy. *Kyklos* (1976), 97–112.

———— and Grace, R. Stabilizing secondary materials markets. *Resources Policy* (1976), 118–27.

Pearson, C. International trade and environmental controls: comment, *Weltwirtschaftliches Archiv* 111 (1975), 564–67.

Pethig, R. Umweltverschmutzung, Wohlfahrt und Umweltpolitik in einem Zwei-Sektoren-Gleichgewichtsmodell, *Zeitschrift für Nationalökonomie* 35, (1975) 99–124.

———. Environmental aspects of trade models. In Walter, I. (ed.) (1976, I), 117–120.

———. Pollution, welfare and environmental policy in the theory of comparative advantage. *Journal of Environmental Economics and Management* 2 (1976, II):160–69.

———. Environmental management in general equilibrium: A new incentive compatible approach. Discussion Paper no. 211. Center for Mathematical Studies in Economics and Management Science, Northwestern University, Evanston (1976, III).

———. Die gesamtwirtschaftlichen Kosten der Umweltpolitik, *Zeitschrift für die gesamte Staatswissenschaft* 133 (1977):322–42.

Ruff, L. E. A note on pollution prices in a general equilibrium model. *American Economic Review* 62 (1972):186–92.

Siebert, H. Environmental protection and international specialization. *Weltwirtschaftliches Archiv* 110: (1974), 494–508.

———. Externalities, environmental quality, and allocation. *Zeitschrift für Wirtschafts- und Sozialwissenschaften,* 1 (1975):17–32.

———. Environmental control, economic structure, and international trade. In I. Walter (ed.), (1976, I), 29–56.

———. Die Grundprobleme des Umweltschutzes. Eine wirtschaftstheoretische Analyse, In H.-D. Haas and B. Külp (eds.), *Soziale Probleme der modernen Industriegesellschaft,* Schriften des Vereins für Socialpolitik NF Bd. 92I, Berlin: Duncker & Humblot, 1977, 141–82.

Tietenberg, T. H. Specific taxes and the control of pollution: A general equilibrium analysis. *Quarterly Journal of Economics* 87, (1973, I):503–22.

———. Controlling pollution by price and standard systems: A general equilibrium analysis. *Swedish Journal of Economics* 75 (1973, II);193–203.

Walter, I. International trade and resource diversion: The case of environmental management. *Weltwirtschaftliches Archiv,* 110 (1974):482–93.

———. Secondary materials, environment, and the international economy. Discussion Paper 75–72. Graduate School of Business Administration, New York University (1975).

———, ed. *Studies in international environmental economics.* New York: John Wiley & Sons, 1976.

Yates, P. L. *Forty years of foreign trade.* London, 1959.

CHAPTER 12

The Prices of Secondary Materials and Recycling Effort

John A. Butlin *

The initial remit for this chapter stated: "Prices of secondary materials are known to fluctuate widely, with important implications for the structure of the recycling industry and the level of investment in plant and equipment. Such instability is critical, both on the supply and demand sides of the recycling loop. This chapter will look at empirical evidence on this issue, and consider what public-policy alternatives may make sense." In essence, the remit requires us to examine both the demand for, and supply of, secondary materials, and to assess whether price fluctuations have adversely affected investment and employment in the secondary materials recovery industry; the extent to which secondary materials have replaced primary materials in manufacturing processes; and the extent to which the solid waste problem has been alleviated by materials recovery and recycling. We seem to have changed a fairly innocuous discussion, as implied by the remit, into a task of broader dimensions. Add to this the need to survey the scant empirical evidence on materials recycling and price fluctuations, and the problem becomes more formidable. Thus, we need to structure the discussion extremely care-

* I gratefully acknowledge the comments of Blair Bower and Toby Page on an earlier draft of this chapter. However, I accept sole responsibility for the content of, errors in, and omissions from this chapter.

fully. We shall approach the topic as follows: first, we shall examine the problem from the point of view of the secondary materials producer. What are the determinants of the output of the secondary materials industry and, in particular, how elastic is the response of this output to secondary materials prices? We need to look at this both as a short-run and as a long-run problem. In the short run, do price fluctuations result in risk-averse behavior by secondary materials producers that is characterized by lower output from the industry than might be the case under a more stable price regime? In the long run, does such risk-averse behavior result in a lower level of investment in plant and equipment in the recycling industry than might otherwise be the case? (That is, is the recycling industry smaller than would be the case if prices had fluctuated less?) On the demand side, we again need to consider the determinants of demand for secondary materials, giving particular attention once more to the price elasticity of demand for secondary materials. We shall consider whether the demand for secondary materials is likely to be affected by the extent of fluctuation in their prices. At this stage, we shall need to enquire a little more thoroughly into manufacturing processes where primary and secondary materials are substitutable, and see if evidence can be adduced as to the elasticity of substitution of raw materials and secondary materials in these processes.

The problem of waste arisings needs to be examined because from these comes (as home, prompt, or obsolescent scrap) the inputs into the secondary materials producing industry. It may be that the root cause of secondary materials price fluctuations is fluctuations in the supply of scrap to the secondary materials industry.

The above discussion will all be theoretically based (although no formal model will be introduced: the discussion is intentionally kept verbal). Its purpose is to provide us with a check list, when investigating the empirical analysis, of factors likely, a priori, to be important. It also will have put price fluctuations in secondary materials markets into context, along with the other factors that have a significant influence on the extent of materials reclamation and recycling.

Following this section is the discussion of the empirical evidence. For a host of reasons, which will be listed prior to the discussion, this section of the paper is the most tentative. The final section, on the "public-policy alternatives that make sense," will also act as a summary of the chapter, and will present its conclusions.

THE SUPPLY OF SECONDARY MATERIALS

At first glance, the supply of secondary materials in the short run would seem to depend, essentially, on three factors: the price of secondary materials, the price of scrap (as well as other inputs), and the state of materials reclamation technology. However, this simple, elementary economics approach to the problem, couched in terms of an ideal, perfectly competitive world, ignores several important factors:

1. There is, in many instances, no "given" supply price. Substantial discounts may be given to particular customers, and these discounts may vary considerably in the course of a year. To a large extent, the discounts are a function of the degree of competition within the industry.
2. The cost of inputs, especially obsolescent scrap, may also vary a great deal. Prompt scrap often arises from fairly large industrial suppliers, and long-term contracts may be negotiated between waste "producers" and scrap dealers.
3. Depending very much upon the material with which we are dealing, and the country under consideration, the structure of the reclamation industry may vary, from an atomistic, competitive industry to a market-sharing oligopoly.

Whilst we can note these complicating factors, we need to keep to the more simple model of the firm if we are to arrive at any a priori understanding of the possible effects of price fluctuations upon a country's materials reclamation and recycling industry.

The simplest way to reach this understanding is to regard increasingly greater price fluctuations (measured by the statistical variance in prices) as producing an increasingly uncertain environment. In this environment, it has been shown [1] that a risk-averse firm, in a competitive industry, will produce less than it would in a certain, or "deterministic," environment. This, in effect, implies a lower rate of materials recovery and recycling than would be the case in a more stable environment. It also is likely to result, in the short run, in a less elastic secondary materials supply curve than might obtain in a deterministic environment. (The argument is simple: a risk-averse, secondary materials producer may "hedge" against the uncertainty of price changes by responding only tentatively to them. For the producer to discount totally the risk of a higher or lower price being short-lived, and, therefore, to run the risk of having to hold large inventories of output, by behaving as if the new price was a signal from a market in stable, short-run equilibrium, would be unwise, unless he could completely cover himself in a futures market).

In the long run, there are two possible ramifications of uncertainty for the secondary materials producer. The first is the possibility that the level of investment will be lower than might otherwise be the case. This result follows intuitively if the greater uncertainty represented by larger price variations is accounted for by inflating the discount rate.[2] This will reduce the present value of the net returns from the investment (for any normal configuration of costs and benefits), and reduce the rate of investment below what it would have been in the more certain environment. For the individual secondary materials producer, this implies a smaller-scale plant than might otherwise be the case, and it also implies a smaller secondary materials producing industry than would exist in the certain environment (again, assuming that at least some of the producers in the industry are risk-averse).

A third interesting possibility arises as a means by which a form of self-insurance against risk can be implemented by producers. Unless the fluctuations in secondary materials prices are in phase, it may be possible for secondary producers to spread the risk by diversifying horizontally into the reclamation of several materials. (It is also possible that users of reclaimed materials may wish to integrate back into materials reclamation. They may then follow a rather different stock-holding pattern than a firm acting solely in the materials reclamation sphere). If price fluctuations are not concurrent, expected profits will not fluctuate as much as they would if production were focused on the reclamation of any single material.

The discussion thus far has been directed very much toward the firm which purchases scrap and then reclaims "useful" material from it. This can be fed back into industrial manufacturing processes. The effect of uncertainty upon the scrap dealer, who collects prompt and obsolescent scrap and sells to the secondary producer, is likely to be considerably different. The main reason for this is that the activities of the dealer relate largely to decisions to buy into, and sell out of, inventory. The decisions that he makes relate, then, to the size of a stock, and the rate at which this should be changed, rather than with the rate of supply flow of scrap.

Having outlined the problem in this way, we can again consider the short-run and long-run implications separately. For simplicity, we shall keep to the convention of assuming that a stock does not change appreciably in size in the short run. The question is, therefore, whether price uncertainty leads the secondary producer to hold a larger or a smaller stock of scrap than he would in a risk-free world (that is, for our purposes, a world where there was no price uncertainty). Rather than enter into an extended discussion on this, we shall simply state a hypothesis, and briefly present the intuitive reasoning behind it.[3] The hypothesis: in a world characterized by wide variations in scrap prices, scrap dealers will hold smaller inventories of scrap than they would in a risk-free world. The intuitive reasoning is again based upon there being at least some risk-averse scrap dealers. In the absence of any other information, they inflate the discount rate they use, in order to account for price uncertainty.[4] They aim to maximize the net present value of the income generated by buying and selling scrap. Inflating the discount rate will lead the scrap dealers to hold smaller inventories than they would in a risk-free world.[5]

The implications of this crude hypothesis are quite broad. If uncertainty causes scrap dealers to hold smaller stocks, the selling price of scrap to secondary material producers will be higher. If this is the case, secondary producers, *ceteris paribus*, will process less scrap, and offer less secondary material on the market than would otherwise be the case. If this is so, less reclaimed and recycled material will be incorporated into manufactured goods than would be the case with a more stable price regime. (We will see later that this hypothesis seems to have important empirical ramifications.)

Thus far, in considering factors affecting the supply of secondary materials, we have not considered technical change. Techniques which make it feasible to increase the percentage of materials recovered from a particular scrap source, or make it possible to recover materials from a hitherto untapped source of scrap, are both likely to increase the volume of secondary materials flowing into industrial processes. It may be that the more uncertain the environment the longer will it take for new reclamations technologies to penetrate into the reclamation sector, but there is no study at hand to confirm this directly. However, the case of the automobile shredder in North America is an interesting example of the effect of an innovation in reclamation technology on the supply of secondary materials.

THE DEMAND FOR SECONDARY MATERIALS

The demand for secondary materials is a function of the price of the particular secondary material, the price of substitute (primary) materials, and the state of technology in the particular "producing" industry. The importance of substitute materials depends on the elasticity of substitution between secondary and primary materials. Obviously, the greater the elasticity of substitution between secondary and primary sources, the higher will be the cross-elasticity between these. Essentially, the elasticity of substitution is determined by the current state of production and reclamation technologies.

Within the terms of reference of this paper, there are two questions of fundamental importance concerning the demand for secondary materials. First, what is the elasticity of substitution between particular primary and secondary materials in particular manufacturing industries? This is a purely empirical question and will be dealt with later. The second question is less easily answered, and asks: do wide variations in secondary materials prices hinder the substitution of these for primary materials, even when it is technically possible and when the average price has fallen relative to the price of the primary material, making such a substitution economically rational?

The discussion around this question must again be at a rather general level. There does not even seem to be any theoretical basis on which we can build the discussion. To guide us, however, there are at least two factors to consider. The first of these is concerned with the magnitude of fluctuations in primary materials prices relative to those of secondary materials. It is apparent that the prices of many primary materials fluctuate significantly. The important parameter of these fluctuations is the magnitude. It would seem more likely that a secondary material would be substituted for a primary source (assuming that the mean price had changed in favor of the secondary material, and that the appropriate technology existed) if the magnitude of the fluctuations in price for the secondary material was less than or equal to that of the primary material. In the event of the price fluctuation of the secondary material being the greater, a risk-averse producer, faced with higher average profits but with a greater associated variance in profits, would seem less likely to make the substitution which in a deterministic environment would be both technically feasible and economically rational.

The other factor that needs to be considered is that price fluctuations apart, the relative prices of secondary and primary materials tend not to reflect the full net societal benefit from using either set of commodities. The prices of primary materials tends to be kept low by depletion allowances to mining companies, accelerated depreciation of capital equipment for primary extractive industries, subsidized exploration, and the like. Measures like this keep the price of primary materials low relative to their secondary substitutes. This tends to militate against the substitution of secondary materials using processes for those using primary materials. Together with such less concrete factors as inertia against switching to different techniques often displayed by industry, and the greater problem of quality control in secondary materials production, the fiscal system being generally biased toward primary materials production produces a strong disincentive against the introduction of secondary materials into many production processes. Such a bias would exist even if there were no uncertainty about the prices of secondary materials. This consideration ought to caution us against attributing too much to uncertainty due to fluctuating materials prices.

From the preceding discussion it is apparent that the amount of recycling and materials reclamation actually achieved in a particular society may be less than the amount which is socially desirable, both because of fiscal biases in favor of primary materials and, possibly, due to fluctuations in the price of secondary materials. An alternative way of looking at this is to enquire whether irregular flows of waste arisings to the reclamation industries could help bring about secondary materials price fluctuations. At an intuitive level, the answer is in the affirmative. Fluctuations in scrap availability will bring about fluctuations both in the volume of scrap recycled and in the price paid for this in a scrap market without long-term contracts or futures trading. Fluctuations in purchased scrap prices will affect both the output and the selling price of secondary materials reclaimed from industrial scrap. Thus, it is possible that fluctuations in waste arisings may affect price stability in the secondary materials market. Whether, in practice, this factor is important depends upon

- the proportion of the scrap arisings not covered by long-term contracts between scrap dealers and the secondary materials industry;
- the elasticity of demand for scrap by secondary materials pro-

ducers, and the elasticity of demand for secondary materials by industry.

Obviously, the more long-term contracts there are, the less variable is the flow of scrap to the secondary materials industry likely to be. Also, the lower the relative input price elasticities of demand are, the greater will be the fluctuations in scrap and secondary materials prices for any given fluctuation in waste arisings. Once again, the matter needs ultimately to be resolved by estimates of the elasticities of demand. Unfortunately, these estimates do not seem to be available.

It is appropriate at this stage, before moving on to consider such empirical evidence as there is, to summarize the main points that arise from our discussion so far:

1. In an uncertain environment characterized by fluctuating prices, the production of secondary materials will be lower;
2. The short-run elasticity of supply of secondary materials will be lower;
3. The rate of investment by secondary materials producers will be smaller;
4. The secondary materials industry will be smaller;
5. Scrap dealers and secondary materials producers will diversify horizontally into the reclamation and recycling of more than one material, and there will also be a tendency for firms using secondary materials extensively to integrate back into the production of secondary materials;
6. Scrap dealers will hold smaller stocks, leading to higher scrap prices and lower volumes of scrap flowing into reclamation and recycling channels;
7. Substitutions of secondary materials for primary materials may be hindered by large price fluctuations;
8. Price fluctuations for scrap and secondary materials may not necessarily be due to factors exogenous to the industry (i.e., demand-induced). It may be that the supply of scrap to dealers, and from them to secondary materials producers, is so erratic as to cause wide variations both in scrap dealers' purchases, and in their sales to secondary materials producers.

This list is fairly extensive, and it is not likely that we will be able to examine all of the points on this "check list." Also, it is not feasible to compare actual experience with what might have been the case in a different (deterministic) environment (although this is the way in which several of the points above are derived). Rather, we shall need to review the evidence at hand and look for certain key characteristics, such as consistently low reclamation and recycling rates; secondary materials prices that, on average, are consistently high in relation to the prices of primary materials for which, technically, they are substitutable; consistently low rates of investment in secondary materials industries. We must also beware of attributing these factors solely to uncertainty brought about by price fluctuations, and bear in mind the general bias against secondary materials that certain fiscal measures build into the economic system of many countries.

THE EMPIRICAL EVIDENCE EVALUATED

We have mentioned that the empirical evidence in this area is sparse. In fact, only one study has been found which actually confronts the problem of price fluctuations of secondary materials and the effects of this on secondary materials producers. Other studies to which we shall refer are concerned with other aspects of waste management but, nevertheless, have some information relevant to the discussion here.

The study that concerns itself with price instability in secondary materials markets was commissioned by OECD's Environment Directorate.[6] Its aim was to use simple, deterministic microeconomic models of alternative price stabilization schemes as usually applied to primary commodities, and to study the implications of these for alternative schemes to stabilize the incomes of those involved in the reclamation and recycling of waste paper.[7] The thrust of this study is that stabilization schemes, although in general having potential social gains in the context of recycling, may, nevertheless, produce greater income instability in the market for a particular secondary material if there are several grades of the material, and if the regulatory authority enters the market for all grades. The paper contains an interesting exercise which is an attempt to evaluate the costs and benefits to the United Kingdom of operating a hypothetical buffer stock scheme for waste paper over the period 1970–74. On top of all this, the paper gives a very useful survey of stabilization schemes for waste paper that have operated in Japan, Holland, the United Kingdom, and Norway.

However, such a brief précis as this cannot do justice to a paper that covers such a broad area. We need to direct our attention to the aspects of the paper of direct relevance to our study. Before doing this, however, we must register a note of dissent on methodology, not only with Pearce, but also with the general approach to modeling problems of price fluctuations and the effect of these on producers plans, both in the short run and the long run. We have argued in this paper that the problems caused by a fluctuating price regime are essentially problems of uncertainty about future prices. If the producer is risk-neutral, then the use of deterministic microstatic models to capture the producers' behavior is perfectly adequate. If, however, at least some of the producers are risk-averse, then it is not appropriate simply to assume that a deterministic model will satisfactorily capture their behavior.[8] We will evaluate the empirical pieces at hand on their own terms, but bearing this proviso in mind.

Pearce's paper has several points which throw some light on the list of effects which, a priori, seemed to us to be possible effects of price instability in secondary materials markets. The first of these relates to the cyclical behavior of waste paper prices. Pearce reports evidence of a recent five-year cycle in paper and board prices. This cannot be explained completely by the close correlation between paper and board prices and gross domestic product. The explanation lies, in part, in the cyclical behavior of United Kingdom trade in waste paper. Pearce has thus brought to notice a specific aspect of the general problem about the source of price instability in waste materials markets. For the United Kingdom market, part of the price instability is brought about by fluctuations on the demand side of the waste paper market. It is apparent that such trade–cycle-generated price instability could operate for other secondary materials markets equally. In the same discussion, and for the case of the United Kingdom waste paper market in 1973–74, Pearce indicates that there was no real difference in waste paper availability. Although only one observation, this nevertheless tends to shed a little doubt on the possibility of price fluctuations being generated by wide variations in domestic waste arisings.

The simulated cost-benefit study in the same paper also provides us with some interesting information. It implies that a stock-holding scheme in operation during the period 1970–74—when the United Kingdom switched from being a net exporter to being a net importer, and then reverted to being a net exporter at the end of the period—would have run at a loss. That is, over the period 1970–74, the average volume of stocks held would have been positive. This conclusion is entirely consistent with an increase in output by risk-averse producers when price uncertainty has been reduced by the operation of a buffer-stock scheme (although it is by no means the only possible explanation).

The final part of this report also holds some interest for us. Brief resumes of buffer-stock schemes indicate that, in Japan, there is a large excess demand for waste paper that is not likely to be alleviated by the buffer-stock scheme at its current level of operation. The existence of excess demand in the long run is again suggestive of insufficient capacity to meet current demands for waste paper, and a rate of expansion too slow to meet the future growth in demand. With a scheme that is so modest as to have a negligible effect on prices (that is, too modest to reduce price uncertainty to any significant degree), these observations are entirely consistent with our discussion in the preceeding section on uncertainty and the size and rate of growth of materials reclamation and recycling industries.

Another piece by the same author [9] provides us with some indirect evidence concerning the effects of price fluctuation on recycling and the recycling effort demonstrated by any particular country. In this paper, Pearce confronts the problem of measuring recycling effort in any particular country. Effort is measured as an index number which is, in essence, a trade-adjusted ratio of the output of secondary materials to the total primary and secondary materials output for any economy. The flow of scrap is measured at the end of the secondary materials production process, rather than as an input into secondary materials production, due to the difficulties in measuring the latter flow. This leads to Pearce's Recycling Effort Index (REI) consistently underestimating a country's recycling effort, a bias that he points out.

With this proviso noted, we find some interesting data in the cross-country REI comparisons. For example, the case of aluminium shows that, from 1963 to 1973, Italy's measured recycling effort increased by 200 percent, due entirely to an increase in secondary recovery from domestic aluminium scrap arisings. Working with proportions can be misleading; but assuming that we are not working with extremely small quantities, this relatively rapid rise in secondary output does not lend support to our hypothesis concerning rates of growth of secondary materials industries.[10] The figures for Japan are even more dramatic, with secondary aluminium production having risen by 400 percent in the same ten-year period. Both West Germany and the United States doubled their production of secondary aluminium during the period. None of this evidence lends any support to our tentative hypotheses about the size and rate of growth of a secondary materials industry operating in an environment where there are significant price fluctuations.

Pearce's discussion on the possible reasons for the downward trend in REIs for copper over the period 1963–73 is extremely interesting. Given the discussion above, we would have suggested that one possible reason for this is the greater magnitude of price fluctuations for the secondary material. Pearce outlines a similar argument, although it is based more on the difference in concentration between the primary and secondary industries, and relies on a conventional oligopoly model to explain why primary prices might be less variable. The data on secondary copper prices must be used with caution; but, for the United States, the data does not seem to support the contention suggested by some that secondary copper prices are, in fact, less variable than primary prices. Pearce concludes that the data suggests that "supply has failed to increase sufficiently to meet demand increases for secondary copper, perhaps because of the fragmented nature of the secondary industry."[11] In the light of our more theoretical discussion above, an entirely plausible alternative explanation is that the "more erratic" secondary copper prices produced sufficient uncertainty to slow down the rate of expansion of the industry.

Sawyer's[12] work on recycling of automobiles provides us with several pieces of information concerning elasticities of supply of scrap. He reports other findings, as well as his own, providing useful comparative data. The information concerns the elasticity of supply of homogeneous grades of ferrous scrap, and not for products manufactured from ferrous scrap. Sawyer reports that Adams[13] estimated a short-run (one- or two-year) elasticity of supply for high-grade shredded scrap of between 5 and 10, which is high by any criterion and which does nothing to support our tentative hypothesis concerning the effect of price uncertainty on the flow supply of secondary materials. For lower quality scrap, the supply elasticity was still high

(c. 8). However, Johnson's [14] findings of a short-run supply elasticity of 0.01–0.02 (virtually completely inelastic) appear to directly contradict this, his reservations about the data notwithstanding. (It is thus difficult to see how a difference of the magnitude that exists between these two estimates can be attributed to poor data. Making even the most lenient allowances for data limitations, Johnson's study implies an extremely inelastic supply curve for ferrous scrap in the United States.)

The third study that Sawyer reports is by the U.S. Bureau of Mines.[15] Their estimate of the short-run elasticity of supply for ferrous scrap is approximately unity, but problems associated with the estimation procedure appear to reduce the value of this study.

Sawyer's own work produces extremely high elasticities of supply for ferrous scrap derived from automobiles.[16] It may seem difficult to reconcile these extremely high elasticities with our tentative hypothesis above. We should remember, however, that Sawyer's estimates come from an input/output model using cross-sectional rather than time-series data. Essentially, most of the tentative hypotheses that we have suggested would need to be tested with time-series data rather than cross-sectional. We cannot completely argue away Sawyer's results, and the implicit refutations of our hypothesis, however. Elasticities of supply of ferrous scrap of between 4 and 20 are extremely high indeed, and, even though postwar ferrous scrap prices have been extremely variable in the United States, there does not seem to have been any short-fall in the supply of ferrous scrap from 1958 to 1970. This does not conform to our hypothesis of an industry expanding slowly in the face of uncertain and fluctuating prices.

There appears to be even less information on the input demand elasticities for reclaimed materials, and their associated cross-elasticities with the relevant primary material. In a recent study, however, Russell and Vaughan [17] publish own-price elasticities for scrap in the United States steel industry, and the cross-elasticity of demand with iron ore. These are typically extremely low for the basic oxygen furnace and electric arc furnace and rather high for the open hearth furnace, reflecting the very limited substitution possibilities of ore for scrap in the electric arc furnace, and of scrap for iron ore in the open hearth. The low elasticities, then, are due to other factors than uncertainty about future scrap prices (although this may have a

TABLE 12–1

OWN-PRICE AND CROSS-ELASTICITIES OF DEMAND BETWEEN SCRAP AND
IRON ORE IN THE U.S. STEEL INDUSTRY

Plant Type	Price Elasticity of Demand for Scrap	Cross Elasticity of Demand for Iron Ore
Open hearth	2.68	0.52
Basic oxygen	0.24	0.03
Electric arc	0.35	n.a.
Basic oxygen/electric arc combination with 100% excess capacity	2.41	0.39

SOURCE: Russell and Vaughan (op. cit.), p. 242.

marginal influence not picked up by the analysis). The elasticities are shown in Table 12–1.

The final, hypothetical case of a combined basic oxygen/electric arc plant points the finger clearly to process constraints being responsible for the low own-price and cross-elasticities. With the plants run in combination, and with no proximate capacity limitations, the elasticities increase significantly, with the same degree of uncertainty about future materials prices.[18]

When we turn to the cause of secondary materials price fluctuations, we seem to be on firmer ground. The tendency of secondary materials demand to fluctuate with business cycles has been generally accepted, if not carefully documented. We also noticed above that fluctuations in the trade of secondary materials could destabilize prices. The possibility of waste arisings fluctuating to the extent that secondary materials prices could be affected was noted in the first major section of this paper. The importance of this would be that the instability would have arisen on the supply side, rather than the demand side of the markets for secondary materials. Policies designed to achieve price stabilization through the demand side of the market would, in this case, obviously be inappropriate. Empirically, the problem depends upon

- the prevalence of long-term contracts between scrap dealers and industries where prompt scrap arises;
- the proportion of the market demand for scrap met by old scrap, for which long-term contracts cannot be established without prohibitive transactions costs to the scrap dealers.[19]

The evidence appears to be that long-term contracts between industry and scrap merchants are the norm rather than the exception. The only fluctuations in scrap availability will, in this case, arise from changes in industrial activity over business cycles. At the same time old ("obsolescent") scrap appears to constitute a relatively small proportion of the total scrap supply for most materials. The proportion of total scrap supply met from domestic sources and obsolete industrial capital equipment (old or obsolete scrap) in relatively small, but in some cases is a sufficient proportion to destabilize the market if it should fluctuate to any degree. For example, in the United States, during the period 1967–73, old scrap averaged 3.3 percent of total aluminium consumption, and 23 percent of total scrap aluminium consumption.[20] Thus, over this period, approximately a quarter of total scrap supplies were not covered by long-term contracts. There is obviously a possibility that this proportion could fluctuate, introducing instability into the price of aluminium scrap. The seven years for which data are at hand shows, however, that the obsolete scrap/total scrap ratio kept between 20 percent and 26 percent, and never changed by more than 3 percent between consecutive years. Whilst the potential for instability exists, experience shows the ratio to be quite stable.

Data on the obsolete scrap/total scrap ratio is not readily available for other metals, but the obsolete scrap/total consumption ratio is available for other metals in the United States for the period 1965–73. These are presented in Table 12–2.

From Table 12–2 it would appear that, for all metals except zinc, tungsten, cobalt, and cadmium, the potential exists for old scrap supply fluctuations to destabilize prices. The data shows that the old scrap/total consumption ratio has been relatively unstable not only for silver (where its use in coinage led to considerable fluctuations) but also for mercury and antimony. The fact that the secular trend in the ratio is falling for antimony, lead, copper, and tin must also be a cause for some concern, even though a fall in such a crude ratio need not necessarily reflect a decrease in recycling effort.

The information on rates of adoption of innovations in reclamation and recycling technology is extremely vague. The best-documented example is the spread of the automobile shredder across North America.[21] Output of shredded ferrous scrap rose from a negligible amount in 1963, the first year for which figures are available, to more than 5 million tons per annum in 1975. The number of shredding

TABLE 12–2

MEAN RATIO OF OLD SCRAP CONSUMPTION/TOTAL CONSUMPTION, U.S.A.,
1965–1973

Metal	Proportion (%)
Antimony	52*
Lead	37*
Copper	23
Silver	20
Tin	19
Platinum	17†
Mercury	15
Zinc	5
Tungsten	4
Cobalt	1
Cadmium	< 1

SOURCE: U.S. Bureau of Mines, *Mineral Facts and Problems*. Bulletin 667, Washington D.C., 1975.

*These high levels are reported to be due to efficient lead-acid battery recycling.
†Platinum data do not include "toll refining," that is, recycling where ownership is retained and a recycling fee paid. If this is included, the proportion for platinum rises to approximately 75%.

plants increased from 29 in December 1966 to 146 in December 1975, a 400 percent increase in twelve years. During the same period, total shredder capacity increased by 300 percent. Throughout the period, considerable excess capacity has existed in the shredding industry. (On a national scale, in 1975, the output of the shredders was only two-thirds of estimated capacity.) Neither the spread of the technology, nor the degree of underutilization of plant are commensurate with our tentative hypothesis concerning rates of adoption of new technology, or about rates of investment and industrial growth. To some extent these effects might be offset by the fact that shredding does not yield just one material but several materials, and by the fact that many shredding plants have been integrated with refining and processing plants for the base metals yielded when automobiles (and other domestic appliances) are processed in this way. Dealing in several distinct types of scrap or further processing them can both be seen as indirect methods of insurance by scrap merchants in order to spread the risk involved in dealing only with one material if prices are fluctuating widely.

There is no direct evidence on elasticities of substitution between primary and secondary materials, but the indirect evidence available suggests that they are, in fact, quite low. In many cases, primary and secondary materials are only substitutable in the production of lower-quality materials. For iron and aluminium, primary and secondary materials are only substitutable in the production of casting products, and not in the production of wrought goods. Reclaimed paper is used largely for the production of poorer-quality paper. Thus, whilst in the processes where they are technically substitutable the elasticity of substitution will be high, and the proportions used determined largely by relative prices, across the broad range of materials produced with the primary material, the elasticity of substitution between it and the secondary material is likely to be quite small.

This concludes our evaluation of the empirical data at hand. At best, the results of this assessment must be regarded as equivocal, in terms of whether or not they lend any weight to our tentative hypotheses. Little information is available to evaluate points 6 and 7. No systematic tendencies have been found; but in several cases, and for particular materials, the evidence allows that uncertainty brought about by wide fluctuations in secondary materials prices *may* lead to a lower level of recycling effort than is socially desirable, although in several cases this is not the only feasible explanation. It is in this vein that we move on to a discussion of alternative possible solutions to the problems that may be raised by price uncertainty, to a summary of the chapter, and to the conclusions therefrom.

SUMMARY, POLICY PRESCRIPTIONS, AND CONCLUSIONS

This chapter represents an attempt to understand the effects of uncertainty about prices on the reclamation and recycling industries in the Western world. The basis for assessing empirical evidence was a set of a priori hypotheses, derived from careful reasoning around a conventional model of behavior by producers, with certain attitudes toward risk in an environment where uncertainty arises from wide price fluctuations, in this case fluctuations in the price of scrap and processed secondary materials. In an uncertain market, without full

futures markets, option schemes or the possibility of complete insurance against changes in profit levels, there is every reason to anticipate a less than socially optimal level of recycling. The primary
materials content of goods will be higher than desirable, and the
consequent rates of depletion will be too high. Rates of reclamation
and recycling being too low means that too many of society's resources will be allocated to the disposal of waste, either as landfill, or
the despoiling of amenity resources because of dumping and abandon-
ment of domestic wastes, or in some other way. We readily concede
that there were many other reasons to expect less than optimal recycling rates, but simply point out that we need to focus some attention on this one problem. There may be objections that the problem
could better be approached with the use of models conventionally used
to analyze commodity stabilization programs. We make no apology
for having chosen an alternative approach. The problem of price
fluctuations is not that prices fluctuate, but that the extent of the
fluctuations is not known, and that, therefore, price fluctuations create
an uncertain environment in which producers may not act as profit
maximizers. The aim of price stabilization schemes is not simply to
delimit income fluctuations of a known extent, but rather to reduce
the uncertainty about future profit levels, and, therefore, enable
better forward planning in the industry.

Considering both the demand for, and supply of, scrap and reprocessed secondary materials, we were able to derive a set of tentative
hypotheses about more specific aspects of the reclamation and recycling
markets. These formed a framework around which our discussion of
the scant empirical evidence was structured. The section on the empirical evidence showed no more than a suspicion that the uncertain
environment produced less than optimal rates of recycling, some evidence of risk-spreading by diversification into several materials, slower
rates of growth and levels of investment in some reclamation and
recycling industries, and a smaller secondary materials industry than
might be the case in the absence of price uncertainty. Given that the
limited amount of empirical work that was available was not intentionally designed to test any of these hypotheses, the possibility of
uncertainty reducing recycling effort should be viewed with some
concern. More cannot be said without the examination of further
evidence that has yet to come to light, or without further investigation
into this area.

This brings us to the point of policy considerations. In the light of this chapter, the most obvious recommendation is that a great deal further investigation is required in this area. The information that is required is fairly modest. We need to know price elasticities of supply and demand, both for raw scrap and for reprocessed secondary materials. Discussions about the simplest stabilization schemes are of little point, in a policy-prescribing context, unless we have some quantitative knowledge of these magnitudes. Indeed, without these, policy-prescription is of little avail. Another magnitude of importance is the elasticity of substitution between primary and secondary materials in various production processes. Unless we have some idea of the value of this parameter, we cannot know, faced with sets of relative prices, what effect a particular scheme to reduce uncertainty about prices will have on the demand for secondary materials, and what this implies for future secondary materials demands, and the size of the secondary materials industry. Thus, the most important conclusion from this study is that a great deal more work needs to be done in this area. This recommendation cannot be emphasized strongly enough. However, we will not stop at this point, as the remit invites the author to "consider what public policy alternatives *may* make sense." Hence, we can consider a whole gamut of possible policy alternatives designed, in one way or another, to reduce the uncertainty in which the secondary materials producers operate, and discuss both their direct and indirect effects.

We should first consider the two most obvious ways of achieving a more certain environment and thus increase rates of recycling, namely the buffer fund and the buffer stock. The first has the disadvantage that, under certain sets of conditions, buffer funds (acting by withholding earnings in buoyant markets and supporting prices in depressed markets) can destabilize rather than stabilize, thereby increasing rather than reducing uncertainty. That we are uncertain about the elasticity of supply, and that, in part, it is on the elasticity of supply that the success or failure of buffer funds depends, suggests that we should not advocate the use of this device. Its close relative, the buffer stock, is generally more appealing, but Pearce [22] suggests that such a scheme for waste paper in Britain, designed largely to encourage local authority involvement in reclamation, would not necessarily be successful (because of a fairly modest increase in demand, and potential excess supply of waste paper by local authorities and private merchants, competing for the higher quality waste paper market). It is also generally possible that, for certain values of supply and demand elasticities, buffer-stock schemes can destabilize income.

We mentioned the possibility that trade fluctuations in secondary materials may have a destabilizing effect upon domestic secondary materials prices. One obvious approach to this is that a buffer-stock scheme could be introduced into which imports are bought at the floor price, and from which stocks can be released during periods when the country is a net exporter. There are several other ways of surmounting the problems introduced into schemes to stabilize domestic prices when trade in the commodity is significant. These schemes vary in their efficacy and their effects, and we do not intend to launch into a discussion of them at this juncture.

Intervention and regulation of the market price to reduce uncertainty is one approach to the problem of uncertainty in secondary materials markets. Another approach would be to provide means to encourage investment in the industry. Investment subsidies and subsidies to finance inventory investment during periods of depressed markets will encourage a faster rate of growth in the secondary materials industry, reduce secondary materials prices, and increase the competitiveness of secondary materials vis-à-vis primary materials. It may also be necessary to subsidize research and development into reclamation technology, as there is some evidence that research and development tends to be intensive in the use of relatively cheap factors of production. We might also expect the R & D bias toward primary materials to be exacerbated by the fiscal bias towards these.

Mention of the bias of the fiscal system towards virgin materials suggests that the removal of this bias, by taking away depletion allowances (and maybe imposing severance taxes), not allowing the extremely high rates of depreciation for capital equipment typical for many primary extractive industries, and so on (or allowing the same rate of depreciation for secondary materials producers) may help to redress the relative price bias for secondary materials, although it will not directly reduce uncertainty to the industry. Another way of reducing uncertainty may be to allow futures trading in secondary as well as primary materials, thus allowing secondary materials producers to hedge against future price changes. We do not advocate this policy strongly at the moment, however, as futures trading by speculators, as opposed to producers or buyers in the market, can easily destabilize the market. A somewhat more comprehensive scheme than any of those in existence at the moment would be necessary.

We thus come to the conclusion of this chapter. If anything is to be emphasized, it must surely be that our knowledge of this area is far too limited. Experience from other national and international agreements for stabilizing the price of primary agricultural products shows that successful schemes are few and far between, and that even the success of these tends to be short-lived, ending when there is some change exogenous to the market. Before a successful scheme can be implemented, the relevant supply and demand elasticities need to be determined with some confidence. It is in this direction that future enquiry needs to be directed, before more detailed consideration is given to public policy programs to reduce the level of uncertainty induced by price fluctuations in secondary materials prices.

NOTES

1. For a summary of this literature, see: J. J. McCall (1971), "Probabilistic Micro-Economics, *Bell Journal,* 2 (no. 2) Autumn, pp. 403–33, and especially pp. 415–17.

2. Although common practice, both in business and in applied economics texts, this rule-of-thumb approach to uncertainty has significant drawbacks. For a discussion of these, see G. M. Heal.

3. The main reason for such cavalier brevity is that an extended discussion on the theory of inventory holding is not likely to yield any more precise hypotheses. Given that the purpose of this section is to provide a basis on which to evaluate the empirical literature, an aesthetic digression into a particular aspect of capital theory does not seem justified.

4. The cautions of note 2 are equally applicable here.

5. It must again be emphasized that this hypothesis is based on intuition rather than strict theoretical reasoning. At a theoretical level, the problem is really one of consistent planning in a stochastic environment. The literature on this subject is growing, but is still so abstract that it is unlikely to yield useful information of the kind we require for our more pragmatic purposes.

6. D. W. Pearce (1975), *Policies for the stabilisation of secondary materials markets: A study of waste paper.* A report commissioned by the Environment Directorate, OECD, Paris.

7. For a review of these schemes, see C. P. Brown (1975), *Primary commodity control,* Oxford University Press, London, chap. 2.

8. See McCall, op. cit., pp. 403–6 for a discussion on the problems and

pitfalls of using deterministic models to capture the behavior of risk-averse producers in an environment of uncertainty.

9. D. W. Pearce (1976), "Environmental Protection, Recycling and the International Materials Economy," chap. 14 in *Studies in International Environment Economics*, I. Walter (ed.), Wiley, New York.

10. This assumes, of course, that the industry grew as a separate entity, without large capital injections from the Italian government, without a governmentally financed stock-holding scheme, and that the industry did not develop as an integral part of a secondary materials consuming industry.

11. Pearce, op. cit., p. 337.

12. J. W. Sawyer (1974), *Automotive Scrap Recycling: Processes, Prices and Prospects*, Johns Hopkins Press (for Resources for the Future), Baltimore, chap. 7.

13. R. L. Adams (1972), "An Economic Analysis of the Junk Automobile Problem." Unpublished Ph.D. dissertation, University of Illinois.

14. W. R. Johnson (1971), "The Supply and Demand for Scrapped Automobiles." *Western Economic Journal* 9, pp. 441–43.

15. U.S. Department of the Interior, Bureau of Mines (1967), *Automobile Disposal, A National Problem*.

16. Sawyer, op. cit., p. 98.

17. See C. S. Russell and W. J. Vaughan (1976), *Steel Production: Processes, Products and Residuals*, Johns Hopkins Press (for Resources for the Future), Baltimore, pp. 225–42.

18. Strictly speaking, as the data is cross-sectional rather than time-series, the reaction of producers to uncertainty about future materials prices will not be captured in this analysis.

19. Implicitly we are assuming that the demand for scrap by merchants and secondary materials producers is at least moderately elastic. If it is, in fact, highly inelastic, then marginal changes in supply could have significant effects on prices. Pearce, op. cit., in a reference to some work by Page (*T. Page: Economics of a Throwaway Society, F.F.F.* Washington, 1975) says:

Page has also stressed the importance of marginal additions to supply having a more than proportionate effect on secondary prices. The general result is to reduce the incentive to recovery.

The inference here is both that the demand for scrap is highly inelastic and that the behavior of the reclamation and recycling industries is characteristically risk-averse. Unfortunately, I have not had an opportunity to see Page's work. This paper would obviously have been the richer had the work been accessible.

20. Source: *Minerals Yearbook*, 1973 aluminium preprint, U.S. Bureau of Mines, Department of the Interior, Washington, D.C.

21. Information for the automobile shredder in North America comes from: I. R. and T. Corporation (1976): *Impacts of Material Substitution in Automobile Manufacture on Resource Recovery*, a Report submitted to the U.S. Environmental Protection Agency, Appendix H: "Shredder Industry Survey."

22. Pearce, op. cit., pp. 42–43.

PART III

Sector Studies

CHAPTER 13

Market Structure and Recycling in the Nonferrous Metals Industries

Donald A. Fink

This paper considers the implication of market structure for the recycling of scrap material in the tonnage nonferrous metals industries. Although casual remarks will be addressed to other metals, attention thus focuses on aluminum, copper, lead, magnesium, tin, and zinc.

Communication will be facilitated by agreement at the outset with respect to a few key terms which recur frequently during any discussion of metals recycling:

Recycling: The collection, segregation, remelting, resmelting, and (possibly also) re-refining of scrap.

Recycling Rate: $\dfrac{\text{Tonnage Recycled Annually}}{\text{Annual Tonnage Available for Recycling}}$

Scrap:
Home Scrap: Scrap generated within the primary and secondary metals industries.
New Scrap: Scrap generated by fabricators in the process of using primary shapes and forms for the manufacture of intermediate

231

and final goods. Sometimes called "prompt industrial scrap."
Obsolete Scrap: Scrap generated by the retirement from use of
products containing the metal in question.

Primary Smelting: The extraction of a metal from its natural ore or
from a concentrate extracted from the ore.

Secondary Smelting: The extraction of a metal from scrap, dross, or
slimes using technologies similar to those utilized in primary
smelting and yield-metals of identical or closely similar composition.

Refining: The advanced treatment of smelted or high-purity scrap
metal to remove impurities and meet standardized specifications.

Market Structure: The basic characteristics of an industry, including
the number and size distribution of firms, the extent of product
differentiation, the height of entry barriers, the nature of demand,
the proportion of fixed costs, and the extent of economies of scale.[1]

The discussion to follow deals mainly with the domestic United
States nonferrous metals industries but takes note of international
relationships where appropriate.

MARKET STRUCTURES IN NONFERROUS METALS

In general, the tonnage primary nonferrous metals industries are
examples of what economists call *undifferentiated small group oli-
gopolies*.[2] This means that capacity and output are dominated by a
small group of large firms producing and selling products and/or
services perceived by their customers to be nearly identical regardless
of source. In the case of nonferrous metals, which are produced and
sold to rigid chemical and physical specifications, the temptation is
strong to substitute "completely" for "nearly" in the previous sentence.
But this would be misleading since buyers of primary metals (for
example, copper) may exhibit preferences (or "loyalties") for certain
sources of supply for reasons having nothing to do with the intrinsic
properties of the supplies in question. United States copper fabricators,
for example, tend to continue buying from domestic primary sources
even when copper is available on the world market at lower prices.
Usually, this is a prudent policy designed to preserve the fabricator's
access to his share of the primary's output during periods of tight

supply. As such, it constitutes, among other things, an implicit recognition of the medium-term supply inelasticity characteristic of copper. From the economist's point of view, however, such behavior means that domestic and imported primary copper are not perfect substitutes in the market place.[3]

Interdependence among producers is generally assumed to vary inversely as the number of participants in the market. This means that small group oligopolists typically possess some individual influence over market prices and are, therefore, acutely aware of one another's capacity, output, and pricing policies and actions. In contrast with monopoly or perfectly competitive market structures, oligopolistic markets are indeterminant from the equilibrium point of view. That is, individual and industry capacity and output/pricing behavior cannot be predicted reliably by means of the static equilibrium models of conventional microeconomic theory. In markets of this kind, specialized types of behavior emerge such as

- *Overt collusion* in the setting of prices, division of markets, and so forth.
- *Covert collusion* in pricing, and so forth.
- *Tacit collusion* of "conscious parallel action" in which firms pursue pricing, output, and marketing policies they perceive as conducive to industry stability and profitability in inherently unstable conditions.
- *Price leadership* in which major pricing decisions are made by a dominant firm which takes into consideration the interests of other industry members in making its decisions.
- *Predatory competition* in which all forms of collusion or cooperation fail and open warfare emerges (e.g., price-cutting wars designed to drive one or more firms from the market).
- *Interdictive resource acquisition* in which existing firms undertake to forestall entry by acquiring scarce resources (e.g., available ore deposits) in advance of current requirements.

Such behavior is always constrained by law and the fact that, at some price, virtually everything besides water has a substitute.

In the United States, market structure is frequently described empirically with the aid of "concentration ratios" of two principal types:

- Ratio of the value-added or value of shipments accounted for by the four or eight largest firms in an industry to the total value-added or value of shipments in the industry over some time period.
- Ratio of the total capacity or output accounted for by the four or eight largest firms to the total capacity or output in the industry.

The value data are made available by the Bureau of the Census, U.S. Department of Commerce, which executes *Censuses of Manufactures* periodically. Capacity and output data are accumulated and published by a number of sources, including trade associations. Table 13–1 summarizes these data for the major nonferrous manufacturing industries as defined in the U.S. Government's *Standard Industrial Classification Manual*. Similar data are not available for the mining sector, although reliable estimates have been developed. These are summarized in Table 13–2. As it happens, the data in Table 13–2 gives the share of the four largest producers of total mine production in lead and zinc but not of copper. For copper, the figure for the four largest firms is 61% +, the plus sign indicating that considerable mine output in 1973 was contributed by mines in which the "Big Four" were involved as partners.

Comparing Tables 13–1 and 13–2 reveals that concentration is roughly the same at the smelting and refining stages of primary copper production but less at the mining level. It is substantially less at the level of fabrication, though still significant. The same can be said of lead and zinc as well. The implication is that entry is easier for all of these metals at the mining and fabricating stages of production than at the smelting and refining stages. Again, this conclusion must be qualified with the reminder that nonintegrated mining firms have to smelt their ores somewhere or else sell them to someone owning a smelter. Hence their independence may be more apparent than real. The differences, however, are only matters of degree. Concentration is still high at the mining stage of production in all of the major nonferrous metals industries and very high in smelting and refining.

With respect to mining, entry remains very difficult for prospective integrated ventures, primarily because of economies of scale at the smelting stage. About the smallest copper smelter that could be con-

TABLE 13–1

DOMESTIC U.S. CONCENTRATION RATIOS FOR MAJOR METALS INDUSTRIES

SIC Code	Industry	Percent of Shipments* Accounted for by		Percent of Capacity Owned by
		4 Largest Firms	8 Largest Firms	4 Largest Firms
	Iron and Steel			
3312	Blast furnaces & steel mills	56	73	. . .
33122	Steel ingot & semifinished shapes	58	79	. . .
33123	Hot-rolled sheet & strip	54	77	. . .
33124	Hot-rolled bars, plates, structural shapes and piling	59	70	. . .
33125	Steel wire	56	81	. . .
33126	Steel pipe & tubes	54	81	. . .
33127	Cold-rolled sheet & strip	45	72	. . .
33128	Cold-finished bars	67	87	. . .
3321	Gray iron foundries	34	42	. . .
3322	Malleable iron foundries	51	62	. . .
3325	Steel castings	22	32	. . .
	Aluminum			
3334	Primary aluminum	80	94	71†
3354	Aluminum extruded products	36	51	. . .
3353	Aluminum sheet, plate and foil	70	86	. . .
33571	Aluminum and aluminum-base alloy wire made in nonferrous wire drawing plants	64	85	. . .
33417	Aluminum ingot produced by secondary smelters	50	69	
33418	Extrusion billet produced by secondary aluminum smelters	80	D‡	
3361	Aluminum foundries	22	28	
34631	Aluminum forgings	76	84	
34694	Aluminum stamped & spun utensils, cooking and kitchen	56	84	
34971	Converted unmounted Aluminum foil packaging products, unlaminated	81	95	

TABLE 13–1, Continued

SIC Code	Industry	Percent of Shipments* Accounted for by		Percent of Capacity Owned by
		4 Largest Firms	8 Largest Firms	4 Largest Firms
34972	Laminated aluminum foil, roll and sheets for Flex packaging	33	53	. . .
34973	Converted aluminum foil for nonpackaging uses and foil and leaf	55	81	. . .
3491	Metal cans	66	79	. . .
	Copper			
3331	Primary copper	60	73	. . .
33311	Copper smelter products, primary	87	D‡	81§
33312	Primary refined copper	82	100	75‖
33412	Secondary copper pig, ingot, shot, etc.	39	62	. . .
3351	Copper rolling and drawing, not including electrical wire	41	60	. . .
33572	Copper electrical wire, bare and tinned, for transmission	56	80	. . .
33574	Communication wire and cable	73	84	. . .
33577	Magnet wire	62	87	. . .
33578	Power wire and cable	45	65	. . .
33620	Copper castings	14	22	. . .
34310	Metal plumbing fixtures	45	62	. . .
34320	Plumbing fixture fittings and trim (brass goods)	23	39	. . .
	Lead			
3332	Primary lead	100	100	100#
33321	Lead smelter products	100	100	100#
33323	Refined primary lead	100	100	100#
33413	Secondary lead	61	75	. . .
3691	Storage batteries	58	85	. . .
	Zinc			
3333	Primary zinc	68	96	. . .
33331	Zinc smelter products	84	98	83**
33334	Refined primary zinc	69	100	. . .
33414	Secondary zinc	48	67	. . .

TABLE 13–1—Continued

SIC Code	Industry	Percent of Shipments* Accounted for by		Percent of Capacity Owned by
		4 Largest Firms	8 Largest Firms	4 Largest Firms
36920	Primary batteries, dry and wet	91	96	. . .
	Magnesium	D‡		100††
	Tin	D‡		100‡‡

* *Concentration Ratios in Manufacturing,* 1972 Census of Manufacturing (Washington: U.S. Department of Commerce, 1975).

† Primary aluminum ingot capacity as of 1 January 1976. *Metal Statistics, 1976* (New York: American Metal Market, 1976).

‡ D = data withheld to avoid disclosure.

§ Data are Arthur D. Little, Inc., estimates for 1972 published in *Economic Impact of Proposed Water Pollution Controls on the Nonferrous Metals Manufacturing Industry,* EPA–230/1–75–041 (Washington: U.S. Environmental Protection Agency, 1975), hereafter referred to as *EPA 1.* Note that at least one old copper smelter (Kennecott's McGill plant) has been closed since 1972, allegedly because of environmental regulations.

‖ *Metal Statistics 1976.* Note that the distinction between primary and secondary refined copper is not significant since there is no metallurgical difference detectable in the market. The percent of total capacity figure reported above therefore refers to the share of the four largest copper refining firms in total U.S. refinery capacity (including secondary) as of 1975.

EPA 1.

** *EPA 1.* Smelter capacity data are somewhat arbitrary in respect to both zinc and lead.

†† *Metal Statistics, 1976.* For all practical purposes, there are only two primary magnesium producers in the United States.

‡‡ *Minerals Yearbook,* vol. 1, 1973 (Washington: U.S. Department of the Interior, 1975), p. 725. Again, there is only one domestic smelter of tin in the United States, which operates primarily on concentrates imported from Bolivia.

sidered economic under present-day conditions, bearing in mind the costs of environmental controls, would be a plant of 80,000 to 100,000 net tons per year of blister capacity. A plant of this size would cost somewhere in the neighborhood of $100–$125 million. To support its feed requirements would require a mine and mill complex costing

TABLE 13-2

DISTRIBUTION OF MINE PRODUCTION BETWEEN INTEGRATED AND
NONINTEGRATED FIRMS

Metal Ore	% of Total Mine Production Accounted for by Integrated Firms	% of Total Mine Production Accounted for by Nonintegrated Firms
	(Metal Content Basis)	
Copper *	81	19
Lead †	80	20
Zinc ‡	77	23
Magnesium §	. .	. .
Aluminum ‖	. .	. .
Tin #	. .	. .

* Arthur D. Little, Inc., Phase II Report, *Analysis of Economic Impact of Proposed Effluent Guidelines for the Metallic Ore Mining and Dressing Industry* (Washington: U.S. Environmental Protection Agency, June 1972).
† ADL, Phase II report.
‡ ADL, Phase II report.
§ Domestic magnesium is recovered from seawater and brines, which are virtually unlimited in supply.
‖ Aluminum is omitted from these calculations because almost all of the domestically used bauxite is imported.
Domestic ore production is nil.

somewhere between $300 and $500 million. This adds up to capital requirements of $400 to $625 million. It is very rare that new firms are able to finance ventures of this magnitude in long-established industries characterized by relatively slow growth in demand and output. The advantage in such industries lies clearly with existing firms who are able to expand incrementally with capacity already in place at one or more stages of production. Capital requirements are not as constraining in lead and zinc, but the market situation in these metals hardly encourages new entry. The domestic zinc industry is under heavy import pressure and cannot be viewed as a profitable target for new entry. Lead demand has grown glacially for many years and may decline in the future as the metal experiences market erosion in the automobile industry and in the production of leaded gasoline. Entry into the aluminum industry at the primary stages is also very difficult because of the virtual nonexistence of competitive sources of ore in the United States. To break into integrated aluminum production, adequate long-term supplies of foreign bauxite must be arranged and a suitable location found for the construction of alumina capacity. This is not as easy as it may sound because the minimum efficient scale of alumina extraction is very large and the requisite facilities are quite expensive. Moreover, the industry now experiences serious siting problems for alumina capacity because of environmental constraints on the disposal of red mud.

Of all the tonnage nonferrous metals industries in the United States, magnesium is the most highly concentrated. In 1976 there were only four primary producers, of which only two were in actual production for a significant period of time.[4] For many years, of course, the Dow Chemical Company had a perfect monopoly in magnesium based on the following entry inhibiting factors:

* Proprietary technology.
* The small size and slow growth of the market (total United States consumption in 1974 did not much exceed the annual capacity of Dow's Freeport, Texas, plant; between 1967 and 1973, total primary production grew only 25.7 percent).
* High capital costs for primary facilities (currently in excess of $22,000 per annual ingot ton).
* Dow's defensive pricing policy.[5]

These are, therefore, highly concentrated industries whose structures bear little resemblance to the competitive model of elementary economic theory. Note, however, that the degree of concentration as measured by the market positions of the four largest firms is substantially less in secondary aluminum, copper, lead, and zinc than in the primary industries in question. The possibility cannot be discarded out of hand, therefore, that the major primary nonferrous metals producers may use their market power in ways which depress the demand for scrap.

MARKET STRUCTURE VERSUS RECYCLING IN NONFERROUS METALS

The high degree of concentration characteristic of the primary nonferrous metals industries implies considerable monopsonistic power in the buying of raw materials. This power might be used to suppress scrap prices and, therefore, to inhibit the substitution of scrap for primary metal.

Available information regarding the structure of nonferrous scrap recovery does not support the above inference.

- Virtually all obsolete *aluminum* scrap is bought and processed by independent secondary smelters.*
- Only about 28 percent of total obsolete *copper* recovered in the United States is bought and processed by the primaries. Secondary smelters account for 50 percent, foundries 10 percent and brass mills 10 percent.
- Virtually all obsolete *lead* scrap is processed by secondary smelters and end-use manufacturers.
- In *zinc,* scrap recovery is also dominated by independent secondaries, although available data are scarce.
- Obsolete magnesium recovery is of so little importance as yet as not to merit discussion in this context.

In short, with the exception of copper, obsolete scrap recovery and processing in the tonnage nonferrous metals is primarily a concern of specialized industries rather than of the primary producers. As noted, these secondary industries are much more competitive in structure than are the relevant primaries.

The relative unimportance of the primaries with respect to obsolete scrap recycling is not difficult to explain:

- In aluminum, magnesium, zinc, and conventional copper smelting, the dominant primary smelting technology does not lend itself to the processing of obsolete scrap.*
- In most of these metals, the geographic location of primary smelting and refining facilities discourages obsolete scrap con-

---

* This situation may change gradually in the future as the recovery of aluminum cans increases. At the present time, 85 percent of the obsolete aluminum recovered from this source is accounted for by a single primary producer—Reynolds.

* Again, this situation may change in copper under the pressure of environmental regulations. EPA's New Source Performance Standards under the Clean Air Act effectively prevent domestic copper producers from utilizing the conventional reverberatory furnace for smelting. If the industry switches primarily to electric smelting, this would tend to encourage greater obsolete scrap usage. On the other hand, if it shifts mainly to flash smelting, obsolete scrap usage would not increase.

sumption because of the burden of transport costs from urban centers, where scrap is generated, to isolated smelter locations.

It has been suggested, though, that the primaries might well have developed more "obsolete scrap intensive" smelting technologies in the absence of public subsidies (e.g., ore depletion allowances) encouraging the development and use of virgin materials. This may be but the issue is more complex than the advocates of this argument appear to be aware in many cases.

In copper, for example, the depletion allowance (and other subsidies) has encouraged the industry to make massive investments in low-grade ore deposits which might otherwise not have been developed. These have, in turn, motivated the industry to take a long-run attitude towards pricing and marketing policies, attempting in the process to minimize substitution and maximize market growth. In the absence of this situation, it is highly likely that domestic copper prices would have fluctuated more violently and trended more consistently upward, to the detriment of total consumption. It is arguable that the secondary copper industry has also benefited from this strategy selection. In any case, the involvement of the primaries in the obsolete scrap market generally acts as a destabilizing factor, on the whole, given the fact that they tend to cut back on scrap purchases relative to total metallics sources when demand slackens and to increase scrap purchases when demand peaks.

But the decisive reason for doubting that market structure as normally interpreted by economists has had much influence on nonferrous metals recycling is simply the fact that most of the nonferrous scraps are valuable commodities. This is indicated clearly in Table 13–3, which includes data for steel scrap by way of contrast. Table 13–4 shows that most nonferrous scrap prices are substantial in relation to the appropriate primary metals prices.

These considerations suggest the need for different explanatory variables.

END-USE AND RECYCLING BY METAL

Aluminum

It has been estimated that, in 1969, aluminum recycled in the United States represented about 48 percent of total available scrap.[6]

TABLE 13–3

SELECTED SCRAP METAL PRICES IN THE U.S., 1958–1975
(Cents Per Pound)

Year	No. 1 Heavy Melting Steel (Chicago)	Dealers' No. 2 Heavy Copper	Heavy Soft Lead	Block Tin Pipe	Scrap Zinc (old)	Aluminum Crank Cases
1958	1.71	. . .	. . .	75.50	. . .	. . .
1959	1.72	22.65	7.95	77.09	. . .	10.75
1960	1.39	21.16	8.03	76.19	. . .	10.25
1961	1.57	21.78	7.19	84.41	. . .	9.40
1962	1.23	21.58	5.80	85.87	. . .	8.70
1963	1.25	22.19	6.92	92.22	. . .	8.33
1964	1.54	25.98	9.82	106.79	. . .	10.13
1965	1.52	34.49	11.26	139.71	7.13	12.15
1966	1.41	44.66	10.80	140.46	5.90	10.30
1967	1.25	33.15	8.31	126.00	4.25	8.40
1968	1.14	32.76	6.40	110.70	3.52	8.41
1969	1.30	42.88	8.60	111.82	3.25	11.48
1970	1.86	39.45	7.13	114.89	3.19	9.79
1971	1.49	27.57	4.36	112.50	3.41	7.00
1972	1.60	39.02	5.65	112.50	4.125	5.52
1973	2.56	50.22	7.66	122.79	7.510	8.58
1974	5.03	54.88	11.44	173.05	14.07	12.78
1975	3.18	33.94	8.94	192.88	9.06	8.01

SOURCE: *Metal Statistics, 1976* (New York: American Metal Market, 1976), appropriate metal chapters. See also *Year Book of the American Bureau of Metal Statistics.*

Since the recovery of old scrap has doubled since 1968–69, in part as a consequence of progress in the recovery of aluminum cans, it is likely that this figure may be somewhat higher today. Nevertheless, the improvement is marginal since obsolete scrap still constitutes no more than about 21–25 percent of total scrap recovery.[7] One reason for this, of course, is that tonnage aluminum has not been around very long and a large percentage of the aluminum placed in service so far in this country is still part of the service inventory. This is especially true of structural aluminum and aluminum contained in transmission cables.

TABLE 13-4

SELECTED PRIMARY METALS PRICES, VARIOUS YEARS

(Cents Per Pound)

	1959	1961	1963	1965	1967	1969	1971	1973
Aluminum *	26.85	25.46	22.62	24.50	24.98	27.18	29.00	25.33
Cadmium sticks				257.17	264.00	328.00	205.06	361.00
Chromium †							156.00	153.70
Copper ‡	30.99	30.32	32.35	36.00	38.10	47.43	52.09	59.53
Lead, Pig	12.21	10.87	11.14	16.00	14.00	14.93	13.89	16.31
Magnesium Ingots	36.00	36.00	36.00	36.00	36.00	36.00	37.00	38.25
Tin, Straits, N.Y.	102.01	113.27	116.64	178.17	153.40	164.43	174.36	227.48
Zinc, Prime Western	11.96	12.05	12.51	15.00	14.35	15.15	16.14	20.84

SOURCE: *Metal Statistics, 1976* (New York: American Metal Market, 1976).

* Virgin ingot.

† Electrolytic.

‡ Electrolytic, U.S. Producers' price.

TABLE 13-5

UNITED STATES ALUMINUM CONSUMPTION BY INDUSTRY

End-Use Industry	Aluminum Consumption (short tons)	% of Total
Building & construction	1,799,000	25.0
Transportation	1,405,000	19.3
Containers & packaging	1,029,000	14.1
Electrical	927,000	13.0
Consumer durables	669,000	9.1
Machinery & equipment	475,000	6.5
Other markets	435,000	6.0
Statistical adjustment	69,000	1.0
Total	6,808,000	94.0
Exports	420,000	6.0
Total	7,228,000	100.0

SOURCE: *Minerals Yearbook*, vol. I, 1973 (Washington: U.S. Department of the Interior, 1975), p. 142.

Table 13-5 is helpful in explaining the obsolete scrap situation in aluminum. It shows, among other things, that packaging and consumers durables consume approximately 23 percent of total aluminum shipments in the United States. This has presented serious problems for aluminum recycling because:

- Nonferrous metals are difficult and costly to separate from automobile hulks and other durable goods.
- At the present time, a large fraction of the annual accession to obsolete consumer appliances in the United States disappears into municipal garbage dumps or into backyard "chicken coops."
- Container utilization of aluminum, which has been growing rapidly, results in the widespread dispersion of the metal, creating serious recovery problems.
- Considerable transportation consumption of aluminum is in military aircraft and (increasingly) in naval vessels. When retired from active service, these tend to go into "moth balls" rather than to be scrapped immediately.

Shredding of auto hulks, which has spread rapidly in the last few years, may lead to increasing yields of scrap, especially as auto manufacturers progressively substitute aluminum for steel and cast iron in an effort to reduce the weight of cars so as to improve gas economy.

Basically, the container recovery problem requires for its solution that housekeepers segregate and collect used cans for delivery to a recycling center, of which there are about 1,300 in the United States. This runs counter to American habits with the result that the bulk of container aluminum eventually lands up in municipal solid waste streams. Moreover, it should be noted that, although cans consume a lot of aluminum in the aggregate, each individual can contains very little. Thus it takes about 15 cans to yield one pound of aluminum, for which the consumer is currently paid about 15.5 cents at aluminum recovery centers. Hence the collector receives only about 1 cent per can—hardly enough to provide much financial incentive for faithful segregation and collection. Thus even Testin, a Reynolds Aluminum executive, reaches the following conclusion regarding aluminum can recycling after a proud discussion of his company's accomplishments in this area:

> Even though continued dramatic gains are expected in percentage and in actual amount of old aluminum scrap recovered through consumer programs as these activities expand still further, it is probable that the majority of this scrap will still end up in the trash heap.

In an interesting convergence of interests, the Federal Energy Administration and the U.S. Environmental Protection Agency are currently supporting legislation calling for mandatory deposits on containers which would impact heavily on the aluminum can business. EPA, of course, wants to reduce pollution, much of which comes from electric power generation. Aluminum production is a massive consumer of electrical power. Consequently, the agency likes the idea of legal arrangements which would tend to discourage the use of aluminum for packaging purposes. FEA, on the other hand, views aluminum packaging as a nonessential use of a highly energy-intensive commodity. A tough piece of legislation in this area would increase the rate of recycling in aluminum simply by eliminating a major dispersive market for the metal.[8]

With respect to the flow of scrap materials in this industry, it is worth noting that secondary smelters are, for all practical purposes, the sole consumers of obsolete scrap aluminum. The primary producers consume considerable new scrap but do not buy much obsolete scrap. The main reason for this is that the bulk of their production goes to wrought end-use markets. These require a very high-purity product which the primaries say they cannot achieve consistently with obsolete scrap. The secondary smelters, on the other hand, are able to blend scrap stocks and, in any case, sell 85 percent of their output to casting alloy markets. These are less demanding metallurgically than are the wrought markets.

Copper

Analysis of recycling in copper is complicated by the fact that there are many ways in which scrap copper can be recycled. Figure 13–1 may help in interpreting the comments which follow.

New Scrap:
1. The fabricator can remelt and re-use his scrap within his own facilities. This is very common in the brass industry.
2. The fabricator can contract with his supplier of refined metal or brass ingot to refine his scrap on a toll basis.
3. The fabricator can sell his scrap to a dealer or broker.
4. The fabricator can also sell directly to a primary or secondary smelter.

Obsolete Scrap:
1. Owners or collectors of scrap can sell it directly to scrap dealers.
2. Owners or collectors of scrap can sell it to junk yards or scrap yards who then resell to scrap wholesalers or dealers who identify it, classify it, sort and grade it, and prepare it for the processor.
3. Considerable obsolete scrap is also collected and reprocessed by major end-users. The telephone industry is a good example.

It is impossible to estimate the number of individuals and firms engaged in the collection and generation of copper scrap. Since the metal is valuable (see Table 13–3) and easily identified, it attracts a lot of attention. It is estimated, however, that there are about 1,500 nonferrous scrap dealers in the United States, indicating that both sides of the market at this level are perfectly competitive.[9] Scrap

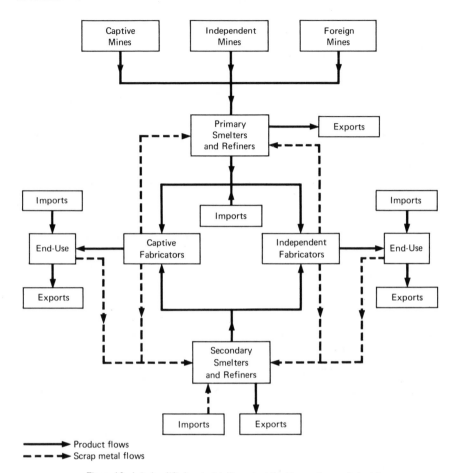

Figure 13–1 A simplified materials flow chart for the nonferrous industries

collection, classification, and preparation, of course, is an inherently labor-intensive process. Entry is easy.

In 1973, approximately 66.3 percent of the secondary copper recovered in the United States consisted of new scrap and the balance, 33.7 percent, was obsolete scrap. Table 13–6 indicates how this scrap flowed through the copper industry.

Obviously, almost 90 percent of the total yield of new scrap is recovered by brass mills and primary producers, mostly from their customers or, in the case of the primaries, from their fabricating subsidiaries. Old scrap, on the other hand, flows primarily to the secondary smelters and the primaries. This is easy to understand considering the fact that obsolete scrap varies widely in quality and gen-

TABLE 13–6

Copper Recovered as Refined Copper, in Alloys and in Other Forms
from Cu-Based Scrap Processed in the U.S., 1973

Processing Sector	% of New Scrap Recovered	% of Old Scrap Recovered	% of Total Scrap Recovered
Primary producers	25.8	28.2	25.3
Secondary smelters	8.1	50.3	22.3
Brass mills	65.6	10.2	47.0
Foundries, etc	.2	10.6	5.1
Chemical plants	.3	.7	.3
	100.0	100.0	100.0

Source: *Minerals Yearbook*, vol. I, 1973 (Washington: U.S. Department of the Interior, 1975), p. 480.

erally requires some metallurgy before it can be re-used. Foundries derive approximately 90 percent of their input metallics from scrap, 69 percent of it from old scrap.[10] These facts are interesting since there are about fifty brass mills and several hundred nonferrous foundries in the United States. There are also about eighty ingot makers and secondary smelters. Approximately 74 percent of the total recovery of scrap copper, therefore, is accomplished by segments of the industry which appear to be at least reasonably competitive.

The Battelle study estimated that about 61 percent of the total available supply of recoverable and available scrap copper was actually recovered in 1969.[11] According to the Battelle analysis, which was executed for the National Association of Secondary Material Industries, the unrecovered copper was accounted for by the following:

- About 16 percent was accounted for by end-uses in which the metal was widely dispersed so that recovery was discouraged by labor and transport costs (e.g., consumer durables such as refrigerators, air conditioners and small appliances).
- About 15 percent went to magnet wire used primarily in small motors which, taken individually, contain little copper but which, in the aggregate, disperse a significant volume.
- About 10 percent disappeared as a sacrificial additive.
- About 8 percent represented unrecovered cartridge brass. This may be inaccurate since the military services recycle considerable

brass internally which may or may not get picked up in the official data on scrap recovery.

• The balance, 51 percent, was accounted for by a catchall "other brass" category consisting of thousands of relatively minor end-uses. Data here are poor and the rate of recovery may be under-estimated.

These facts suggest that it is mainly end-use dilution and dispersion which account for the bulk of scrap copper not recovered in the United States.

It is worth noting that rising energy costs seem likely to provide additional commercial incentive for the recycling of both copper and aluminum. These are highly energy-intensive industries at the primary levels of production (see Table 13–7). Actually, the unit energy consumption factor for copper somewhat underestimates the energy intensity of primary copper production because one important stage of the overall smelting process, conversion, is exothermic. This tends to obscure the heavy energy requirements per unit of production char-acteristic of the other stages of the smelting process. Energy con-sumption per pound of metal recycled from obsolete scrap is estimated by industry sources to be about one-third that required to smelt virgin concentrate. This is in close agreement with the unit energy con-sumption figure for Secondary Nonferrous Metals (SIC 3341) in Table 13–7. In aluminum, the energy advantage of secondary pro-duction is even greater. According to Testin, energy consumption per pound output in manufacturing aluminum from scrap averages about 3,000 to 4,000 BTU compared with 90,000 BTU in extracting aluminum from bauxite.

Lead

According to the Battelle study, only about 40 percent of the total lead available for recycling was being recovered in the 1969–70 time frame. Affairs have probably not changed significantly since the Battelle research was conducted. The main reasons for the relatively low recycling rate in lead appear to be the following:

• Large volumes of lead are consumed in industries or end-uses that are dispersive, dilutive, or sacrificial (see in this connection Table 13–8, where the consumption data for 1974 for such end-uses have been indicated with an asterisk). The total of such

TABLE 13–7

ESTIMATED TOTAL ENERGY CONSUMED AND UNIT ENERGY FACTORS IN THE
NONFERROUS METALS INDUSTRIES, 1973

SIC Code	Industry	Total Energy * Consumed 10^{12} BTU	Unit Energy * Consumed 10^6 BTU/ST †
3331	Primary copper [a]	107.3	59.6
3332	Primary lead [a]	9.8	13.1
3333	Primary zinc [a]	47.2	69.9
3334	Primary aluminum ‡ [a]	590.0	130.0
3339	Primary nonferrous NEC [a]	11.5	45.5
3341	Secondary nonferrous metals [a]	37.5	19.9
3351	Copper rolling and drawing [a]	60.2	24.0
3352	Aluminum rolling and drawing [a]	147.2	22.7
3356	Nonferrous NEC rolling and drawing § [a]	7.7	122.4
3357	Drawing and insulating of wire [a]	43.6	23.2
	Hi-carbon ferrochromium [b]	15.8	61.0
	LO-carbon ferrochromium [b]	19.5	129.0
	Magnesium metal [b]	42.0	358.0
	Ferromanganese [b]	33.0	49.5
	Molybdic oxide [b]	5.9	145.0
	Electrolytic nickel [b]	18.0	144.0
	Titanium sponge [b]	8.2	408.0

SOURCES: (a) *Study of the Energy and Fuel-Use Patterns in the Non-ferrous Metals Industries* (Columbus: Battelle Memorial Institute, 1975); (b) *Energy Use Patterns in Metallurgical and Nonmetallic Mineral Processing* (Columbus: Battelle Memorial Institute, 1974)
* Expressed as fossil-fuel-equivalent energy.
† ST=short ton of production.
‡ Values for aluminum assume that 35% of electrical energy is hydroelectric.
§ Data are only for nickel rolling and drawing.

end-use consumption lines in 1974 was 486,566 tons, or fully 35 percent of total consumption. Actually, these figures underestimate the total volume of lead consumption falling into this category since the "miscellaneous uses" line item includes many applications that are also economically non-recyclable.

• Lead is highly immune from chemical attack and, therefore, tends to remain in the service inventory for great periods of time. This makes it especially difficult to develop accurate estimates of the volume of obsolete scrap becoming available each year.

Donald A. Fink   251

TABLE 13–8

Lead Consumption in the U.S. by Product, 1965/70/74
(Metric Tons)

Metal Product: (1)	1965	1970	1974
Ammunition	52,002	65,976	79,113 *
Bearing metals	19,595	14,813	11,218 *
Brass and bronze	21,499	17,170	15,665
Cable covering	54,109	46,059	34,846
Caulking lead	60,404	31,396	14,007 *
Casting metals	4,578	6,802	3,974 *
Collapsible tubes	9,882	9,900	2,011 *
Foil	4,359	5,009	3,995 *
Pipes, siphons, bends	17,996	16,228	11,914
Sheet lead	25,010	19,096	16,576
Solder	70,596	63,237	48,924 *
Storage batteries	413,084	538,371	669,012
Type metal	30,314	22,204	16,130
White lead	7,633	5,385	1,908 *
Red lead and litharge	72,441	70,048	80,137 *
Other pigments †	18,703	14,138	14,027 *
Tetraethyl lead	204,301	252,656	227,252 *
Other chemicals	314	566	. . . *
Miscellaneous uses	39,434	35,218	140,126
Grand Total	1,126,254	1,234,272	1,390,835 ‡

Source: *Metal Statistics, 1964–1974* (Frankfurt: Metallgesellschaft Aktiengesellschaft, 1975), p. 162. MA data based on U.S. Bureau of Mines
estimates.
* Includes remelted lead, lead in alloys, lead in scrap and residues and in ores
used directly in the manufacture of lead compounds.
† Includes lead content of leaded zinc oxide production.
‡ Data for 1974 are preliminary.

- Since lead is relatively easy to recover, substantial volumes may
  be recycled by end-users without being reported via official
  channels. Hence the data may underestimate the rate of recycling somewhat.
- Apparently, significant numbers of lead-containing batteries are
  lost (chicken coops again?) in both the civilian and military
  sectors.

If one adds the lead lost to dispersive, dilutive, and sacrificial end-
uses to that actually recycled, it turns out that only about 20 percent

of the lead estimated to be available for recycling escapes recovery each year.

Table 13–9 indicates the breakdown of lead recovery as between new and old scrap. These data show that new scrap accounts for only about 18 percent of total scrap recovery in the United States. Furthermore, the table also shows that virtually all of the annual recovery is accomplished by secondary smelters and refiners or by end-use manufacturers. Obviously, this is because lead recovery is a simple melting and skimming operation, for the most part, requiring none of the metallurgical talents of the primary lead sector. Furthermore, the primary lead industry is located in remote areas at great distance from the heavily populated sections of the country in which most obsolete lead is recovered. Transport costs, therefore, encourage regional recycling. Note in this connection that battery manufacture is also regionalized in the United States.

One unique aspect of the recycling situation in lead is worth attention in passing. This is the fact that one of lead's end-uses, automobile batteries, generates a nearly automatic collection system. Most batteries have a three- to four-year life cycle at the end of which they are traded in for new replacements at the neighborhood gasoline station or Sears parts department.

Again, it seems clear that the structural characteristics of the lead

TABLE 13–9

SECONDARY LEAD RECOVERED FROM SCRAP MATERIAL 1965/70/73
(Metric Tons)

	1965	1970	1973
Total recovered from *new* scrap	72,700	82,700	105,000
Total recovered from *old* scrap	449,700	459,200	488,600
Total Recovered	522,400	541,900	593,600
Of which recovered at primary plants as refined metal	11,900	4,000	—
Of which recovered at secondary plants as refined metal	118,400	122,000	135,400
Of which remelted lead at primary plants	17,500	6,900	1,000
Of which remelted lead at other plants	228,000	309,100	339,900
Of which recovered in other alloys	111,900	81,500	83,800

SOURCE: *Metal Statistics, 1964–1974* (Frankfurt: Metallgesellschaft Aktiengesellschaft, 1975), p. 162. MA data based on U.S. Bureau of Mines estimates.

Donald A. Fink   253

market have little effect on the rate of scrap recovery. Scrap lead is
easy to collect and reprocess, and its recovery is apparently not subject to strong economies of scale. Transport costs encourage its reprocessing at facilities located in close proximity to its sources.

Zinc

According to the Battelle study, only about 10 percent of the zinc
potentially available for recycling is actually recovered. The main
reasons for this, most of them associated clearly with the end-use
characteristics of the metal, are the following:

- Considerable zinc is consumed in chemicals and pigments and
  results in a high rate of metal loss.
- The largest single use of zinc—galvanizing—is sacrificial in
  character and also results in a high rate of metal loss.
- Considerable zinc is also lost in the form of flue dust during
  various pyrometallurgical activities. This material is fluffy and
  high in chlorine, rendering it costly to recycle.
- Much zinc is also consumed in the manufacture of small items
  such as dry cell batteries. These are difficult and costly to collect,
  because of spatial dispersion, and may also be costly to dis-
  assemble.
- The most rapidly growing major application of zinc—die cast-
  ings for automobiles—has presented serious recycling problems
  in the past because of the difficulty of separating nonferrous
  metals from automobile hulks. New technologies are now emerging, however, for recovering nonferrous values from shredded
  auto scrap.

TABLE 13–10

ZINC CONSUMPTION IN THE U.S. BY END-USE: 1965/70/74
(Metric Tons)

End-Use:	1965	1970	1974
Galvanizing	437,645	430,231	448,368
Brass and bronze	115,075	115,890	160,642
Zinc-base alloys	578,757	420,604	390,502
Rolled zinc	41,623	37,254	35,061
Zinc oxide	23,388	39,761	59,979
Other uses	31,924	33,044	78,448
Grand Total	1,228,412	1,076,784	1,173,000

SOURCE: United States Bureau of Mines.

TABLE 13–11

Secondary Zinc Recovered from Scrap Material 1965/70/73
(Metric Tons)

	1965	1970	1973
Total recovered from *new* scrap	246,200	242,600	266,900
Total recovered from *old* scrap	74,400	65,400	84,700
Total Recovered	320,600	308,000	351,600

Source: *Metal Statistics, 1964–1974* (Frankfurt: Metallgesellschaft Aktienge-sellschaft, 1975), p. 279. MA data based on U.S. Bureau of Mines estimates.

• In part because of static total demand for the metal, zinc prices (primary and secondary) have been low for many years. This does not encourage recycling.[12]

Tables 13–11 and 13–12 reproduce useful information on the end-use consumption of zinc and on secondary recovery. Scrap data for zinc are not very good. They do show that about one-quarter of total secondary zinc recovery in the United States consists of acquisitions from the service inventory. For the most part, therefore, zinc recovery is confined at present to prompt industrial feedback of virgin scrap. Virtually all of the old scrap recovered is processed by distillers and smelters while approximately 25 percent of the new scrap recovered each year is processed by chemical plants, foundries and other manufacturing activities.

Magnesium

Recycling of magnesium is of no great importance as yet (see Table 13–12) for two fairly obvious reasons:

TABLE 13–12

Magnesium Recovered from Scrap in the U.S., 1974
(Short tons)

From new scrap	9,155
From old scrap	5,719
Total	14,874

Source: *Metal Statistics, 1976* (New York: American Metal Market, 1976), p. 144.

- Relatively new on the industrial scene, magnesium does not yet have a large in-service inventory.
- Over 78 percent of total magnesium consumption is accounted for by sacrificial uses.

The preponderance of sacrificial uses is important because magnesium is difficult and costly to extract from its alloys in usable forms. It does not appear, therefore, that market structure has played a significant role in this metal's recycling history to date.

CONCLUSIONS

The conclusion which seems to emerge from this analysis, introductory as it is, is that the rate of recycling in nonferrous metals is determined primarily by:

- The structure of the end-use spectrum peculiar to each metal.
- The magnitude and average age of the in-service inventory of each metal.
- The price of both primary and secondary metal.
- Cyclical fluctuations in the level of economic activity.

The degree of competition in the primary originating industry does not appear to have much of a bearing on the rate of recycling.

This is an interesting conclusion from the policy point of view. It means, among other things, that positive actions designed to increase the rate of recycling will have to be focused mainly on the demand side, that is, on the end-use spectrum for each metal. Most promising in this respect are standards specifications, taxes, and other measures which would have the effect of discouraging sacrificial consumption. A ban on the use of tetraethyl lead in gasoline, for example, would sharply reduce the sacrificial loss of lead since about 17 percent of the total consumption of lead in the United States is accounted for by this application. Bear in mind, however, that drastic and sudden reductions in end-use demand are certain to have adverse impacts on recycling because of their implications for prices.

A second major point emerging from the analysis is that the rapidly rising cost of energy provides a strong stimulus to nonferrous metals scrap recovery.

NOTES

1. *Aluminum Prices: 1974–75* (Washington: Executive Office of the President, Council on Wage and Price Stability, 1976), p. 242.

2. W. Fellner, *Competition Among the Few* (New York: Alfred Knopf, 1949).

3. D. McNicol, "The Two-Price Systems in the Copper Industry," unpublished Ph.D. thesis, Massachusetts Institute of Technology, February, 1973.

4. Industry sources.

5. Charles River Associates, *An Economic Analysis of the Magnesium Industry,* Cambridge, Mass., 1967.

6. Battelle Memorial Institute, Columbus Laboratories, *A Study to Identify Opporunities for Increased Solid Waste Utilization,* 1972.

7. R. F. Testin, "Recycling Opportunities and Challenges for the Aluminum Industry," American Chemical Society Symposium on Energy and Materials, June 11, 1975, p. 5.

8. T. H. Bingham, M. S. Marquis, P. C. Cooley, A. M. Cruze, E. W. Hauser, S. A. Johnston, and P. F. Mulligan, *An Evaluation of the Effectiveness and Costs of Regulatory and Fiscal Policy Instruments on Product Packaging* (Washington: EPA, 1974).

9. R. L. Gordon, W. A. Lambo, and G. H. K. Schenck, *The Collection of Nonferrous Scrap: A Literature Review of the Copper and Aluminum Sectors* (University Park: Pennsylvania State University, 1972). E. S. Bonczar, and J. E. Tilton, *An Econo-Analysis of the Determinants of Metal Recycling in the U.S.: A Case Study of Secondary Copper* (University Park: Pennsylvania State University, 1975). F. V. Carrillo, M. H. Hibshman, and R. D. Rosenkranz, "Recovery of Secondary Copper and Zinc in the United States," U.S. Bureau of Mines, Information Circular IC 8622, 1974.

10. See Battelle, 1972, p. 20.

11. Ibid., p. 119.

12. McMahon, "The U.S. Zinc Industry: A Historical Perspective," U.S. Bureau of Mines, Information Circular IC 8629, 1974.

CHAPTER 14

Ferrous-scrap Recycling

Liselotte Lichtwer

Numerous excellent reports have been published in recent years describing, in considerable detail, technical and economic aspects of the processes and industries involved in ferrous scrap generation, processing, marketing, and consumption. No attempt will be made in this paper to provide comprehensive information on these aspects. This paper is aimed at providing a rough overall picture of the technical and economic features of the market for ferrous scrap and drawing some conclusions as a basis for further discussion.

The paper is primarily based on a study carried out by Battelle-Frankfurt for the Ministry of the Interior in 1973 dealing with the situation of motor-vehicle scrap recycling in the Federal Republic of Germany.[1] The principal aim of the study was to find out whether the problem of automobile scrap recycling can be solved by the market or whether political intervention is unavoidable.

ECONOMIC AND TECHNICAL FACTORS INFLUENCING THE USE OF FERROUS SCRAP

Recycling in this volume is viewed in the context of resource conservation on the one hand and protection of the environment on the other. This point of view is relatively new compared with recycling activities initiated for economic or technical reasons.

Apart from aspects of resource conservation and environmental protection, ferrous scrap is a traditional input in the iron and steel industry. The alternative to scrap in iron- and steelmaking is pig iron. Although these materials are interchangeable in production within certain limits which are technically determined, the ratio between the use of pig iron and scrap remained more or less stable over the last decade.

Nevertheless, as can be seen in Table 14–1, the share of scrap in iron- and steelmaking processes differs considerably from one country to another. This is mainly due to different process patterns of crude steel production. Thomas and Bessemer converters as well as basic oxygen LD converters are pig–iron-intensive, whereas open-hearth furnaces and electric furnaces are scrap-intensive processes. Since pig–iron-intensive Thomas converters and scrap-intensive open-hearth furnaces are replaced worldwide by pig–iron-intensive LD processes and scrap-intensive electric furnaces, the total specific scrap consumption remained nearly unchanged. Changes in process pattern of crude steel production will continue as in the past: less open-hearth plant, more electric furnaces. Thus, in the near future scrap demand will depend mainly on the development of iron and steel production.

Tables 14–2 and 14–3 illustrate the structure of steelmaking and the resulting consumption figures for scrap in the Federal Republic of Germany in 1974. Crude steelmaking constitutes about 80 percent of the total consumption, by far the main consumption sector for scrap. Scrap input dominates in the electric furnaces and open-hearth furnaces (with shares of 96.8 and 68.8 respectively).

ECONOMIC AND TECHNICAL FACTORS AFFECTING SUPPLY OF FERROUS SCRAP

There are three main sources of scrap:

* the iron and steel industry itself
* the steel-manufacturing industry
* consumers of steel-containing products

As can be derived from the ferrous materials flow chart (Fig. 14–1), about 50 percent of the scrap input arises from steelworks themselves.

TABLE 14–1

CONSUMPTION OF PIG IRON AND SCRAP IN CRUDE STEELMAKING IN 1974
(In Thousands of Tons)

Country	Total	Pig Iron	Scrap	Scrap as Percentage of Total
Belgium	17,924	13,136	4,788	26.7
Denmark	593	70	523	88.2
Fed. Rep. of Germany	57,325	36,952	20,373	35.5
France	30,001	20,431	9,570	31.9
Ireland	132	22	110	83.3
Italy	26,340	11,782	14,558	55.2
Luxembourg	7,236	5,485	1,751	24.2
Netherlands	6,504	4,576	1,928	29.6
United Kingdom	25,136	12,940	12,196	48.5
Total EEC	171,191	105,394	65,797	38.4
Austria *	4,546	3,012	1,534	33.7
Finland *	1,778	1,207	571	32.1
Norway *	978	558	420	42.9
Portugal †	469	348	121	25.8
Spain *	12,044	5,924	6,120	50.8
Sweden	6,344	2,824	3,520	55.5
Yugoslavia	3,139	1,588	1,551	49.4
Total Western Europe	200,489	120,855	79,634	39.7
German Dem. Republic ‡	1,774	1,119	655	36.9
Hungary	3,830	2,115	1,715	44.8
Poland	15,905	7,967	7,938	49.9
Romania *	9,188	6,484	2,704	29.4
Canada	15,688	8,701	6,987	44.5
United States	148,894	81,499	67,395	45.3
Japan	127,247	88,105	39,142	30.8

SOURCE: Organization for Economic Cooperation and Development.
* 1973.
† 1971.
‡ 1969.

The so-called circulating scrap is generated during iron and steel production (ingot croppings, sheet trimmings, foundry gates, and risers). The quantity thus generated is fully recycled.

Despite numerous improvements in iron- and steelmaking tech-

TABLE 14–2

SCRAP CONSUMPTION IN THE FEDERAL REPUBLIC OF GERMANY IN 1974

	Scrap Input 1,000 Tons	% of Total
Blast furnaces	558	2.2
Steel works	20,378	79.7
Thomas converters	(155)	(0.6)
Open-hearth furnaces	(6,738)	(26.4)
LD converters	(8,501)	(33.2)
Electric furnaces	(4,979)	(19.5)
Foundries	4,636	18.1
Total Scrap Consumption	25,572	100.0

SOURCE: Battelle Memorial Institute, Frankfurt.

nology, the rate of circulating scrap increased. This is mainly due to the following factors:

- increasing number of finishing operations
- more rigid product specifications
- faster production processes

In the recent past, some factors have caused a reduction of circulating scrap, that is:

- growing use of the continuous casting process
- growing proportion of rimming and semi-killed steel

TABLE 14–3

CONSUMPTION OF PIG IRON AND SCRAP IN CRUDE STEELMAKING
IN THE FEDERAL REPUBLIC OF GERMANY IN 1974
(In Thousands of Tons)

	Total	Pig Iron	Scrap	Scrap as Percentage of Total
Thomas converters	1,772	1,617	155	0.9
Open-hearth furnaces	9,797	3,059	6,738	68.8
LD converters	40,612	32,111	8,501	20.9
Electric furnaces	5,144	165	4,979	96.8
Total steelmaking	57,325	36,952	20,373	35.5

SOURCE: Battelle Memorial Institute, Frankfurt.

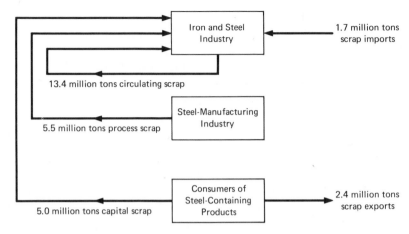

Figure 14–1 Ferrous scrap balance in the Federal Republic of Germany in 1974

- use of larger slabs and billets
- increasing rationalization of production processes

The growing use of the continuous casting process will effect a certain reduction in total scrap generated in the iron and steel industry. Whereas the conventional primary rolling process yields about 20 percent of scrap, continuous casting only provides 6 percent.

The second major source of scrap for the iron and steel industry is process scrap. It is generated during the processing of mill products for industrial and consumer products by metal-working firms (stampings, cuttings, turnings). Since quality and composition are high and known, process scrap flows relatively easily in the recycle chain (approximately 95 percent is recycled). Different steel-consuming sections yield varying amounts of scrap. Thus, the volume of process scrap generated is critically influenced by the sector pattern of steel consumption. For the United States, the following rates of scrap (percentages of finished steel consumption) were derived:

Construction, mining, quarrying	3%
Motor vehicle manufacture	31%
Shipbuilding and marine equipment	23%
Engineering industry	26%
Agricultural machinery	19%
Appliances, utensils, and cutlery	17%
Other domestic and household equipment	15%
Containers	12%

According to these figures, it is obvious that in highly industrialized economies with important motor-vehicle, shipbuilding, and engineering industries, the generation of process scrap is much higher than in less-developed countries. On the other hand, efforts made toward improved rationalization and the fact that finished steel products are increasingly supplied in optimum dimensions result in a reduction of process scrap. These two effects may compensate each other. While circulating scrap and process scrap (because of their high quality and homogeneous nature) are completely recycled without great difficulty, the third category of scrap, the so-called capital scrap, constitutes a problem in the scrap market.

Capital scrap comes from discarded fabricated products containing iron and steel (obsolete motor vehicles, scrap from railroad cars, dismantling and demolition projects, and other obsolete consumer and industrial products). There are two main reasons for the problems.

Economic reason: As opposed to circulating and process scrap, which arise in conjunction with the activity in the iron and steel industry and the iron- and steel-consuming sectors, capital scrap is based on the development in the past. As a consequence, scrap demand and scrap supply may be unbalanced temporarily. This occurs in periods of sudden increase in demand for iron and steel, leading to a temporary shortage of pig-iron capacity. Such periods are characterized by increasing scrap prices (see Fig. 14–2). As can be seen from the figure, such high-price periods are relatively short and, therefore, should be neglected in the discussion of economic aspects of capital scrap recycling.

Technical reason: The main problem of capital scrap recycling is the low and even decreasing scrap quality due to the increasing proportion of coated and painted light flat products. In addition, light scrap, particularly from passenger cars and consumer durables, causes numerous problems because of its copper and tin content. The upper limit of impurity concentration depends on the quality of steel produced and the steelmaking process. On the average, the content of copper plus the eightfold of tin should be 0.4 percent. For unalloyed carbon steel, the maximum content is 0.15 percent copper and 0.02 percent tin.

Since capital scrap often arises from many different sources, it is difficult to assess the impurity content. As a consequence, capital

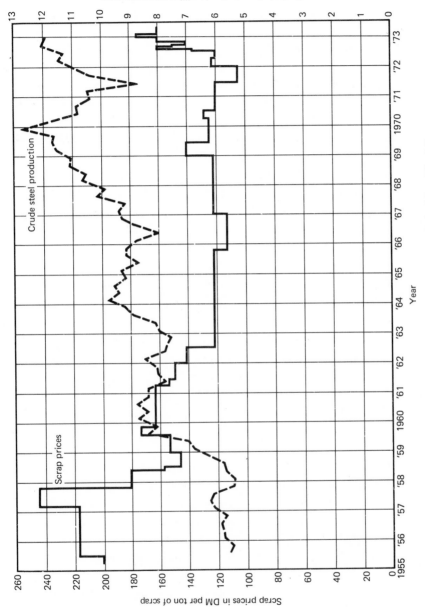

Figure 14—2 Scrap prices and crude steel production in the Federal Republic of Germany

scrap from known sources like shipyards or steel bridges, which are homogeneous and of known quality, are considered as circulated scrap and are sold easily.

The difficulties encountered due to the heterogeneity of light capital scrap can be overcome by improved methods of sorting and preparation, that is, shredding. This increased effort in scrap processing leads to higher expenditure which can only be recouped via higher scrap prices.

In low price periods, lower grades of capital scrap arising from production of consumer durables may remain uncollected and unprocessed. Consumer goods such as stoves, washing machines, refrigerators, and dishwashers account for up to 30 percent of the total capital light scrap.[2] These complex final products contain various impurities, mainly plastics and tin. In the Federal Republic of Germany, about 7 percent of the total rolling mill products are surface-coated (galvanized, tin-plated, plastic coated). About 50,000 tons of zinc, 900 tons of tin and 7,000 tons of polymers are used for surface coating per year.

Besides the technical problem of recycling this kind of light capital scrap, there exist some economic barriers. Owing to the vast number of sites where this type of scrap is generated, the cost of collection is prohibitive. This is why obsolete metallic durables are to some extent not recycled in low price periods but deposited in sanitary landfills.

WORLD TRADE IN FERROUS SCRAP

World trade in ferrous scrap made up around 5 percent of the total world scrap consumption in the past. The major deficit countries are Italy, Japan, and Spain, whereas the United States, Soviet Union, and France have an export surplus. The United States accounts for about 45 percent of the world exports of scrap.

A characteristic feature of foreign trade in scrap is that it takes place mainly in the same industrial region, that is, USA-Canada, USA-Mexico, USSR-Finland, FRG-Belgium-Luxembourg-Netherlands-France; Southern France-Southern Germany-Northern Italy. This is due to the important role of transportation cost in scrap supply. Dealers in Southern Germany prefer to supply Northern Italy rather than Northern Germany. Iron- and steelworks in Southern Italy prefer imports from the United States despite the presence of potential suppliers in Northern Italy.

Since transportation cost will continue to be a decisive factor in future international trade, the main trade flows will be stable. In most countries however, the trade volume in scrap is so small that it does not substantially affect the national supply and demand situation.

Apart from considering direct scrap trade, the so-called indirect scrap exports and imports have to be taken into account when analyzing the national materials balances. The high share of exports of steel-containing products (equipment, mechinery, and motor vehicles) of the Federal Republic of Germany results in a lower generation of capital scrap compared with steel production. Hence, in the Federal Republic of Germany, the capital scrap arising can be sold easier than in other countries. An extremely difficult market situation can be expected in industrial countries without an important steel industry.

SCRAP BALANCE FOR THE FEDERAL REPUBLIC OF GERMANY

Based on estimates of steel production and consumption figures, as well as forecasts on foreign trade in scrap, Battelle calculated the following scrap balance for 1980 in million tons:

Scrap demand		Scrap supply	
steelworks	21.4	circulating scrap	14.1
foundries	5.0	process scrap	6.7
blast-furnaces	0.6	imports	1.0
Total inland	27.0	demand for capital	21.8
exports	2.2	scrap	7.4
	29.2		29.2

As a result, the gap in the supply of circulating and process scrap which equals the demand for capital scrap makes up 7.4 million tons. The generation of light capital scrap in 1980 is estimated at 2.2 million tons, of which 1.5 million tons is scrap from discarded motor vehicles and the balance constitutes scrap from steel consumer durables. Thus, even taking into account a high share of heavy scrap—like shipyards, railroads and dismantled bridges—there seems to exist no quantitative problem in the light capital scrap market.

Since light capital scrap in the Federal Republic of Germany is mainly processed in shredders (twenty-two shredders are installed in the Federal Republic of Germany) the most serious quality problems have likewise been overcome.

Thus, the quantitative and qualitative aspects of scrap supply can be judged with confidence. But there is one question left: do the prices for capital scrap of shredder quality cover the transportation and processing costs?

The Battelle study gives comprehensive and detailed cost calculations for the different technical solutions for scrap processing. The costs are calculated by type (e.g., shredder) and capacity (tons per day, month, and year). The following cost components are considered separately; capital cost, personnel cost, energy cost, disposal costs for impurities, maintenance costs, overhead costs.

In 1973 the following costs were calculated: shreddings DM 54–DM 63 per ton, transportation costs (as a function of distance between place of generation, shredder location, and location of steelworks) from DM 55 to 150 per ton of scrap. Prepressing costs DM 8 per motor vehicle. Assuming an average price for shredder scrap of DM 170 (including income from nonferrous metals sales), up to DM 52 per ton of scrap (or DM 36 per motor car) is gained. On the other hand, losses up to DM 43 per ton of scrap (DM 29 per motor vehicle) have likewise been encountered. The losses only occurred in unfavorable places of generation. In periods of high scrap prices, such as 1974 when scrap prices went up to DM 225 per ton, gains were possible even in these unfavorable locations.

At present, all motor vehicles and most of the steel containing consumer durables are collected and processed to scrap owing to the large shredder capacity. Even in low price periods, collection is not interrupted, but the collected scrap is stored until prices go up.

CONCLUSIONS

From this short glance at the ferrous scrap situation in the Federal Republic of Germany, we can note that for economic and technical reasons the request for recycling in this field is satisfied to a high extent. Only when ferrous material is combined with other materials like concrete (construction industry) or has low metallurgical value due to impurities, does ferrous scrap recycling become uneconomical.

Increased proportions of coated and painted steel or composite material can reduce the prospects of scrap recycling. Efforts aimed at the construction of motor vehicles or other consumer durables suitable for recycling must, therefore, be regarded with interest. These activities should be supported by government R & D policy.

Also, government financed R & D activities aimed at sorting municipal solid waste—before collection by the household or after mechanical collection—may increase the share of ferrous metals which can be recycled. But this increase can only be marginal.

These statements are valid for the Federal Republic of Germany. As can be seen from this example, the following conditions seem to guarantee a high share of ferrous scrap recycling:

- an important iron and steel industry which use scrap intensive steel processes like electric furnaces
- a highly developed steel manufacturing industry
- a good organization of scrap collection and processing, that is, large scrap dealers
- a shredding capacity which yields high-quality scrap

When these conditions are supplemented by legislation which penalizes "littering," the environmental problem of ferrous scrap seems to have been solved, and the question of resource conservation can be answered in positive terms.

NOTES

1. Untersuchung über den derzeitigen Stand der Autowrackbeseitigung in der Bundesrepublik Deutschland.

2. According to a Battelle Study "Planungsgrundlagen für die Beseitigung von Autowracks und metallischem Sperrgut in Bayern" ("Basic Planning Data for the Disposal of Wrecked Cars and Bulky Goods in Bavaria").

CHAPTER 15

Alternative Institutional Approaches to Recycling Used Oil

William A. Irwin

One could not launch a program for used oil recycling without defining both *used oil* and *recycling*. A paper on the subject should begin by facing the same task. *Recycling* has at least two meanings and *used oil* can have many more than that. Recycling can mean reconditioning and re-use of a material or product for its original purpose, for example, a returnable bottle; or it can mean re-use of the material or product in a way that substitutes for the use of other material, for example, using broken one-way bottles to make glass wool. Perhaps one should not make too much of this distinction, and simply be content to define recycling as re-use of used products and raw materials, but economics often makes the difference between whether one or both is feasible. Used lubricating oils derived from petroleum can be recycled either by re-refining them into similar products or by re-using them for other purposes, for example, as a supplemental fuel, as a constituent in making asphalt, or as a road–dust-suppressant. Both kinds of recycling are discussed in this paper.

Defining *used oil* is difficult only because there are many kinds of oil. As with many definitions, the simpler a definition of used oil is, the more likely that it will make a program more difficult to administer. One must decide what to include and exclude. Here is a sample of existing definitions of used oil which have emerged from the give-and-take of legislative drafting:

1. "used mineral oils and used liquid mineral oil products as well as mineral oil-containing wastes from storage, business, and transportation receptacles" [1]
2. "used engine, machine, cooling, and similar waste oil" [2]
3. "any oil which has been refined from crude oil, has been used, and as a result of such use has been contaminated by physical or chemical impurities" [3]
4. "any semi-liquid or liquid used product totally or partially consisting of mineral or synthetic oil, including the oily residues from tanks, oil-water mixtures and emulsions" [4]
5. "a petroleum-based oil which through use, storage or handling has become unsuitable for its original purpose due to the presence of impurities or loss of original properties" [5]

This selection of definitions illustrates some of the basic choices in determining the scope of a program. Numbers 1, 3, and 5 specify a petroleum-based oil, thus excluding animal and vegetable oils; number 4 specifically includes synthetic oil. Numbers 1 and 4 include products but specify they must be liquid, thus excluding grease, asphalt, and so forth. Numbers 1 through 4 specify "used" oils, thus excluding refinery wastes. Number 4 includes emulsions; numbers 1, 4, and 5 include storage and transportation oil-containing wastes (but, for numbers 1 and 4, only if used). This paper is not limited to any one of these definitions, although Number 4 most closely defines its scope.

WASTE AND DAMAGE FROM IMPROPER USE OR DISPOSAL OF USED OIL

Failure to recycle used lubricating oils wastes a valuable fraction of crude oil and contributes to one or more kinds of damage to natural resources, depending on how they are otherwise used or disposed of. For a time certain oil industry representatives were concerned about shortages of lube oil fractions.[6] Now the predictions are less urgent,[7] but the fact remains that the supply is not inexhaustible.

Damage from incautious use or disposal varies, of course, with quantity, contaminants, and method of disposal.[8] If used oils are dumped in or near watercourses, they cause considerable biological oxygen demand,[9] adversely affect assimilative capacity,[10] are fatal or harmful to water-related biota,[11] and contribute oil and chemical constituents, some of them toxic or carcinogenic, which render the water unpleasant [12] or dangerous [13] to drink. These constituents are difficult and costly to remove from drinking water supplies. If used oils are dumped into drains or sewers, they foul sewerage and sewage treatment plants, increasing maintenance, reducing treatment plant efficiency (hence contributing to the discharge of other pollutants), and sometimes causing shutdowns.[14] Disposal on land may render the land itself unproductive [15] and contaminate ground water supplies.[16] Uncontrolled burning of untreated used oils, particularly automotive lubricants, causes emissions of heavy metal particulate, principally lead, and may foul the burning equipment.[17] In addition, burning may present risks of fire or explosion.[18]

KINDS OF USED OIL, BARRIERS TO RECYCLING THEM, AND TECHNICAL PROCESSES FOR PREPARING THEM FOR RECYCLING

The available figures differ among industrialized nations but, in general, about half the lubricants used are not consumed in use.[19] The breakdown between industrial and automotive lubricants in a particular nation depends on the kind and extent of industrialization and its automotive population, but used automotive oils average about 60 percent of the total.[20] Automotive lubricants can be treated as a category, but industrial lubricants should not be: the latter term comprises metal-working oils, hydraulic oils, gearbox oils, spindle oils, electrical oils,[21] and process oils used in tanning, making rubber and textiles, and so forth.

The chief barriers to recycling used automotive lubricants are that they are widely dispersed [22] (and thus often not collected) and frequently not segregated from other wastes. The dispersion makes them expensive to collect. The fact that they are not segregated means that, in addition to the chemical additives mixed with the oil at the time of manufacture, there is other foreign matter which is also expensive to remove.

Although the composition of used industrial lubricants depends on their use and extent of segregation, they are generally less dispersed than automotive oils and, therefore, more readily kept available for recycling or use in-plant as lower-grade lubricants. One large problem area in recycling industrial oils is emulsions.[23] These are stable suspensions of about 5 percent oil in water which serve to lubricate, cool, and cleanse in various metal-working operations such as milling, drilling, rolling, and drawing. Similar, although less stable and often higher in oil content, are the oily liquids which result from washing tanks. In order to recover these oils, the emulsions must be "broken" by a special process involving chemicals and sometimes heat. Central plants for this purpose are more efficient and effective but involve transportation and service costs individual plants are often unwilling to bear. Facilities at individual plants, however (if extant), have been found to perform poorly. As a result, emulsions and oil wash waters usually end up as waste waters.[24]

The technical processes for treating used industrial oils so they can be recycled vary with the kind of oil involved.[25] For used automotive lubricants as a category, however, there is a standard re-refining theme with variations. First, the sediment is allowed to settle, then the oil is decanted and heated under pressure to evaporate the water and vola-tile components. Then the oil is treated with sulfuric acid, which precipitates the impurities. The acid sludge is drained off, and the oil then steamed, mixed with decoloring clay, and filtered. The result-ing "base stock" oil then may be blended with virgin oil and whatever additives are needed to bring it to the desired lubricant specifications. One variation is to substitute centrifuging and vacuum distillation for the acid treatment stage; instead of acid sludge, this method re-sults in a high-ash fuel as a by-product. Another variation is to intro-duce propane into the oil before the acid treatment stage; the oil dis-solves in the propane, the solution is extracted from the impurities, and the oil then separated from the propane. Then the oil is subjected to the acid and clay treatment stages, but only about half as much acid and clay is needed. There are variations being developed which would treat vacuum-distilled oil with hydrogen (instead of clay); the by-product is sufficiently high in lead content to be useful in lead smelting.[26]

These re-refining technologies are to be distinguished from "re-processing," that is, comparatively inexpensive treatment of used oil by settling, heating, and/or filtering to remove water, volatiles, and sediment only. Reprocessing does not remove metallic and chemical components of used oils. Reprocessed used oil is usually used as a fuel supplement.[27]

One of the by-products produced by the standard re-refining method

—acid sludge—is difficult to dispose of. It is dangerous to handle and contains materials which require a landfill suitable for hazardous wastes. It should preferably be neutralized before being disposed of. Hazardous waste disposal sites are scarce, however, and neutralization is expensive. These facts constitute a barrier to recycling via re-refining, at least for the predominant technology.[28]

IMPACT OF THE OIL EMBARGO ON HOW USED OIL IS RECYCLED

Efforts to collect and recycle used oil increased significantly after the 1973–74 oil embargo. Prices of products made from virgin oil rose. As a result, it became worthwhile for people to drive further to collect used oil and even to pay to get it. (Previously, most sources of used oil, such as service stations, had to pay collectors to take it.[29]) Since prices for virgin fuel oils had increased more sharply than for lubricating oils, in general fuel oil dealers could offer collectors more for their used oil than could re-refiners. (In addition to the smaller increases in prices for lubricating oils, re-refiners' process costs are higher than fuel oil dealers', thus leaving re-refiners less able to offer collectors prices for used oil which are competitive with those offered by fuel oil dealers.) As a result, the increase in used-oil recycling via use as a supplemental fuel has been greater than re-refining.[30] Some re-refiners have made efforts to assure a continuous supply of used oil (necessary to conducting their operations as nearly at full capacity and efficiency as possible) by purchasing their own collection trucks, rather than relying on independent collectors. But the competition is intense and sometimes unscrupulous. For example, one re-refiner in Florida sought to increase his supplies by placing collection tanks at shopping centers, only to find that "gypsy" collectors cut off the locks at night, pumped out the oil, and then drove up to his plant to sell it to him. Standard Oil of Ohio also had problems of theft by scavengers from its service stations in the Cincinnati area. In the face of an unfavorable market position vis-à-vis fuel oil dealers, compounded by unfair tactics such as these, some re-refiners have decided to convert their plants to be able to reprocess more used oil for sale as fuel rather than re-refine it.[31]

ALTERNATIVE MEANS FOR ACHIEVING USED-OIL RECYCLING POLICY GOALS *

Over the years several different approaches have been instituted to promote used-oil recycling. There are several policy objectives which these approaches are designed to achieve, usually concomitantly. Particularly since 1974, nations which consume more oil than they produce have sought more self-sufficiency. Recycling can help reduce demand for oil imports and concomitantly hold down balance of payments deficits.[32] Some countries wish to encourage recycling in order to protect the jobs and capital investment involved in the re-refining industry particularly. They also wish to support the industry because re-refineries can produce certain special products more readily and other products more cheaply than major refineries. Finally, prevention of water, soil, and air pollution from improper disposal has become an increasingly important objective.[33]

European Approaches to Used-Oil Recycling Developed Prior to the 1975 EEC Directive on Used Oil

Because they are more vulnerable to shortages of oil, because they have less capacity to absorb the environmental impacts of improper used-oil disposal and because the high price of oil products encouraged the early development of a tradition of recycling, some European nations took steps to promote collection and re-use of used oil before other industrialized nations faced the problems involved.

Italy, for example, exempts products made from used oil from 75 percent of the tax levied on those made from new oil. If a company authorized to re-refine its own oil meets certain standards for the product, even the remaining 25 percent of the tax is waived.[34] Similarly, as a matter of tax law (rather than recycling policy), France does not apply its excise tax on oil to products made from used oil. The effect is the same as in Italy, though to a lesser degree:

---

* Other helpful sources of information on this topic are D. Pearce, "The Recovery of Waste Lubrication Oil: A Comparative National Analysis," *Resources Policy,* June 1975, pp. 213–29, and *Collection and Re-use of Waste Oils,* published by the Commission of the European Communities, Directorate-General "Scientific and Technical Information and Information Management," Luxembourg, September 1976, EUR 5625 d–e–f–i, pp. 213–307.

the indirect subsidy enables recyclers to sell their products at lower prices than comparable ones produced by new oil refineries. In France there is also an order, issued in November 1956 by the Secretary of State for Industry and Commerce, which states that used oils are destined for re-refining and for no other use. This order appears to have been provoked by the Suez crisis, forgotten for nearly twenty years, then rediscovered after 1973. Since then it has been characterized both as applicable law and as null and of no practical effect.[35]

In Denmark local governments must establish used-oil collection facilities. All persons have an obligation not to cause pollution by storing, transporting, or disposing of used oil, and all except businesses which generate more than 300 liters a year may take used oil to municipal collection facilities free of charge. A business which generates more than 300 liters of used oil must inform the municipal council about kinds and amounts and must deposit it at a municipal collection facility (for a fee based on rates which would cover costs of operating the facility) unless the business can demonstrate it is taking proper care of it on its own.[36]

West Germany, after encouraging re-refining by tax preferences and subsidies for twenty years, enacted a comprehensive, self-supporting national system in 1968. That system is fairly easy to summarize.[37] All who import or produce certain lubricating oils (including re-refiners) in Germany pay a compensation fee of 9 Deutsche Mark (about \$3.60) per 100 kilograms of product to the federal government in addition to the tax on mineral oils. This money goes into a special fund reserved for the support of the disposal of used oils by controlled burning or recycling, the two ways deemed safe from environmental and public health viewpoints. The fund also supports the administrative expenses of the Federal Office.

Recycling and burning enterprises under contract with the Federal Office for Trade and Industry are entitled to apply for payments to cover the costs of collection, transportation, and disposal not otherwise covered, for example, by selling the re-refined products. Payments are made at standard rates, 10 DM for each 100 kilograms of used oil which is re-refined into lubricating oils, 10 DM for oil products other than lubricants, and 10 DM for each 100 kilograms incinerated. (Re-refiners received more in earlier years but now receive less because their uncovered costs are less.) It is assumed that re-refining yields 70 percent of the used oil by weight, so the re-refiners' payments are made on the basis of figures for the weight of a month's re-refined products in the application. Incinerators are paid on the basis of how much of what they burn is oil. The Federal Office's lab analyzes the contents of special drip devices on a monthly basis, and the proportion of the sample which is oil is the basis for figuring the weight of oil burned, for which payments can be made. ·

The obligations imposed on the disposal firms by their contracts are many. They must: (1) pick up all amounts of used oils over 200 liters in the district assigned to them; (2) do so at no charge to the user unless the oils contain more than 10 percent foreign matter; (3) provide suitable containers for lesser amounts so they can be collected later; (4) keep records of their costs and make their books and other relevant information available to the Federal Office, or to the auditors it appoints; (5) file their application for payments monthly; (6) maintain equipment specified by the Federal Office for purposes of checking their output (the special drip devices mentioned above); (7) give notice of any re-refined products shipped to other member nations of the European Economic Community and repay any payments received for producing these products (this requirement was imposed by the EEC to avoid favoring German re-refiners in violation of the Treaty of Rome); (8) give receipts for used oils collected which contain more than 10 percent foreign matter.

Those who generate or pick up more than 500 liters of used oils containing more than 10 percent of foreign matter (which is not picked up for free) must also keep records on kind, amount, and disposal of the oil, so that it is possible to trace the chain of disposal from a source through collection to final disposition.

Since only lubricating oils subject to the mineral oil tax are also subject to the disposal fund compensation fee, the paperwork, procedures, and personnel for levying the fee are integrated almost completely with the payment of the mineral oil tax. This results in substantial savings of administrative costs.

The 1975 EEC Directive on the Disposal of Waste Oils

Several elements of the West German system influenced the contents of the Directive on the disposal of waste oils issued by the Council of the European Communities in June 1975.[38] The directive requires the nine member nations to implement measures within two years which will ensure: (1) safe collection and disposal of used oil; (2) disposal by means of regeneration or combustion other than for destruction; and (3) prohibitions of discharges of used oil into surface waters, ground water, coastal waters, and drainage systems, of deposits harmful to soil, of uncontrolled discharges of residues from processing used oil, and of processing of used oil by means which cause illegal air pollution. To assure that these prohibitions are obeyed, within four years the member nations are to issue permits to any undertaking which disposes of used oil and to impose conditions required by "the state of technical development." Authorized disposers of used oil must conduct their operations so as to prevent unavoidable risk of water, air, or soil pollution, as must those who collect it (although collectors need not be licensed). The member nation authorities are obligated to inspect the facilities for compliance periodically.

Any person holding used oil who cannot comply with the measures providing for these prohibitions must give his used oil to a disposer who holds a permit. Holders of certain quantities of used oil containing more than a percentage of impurities specified by national authorities must segregate them.

Those who generate, collect, or dispose of more than 500 liters of used oil a year must keep records of its quantity, quality, origin, location, and dispatch and receipt or provide this information to the authorities when they request. Disposers must provide information when requested about where used oils or used-oil processing residues are disposed of.

If safe collection, disposal, regeneration, or combustion, and the prohibitions mentioned above cannot be realized without government intervention, the member nations are to take the steps necessary to ensure collection and disposal, perhaps by assigning enterprises to certain zones. The uncovered costs of rendering this service, plus a reasonable profit, may be paid to the enterprises as indemnities. The indemnities must be financed within the member nations in accordance with the "polluter pays" principle, perhaps by charges imposed on used oil or on products which cause or become used oil.

The implementation of the Council Directive will be an interesting case study of the effectiveness of EEC efforts to harmonize member nations' laws in order to reduce "unequal conditions of competition" and to achieve "one of the aims of the Community in the sphere of

protection of the environment." [39] There are many issues of interpretation and enforcement, including whether the measures taken
may reasonably be expected to ensure recycling "as far as possible"
or to ensure compliance with the required prohibitions, as well as
whether the financing of indemnities is "in accordance with 'polluter
pays' principle" and whether the amount of the indemnities does "not
cause any significant distortion of competition or . . . give rise to
artificial patterns of trade in the products."

Response of Some Member Nations to the EEC Directive
Although not all member nations have fully developed their plans
for implementing the EEC Directive, what can be learned about proposed legislation in some of them indicates interesting patterns and
variations in approaching the problems posed by used-oil collection
and recycling.

The Netherlands enacted a law concerning chemical wastes in
February 1976 with provisions applicable to used oil which closely
parallel the EEC Directive. A person may not transfer used oils to
one not licensed to collect them or to "store, treat, process, or destroy"
them. Both the transferer and transferee must notify the Minister of
Health and Environmental Hygiene of the names and addresses of
parties involved, date, nature, and amount of oils and place and
means of delivery involved in each transaction. Licensed collectors
will be limited to one of approximately fifteen designated zones (which
together will cover the country) and must collect amounts of oil
above a certain minimum without charge in this zone unless a license
specifically authorizes charging for collection in accordance with
authorized rates. (The zones may overlap to encourage competition
among collectors.) The government plans to limit licensed recyclers
or disposers to a number which will assure an efficient balance with
the number of collectors. That is, no more recyclers or disposers will
be licensed than are needed to handle what the collectors collect. The
collector's license may designate a recycler or disposer to whom he is
required to deliver what is collected, in order to assure the recycler a
sufficient supply. Similarly, a recycler's license will designate the
zones or collectors from which he must accept used oil. Thus, the
system is designed to harmonize supply and demand of used oils on a
national basis. The law provides for reasonable indemnities for a
licensee who must bear unreasonable costs or losses he would not

otherwise be compensated for as a result of a decision by the government about the license. These indemnities and other costs entailed in the implementation of measures adopted in the interest of effective disposal of used oil will be financed by an "oil penny" levied on persons who import, manufacture, use, sell, or deliver lubricating and insulating oils, based on the quantity and nature of oils involved. A Used Oil Policy Advisory Committee, made up of not more than eleven members who produce, sell, use, or dispose of these oils, will assist the Minister in implementing this law. The Committee would presumably be useful in advising the Minister on the use of his authority to make exemptions from the general prohibition on depositing used oil in or on the soil (whether or not in containers) if necessary in the interest of effective disposal of used oil and if not in conflict with the interest of protection of the environment.[40]

As of July 1976, the government of the Netherlands had not announced whether it would continue to prefer that used oil be reprocessed for use as a fuel or whether it would initiate a policy of granting indemnities to support the extra costs of re-refining.

In Italy there are tentative plans for an interministerial committee on used oils (with representation from interested parties, too) which, among other duties, would establish payments to sources and re-refiners of used oil (and means for financing the payments) and authorize private and public companies to collect and use used oils. The legislation creating the committee would require sources to segregate their oil according to class of usage. Collectors and users of used oil would be assigned exclusive zones for their operation, that is, collectors would collect and users receive all used oil in a zone, but neither could operate outside it. Ultimately a user would have to locate his plant in his exclusive zone (presumably to reduce the costs and risks of transportation), but in transition stages he would participate in assigning used oils to their destination. Collectors would be permitted to operate incinerators as well.

France, too, reportedly plans to subdivide its territory into collection zones and contract for a three-year term of collection of all used oil in a zone. (In France the licensed collector could subcontract 70 percent of his work, in Italy 50 percent.) Collectors would sell their oil (at a price set by an interministerial committee composed similar to Italy's) to a publicly controlled national company authorized by the Ministry of Industry for five years to sell at fixed prices (and transport) used oils to those authorized by the committee to re-refine, heat with, or incinerate used oils. Re-refiners would receive quantities fixed annually by the committee and would bid to receive any eventual surplus quantities. One would be prohibited from burning his own used oil; only licensed persons would heat with used oil or incinerate nonrecyclable oil.[41]

In July 1976, England's Department of the Environment issued one of its waste management paper series entitled "Mineral oil wastes: A Technical Memorandum on Arisings, Treatment, and Disposal including a Code of Practice." [42] The Code of Practice for Mineral Oil Wastes is advisory only and intended for adaptation to local circumstances. Among other things, it advises that "the economics of collection could be improved by the provision of reception points at Civic Amenity Sites and of joint storage facilities for example on industrial trading estates." The Code also recommends co-operation between government waste disposal agencies, used-oil generators, and used-oil recovery firms to enhance "the efficiency of oil recovery operations." It also discourages the burning of used oils in small burners: "Waste of lower oil content may also be burned as supplementary fuel in suitably equipped installations. In the combustion of the waste, account should be taken of any contaminants present which could give rise to objectionable emissions and possible health hazards. . . . [S]pecifically, spent motor oils contain lead, a dangerous cumulative poison, and the control of emissions from combustion of spent motor oils requires careful consideration. . . ." [43]

The German Ministry of Economics has proposed several amendments to the 1968 law which are of particular interest because they in part constitute suggested improvements of the system that served as a model for the EEC Directive, based on experience with that system.[44]

The Ministry seeks authority to reduce the size of a collector's mandatory pick-up districts from that established in his contract. Its checking of firms' costs shows that collection and transportation costs are lowest for enterprises which collect within a radius of 100 kilometers. Many firms have contractually fixed districts much larger than this and seek compensation for the costs of collection from, in one instance, as large an area as the entire nation. The Ministry's viewpoint is that higher than normal collection costs must be offset by savings in process costs due to increased use of capacity, not by higher compensation from the fund. To this the association of German re-refiners argues that the thrust of the Ministry's proposal would result in a national plan for optimal collection and disposal which would require monthly revision based on individual plant capacity, location, collection costs, process costs, and amounts of used oil generated in the area—a result they argue neither the Parliament nor the Ministry (nor, for that matter, the re-refining industry) wants.

In this connection, the Ministry has also proposed that the firms make available on demand information concerning costs of disposal and profits or other receipts. They request this authority because the firms have not made available to federal accountants all their profit and loss figures, particularly those concerning collection costs, which the Ministry argues are inflated because the firms travel too far outside their districts, forego fees they are entitled to for collection of oil with more than 10 percent contamination, and make extralegal payments to those having clean used oil.

The Ministry also proposes to eliminate the requirement that the federal government be reimbursed for compensation paid for re-refined products exported to other EEC member nations, if the other nation has provisions authorizing payment of indemnities in accordance with Article 13 of the Council Directive. If France compensates re-refiners, for example, then there would no longer be any reason for a German re-refiner to refuse compensation on the grounds he would be distorting competition within the Market.

The Ministry has also proposed that only recyclers with contractually fixed districts for mandatory pick-up of used oil serve as collectors. Independent collectors would only be entitled to operate if their services were contracted for by the government. These contracts would require a collector to allow government accounting of collection and transportation costs and to keep records on the source, kind, amount, storage, and disposal of collected oils.

In the summer of 1976, Germany amended its waste disposal law by adding provisions governing so-called special (i.e., hazardous) wastes.[45] In order to prevent people from avoiding these controls by mixing their special wastes with used oils which would be picked up in accordance with the Used Oil Law, the Ministry proposes limiting the definition of used oils which would be picked up for free to those containing not more than 15 percent *use-related* foreign matter. Those with more than 15 percent would have to be stored separately (as required by the Directive) in accordance with regulations issued by *Länder* officials. Used oils containing foreign matter unrelated to use would be handled in accordance with regulations governing wastes or special wastes, depending on the nature of the foreign matter. These proposed amendments lend urgency to the need for Ministry regulations authorized by the law which would prescribe means for determining proportions of foreign matter in used oil.

Three further amendments are designed to improve supervision of used oil generation, collection, and disposal. One—designed to implement Article 10 of the EEC Directive—would authorize *Länder* officials to require all those possessing used oil to provide information about its source, kind, amount, storage, and disposal, not just commercial enterprises. Another would require all commercial or public enterprises which generate or collect used oil to give notice to officials of these activities, in order that the officials would know who should be keeping records rather than having to determine this by investigation. A third would require recyclers of used oil to provide information on request about the source, kind, amount, storage, and disposal of oils they receive.

Finally, the Ministry's proposals are noteworthy for an amendment they do not include, one which might have read "One who sells new oil shall accept the return of used oil." Several members of Parliament had suggested a law, designed to prevent improper disposal of used oil by those who change their own oil, which would require that sales or changes of oil could only be made at service stations or repair shops. The Ministry had resisted this, on the grounds that it would be unenforceable and would lead to the disappearance of cheaper lubricating oils from the market. Armed with the threat of such legislation, Ministry officials called in representatives of those who sell oil and other interested parties to work out a voluntary program for providing convenient disposal opportunities to those who change their own oil. The results vindicated the Ministry's belief that legal requirements cannot substitute for voluntary initiatives taken by those directly responsible for the realization of a solution. The national association of retailers committed itself to providing everyone who purchases oil for purposes of performing his own oil changes a place to take his oil, if possible at the place of sale. Where not possible via retailers themselves, places would be arranged with municipalities, service stations, and repair shops. The retailers would inform their customers of the disposal opportunities available. For their part, municipalities intensified their efforts to provide public collection facilities. Major oil companies offered to make available at service stations a new device for oil collection at no cost even to persons not requesting service; unfortunately this offer has only been realized in a few instances. The success of these efforts was considerably facilitated by the efforts of the media and automobile clubs to provide information about the problems caused by improper disposal of self-changed oil and the possibilities for proper disposal.[46]

Used-Oil Recycling in the United States

In the United States, until quite recently, national policy concerning used-oil recycling has not developed as it had in Europe, in part because neither the energy conservation nor the environmental justifications for recycling seemed sufficiently important to policy makers and in part because of persistent doubts about the quality of re-refined products.[47]

A principal barrier to recycling (specifically, re-refining) is an interpretation of the 1965 federal Excise Tax Reduction Act. Section 6424 of the Internal Revenue Code provides for a six-cent per gallon excise tax rebate on virgin lubricating oils "used otherwise than in a highway motor vehicle." But a Department of Treasury ruling denies the rebate to re-refiners who use virgin oil for blending with re-refined base stocks on the grounds that their use of it for blending was not one "through which the oil is consumed or rendered unfit for further use as a lubricant"—a distinction without basis in the legislative history of the act. The ruling also denied the rebate to purchasers of blended virgin and re-refined oil on the virgin portion of the oil on the grounds that it was no longer virgin, having been used for blending. The effect of this ruling is to make the cost of recycled oil used for "off-highway" purposes more than that of virgin oils sold for these purposes.[48] A provision which would have alleviated this problem by exempting virgin oils purchased for blending with re-refined oil from excise taxes was passed by the House of Representatives but not included in the Conference Committee version of the tax reform act which was reported for approval by the House and Senate in mid-September 1976 and subsequently enacted.[49]

At about the same time as the Treasury Department ruling, the Federal Trade Commission adopted a trade regulation rule requiring lubricating oil products made from used oil to be clearly advertised and labeled as "previously used." This was done on the basis of a commission finding that consumers prefer virgin lubricating oils, that they assume they are buying such products unless they are otherwise labeled, and therefore that it is an unfair method of competition and a deceptive trade practice to fail to label them as previously used. Although the text of the commission's rule says that neither the value of the recycling industry's service (in providing proper disposal of used oil) nor the equality of its products with virgin oil products were "germane" to its decision, subsequent statements by Commission Chairman Kirkpatrick indicate a commission belief, based on some defense agency research, that the reliability of performance characteristics (such as durability) of re-refined motor oils is questionable, because of "the unknown origin of the waste oil," and cannot be determined without performance testing.[50] The FTC is not inclined to alter its rule until "valid, impartial scientific tests" are available to demonstrate the equivalence of rerefined and virgin oil products.[51] For this reason the Congress enacted a provision in December 1975 requiring the National Bureau of Standards, "as soon as practicable," to "develop test procedures for the determination of substantial equivalency of re-refined or otherwise processed used oil or blend of oil . . . with new oil for a particular end use" and to report the procedures to the commission.[52] There is considerable doubt whether this assignment can result in simple, inexpensive tests, particularly since the major oil companies have been trying unsuccessfully to develop simple quality tests for decades, but if and when the NBS reports to the FTC,[53] the FTC is required to prescribe labeling standards within ninety days which "permit any container of recycled oil to bear a label indicating any particular end use for which a determination of substantial equivalency has been made" in accordance with test procedures the FTC adopts by rule on the basis of the NBS report.[54] Within the same period, the Environmental Protection Agency is required to adopt standards for labeling of *all* containers of oil "relating to the proper disposal of such oils after use . . . [which] shall be designed to reduce, to the maximum extent practicable, environmental hazards and wasteful practices associated with the disposal of such oils after use." [55]

Once the FTC rules governing labeling of recycled oil go into effect, they pre-empt any inconsistent rule of the commission or state or local law.[56] In addition, all federal officials "shall act within their authority" to revise procurement policies "to encourage procurement of recycled oil for military and nonmilitary Federal uses" whenever it is available at prices competitive with new oil for the same end-use. (Some military procurement specifications prohibit the purchase of products containing recycled oil.) Further, all federal officials are also supposed to educate persons in both the public and private sectors on "the merits of recycled oil, the need for its use in order to reduce the drain on the Nation's oil reserves, and proper disposal of used oil to avoid waste of such oil and to minimize environmental hazards associated with improper disposal." [57]

In anticipation of this public education assignment (and in response to several dozen inquiries from congressmen in early 1975 about the agency's policy), the Federal Energy Administration prepared a short "fact sheet" about used oil, and sponsored the preparation of a handbook to guide persons wishing to organize voluntary collection and recycling efforts at the local level,[58] and a model bill for state and local legislatures to consider in developing used oil recycling legislation.[59] The model bill states as its policy that "used oil shall be collected and recycled to the maximum extent possible, by means which are economically feasible and environmentally sound." It defines *recycle* as "to prepare for reuse as a petroleum product . . . or to use in a manner that substitutes for a petroleum product made from new oil." The bill would require a government agency to issue rules which "prescribe means for the provision of safe and conveniently located collection facilities for the deposit of used oil by persons possessing not more than 5 gallons at one time at no cost." Rules would also require sellers of lubricating oils to post signs telling customers where such collection facilities are. The agency would also have to conduct a public education program and a licensing program. The former would involve assigning a person to inform people about the law and where to dispose of used oil and to encourage and assist the development of voluntary local recycling programs. The licensing program is designed to direct the flow of used oil via approved collectors only to approved recyclers or disposers. (A person who disposes of more than a certain amount of used oil by means other than recycling, e.g., road oiling, incineration, or landfilling, would have to obtain a special permit instead of a license.) In deciding whether or not to grant an application for a license or special permit, the agency would have to determine "that the proposed means for collection, transport, transfer, storage, recycling, use, or disposal is operationally sound and consistent with the policy of this Act" and would have to "impose terms . . . necessary to insure continuous compliance with existing laws and regulations." Licensed collectors and recyclers would leave receipts and keep records of their transactions and submit annual reports to the agency, in order that the agency would be able to monitor and eventually manage used oil flows. The agency would also provide an annual report to the legislature on the law's effectiveness. The model bill would authorize recycled oil products to be represented as substantially equivalent to new oil products if they meet new oil product specifications (or have been determined to be so under FTC rules) and would require government officials to encourage the purchase of substantially equivalent recycled oil products. Finally, the bill prohibits disposal of used oil by discharge to sewers, surface or ground waters, or marine waters, and by incineration or land deposit unless in accordance with a special permit.

Many controls similar to those suggested in the model bill will become federal law if used oil is included in the list of hazardous wastes EPA must promulgate by April 1978 in accordance with the Resource Conservation and Recovery Act of 1976.

CONCLUSION

The model used–oil-recycling act did not include provisions for tax incentives or subsidies for used-oil collection or recycling because the bill was designed for consideration by any jurisdiction, and it cannot be decided a priori for any jurisdiction what level of collection and what kinds of recycling are worth public financial support. One must know at least generally the particular circumstances of a jurisdiction —kinds and amounts of used oils generated and collected, and current means of recycling or disposal, and nature and extent of damages or risks to public or environmental health or other resources—before adopting a program of public control or support or both.

As is frequently the case, a principal problem in evaluating what approach to adopt for used oil is that the costs of the alternative approaches are much more susceptible to careful estimation than either the effectiveness of the approaches or the benefits to be achieved. It is more feasible—though difficult enough—to project the quantities and value of oil saved by one degree or kind of recycling or another than it is to predict the environmental and health damages avoided. The difficulty of this prediction is compounded because of the toxic components of used oil: lead and carcinogens such as polycyclic aromatic hydrocarbons, benzpyrenes, benzathracenes, and dibenzanthrazenes.

In the United States, policy toward lead has been formulated under the Clean Air Act. On the basis of determining that automotive emissions of the lead in gasoline present a "significant risk of harm to public health," the Environmental Protection Agency promulgated regulations providing for the phased reduction of lead content in gasoline. When the regulations were challenged, the Court of Appeals upheld them, saying that the language of the statute "is precautionary and does not require proof of actual harm before regulation is appropriate." [60] The Court observed that "public health may properly be found endangered by a lesser risk of a greater harm and by a greater risk of a lesser harm," although it cautioned that "even the absolute certainty of *de minimis* harm might not justify government action." [61]

The regulatory approach to controlling carcinogens has been even more stringent and likewise withstood judicial review. The Environmental Protection Agency has canceled the registration and use of some pesticides on the scientifically defensible, though debatable, grounds that the substance has caused cancer in animals and, therefore, is a "no-threshold" substance, that is, may cause cancer in humans at any level of exposure above zero.[62]

In promulgating standards governing emissions of vinyl chlorides, also shown to cause cancer, however, the EPA did not impose a zero emission limit, even though section 112 of the Clean Air Act calls for hazardous air pollutant standards to protect public health "allowing an ample margin of safety." Its reasoning was

> In view of the beneficial uses of vinyl chloride products for which desirable substitutes are not readily available, the potentially adverse health and environmental impacts from substitutes which have not been thoroughly studied, the number of employees, particularly in fabrication industries, who would become at least temporarily unemployed, and the availability of control technology which is capable of substantially reducing emissions of vinyl chloride into the atmosphere, EPA concluded

that setting zero emission limits would be neither desirable nor necessary.

An alternative interpretation of section 112 is that it authorizes setting emission standards that require emission reduction to the lowest level achievable by use of the best available control technology in cases involving apparent nonthreshold pollutants, where complete emission prohibition would result in widespread industry closure and EPA has determined that the cost of such closure would be grossly disproportionate to the benefits of removing the risk that would remain after imposition of the best available control technology. EPA recognizes that consideration of technology in standard setting is not explicitly provided for under section 112. Congress never discussed the particular problem associated with apparent nonthreshold pollutants. EPA, however, believes that Congress did not intend to impose the costs associated with complete emission prohibition in every case involving such a pollutant.[63]

Thus, although EPA is legally required by the Clean Air Act to ignore technical feasibility and costs in setting standards which protect public health with an adequate margin of safety [64] and may prohibit at great cost activities which present significant risks to public health, it has chosen not to do so after balancing the benefits to health against the costs to other aspects of the public interest. The trend in the United States Congress as evidenced, in the more recent Safe Drinking Water Act, the amendments to the federal Insecticide, Fungicide, and Rodenticide Act, and the recently enacted Toxic Substances Control Act, is to require consideration of technical feasibility and economic costs in regulating to protect public health.

This pragmatic approach is also reflected in the principles established by the German *Altölgesetz* and the Council of the European Communities 1975 Directive. Based neither on a rigorous cost-benefit analysis nor on an unreasonable effort to protect public and environmental health from all possible risks, these principles seek a gradual maximization of resource conservation and a gradual minimization of environmental damages. They place the financial burden of support for used-oil collection and recycling on the shoulders of those responsible for creating the problems that necessitate the programs— those who use the oil. They provide for record-keeping which not only facilitates compliance with and supervision of the system but also generates information about its operations and effects which is essential to determining what adjustments are needed to make it more efficient and effective. These principles, with appropriate adaptation based on the peculiar characteristics of different resources and their patterns of use, can be applied to the management of other recyclable materials or products.[65]

Within the limits of the EEC Directive, each member nation is free to decide both what balance it wishes to achieve between conservation of resources and protection of health and the environment—based on its own consideration of fairness, efficiency, political opportunity, and responsibility, and perhaps even common sense—and what mixture of public and private institutional means it wishes to employ. Whatever the details of the system adopted, there will be a need for reforms and refinements based on the experience of implementing it. This has been true for Germany, as discussed, and the plans of other nations indicate an awareness of this experience. It makes little economic sense for an uncontrolled number of recyclers to compete to collect a limited amount of used oil or for even a limited number to go to great lengths or pay significant amounts to do so. Germany's proposed answer to this problem (which problem is analogous to exploitation of fisheries and other common property resources) is to limit the size of the areas in which collection is mandatory and to limit the number of collectors, both in an effort to discourage escalation of costs due to longer trips and payments made for good-quality used oil (and fees foregone for collecting poor-quality oils) by existing collectors. (The availability of a fund to cover all uncovered costs accrued encourages all recyclers to expend more resources collecting used oil than if there were no reimbursement for these costs.) France and the Netherlands have a more far-reaching answer—to limit entry into both the collection and recycling businesses and to regulate their conditions of operation, especially their sources of supply and outlets of used oil. (There are models to follow in establishing the areas in which used-oil collection and recycling are conducted to an extent consonant with an efficient allocation of resources,[66] but ultimately the size depends on particular circumstances.) Other nations also plan to institutionalize inputs to the formulation and administration of used–oil-recycling policies more formally than Germany has so far chosen to do, but whether these advisory committees will be more help than hindrance remains to be seen. The German experience has also shown that it is necessary to require the segregation of used oils from other wastes, both to avoid difficult or costly problems for recyclers and to prevent inappropriate disposal of toxic wastes.

NOTES

1. § 3(2), Gesetz über Massnahmen zur Sicherung der Altölbeseitigung (Altölgesetz) vom 23. Dezember 1968, Bundesgesetzbl. I, S. 1419 (Federal Republic of Germany).

2. § 104(m)(1)(A), Federal Water Pollution Control Act Amendments of 1972, P.L. 92–500, 33 U.S.C. 1254(m)(1)(A) (United States).

3. § 383(b)(1), Energy Policy and Conservation Act, P.L. 94–163, 42 U.S.C. 6363(b)(1) (United States).

4. Article 1, Council Directive of 16 June 1975 on the disposal of waste oils (75/439/EEC), Official Journal of the European Communities No. L 194/23.

5. § 2(2), A Model Used Oil Recycling Act, by William A. Irwin (available from Environmental Law Institute, 1346 Connecticut Avenue, N.W., Washington, D.C. 20036).

6. David W. Twomey, "The Source and Supply of Virgin Lubes" in *Waste Oil Recovery and Reuse*, Proceedings of the International Conference on Waste Oil Recovery and Reuse, February 12–14, 1974 (available from Information Transfer, Inc., 1625 Eye Street, N.W., Washington, D.C. 20006).

7. Thor S. Johnson, "World Lube Oil Outlook," in *Waste Oil. Headache or Resource?* Proceedings of the Second International Conference of Waste Oil Recovery and Reuse, February 24–26, 1975 (available from the Association of Petroleum Re-refiners, 1730 Pennsylvania Avenue, N.W., Washington, D.C. 20006), at page 13. *See also,* Moore, "Recycled Oil: More Respectability But Less Urgency," *Oil Daily,* September 16, 1976, at page 9.

8. John A. Jaksch, "The Waste Oil Industry: A Discussion of Some Issues to Consider in Performing an Economic Analysis" in *Waste Oil Recovery and Reuse, supra,* note 6, at page 398.

9. J. J. Hopmans, *The Problem of the Processing of Spent Oil in the Member States of the European Community* (ENV/3/74–E), The Hague, March 1974, Appendix III. One kilogram of used oil exerts the same BOD_5 as the sewage from forty persons.

10. *Id.,* at page 5 and Appendix VI, pages 3–7.

11. Environmental Protection Agency, *Report to Congress: Waste Oil Study,* April 1974, Section VIII, "The Effects of Waste Crankcase Oil on Selected Marine and Freshwater Organisms," pages 74–77; Sonia P. Maltezou, *Waste Oil Recycling: The New York Metropolitan Area Case,* March 1976 (available from the Council on the Environment of New York City, 51 Chambers Street, New York, New York 10007), at pages 31–32.

12. Hopmans, *supra,* note 9, at page 6, ("[T]he prevailing view assumes that oil concentrations of 1-2 mg/l in drinking water . . . make it unpalatable to a large section of the population."), and Appendix IV.

13. Irwin and Liroff, *Used Oil Law in the United States and Europe,* EPA–600/5–74–025 (July 1974) (available from the Superintendent of Documents, U.S. Government Printing Office, Washington, D.C. 20402), at 16–20; Hopmans, *supra,* note 9, at page 2 and Appendix VI; W. Zimmermann, *Pollution of Water and Soil by Miscellaneous Petroleum Products* (General Report No. 2, International Water Supply Congress and Exhibition, Stockholm, June 1–19, 1964, published by the International Water Supply Association, 34, Park Street, London, England) at pages B53–54: ". . . Statistical data show that adults drinking purified surface water [from the Rhine and Lake Constance] take with the drinking water between 0.1 and 1 mg. carcinogene hydrocarbons per year. . . ."

14. Maltezou, *supra,* note 11, at page 34.

15. Zimmermann, *supra,* note 13, at pages B38–54.

16. Maltezou, *supra,* note 11, at page 32.

17. *Id.,* at pages 20–29.

18. Hopmans, *supra,* note 9, at pages 21–22. For a more complete discussion of potential environmental and public health damages from improper use or disposal of used oil, *see* Chapter 3 of Maltezou, *supra,* note 11.

19. Hopmans, *supra,* note 9, at page 8 (Table 1); Environmental Protection Agency, *supra,* note 11, at page 4.

20. Hopmans, *supra,* note 9, at page 12 (Table 3); Environmental Protection Agency, *supra,* note 11, at page 11 (Table 5).

21. These include turbine oils and transformer insulating oils. The latter contain polychlorinated biphenyls and trichlorobenzene; these are persistent toxic chemicals which require special disposal.

22. Disperson is increasing as more oil is sold to individuals by retail stores for "do-it-yourself" oil changes.

23. Hopmans, *supra,* note 9, at page 14 refers to recycling of emulsions and disposal of rerefining byproducts, discussed below at note 28, as "the Achilles heel of the spent oil problem." Another large problem is that industrial oils are often not segregated from other wastes, many of which are hazardous or toxic.

24. *Id.,* at pages 13–15 and Appendix VII.

25. For a brief summary of methods of recycling used industrial lubricants, see Environmental Protection Agency, *supra,* note 11, at pages 18–20.

26. Environmental Protection Agency, *supra,* note 11, at pages 35–44; Hopmans, *supra,* note 9, at page 16 and Appendix VIII; Maltezou, *supra,* note 11, at pages 37–40.

27. Maltezou, *supra,* note 11, at page 38.

28. Hopmans, *supra,* note 9, at pages 23–24, discusses research under way to help solve the problem of acid sludge disposal. The Environmental Protection Agency, *supra,* note 11, at page 44, concluded that "landfilling of acid sludge . . . appears to be a reasonable method of disposal, provided sufficient safeguards are used to protect personnel, groundwater, and nearby streams."

EPA's Division of Hazardous Waste Management is currently sponsoring a study of used–oil-recycling by-product disposal.

29. Maltezou, *supra*, note 11, at page 61.

30. *Id.*, at pages 69, 71, 82, 85, 107.

31. *Id.*, at pages 78–79, 85. For a thorough case study of these factors in the New York City area, *see* Maltezou, *supra*, note 11, Chapters 2 ("Costs and Benefits of Recycling"), 5 ("Factual and Statistical Survey of the Waste Oil Problem in the New York Metropolitan Area"), 6 ("The Public and Private Decision to Recycle Waste Oil in the New York Metropolitan Area (NYMA)"), and 7 ("Concluding Remarks").

32. Ingo Walter and Sonia P. Maltezou, "Resource Recovery and U.S. International Trade: The Case of Waste Oil," 3 *Environmental Affairs* 433 (1974). A report by Britain's Waste Management Advisory Council concludes that recovery of the approximately 65,000 tons of high-quality used oil generated but uncollected each year would result in an improvement in the balance of payments of 1.7–2.2 million pounds. The report adds:

> This estimate is tentative because of the difficulty of assessing what categories of crude or refined oil imports will be substituted at the margin when more waste oil is recovered, and because the estimate takes no account of indirect balance of payments effects such as the import content of extra resources employed in the re-refining process.

33. Irwin and Liroff, *supra*, note 13, at pages 84–85. For a study showing the savings in energy of rerefining over refining, *see* Cukor, Energy Consumption in Waste Oil Recovery, Report No. EEED 109, Teknekron, Inc., 2118 Milvia Street, Berkeley, California 94704.

34. *Id.*, at page 134.

35. *Id.*, at pages 131–132.

36. *Id.*, at pages 121–122.

37. For a complete description of the German law and its implementation, *see* Irwin and Burhenne, "A Model Waste Oil Disposal Program in the Federal Republic of Germany," 1 *Ecology Law Quarterly* 471 (1971) and Irwin and Liroff, *supra*, note 13, at pages 85–120, 188–248.

38. Council Directive of 16 June 1975, *supra*, note 4. For background on the Directive, *see* Irwin and Liroff, *supra*, note 13, at pages 122–126.

39. The quoted phrases are from the preamble to the Directive.

40. Articles 1, 2, 17–31, 35–37, Chemical Wastes Act. Other procedural and substantive matters are covered in sections 38, 42–45, 48, 49, 51, 54 and 57. For the background of this law, *see* Irwin and Liroff, *supra*, note 13, at pages 126–130.

41. This summary is principally based on an address by Mr. P. Brassart, President Directeur General de l'Union Française des Petroles of Paris, at the First European Congress on Waste Oils, sponsored by the Commission of the European Communities and the European Union of Independent Lubricant Manufacturers, in Brussels, March 18–19, 1976, on March 19. The information in the preceding paragraph was contained in a private communication from Italy.

42. Department of the Environment, Waste Management Paper No. 7, available from Her Majesty's Stationery Office, 49 High Holborn, London WC1V6HB, England. The foreword says "the advice given in the memorandum accords with the approach established in the EEC Directive" and states that "compliance with the requirements of the Directive *will be* achieved largely by the implementation of Part I of the Control of Pollution Act, in particular regulations will be made *as necessary* under Section 17" (emphasis added). Section 17 obligates the Secretary of State for the Environment to promulgate regulations for disposal of any waste he regards as particularly dangerous or intractable. Although mineral oil wastes do not usually warrant this characterization, the section offers the Department convenient statutory authority.

43. *Id.,* §§ 5.7.3, 5.7.4, 5.7.5, and 3.1.9. A report on a case study of the economic prospects for increased recovery of used oil in England, issued by the Waste Management Advisory Council in the autumn of 1976, concludes:

> There are several imperfections that exist in the current market situation preventing the recovery of . . . 65,000 [tons per year of reasonably high quality used oil currently unrecovered]. These relate to: i. The small nature of individual arisings and the lack of information about the best means of disposal for Do-It-Yourself motorists; and ii. The problems of contamination of industrial waste oil arisings by other wastes which present technical and economical barriers to recovery.

The report suggests that providing and publicizing collection centers would solve the first problem (and reduce illegal disposal of small amounts of industrial used oils) and that following the advice in the Technical Memorandum will alleviate the second problem. In addition, a handbook will be forthcoming in early 1977 to "help voluntary organizations and local authorities . . . decide whether they can provide collection facilities and sell the oil they recover through the trade."

44. The following summary is based on the 31 October 1975 version of an Entwurf eines Zweiten Gesetzes zur Aenderung des Altölgesetzes prepared by Referat III D 5 of the Bundesministerium für Wirtschaft, 53 Bonn-Duisdorf, Postfach, Federal Republic of Germany. This version was circulated to all interested parties for comment and amended slightly. The Ministry's November 9, 1976 version, with Begründung, will be submitted to the current session of Parliament.

45. Gesetz zur Aenderung des Abfallbeseitigungsgesetzes vom 21. Juni 1976, Bundesgesetzblatt I, page 1601. *See* Artikel 1, No. 1.

46. For further background on German efforts to solve the "do-it-yourselfer problem," *see,* Zweiter Bericht der Bundesregierung über die Tätigkeit des Rückstellungsfonds nach dem Altölgesetz, insbesondere über die Möglichkeiten einer Ermässigung der laufenden Zuschüsse und der Ausgleichsabgabe, Deutscher Bundestag, Drucksache 7/3455, 9 April 1975, at pages 6–7, and Irwin and Liroff, *supra,* note 13, at pages 90–93.

47. For a recent summary of the U.S. situation, *see* Thomas H. Maugh, "Rerefined Oil: An Option that Saves Oil, Minimizes Pollution," 193 *Science* 1108 (17 September 1976).

48. For a summary of the complicated history of federal tax treatment of recycled oil products, *see* Irwin and Liroff, *supra,* note 13, at pages 28–39.

49. H.R. 10612, § 2008.

50. Performance testing is distinct from so-called bench testing, *i.e.,* lab tests of chemical and physical properties. Performance tests involve automotive engine sequence tests. "In them, oil to be tested serves as a lubricating agent in an engine that is run through a specific sequence of operations for an extended period. The engine is then disassembled and checked for wear, corrosion, and so forth. These tests can cost as much as $20,000 for one oil sample, so rerefiners have not been able to afford to demonstrate the quality of their products." Maugh, *supra,* note 47, at page 1110.

51. Irwin and Liroff, *supra,* note 13, at pages 39–55. *See also,* Environmental Protection Agency, *supra,* note 11, at pages 138–40 (Section X, "Federal Procurement of Products Made From Waste Oil"), and Cukor, Keaton and Wilcox, *A Technical and Economic Study of Waste Oil Recovery,* Part I, (available as Report # PB 236–618 from the National Technical Information Service, Springfield, Virginia) at pages 13–14. This concern has apparently been settled in Europe:

> Formerly the question whether this recovery product could in fact be regarded as qualitatively on a par with the "new oil" made from crude in the refineries of the big oil companies was the subject of heated discussion. Today there is no doubt for the objective observer that in fact regenerated base oil—known in the Federal Republic as "Zweitraffinat" —is in no way inferior in quality to the product from crude. That is, however, conditional on the regeneration process being performed carefully and expertly. Not only chemical, physical and mechanical examination of the regeneration product has proved that it is the equal of new oil. Another point in favour of this is that various large consumers who must be considered able to pass a very good judgement on the quality of luboil use this product. These big consumers include the Bundesbahn, the Societe Nationale des Chemins de fer, Charbonnages de France, the United States Air Force, General Electric, large car manufacturers etc. Regenerated oil is also supplied to a number of large oil concerns.

Hopmans, *supra,* note 9, at pages 16–17. *See also,* Irwin and Liroff, *supra,* note 13, at page 93.

52. P.L. 94–163, *supra,* note 3, § 383(c).

53. Uncertainties about the priority for and funding of this research have postponed its beginning. As of September 1976, the National Bureau of Standards had initiated a multiyear program of review and evaluation of existing oil test procedures, and research into new and revised test procedures where required. Initial efforts will be for recycled oil used as fuel, with other types of recycled oils (industrial, hydraulic, and engine) to follow.

54. P.L. 94–163, *supra,* note 3, § 383(d)(1)(B).

55. *Id.,* § 383(d)(2).

56. *Id.,* § 383(e).

57. P.L. 94–163, *supra,* note 3, § 383(f).

58. Voluntary used–oil-recycling programs may be sponsored by municipalities, private organizations or corporations. The first step in the establishment of such a program is to obtain the use of used-oil collection facilities. Usually, service stations—most of which have underground storage tanks—provide this facility. In some cases, re-refiners supply collection tanks. The next step is to publicize the program. This is accomplished through distribution of press releases, publicity pamphlets, posters, bumper stickers, etc. Frequently, newspaper articles in local papers serve an important publicity function, and occasionally radio and television advertising are used. Finally, arrangements must be made for hauling away the used oil. In most instances, re-refiners have this responsibility. At the present time, re-refiners usually pay several cents per gallon of used oil collected. Many of the voluntary programs donate the money received to charitable organizations.

59. Irwin, *supra,* note 5.

60. *Ethyl Corporation v. EPA,* 6 *Environmental Law Reporter* 20267, at page 20275 (D.C. Circuit, 1976).

61. *Id.*

62. *EDF v. EPA,* 510 F.2d 1292 (D.C. Circuit, 1975).

63. 40 Fed. Reg. 59532, at page 59534 (December 24, 1975).

64. *Union Electric v. EPA,* 6 *Environmental Law Reporter* 20570 (U.S. Supreme Court, 1976).

65. A person who is both a reconditioner of steel drums and a re-refiner familiar with the Altölgesetz, for example, has proposed its adaptation from the oil industry to the steel industry, to "serve the national interest by conserving energy and natural resources":

In the case of drums, the charge should be collected from the steel industry, or its drums manufacturing subsidiaries. It should be imposed on top of prevailing prices. The filler would have to pay an accordingly increased price, thereby making the throw-away drum lose part of its commercial attraction against the resusable all-18-gauge drum, which would regain interest.

The specific amount of this charge should be worked out in the form of a sliding scale, considering weight or metal thickness. The lower the weight, the higher the charge. . . .

In the case of drums, the fund should be instituted by a special body and used for such purposes as: extra non-profitable collection cost of empty, non-reusable drums, cost of storage, transport and handling, or possible reforming of those drums, from which the only return is the low scrap metal value, into metal bales. The operation of such a non-profit service cannot be organized efficiently by a private drum reconditioning firm without being subsidized, which subsidy should be provided from the fund.

Jochanon Katz, "A proposal to encourage the reuse of steel drums, based on the 'Used Oil Recycling Act,' " in the Proceedings of the Third International Conference on Steel Drums, May 29–June 3, 1976 (available from the National Barrel and Drum Association, 1028 Connecticut Avenue, N.W., Washington, D.C. 20036), at pages 83–86.

66. Martin and McMillan, "An Economic Model of Waste Oil Recovery, Reprocessing and Distribution Systems" in *Waste Oil Recovery and Reuse, supra,* note 6, at page 405. For the full report on which this article was based, *see* Martin and Gumtz, *State of Maryland Waste Oil Recovery and Reuse Program,* EPA–670/2–74–013, January 1974 (available from the Superintendent of Documents, U.S. Government Printing Office, Washington, D.C. 20402, for $2.70).

CHAPTER 16

The Economics of Waste Paper Recycling

R. Kerry Turner, R. Grace, and D. W. Pearce *

While no social policy toward the recycling of waste materials can be considered in isolation of an overall materials policy (Page, 1977), most developed countries are investigating the potential for further use of secondary materials. Motivations vary from outright concern about the physical availability of virgin material supplies to more nationalistic desires to reduce balance of payments costs. Whether a country is naturally endowed with virgin material supplies or has to import them, this concern still exists. In the former case, it may be prompted by the desire to ration a resource with a limited life (reportedly, this was one of the factors underlying the OPEC action on oil prices). In the latter case, it tends to reflect the severe balance of payments problems that have arisen for oil-importing countries since 1973. Nonetheless, it is not surprising that "recycling effort" tends to be inversely related to virgin material endowment, with countries such as the United Kingdom heavily dependent upon imports of all basic new materials, being significantly more active in the recycling field than others (Pearce, 1976a). Of course, many other factors affect the picture—secondary materials collection is costly in

* This work is supported by a grant from the Social Science Research Council.

less densely populated countries, the nature of the final product and its associated ease of recycling will vary (lead in petrol is nonrecyclable, paper in construction board tends to be "embodied" in the final product and is not easily reclaimed), and so on.

The purpose of this paper is to take one secondary material, waste paper ("paperstock" in North American parlance), and consider the extent to which recycling *actually* takes place, the desirability of increasing that rate, and the mechanisms by which increased recycling might be brought about. While much of the material relates directly to the United Kingdom, we have drawn on international experience wherever possible.

We also consider the international trade dimensions, since trade must ultimately be thought of as a means of increasing recycling rates.

WASTE PAPER RECYCLING RATES

The concept of a "recycling rate" is far from being unambiguous,[1] but we shall make use of two measures in common usage. The first is the *utilization* rate, and the second is the *recovery* rate. These are conventionally defined for any one country as

$$(1) \qquad U = \text{utilization rate} = \frac{\text{Waste paper usage}}{\text{Total fiber usage}}$$

so that
$$U = \frac{W_D - W_X + W_M}{TFU}$$

where W_D = domestically recovered waste paper
W_X = exports of waste paper
W_M = imports of waste paper

$$(2)$$
$$R = \text{recovery rate} = \frac{\text{Domestically recovered waste paper}}{\text{Apparent consumption of paper and board}}$$

so that
$$R = \frac{W_D}{B_D + B_M - B_X}$$

where B_D = domestically produced paper and board
B_M = imported paper and board
B_X = exported paper and board

If we let $TFU = B_D$, then a closed economy will have *

$$U = \frac{W_D}{TFU}$$

and

$$R = \frac{W_D}{B_D}$$

so that $U = R$.

It will be seen immediately that trade serves the function of "absorbing" the disparities between U and R (Grace, Turner, and Walter, 1976). Ignoring trade in waste paper, countries which are net importers of paper and board will have U in excess of R, while net exporters will have U less than R. We reserve a discussion of the actual importance of trade for a later section. For the moment, we take the above definitions and show in Table 1 the trends in U and R for selected OECD countries.

The first thing to be noted from Table 16–1 is that, by and large, most developed countries have recovery rates in excess of 20 percent, with Japan, Switzerland, and the Netherlands securing rates close to, or above 40 percent. Population density and the general absence of virgin pulp sources would seem to be particularly relevant here. Other countries, such as Eire and Italy, are notable for the rapid escalation of the recovery rate over time, while only Canada exhibits any evidence of comparatively low recovery rates. Greater variation is notable among utilization rates, with European Economic Community (EEC) countries (Belgium apart—which is a significant waste paper exporter) exceeding 40 percent utilization rates, and with Japan and Switzerland again in approximately the same category. The traditional pulp producers, such as the Scandinavian countries and Canada, have very low utilization rates, as we would expect.

Against this factual background we now need to determine the desirability and potential for increased recycling.

THE DESIRABILITY OF INCREASED RECYCLING

It is difficult to generalize about the increased *private* returns to mills from the use of extra recycled fiber. By and large, studies of *existing* plants do not exist so that it is possible to comment on the returns

---

* Typically, $TFU = a \cdot B_D$ with $a < 1$ since these are losses in conversion.

TABLE 16-1a

PERCENTAGE OF RECOVERY RATES IN WASTE PAPER

Countries	1960	1963	1965	1966	1967	1968	1969	1970	1971	1972	1973	1974
F.R. of Germany	26.7	26.0	27.4	25.2	28.6	28.6	28.8	30.0	30.1	29.6	30.0	31.9
Belgium-Luxembourg	25.6	22.9	27.0	27.7	30.9	27.2	27.1	30.3	26.1	30.6	29.6	29.9
Denmark	21.4	20.1	12.7	14.4	13.7	14.2	17.8	18.1	18.9	23.9	24.5	27.7
France	27.1	27.0	26.8	26.5	26.8	27.0	25.9	27.5	27.7	27.2	26.6	30.6
Eire	8.3	10.0	10.2	9.5	9.4	9.7	8.7	9.0	25.6	30.7	26.6	21.5
Italy	14.9	13.6	16.6	19.7	21.3	20.9	20.6	20.5	21.3	22.6	21.2	27.8
Netherlands	34.1	33.5	33.9	34.9	40.5	38.6	39.0	39.6	42.1	40.5	42.0	46.0
U.K.	27.8	27.5	28.6	27.1	26.5	27.0	27.0	28.7	28.7	27.0	27.5	27.6
EEC	26.1	25.4	26.3	25.7	27.0	27.0	26.9	28.2	28.5	28.2	28.1	30.6
Austria	21.9	23.4	24.6	26.3	30.0	30.3	32.1	29.8	32.7	33.3	32.1	30.2
Spain	25.3	29.2	27.8	26.7	29.9	36.4	26.0	27.6	25.9	33.6	29.4	31.8
Finland	20.5	17.3	19.7	21.0	18.7	19.1	15.1	22.2	15.2	13.5	13.8	17.2
Norway	15.5	16.9	20.0	17.1	17.5	17.8	18.0	17.4	18.0	18.6	21.2	20.5
Sweden	25.7	20.5	21.1	26.5	19.9	23.0	21.6	22.2	24.0	26.5	24.5	28.0
Switzerland	32.5	35.0	32.6	35.0	32.9	34.5	33.2	30.9	34.5	35.2	36.1	40.4
Canada	16.0	15.2	14.7	13.0	12.9	12.2	12.5	18.6	21.0	19.6	20.5	12.0
U.S.A.	n.a.	n.a.	21.7	19.8	19.6	19.8	19.9	21.3	20.5	22.6	20.4	22.3
Japan	n.a.	n.a.	37.4	39.2	37.3	36.6	38.1	38.5	35.9	38.0	40.2	39.2

SOURCE: OECD, *The Pulp and Paper Industry*, Annual Reports (Paris: OECD).

Note: n.a. = not available.

TABLE 16–1b

PERCENTAGE OF UTILIZATION RATES IN WASTE PAPER

Countries	1960	1963	1965	1966	1967	1968	1969	1970	1971	1972	1973	1974
F.R. of Germany	39.9	41.7	45.6	44.6	44.1	46.0	44.6	43.8	46.4	45.9	45.9	45.2
Belgium-Luxembourg	29.7	26.5	27.6	25.3	25.2	21.8	21.8	22.4	18.7	18.5	18.7	18.4
Denmark	34.3	29.3	16.1	22.2	21.7	22.7	32.9	32.0	40.3	48.5	48.7	48.6
France	28.2	30.0	30.9	31.5	32.0	31.7	31.4	32.2	35.0	35.2	35.7	36.0
Eire	29.0	28.0	41.7	35.6	37.3	35.6	39.5	34.5	n.a.	n.a.	41.3	66.4
Italy	21.6	22.0	24.5	28.1	28.9	27.1	28.3	28.8	32.4	33.2	34.3	40.6
Netherlands	20.3	22.7	23.1	24.5	31.0	31.7	33.2	34.0	40.0	38.2	40.4	42.6
U.K.	32.3	34.1	35.7	34.4	35.7	36.0	37.9	38.2	43.2	41.8	44.3	45.8
EEC	31.2	32.2	34.2	34.0	34.9	35.2	35.6	35.9	39.3	38.8	40.1	41.4
Austria	17.2	18.1	19.5	19.8	21.5	18.3	22.7	24.6	25.2	26.4	26.0	24.3
Spain	28.4	32.8	32.4	26.4	33.2	34.6	29.3	30.1	29.4	36.2	34.1	37.5
Finland	4.0	2.9	4.1	4.2	3.3	3.2	2.9	4.6	3.3	2.8	2.8	3.2
Norway	5.4	6.1	7.1	7.2	6.9	6.6	6.5	6.7	7.1	6.7	7.1	7.4
Sweden	7.9	5.5	5.9	6.5	5.5	6.7	6.3	6.0	6.1	6.8	6.7	7.3
Switzerland	30.8	31.5	31.5	31.9	31.3	31.6	31.2	30.6	35.1	34.6	36.1	40.0
Canada	3.4	3.3	4.2	3.4	2.7	2.9	3.3	5.0	6.0	6.0	6.3	6.4
U.S.A.	n.a.	n.a.	23.0	21.3	21.1	20.6	20.1	21.1	21.2	22.1	20.8	20.6
Japan	n.a.	n.a.	35.3	34.9	35.4	36.2	35.7	35.0	33.8	35.1	37.6	37.1

SOURCE: OECD, *The Pulp and Paper Industry*, Annual Reports (Paris: OECD).
Note: n.a. = not available.

from sustained increases in the use of secondary fiber in the "mix." In the normal course of events, the mix is varied over the waste paper cycle as virgin or secondary fiber becomes more or less attractive in terms of price and availability. In turn, however, such variations take place within "limits" set by the nature of existing plant and machinery and by the quality specification of the product.

The most detailed study of the comparative economies of *new* plant with variable secondary and virgin mixes is contained in Arthur D. Little (1975). Table 16–2 summarizes the main findings of that report. It should be noted that (1) the figures relate to new plants in the United States; (2) the hypothesized plant size varies so that unit cost differences can result from scale factors; (3) each result is sensitive to the relevant cost components; (4) each result depends on whether integrated or nonintegrated mills are under consideration.

Despite all the limitations involved in making comparisons, some general conclusions can be drawn from Table 16–2. First, 100 percent secondary fiber use appears uneconomic for all products save newsprint. In 1967–69 only 11–12 percent waste paper was used in newsprint production, suggesting that (1) increased use of waste paper is inhibited by beliefs about "consumer resistance" and (2) that considerable increases in waste paper usage could be secured in this sector. "Blends" of secondary and primary fiber would appear economically sensible for linerboard, printing papers, and kraft bags. The margins of difference also appear small for corrugating medium and perhaps bond paper.

Thus, while it is difficult to comment on the potential for internal economies in existing plant, there would appear to be a potential for competitive use of waste paper in containerboard, newsprint, tissue, and some printing and writing papers. This, indeed, is the conclusion reached by Arthur D. Little (1975). But the potential is, as they correctly pointed out, limited by the economics of recovery—that is, on the delivered price of waste paper to mills being competitive with virgin pulp supplies. This in turn depends on the economics of recovery, which we consider later, and on the future of pulp prices.

Views on the future availability and price of pulp in the United States have varied. Midwest Research Institute (1973) took an optimistic view on pulp supplies, especially in light of the economies of scale from operating large mills as opposed to the necessarily smaller waste paper based mills. On the other hand, while accepting that

TABLE 16–2

COMPARATIVE ECONOMICS OF SECONDARY AND VIRGIN FIBER USE
IN NEW PLANTS (U.S.A.)

	Pretax Rate of Return on Investment (%)		
Linerboard	V = 1	V = 0	V = 0.8
Kraft liner	17.9	—	—
Jute liner	—	8.7ni	—
Blended liner	—	—	17.6–20.7
Corrugating medium	V = 0.85	V = 0	V = 0.57
	13.7	11.8ni	12.7
Newsprint	V = 1	V = 0	V = 0.67
	6.2	10.6ni	7.4
Uncoated printing paper	6.3	− 6.1ni	6.3
Tissue (box, facial, and toilet roll)	21.0	6.9ni	16.8
Boxboard	11.3	9.3ni	—
Bond paper	22.5	4.2ni	20.5
Unbleached kraft bags	V = 1	V = 0	V = 0.7
	3.4	− 7.2ni	3.2
	− 49.0ni	− 7.2ni	

SOURCE: A. D. Little (1975), vol. 2.
NOTE: V = 1 = 100% virgin fiber; V = 0 = 100% secondary fiber; V = 0.7 = 70% virgin/30% secondary fiber. The notation "ni" refers to nonintegrated production. In general, it has been assumed that 100% secondary fiber use corresponds to a nonintegrated structure. For illustration, the costs of nonintegrated production for 100% virgin fiber production are sometimes shown.

"adequate" supplies exist in the United States for lumber and pulpwood uses up to 1985, Arthur D. Little (1975) predicted significant increases in pulpwood costs—increases which will exceed the rate of inflation (Little, 1975, vol. 1, p. IV–41). They put this rate of price increase at 3–4 percent above that of the general rate of inflation. This suggests that the competitive role of waste paper will, in the United States anyway, depend critically upon the delivered prices of waste paper, which in turn depend on the economics of recovering waste.

How far the United States situation reported above is applicable elsewhere is unknown since comparable costings appear not to exist.

There is, however, a presumption that, at least in newsprint and tissue manufacturing, in Europe increased usage of waste paper will occur, especially in light of government assistance to the paper industry in Europe.

Thus it would be wrong to ignore potential private cost savings from increased recycling rates, but the presumption must remain that the social desirability of increased recycling is to be justified on a basis other than that of private profitability.

Motivations for sustaining or increasing recycling rates have, in fact, varied widely from country to country. In the Netherlands, a buffer stock scheme (these schemes are discussed later in this chapter) was justified in part in terms of export earnings (about 36 percent of domestically recovered paper was exported in 1974). Concern with import bills has been notable, particularly in the United Kingdom.[2] Turner and Grace (1976) have suggested a balance of payments saving of at least £30m for the United Kingdom if the newspaper content of a 25 percent increased household recovery rate could be de-inked and substituted for mechanical pulp. It is significant that the United Kingdom government has now authorized expanded capacity in de-inking plant. In Japan, much of the concern for maintaining household paper waste recycling has emanated from a desire to sustain minimum income levels for the low-income workers who traditionally collect waste paper. Any, or all, of these motivations are legitimate if we construe them as reflecting some equity objective, or some feeling that shadow import prices diverge from market prices, although for the United Kingdom the latter must now be a somewhat arguable point.

The environmental aspects of recycling have perhaps been the ones most to the fore in public debate on waste paper. Apart from the feeling of the public that a potential resource is in some sense being "wasted"—a feeling which is often not paralleled by a recognition that recycling is not costless—much recycling offers environmental gains in terms of air and water pollution and solid waste generation.

Tables 16–3 and 16–4 show one comparison of environmental impacts for manufacturing 1,000 (U.S.) tons of low grade paper. The tables show the environmental impact comparisons for (1) manufacturing 1,000 tons of low grade paper using either virgin pulp or repulped waste paper (Table 16–3), and (2) manufacturing 1,000 tons of bleached virgin kraft pulp and its equivalent from

TABLE 16–3

ENVIRONMENTAL IMPACT COMPARISON FOR 1,000 TONS
OF LOW GRADE PAPER

Environmental Effect	Unbleached Kraft Pulp (virgin)	Repulped Waste Paper (100%)	Change from Increased Recycling (%)*
Virgin materials use (oven-dry fiber)	1,000 tons	0	−100
Process water used	24 mill. gallons	10 mill. gallons	−61
Energy consumption	17,000 ×10⁶ BTU	5,000×10⁶ BTU	−70
Air pollutants † effluents (transportation, manufacturing, and harvesting)	42 tons	11 tons	−73
Waterborne waste discharges—BOD †	15 tons	9 tons	−44
Waterborne waste discharges—suspended solids	8 tons	6 tons	−25
Process solid wastes generated	68 tons	42 tons	−39
Net postconsumer wastes generated	850 tons ‡	−250 tons §	−129

SOURCE: Midwest Research Institute,"*Economic Studies in Support of Policy Formation on Resources Recovery,*" Unpublished data, 1972.
* Negative numbers represent a decrease in that category, or a positive change from increased recycling.
† Based primarily on surveys conducted in 1968–1970.
‡ This assumes a 15% loss of fiber in the papermaking and converting operations.
§ This assumes that 1,100 tons of waste paper would be needed to produce 1,000 tons of pulp. Therefore, 850−1100=−250 represents the net reduction of postconsumer waste.

de-inked pulp (Table 16–4). Table 16–3 suggests that all constituent environmental impacts are reduced if waste is used for the manufacture of low grade paper and that most impacts are reduced if higher grade paper is manufactured but that the de-inking process in the

TABLE 16–4

ENVIRONMENTAL IMPACTS RESULTING FROM THE MANUFACTURE OF
1,000 TONS OF BLEACHED VIRGIN KRAFT PULP AND EQUIVALENT
MANUFACTURED FROM DE-INKED AND BLEACHED WASTE PAPER

Environmental Effect	Virgin Fiber Pulp	De-inked Pulp	Increased Recycling Change (%)*
Virgin materials use (oven dry fiber)	1,100 tons	0	−100
Process water used	47,000 × 10 ‡ gallons	40,000 × 10 ‡ gallons	−15
Energy consumption	23,000 × 10⁶ BTU	9,000 × 10⁶ BTU	−60
Air pollutants (transportation, manufacturing, and harvesting)	49 tons	20 tons	−60
Waterborne wastes discharged—BOD †	23 tons	20 tons	−13
Waterborne wastes discharged—suspended solids	24 tons	77 tons	+222
Process solid wastes	112 tons	224 tons	+100
Net postconsumer waste disposal	850 tons ‡	−550 tons §	−165

SOURCE: Midwest Research Institute, op. cit.
* Negative numbers represent a decrease in that category resulting from recycling.
† Based on surveys conducted in 1968–1970.
‡ This assumes a 15% loss of fiber in paperworking and converting operations.
§ This assumes that 1,400 tons of waste paper is needed to produce 1,000 tons of pulp. Therefore, 850−1,400 = −550 represents the net reduction in post-consumer solid waste.

latter case gives rise to significant increases in process solid wastes and in waterborne suspended solids. In both cases, energy "costs" (i.e., expressed in energy units) are reduced.

Table 16–4 indicates the well-known problem that de-inking tends to generate a water pollution problem in the form of suspended solids.

Work on the construction of so-called residuals management models by Resources for the Future (see B. T. Bower et al. [1971], B. T.

Bower et al. [1973] and B. T. Bower [1975]) suggests that a much more detailed analysis of the pulp and paper industry is required before any meaningful conclusions can be drawn on residuals generation. Bower et al. state that residuals generation in the pulp and paper industry is a function of seven major variables (the list being reduced to six if waste paper is used as a raw material input).

$$R = f(RM, WPP, B, PM, C, PO)$$

where R = the vector of residues generated
   RM = type of raw material
   WPP = waste paper processing
   B = bleaching sequence
   PM = papermaking process
   C = converting operation
   PO = final product specifications

From this list of variables, Bower selects two, PO and B, as being especially significant factors. The desired paper product characteristics (PO) can be obtained by some combination of the above factors (production combination). However, certain product characteristics can only be achieved with a given production combination. For example, final product "brightness" (an "aesthetic" characteristic) requires some combination of brightness of the pulp stock plus additives in the form of coatings.

Bower et al. explore the implications for residuals generation if the level of product brightness is varied. The practicality of these simulated changes in brightness is, of course, essentially a "marketing" problem. There is, unfortunately, a dearth of information concerning the likely implications, in terms of consumer reaction, of any reductions in product brightness. The two variables PO and B are in fact interrelated. Any trend toward an increased final product brightness specification brings a parallel increase in the use of bleaching processes (B). Moreover, the bleaching sequence is itself a substantial generator of residuals.

The Resources for the Future (RFF) Pulp and Paper Industry Model suggests that when a mill makes increased use of waste paper (old news) in order to produce newsprint, the result is likely to be an increased generation of some residuals, if the currently high brightness specifications are held constant or reduced by only a small amount. All gaseous residuals are eliminated, but the generation of dissolved organic and inorganic solids plus suspended organic solids residuals is increased. Only when brightness is substantially reduced does residuals generation decrease substantially in newsprint production. In the production of tissue paper, a large reduction in the brightness specification allows the use of 100 percent No. 1 mixed waste paper (a combination of newsprint, old news, and used corrugated). Utilizing this production combination would again eliminate all gaseous residuals and also reduce dissolved organic and inorganic solids generation, but would still lead to an increase in suspended inorganic solids generation.

Bower et al. stress, however, that there does exist a major short-run variation problem in the residuals generation process. The use of waste paper entails inevitable random variations in raw material input quality, and this results in wide variations in residuals generation. Other factors like the extent to which equipment is "pushed," the effectiveness of water reclamation systems plus tight management and good housekeeping also contribute to the short-run variations in residuals generation. Bower et al. (1971) conclude that "the reuse of paper residuals is not a panacea with respect to managing environmental quality. Whatever the product specifications, it results in the generation of substantial quantities of residuals." Thus the environmental case for waste paper remains ambiguous, and a number of further detailed studies are required.

Significant in Tables 16–3 and 16–4 are the savings in postconsumer solid wastes. The savings here can be substantial. There are a priori reasons for supposing that municipal waste *collection* costs will not be significantly affected. First, separate waste paper collection from households is likely to be a municipal responsibility if it is taken on at all, although voluntary agencies have been active in this field with varying degrees of success. As such, the municipality will find itself collecting the same volume/weight of refuse but using separate trailers or "racks" to keep the paper separate. This can actually *add* to collection costs. Second, there will be indivisibilities in collection costs— removal of, say, newspapers from domestic waste, would reduce the weight of refuse; but since refuse tends to be placed in containers, it is unclear that any reduction in the number of containers to be collected would occur. On the other hand, depending on the form of separate collection, any refuse truck should now have an extended area of coverage.

While the impact on *collection* costs is ambiguous, the impact on *disposal* costs should be a clear benefit. The exact size of any savings in disposal costs is again, however, not at all clear. In the United Kingdom, landfill without prior shredding remains an extremely cheap form of disposal, averaging some £0.9 per ton (Pearce, 1976b). There is probably something like 4.4 million tons of unrecovered domestic and commercial paper in the United Kingdom municipal waste stream.[3] Taking a hypothetical recovery scheme aiming to secure 25 percent of these supplies, 1.1m tons of waste paper need not reach municipal dumps or incinerators. This suggests a minimum saving of £0.9m per year in disposal costs if all disposal is to landfill. There are obvious dangers, however, in using an average cost figure as opposed to a marginal cost figure in this context. Marginal costing is not widely practiced by United Kingdom local authorities and, therefore, the levels of cost savings are not known with any accuracy. As far as landfilling operations are concerned, the amount of labor and capital equipment being utilized on the dump is small and, therefore, not amenable to marginal cutbacks—whereas the life of the dump itself is obviously extended and this means that in the long run the total amount of land required is reduced. Nevertheless, it is also true that completed dumps are more valuable if they are reclaimed earlier rather than later. The average cost of incineration in the United Kingdom appears to be some £7 per ton, suggesting an upper limit of £7.7m in disposal cost savings. Again, however, on a marginal cost basis, the exact level of any savings is not known. Incineration processes have high fixed-capital costs, and thus any marginal savings are likely to be small unless the plant is running near to or over capacity.

Looking at the issue from another point of view, the 4.4m tons of waste paper disposed of in the United Kingdom municipal waste stream costs something like £10 per ton to collect and £2 per ton to dispose of. At £12 per ton, then, there is a cost "external" to the purchasers of paper products equal to some £53m. One United States report (Miedema, 1976) estimates that some 44m tons of paper waste entered the municipal waste stream in 1973 at an average collecting and disposal cost of about $27, suggesting a $1,200m "external cost" which can be debited to paper products. In terms of an average "external cost charge," the United States report suggests that these costs would add 15 percent to the price of paper products. A similar analysis for the United Kingdom suggests a 9 percent increase in paper product prices.

It seems clear that the social desirability of extra waste paper recycling must rest largely with the arguments that there will be savings in disposal and possible collection costs plus, of course, any balance of payments or equity arguments that relate to individual countries. The environmental argument is not a powerful one until we know more about the cost of controlling pollution from upgrading technologies. The argument about resource cost savings depends critically upon the use of such technologies to make products publicly more acceptable. Finally, while calculations of the total external cost of paper disposal have relevance to policies on "product charges" (Smith, 1977), what matters for our analysis are the savings that would emanate from a feasible policy of additional collection and re-use.

Moreover, we must be sure that the extra supplies of waste paper match the likely grade-composition of demand, for low grades of waste paper are not substitutes for higher quality pulp-using products. We turn briefly to the likely supply and demand aspects.

FUTURE SUPPLY AND DEMAND FOR WASTE PAPER

This section reports estimates of the future supply of and demand for waste paper in various countries.

The application of the "materials balance" principle to paper waste generation suggests that the amount of paper discarded each year in each country will bear a direct relationship to the amount of "apparent consumption" of paper and board in each country each year (Smith, 1975). If we omit building board (which is "embodied" in durable products and is, in any event, generally not recycled) we obtain the following estimates of paper waste in selected OECD countries. The figures should be treated with some caution but are indicative of the orders of magnitude involved.

If projections of apparent *consumption* of paper and board in these countries were available, it would be possible to use the approach adopted in Table 16–5 to estimate paper in the waste stream in the future. Various forecasts exist for the United States: Massus (1974) provides one estimate for the EEC in 1980, and BIS (1975) another

TABLE 16–5

PAPER IN THE WASTE STREAM: MATERIALS BALANCE APPROACH—SELECTED
OECD COUNTRIES, 1972
(In Millions of Tons)

	U.S.A.	U.K.	EEC
Apparent consumption of paper board	58.4	7.5	28.0
Less nonrecoverable *	8.8	1.1	4.2
Equals net discards	49.6	6.4	23.8
Less amount recovered	12.4	2.0	7.9
Equals amount discarded to waste stream	37.2	4.4	15.9

SOURCE: Leicester University Pulp and Paper Study.
* Estimates of what is "nonrecoverable" vary. Smith (1975) implicitly uses a
22.3% rate. Massus (1974) suggests 20.5% for the EEC, but BIS (1975)
suggest only 16%. Darnay (1972) suggests 12.4% for the U.S.A. We have used
15%. This may exaggerate losses in U.K. and the EEC where construction
board accounts for very small proportions of the market. The most detailed
estimates, however, are contained in Miedema (1976) for the U.S.A. These
suggest a 1973 figure of 13.6% "nonrecoverable" with the ratio varying only
between 12.5% (1966) and 15.2% (1958).

for the EEC for 1983. These are shown in Table 16–6. Figures for
the United States have been converted from short tons to metric tons.
The implied annual growth rates in Table 16–6 are reasonably
uniform, although there are clearly wide disparities in the forecasts

TABLE 16–6

FORECAST PAPER AND BOARD APPARENT CONSUMPTION—
SELECTED COUNTRIES
(In Millions of Tons)

	U.S.A. *	U.S.A. †	U.S.A. ‡	EEC §	EEC ‖
1980	72.6	83.7	—	39.0	—
1983	—	—	82.4	—	44.8
1985	86.2	98.6	—	—	—

* B. Slatin (1975).
† Miedema (1976).
‡ A. D. Little (1975).
§ Massus (1974).
‖ BIS (1975).

of growth in paper and board consumption in the United States economy between now and 1985. From 1980 to 1985 a rate of about 3.5 percent is suggested for the United States. Massus' forecast for the EEC suggests a 3.7 percent growth rate to 1980. With the exception of Miedema (1976), all the projections were made before the onset of the major slump in the paper and board industry of 1975. This does not affect expected growth *rates* as such, but will alter the absolute magnitude involved, and these are relevant for our estimation of future waste. Hence we adjust the growth rates downward.

We therefore propose to use a 3 percent growth rate as generally applicable, with the exception of the United Kingdom, where a 1 percent growth rate is applied overall. Tables 16–7a, 16–7b, and 16–7c show the magnitude of paper in the waste stream projected to 1980, 1985, and 1990 on the above assumptions. Note that the use of overall growth rates is justified as long as we are concerned solely with the total *weight* of paper in the waste stream.

Estimates of how much of this waste could be recovered vary. Massus (1974) argues that a 25 percent recovery rate could be achieved for existing unrecovered paper in the EEC. Darnay (1972) estimates that some 57 percent of discards could "technically" be

TABLE 16–7a

PROJECTED WEIGHT OF PAPER IN THE WASTE STREAM: U.K. *
(In Millions of Tons)

	1975†	1980	1985	1990
Consumption of paper and board	6.3	7.3	8.5	9.8
Less nonrecoverable ‡	1.0	1.1	1.3	1.5
Equals net discards	5.3	6.2	7.2	8.3
Less amount recovered §	2.0	2.2	2.3	2.4
Equals amount discarded to waste stream	3.3	4.0	4.9	5.9

SOURCE: Leicester University Pulp and Paper Study.
* Assuming 1% growth rate in paper and board apparent consumption overall.
† 1975 was, in fact, a slump year. The trend rate of growth 1963–74 was 3% per year (consumption in 1974 was 8.3 million tons). For 1963–75 it was < ½%, indicating the magnitude of the slump. The procedure here is to assume that consumption will grow at 3% per year from 1975.
‡ At 15%.
§ A recovery rate of 27% is assumed to apply throughout.

TABLE 16–7b

PROJECTED WEIGHT OF PAPER IN THE WASTE STREAM: EEC *
(In Millions of Tons)

	1972	1980	1985	1990
Consumption of paper and board †	28.0	35.5	41.1	47.8
Less nonrecoverable ‡	4.2	5.3	6.2	7.2
Equals net discards	23.8	30.2	34.7	40.6
Less amount recovered §	7.9	9.9	11.5	13.4
Equals amount discarded to waste stream	15.9	20.3	23.4	27.2

SOURCE: See Table 16–7a.
* The "EEC" is treated as if the current nine countries also comprised the membership in 1972.
† Assuming 3% growth rate in paper and board consumption.
‡ At 15%.
§ A recovery rate of 28% is assumed to apply throughout.

recovered, but that 29 percent is a figure relating to what is "most likely." The United States EPA (1975) quotes a rate of between 25.8 percent and 32.3 percent for the United States provided source separation is practiced. Arthur D. Little (1975) estimated 44 percent of the "collectable tonnage" of old corrugated containers could be achieved, 34 percent of news waste, 87 percent of higher grades, and 16 percent of mixed papers. The overall average is 34 percent. It seems safe, therefore, to use the 25 percent rate as being generally applicable. Table 16–8 shows the effect of this on an average of the estimates in Tables 16–7a to 16–7c for the United Kingdom, European Economic Community, and United States.

We may also estimate the grade composition of the supplies. Massus

TABLE 16–7c

PROJECTED WEIGHT OF PAPER IN THE WASTE STREAM: U.S.A.*
(In Millions of Tons)

	1972	1980	1985	1990
Total discarded to waste stream	37.2	47.5	55.3	64.4

SOURCE: See Table 16–7a.
* Ancillary calculations are similar to those made in Tables 16–7a and 16–7b.

TABLE 16–8

MAGNITUDE OF WASTE PAPER RECOVERED IF 25% RECOVERY RATE IS APPLIED
(In Millions of Tons)

	1975	1980	1985	1990
U.K.				
Extra paper waste recovered	0.8	1.0	1.2	1.5
EEC	(1972)			
Extra paper waste recovered	4.0	5.1	5.9	6.8
U.S.A.	(1972)			
Extra paper waste recovered	9.3	11.9	13.8	16.1

SOURCE: See Table 16–7a.

(1974) suggests a breakdown for the EEC in 1980 (based largely on United Kingdom data) and Darnay (1972) for the United States, as in Table 16–9a.

Table 16–9b presents the likely future grade composition of supply for the United Kingdom, European Economic Community, and United States.

The municipal waste stream source generates essentially low grade papers, and while the proportions of the total paper waste stream accounted for by newspapers, old corrugated and mixed papers may differ between countries, the types of paper residuals found do not. The same appears not to be true for "untapped" sources of higher grade paper residuals. In the United Kingdom discussions with merchants and local authorities suggest that some large retail outlets are covered by contracts which operate only in times of buoyant demand, so that kraft-grade material is disposed of to the municipal waste stream in times of low demand. Some United Kingdom local authorities believe that a separate waste paper collection scheme in their

TABLE 16–9a

PERCENTAGE OF GRADE COMPOSITION OF EXTRA PAPER SUPPLIES

	Massus	Darnay
Newspapers, magazines, directories	36	27
Corrugated and kraft waste	46	38
Mixed papers	18	32

SOURCE: See Table 16–7a.

TABLE 16–9b

GRADE COMPOSITION OF EXTRA RECOVERED WASTE PAPER
(In Millions of Tons)

	1980	1985	1990
U.K.			
Newspapers, etc.	0.36	0.43	0.54
Corrugated and kraft	0.46	0.55	0.69
Mixed papers	0.18	0.22	0.27
Total	1.00	1.20	1.50
EEC			
Newspapers, etc.	1.84	2.12	2.45
Corrugated and kraft	2.35	2.71	3.13
Mixed papers	0.92	1.06	1.22
Total	5.11	5.89	6.80
U.S.A.			
Newspapers, etc.	3.21	3.73	4.35
Corrugated and kraft	4.52	5.24	6.12
Mixed papers	3.81	4.42	5.15
Total	11.54*	13.39*	15.62*

SOURCE: See Table 16–7a.
* Does not add up to 11.9 (see Table 16–9a) since Darnay (1972) suggests 3%
of residential and commercial waste would be of higher grades.

area could salvage fair quantities of residuals from small retail outlets. Overall, however, it would appear that the majority of large
generations of higher grade paper wastes are either already covered
by the merchants or are inhibited by difficulties with unionized labor
from sorting the paper residuals in their factories. The fact that sorting is a skilled task requires the factory to pay higher wage rates
and, as pay differentials are adjusted, can cause an appreciable escalation in the total wage bill. In the United States, on the other hand,
there do appear to be more significant "untapped" sources of higher
grade paper particularly in office establishments.

Forecasting the demand for waste paper is even less straightforward
than forecasting supply. One approach is to take forecasts of the
production of paper and board products and relate these to technical
waste paper utilization input-output coefficients. Technically we multi-
ply the matrix of technical coefficients (adapted for technical change)

TABLE 16–10a

OUTPUT OF PAPER AND BOARD: EEC
(In Millions of Tons)

	Production of paper and board *	Of which printing & news-print	Papers for corrugated	Other packaging	Boards	Other
1973	22.8					
1980	28.0	11.2	6.9	2.4	4.9	2.6
1985	32.5	13.0	7.96	2.76	5.68	3.08
1990	37.6	15.04	9.21	3.91	6.58	3.19

SOURCE: See Table 16–7a.
* Growing at 3% per year.

by a final demand vector derived from the forecasted growth rates of paper and board products. Massus (1974) has, in fact, produced a set of coefficients for individual EEC countries and for the EEC as a whole. He also allows for changing coefficients over time, using industry assessments of what is likely in terms of technological change and assessments of "saturation" levels for waste paper usage. Table 16–10a shows estimates of paper and board production for the EEC. Massus (1974, vol. 1, p. 9) estimates production to be growing at an annual rate of 4.3 percent; other sources, however, quote much lower rates. We propose to use a 3 percent growth rate. Table 16–10b illustrates the demand for waste paper in 1980 by final product category using the EEC input-output table. Table 16–10c and 16–10d illustrate the United Kingdom situation.[4]

The input-output coefficients used to arrive at the figures for 1980 in Table 16–10b and 16–10d only allow for limited technological

TABLE 16–10b

WASTE PAPER DEMAND: EEC
(In Millions of Tons)

	Printings	Papers for corrugated	Other packaging	Boards	Other	Total
1980	0.78 +	5.86 +	0.96 +	3.87 +	0.8 =	12.27

SOURCE: See Table 16–7a.

TABLE 16–10c

OUTPUT OF PAPER AND BOARD: U.K.

(In Millions of Tons)

	Production* of paper and board	Of which printings	Papers for corrugated	Other packaging	Boards	Other
		36%	24%	7%	21%	12%
1973	4.6	1.7	1.1	0.3	1.0	0.6
1980	4.9	1.8	1.2	0.3	1.0	0.6
1985	5.2	1.9	1.2	0.4	1.1	0.6
1990	5.4	1.9	1.3	0.4	1.1	0.7

SOURCE: See Table 16–7a.
* Assumed to grow at 1% per year.

change. For the period beyond 1980, it is right to consider what types of upgrading technology may come into force. De-inking techniques will be developed in the EEC and the United Kingdom, and perhaps more optimistically let us assume that cooking and bleaching technology develops to the stage where corrugated and mixed paper residuals can be more fully utilized. On the basis of these assumptions, Table 16–11a illustrates what Massus (1974) considers to be optimistic coefficients for the EEC and the United Kingdom (post-1980) and Table 16–11b gives the United States position.

Using these "optimistic" input-output coefficients, Tables 12a and 12b indicate what the likely demands for waste paper in the United Kingdom and the EEC would be in 1985 and 1990.

We now bring together our demand for and supply of waste paper estimates for the United Kingdom and the EEC in Table 16–13.

Table 16–13 suggests a state of excess supply for waste paper in the United Kingdom even assuming the rapid technological change in

TABLE 16–10d

WASTE PAPER DEMAND: U.K.

	Printings		Papers for corrugated		Other packaging		Boards		Other		Total
1980	0.2	+	1.0	+	0.1	+	0.9	+	0.1	=	2.3

SOURCE: See Table 16–7a.

TABLE 16–11a

INPUT-OUTPUT COEFFICIENTS: EEC AND U.K. (POST-1980)

	EEC	U.K.
Printings	0.33	0.33
Papers for corrugated board	0.85	0.86
Other packaging	0.60	0.60
Boards	0.81	0.88
Other	0.52	0.52

SOURCE: Massus (1974), vol. 1, p. 36.

TABLE 16–11b

INPUT-OUTPUT COEFFICIENTS: U.S.A. (1985)

	1972	1985
News	0.12	0.42
Other printings	0.08	0.09
Packaging papers	0.08	0.08
Corrugated board and solid fiberboard	0.35	0.49
Buildings papers and boards	0.34	0.34
Tissues	0.23	0.43

SOURCE: Massus (1974), vol 1, pp. 38–40.

TABLE 16–12a

WASTE PAPER DEMAND: U.K. (OPTIMISTIC TECHNOLOGY)
(In Millions of Tons)

	1985	1990
Printings	0.63	0.63
Papers for corrugated board	1.03	1.12
Other packaging	0.24	0.24
Boards	0.97	0.97
Other	0.31	0.36
	3.18	3.32

SOURCE: See Table 16–7a.

TABLE 16–12b

WASTE PAPER DEMAND: EEC (OPTIMISTIC TECHNOLOGY)
(In Millions of Tons)

	1985	1990
Printings	4.29	4.96
Papers for corrugated board	6.67	7.82
Other packaging	1.65	1.91
Boards	4.60	5.32
Other	1.60	1.65
Total	18.90	21.66

SOURCE: See Table 16–7a.

the upgrading technologies is likely to increase the demand for paper
residuals. Thus the hypothesized 25 percent waste paper recovery
drive would produce too much waste paper in the United Kingdom
situation. The level of extra recovery effort necessary if supply and
demand are to balance out is computed in Table 16–14.

TABLE 16–13

SUPPLY AND DEMAND FOR WASTE PAPER: U.K. AND EEC
(In Millions of Tons)

U.K.	1980	1985	1990
Demand	2.3	3.18	3.32
Supply			
"Normal recovery"	2.2	2.3	2.4
Extra recovered	1.0	1.2	1.5
	3.2	3.5	1.5
Excess supply	0.9	0.3	0.6
EEC			
	1980	1985	1990
Demand	12.27	18.90	21.66
Supply			
"Normal recovery"	9.9	11.5	13.4
Extra recovered	5.1	5.9	6.8
	15.0	17.4	20.2
Excess supply	2.73	Excess demand 0.50	Excess demand 0.46

SOURCE: See Table 16–7a.

TABLE 16–14

EXCESS OF WASTE PAPER DEMAND OVER "NORMAL" SUPPLY: U.K.
(In Millions of Tons)

1980	1985	1990
0.1	0.9	0.9

SOURCE: See Table 16–7a.

Currently United Kingdom local authorities recycle about 300,000 tons; thus to meet the likely demand for waste paper in 1980, only a marginal increase in effort is required. If, however, the 1985 and 1990 demands are to be met, local authorities would need to treble their current collection rates. These demands are, of course, dependent on the "optimistic" technological changes in upgrading technology actually occurring. Further, we have so far neglected the crucial grade composition of waste problem and the possible increase in supplies from United Kingdom commercial sources, the evidence for which is not clear-cut.

As far as the EEC is concerned, a situation of excess demand could develop in 1985–90 if the rapid technological changes do occur. However, once again this conclusion is dependent on the grade composition of the extra supply and demand, and it is to this problem that we now turn. First, we need to know which grades of waste paper will be used in each final paper and board product. Table 16–15 estimates

TABLE 16–15

GRADE INPUT-OUTPUT TABLE EEC: POST-1980 "OPTIMISTIC" TECHNOLOGY

Waste Paper	Printing & Newsprint	Corrugated	Other Packaging	Boards	Other
Mixed paper	0.03(0.01)*	0.44(0.47)	0.36(0.26)	0.53(0.55)	0.37(0.26)
Corrugated	0.40(0.08)	0.36(0.37)	0.24(0.18)	0.15(0.15)	0.28(0.14)
Newspapers	0.46(0.33)	0.07(0.06)	0.11(0.15)	0.23(0.22)	0.11(0.20)
Printers waste	0.10(0.51)	0.03(0.03)	0.13(0.20)	0.06(0.06)	0.18(0.29)
Kraft	0.01(0.07)	0.01(0.07)	0.14(0.20)	0.02(0.02)	0.06(0.11)
Waste paper pulps	—	—	0.02(0.01)	0.01(—)	0 (0)

SOURCE: Massus (1974), vol 1, p. 4 for 1973 data, p. 36 for "optimistic" technology data.
* Figures inside parentheses refer to 1973 data.

TABLE 16–16

INPUT-OUTPUT COEFFICIENTS: EEC (1980)

Waste Paper	Printing & Newsprint	Papers for Corrugated	Other Packaging Papers	Boards	Other Papers and Boards
Mixed papers and boards	0.01	0.44	0.25	0.52	0.28
Corrugated	0.06	0.37	0.16	0.15	0.12
Newspapers, brochures, directories	0.36	0.07	0.16	0.24	0.19
Printers waste	0.51	0.03	0.20	0.06	0.30
Kraft, tabulating cards, listings	0.06	0.10	0.21	0.02	0.11
Waste paper pulps	—	0.1	0.03	0.01	—

SOURCE: Massus (1974), vol. 1, p. 26.

the relevant input-output coefficient on the assumption that the upgrading technologies like de-inking, cooking, and bleaching are developed to the stage whereby the lower waste paper grades can be fully utilized after 1980.

Table 16–16 presents the input-output coefficients for 1980 on the

TABLE 16–17

DEMAND FOR WASTE PAPER BY GRADE: EEC IN 1980, 1985, AND 1990
(In Millions of Tons)

	1980	1985 (assuming optimistic technology)	1990 (assuming optimistic technology)
Mixed papers and boards	5.1	6.7	7.6
Corrugated	3.0	5.7	6.3
Newspapers, brochures, directories	1.9	3.8	4.8
Printers waste	1.2	1.4	1.6
Kraft, tabulating cards, listings	1.0	0.5	0.5
Waste paper pulps	0.6	0.1	0.1
Total *	12.8	18.2	20.9

SOURCE: See Table 16–7a.
* Errors due to rounding. Total in each column should correspond to totals in Tables 16–10b and 16–12b.

TABLE 16–18

PERCENTAGES OF TOTAL WASTE PAPER BY GRADE: EEC 1973

Mixed papers	42.8
Corrugated	23.2
Newspapers, etc.	15.5
Printers waste	11.0
Kraft, etc.	7.0
Waste pulps	0.5
	99.0

SOURCE: Massus (1974), vol. 1, p. 22.

TABLE 16–19

SUPPLY AND DEMAND FOR WASTE PAPER BY GRADES: EEC
(In Millions of Tons)

		(assuming "optimistic" technology)	(assuming "optimistic" technology)
a)	*Mixed Papers*		
		1980	1985	1990
	Supply: normal recovery *	4.2	4.9	5.7
	extra recovery †	2.2	2.5	2.9
	Demand	5.1	6.7	7.6
	Excess Supply	1.3	0.7	1.0
b)	*Corrugated and Kraft*		
		1980	1985	1990
	Supply: normal recovery	3.0	3.5	4.1
	extra recovery	1.5	1.8	2.1
	Demand	4.0	6.2	6.8
	Excess Supply	0.5		
	Excess Demand		0.9	0.6
c)	*Newspapers, Brochures and Directories*		
		1980	1985	1990
	Supply: normal recovery	1.5	1.8	2.1
	extra recovery	0.8	0.9	1.1
	Demand	1.9	3.8	4.8
	Excess Supply	0.4		
	Excess Demand		1.1	3.6

SOURCE: See Table 16–7a.
* See Table 16–13.
† See Table 16–13.

TABLE 16–20

INPUT-OUTPUT COEFFICIENTS: U.K. (1980)

Waste Paper	Printings	Papers for Corru- gated	Other Pack- aging Papers	Boards	Other Papers and Boards
Mixed papers and boards	0.03	0.06	0.15	0.71	0.32
Corrugated	—	0.28	0.46	0.16	0.08
Newspapers, brochures, directories	0.45	0.05	0.01	0.1	0.1
Printers waste	0.4	—	0.3	0.02	0.32
Kraft, tabulating cards, listings	0.1	—	0.06	0.0	0.17
Waste paper pulps	—	—	—	—	—

SOURCE: Massus (1974), vol. 1, p. 63.
NOTE: The resulting demands are shown in Table 16–21.

assumption that any radical technological changes have not had sufficient time to reach full operational efficiency.

The EEC's waste paper demand, differentiated by grade, can now be computed by multiplying the components of Tables 16–10b and 16–12b by the relevant input-output matrix, that is, Tables 16–16 and 16–15 respectively. The results are presented in Table 16–17.

In order to compare the supply and demand situation in terms of

TABLE 16–21

DEMAND FOR WASTE PAPER BY GRADE: U.K. IN 1980
(In Millions of Tons)

	1980
Mixed papers and boards	1.03
Corrugated	0.5
Newspapers, brochures, directories	0.24
Printers waste	0.16
Kraft, tabulating cards, listings	0.05
Total *	1.98

SOURCE: See Table 16–7a.
* Errors due to rounding. Total should correspond to total in Table 16–10d.

grade composition, we need to know the grade composition of existing waste paper usage. Massus (1974) suggests the proportions for EEC countries in 1973, as shown in Table 16–18.

For all three major grades involved in municipal waste (mixed papers, corrugated and kraft and newspapers, brochures and directories), we have the results shown below in Table 16–19.

For the United Kingdom no detailed input-output breakdown is available comparable to Massus' optimistic technology matrix. Certainly de-inking plants will be "on stream" by 1980, but the capacity of any such plants and the existence of improved and operational cooking and bleaching plants is an open question. What we have done is to analyze the United Kingdom situation in 1980 on the assumptions that a limited amount of technological change will take place and there is a 25 percent waste paper recovery drive in operation. The United Kingdom's 1980 waste paper demand, differentiated by grade, can be computed by multiplying the components of Table 16–10d by the relevant input-output coefficients in Table 16–20. The resulting demands are shown in Table 16–21.

Again, using Massus' (1974) grading scheme (see Table 16–18),

TABLE 16–22

Supply and Demand for Waste Paper by Grades: U.K.
(In Millions of Tons)

	1980
a) *Mixed Papers*	
Supply: normal recovery	0.94
extra recovery	0.42
Demand	1.03
Excess Supply	0.33
b) *Corrugated and Kraft*	1980
Supply: normal recovery	0.66
extra recovery	0.30
Demand	0.55
Excess Supply	0.41
c) *Newspapers, Brochures, Directories*	1980
Supply: normal recovery	0.34
extra recovery	0.15
Demand	0.24
Excess Supply	0.25

Source: See Table 16–7a.

the demand and supply situations for the three "municipal" waste paper grades are shown in Table 16–22. The results are clear excess supply situations in all the "municipal" grades.

Table 16–23 presents a summary of the waste paper demand and supply situation in the United States.

It will be seen that the major advances are thought likely to occur in containerboard (which includes corrugating medium) and printings. The considerable contrast between these coefficients and those for the EEC/United Kingdom (the latter being much higher) can be explained by two main reasons. First, the Arthur D. Little data represent projections of what is *likely* to happen whereas the EEC coefficients reflect *potential*. Second, the ADL projections allow for the existence of indigenous pulp supplies. In short, the contrast between the United States and EEC/United Kingdom matrices reflects the

TABLE 16–23
INPUT-OUTPUT COEFFICIENTS: U.S.A.
(In Millions of Tons)

	Production	Waste Paper Consumption	Input-Output Coefficient	Production	Waste Paper Consumption	Input-Output Coefficient
Container board	19.4	3.2	0.16	27.5	7.6	0.28
Printings	4.9	0.6	0.12	6.1	1.2	0.20
Tissue	4.0	1.2	0.30	5.2	1.7	0.33
Folding box board	7.7	4.6	0.60	9.5	5.7	0.60
Other printing *	11.8	0.9	0.08	16.9	1.8	0.11
Industrial packaging	7.4	1.5	0.2	9.5	2.3	0.24
Construction paper & board	6.6	2.4	0.36	9.3	3.4	0.37
Total	61.7	14.3	0.23	83.9	23.5	0.28

SOURCE: A. D. Little (1975).
* Nongroundwood printings.

availability of pulp supplies in the United States. Nevertheless, even if the input-output coefficients do not change, demand for waste paper will rise in the United States as paper and board production increases. Table 16–23 shows a rise in demand for waste paper from around 14 million tons in 1973 to over 23 million tons in 1983.

Estimates of the kind produced so far on the demand and supply situation for waste paper are clearly unsophisticated, despite the formidable informational requirements necessary to produce them, mainly in respect of demand forecasting. Interestingly, the forecasting of demand for secondary materials in general has been a grossly neglected issue (at least outside the United States). Turner and Grace (1977) have secured econometric estimates for the United Kingdom which suggest a simple relationship between waste paper demand and general indices of economic activity.[5] The grades of paper used in this exercise differ slightly to those normally used. The comparison of grade nomenclature is given below.

	Higher Grades	*Grade Heading*
WP1	Printers waste	1 + 2
WP2	Tabulating cards and listings	3 + 4
	Ordinary Grades	*Grade Heading*
WP3	Newspapers, brochures, and directories	5
WP4	Corrugated paper board waste, kraft paper	6
WP5	Mixed papers and boards	7 + 7a

Both long-term and short-term forecasts were secured. Strong time trends in both series (waste paper consumption and gross domestic product) produced high correlations for the long-term forecasts, but, interestingly, the detrended correlations performed well. The long-term forecasting equations are shown in Table 16–24.

These forecasts serve to cast severe doubt on official United Kingdom forecasts of some 3.2m tons demand by 1980 or thereabouts. Indeed, Turner and Grace's forecasts (assuming 3.8 percent per year increase in gross domestic product) suggest a demand of 2.4 metric tons by 1985. Interestingly, the 1980 figure is in accord with the industry federation's own revised (1976) forecast for that year.

TABLE 16–24

LONG-TERM DEMAND FORECASTING EQUATIONS FOR WASTE PAPER: U.K.

WP1 (index) = $-3.04 + 1.04$ GDP (index), $r^2 = 0.92$, DW = 1.27
WP2 (index) = $-80.33 + 1.72$ GDP (index), $r^2 = 0.88$, DW = 1.16
WP3 (index) = $-102.11 + 1.88$ GDP (index), $r^2 = 0.91$, DW = 1.43
WP4 (index) = $-198.4 + 2.96$ GDP (index), $r^2 = 0.94$, DW = 0.74
WP5 (index) = $36.26 + 0.58$ GDP (index), $r^2 = 0.95$, DW = 1.97
WP TOTAL (index) = $-29.66 + 1.2$ GDP (index), $r^2 = 0.95$, DW = 1.74

SOURCE: See Table 16–7a

While long-term forecasts are useful in planning investment decisions (there was, for example, a serious danger of overencouragement of supplies because of the erroneously high forecasts produced in 1975 and repeated as late as January 1976), industry and municipalities are of the view that the household sector will not be a source of extra supplies, at least on a significant scale, unless fluctuations in price are "ironed out." The argument is essentially that local authorities and charities are encouraged into the market in times of buoyant demand and high prices, only to find that the boom collapses and they are left with serious financial losses. This has, indeed, been the experience in Europe generally, although municipalities are involved in collection to varying degrees. It has certainly been made virtually a condition of re-entry to the market in the United Kingdom.

Because of this, it is valuable to secure short-term forecasts. Turner and Grace's work has enabled the cycles to be identified very accurately in the United Kingdom, and their forecasting equations have so far proved successful in predicting quarterly demand. Detrended series of waste paper consumption were correlated with detrended series for industrial production with the following result for overall waste paper consumption:

$$WP \text{ total} = 246.7 + 2215.9 \text{ (Industrial Production)}$$
$$r^2 = 0.57$$
$$DW = 1.35$$

The variable industrial production is statistically significant at the 5 percent level, but the low value of the Durbin-Watson statistic shows that positive serial correlation exists in the residual. It is clear that it is possible to explain more of the variation than has as yet been achieved. Variables such as the levels of stocks and waste paper

R. Kerry Turner, R. Grace, and D. W. Pearce   327

prices could be brought into the model to improve the predictive power of the analysis. However, lack of detailed data, particularly prices, has meant this has not been possible.

The amplitude of the waste paper cycle is greater than that of general economic activity, which indicates that a boom in the economy as a whole is reflected by a greater boom in waste paper usage; similarly slumps in waste paper usage are also greater than those experienced by the general economy. Another factor of the waste paper cycle is the tendency for the recovery and expansion phase toward a boom to have a considerably longer duration than the contraction and depression phase toward a slump and, consequently, the impact of a slump is felt more noticeably than a boom by the industry. The frequency of the cycles is not constant and has a range between 4 and 5 years from slump to slump with the duration of the upswing varying from 2 to 3½ years and the downturn varying between 1 and 2½ years.

As with the long-term forecast, this short-term forecast can be extended further to disaggregate the overall grade composition of waste paper, and this has been done for the lower quality grades, that is, those grades which have potential for further growth should the social benefits of increased recycling be shown to outweigh the costs.

The results are given below:

WP3
$$\text{Exponential: } WP3 = 9108\, e^{1.256t}$$
Detrended series

$$WP3 - \text{exponential} = 82.3 + 336.8 \text{ Industrial Production}$$
$$r^2 = 0.45$$
$$DW = 0.7$$

WP4
$$\text{Exponential: } WP4 = 14740\, e^{2.04t}$$

Detrended series

$$WP4 - \text{exponential} = 63.2 + 470.2 \text{ Industrial Production}$$
$$r^2 = 0.39$$
$$DW = 1.15$$

WP5

Exponential: $WP5 = 82760\,e^{22.33t}$

Detrended series

$WP5$ − exponential $= 169 + 1355.6$ Industrial Production
$$r^2 = 0.61$$
$$DW = 1.74$$

STABILIZING THE WASTE PAPER MARKET

As noted above, the most widely quoted obstacle to increased recycling is the cyclical variation in prices. The previous section has shown that this in turn is simply a fairly accurate reflection of the standard business cycle: there is little other than this causing the fluctuations. These findings are borne out by other studies of fluctuations, for example, the study carried out by Tractionel in Belgium (1976). Accordingly, much attention has been paid to schemes for stabilizing the price fluctuations. The schemes considered are direct counterparts of those traditionally considered for primary commodity control —long-term contracts, buffer funds, and buffer stocks. The buffer stock scheme has attracted most attention and schemes exist in infant form in Norway, the Netherlands, and Japan (for a brief discussion of these schemes, see Pearce [1976c]). The industry's request for such a scheme was rejected in the United Kingdom, but recommendations that there be such a scheme have been made in Belgium (see the report by Tractionel [1976]) and Denmark.

This section takes a closer look at the buffer stock concept since this is the technique most widely advocated, even though it may not be the best candidate.

A buffer stock scheme requires that stocks be accumulated at times of low demand (or excess supply) and resold at times of high demand (or low supply.) The analytics of the scheme can be understood with the aid of a simple supply and demand diagram. Figure 16–1 deals with a situation in which demand shifts over time but the supply fuction stays constant. The uncontrolled market prices are P_1 and P_2. We now assume that the authorities establish a buffer stock scheme the aim of which is to hold prices within the range P^*_1 P^*_2. At the time of low demand (D_1) the scheme offers the price P^*_1, which, in this case, is above the price that would have ruled in the market, P_1.

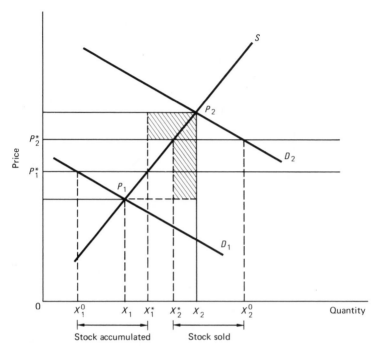

Figure 16–1 Operation of a buffer stock scheme

This restricts market demand to X_1^0 but suppliers supply X_1. The excess supply is, therefore, stored by the authorities and is released by them when demand shifts to D_2. Since the authorities do not wish the price to rise above P_2^* they can hold the price there by releasing the stock accumulated in period 1 as soon as price reaches P_2^* in the market. In this way they will unload their entire stock and will supply the market with more waste paper than uncontrolled market forces would have done—that is, X_2^0 instead of X_2.

We may list the immediate results of the simple analysis in Figure 16–1 since these are important:

1. The free-market price fluctuation P_1P_2 has now been reduced to $P_1^*P_2^*$;

2. The stock-holding agency has broken even in terms of physical stocks and has made a profit of $P_1^*P_2^*X_2^0$ *less* storage, insurance, handling, and physical deterioration costs. The trade profit must also be expressed in present value terms;

3. *Physical* sales are less in the low demand situation in the controlled market, but higher in the high demand situation;

4. *The supplier's income* (financial sales) is actually *less* than netted out over the two periods.

Conclusion (4) is important and should perhaps be explained, under the simplifying assumptions of Figure 16–1 $P_1P^*_1 = P_2P^*_2$. Industry income in the controlled market is, over the two periods,

$$P^*_1 X^*_1 + P^*_2 X^*_2$$

and in the uncontrolled market it is

$$P_1 X_1 + P_2 X_2$$

The difference between these two aggregate magnitudes is in a *loss* equal to

$$(X^*_1 X_2) (P_2 P^*_2) + (P_1 P^*_2) (X^*_2 X_2)$$

This is shown in Figure 16–1 as the shaded area.

This conclusion, that the supplier may lose income under a stabilization scheme, is dependent on the specific assumptions made about elasticity in Figure 16–1. Accordingly, no conclusion about the virtues of a stabilization scheme from the supplier's standpoint can be reached without knowledge of demand conditions and elasticities.[6] Further, if the stabilization scheme has the effect of increasing supply, the analysis becomes more complex.[7] Figure 16–2 shows the essentials. For convenience, the diagram is drawn so that the break-even stock disposition requirement brings about a unique stabilized price P rather than a range. Now because of the stabilization scheme, it is assumed that there is an immediate shift in supply from S_1S_2.

Under the stabilization scheme, the supplier gains the shaded area $C + D$ in period 1. In the second period he would have secured a revenue of P_2X_2 had the stabilization scheme not existed. Instead, he now secures a revenue of P^*X^*, so that he gains area B but loses area A. Over the two periods, his net gains (losses) are $C + D + B - A$.

In the longer run we may also note that exactly the same conclusion could apply to those supplying agencies which stabilization schemes are designed to assist. For example, if the aim is to encourage local authorities to participate in preseparation or mechanical separation schemes in order to supply waste paper, then a stabilization scheme *could* well mean that they would make less income with stabilized prices than if they operated in a free market with widely

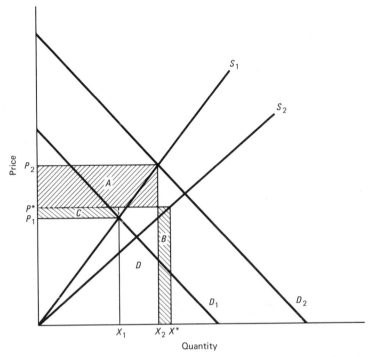

Figure 16–2 Operation of a buffer stock scheme with generated increased supply

fluctuating prices. In short, the widely accepted view (in the United Kingdom, at least) that local authorities are deterred from entering the supply market because of price instability could be erroneous in the sense that no real comparison between the potential revenues for local authorities in stabilized and unstabilized markets has been made. The *belief* by local authorities that stabilized markets will be more beneficial to them is totally understandable, but it need not be founded in fact. This does not, of course, mean that local authorities have not lost in the past by supplying a fluctuating market, merely that those losses may well not be reduced by stabilizing the market.

Turner and Grace (1976a), modifying and extending the earlier analysis of Pearce and Grace (1976), have analyzed the operations of a simulated buffer stock scheme for waste paper in the United Kingdom. The analysis is *ex post* in the sense that it looks at how a buffer stock scheme would have behaved if it had existed. (We consider an *ex ante* approach described in Tractionel (1976) for Belgium shortly.)

First, a series of residual variations in waste paper consumption is calculated (i.e., consumption with the trend and seasonal factors removed). This establishes the quantities which it is assumed the hypothetical agency must buy and sell, the basic idea being that purchases and sales of such residual amounts will generate price movements closer, if not equal, to the "natural" price trend. In other words, such behavior will reduce or remove the price cycle. The agency faces costs of buying in stocks, handling charges, storage charges, insurance, and, of course, the capital investment necessary for warehousing capacity. In turn, in boom times it secures the revenue from sales.

Table 16–25 shows the balance sheet for the buffer stock agency. In the absence of detailed prices for grades, assume the agency buys and sells paper at the overall price of waste paper. Two problems arise with this. First, from our previous analysis we assume that any agency would, in fact, deal largely, if not entirely, in the lower grades. Hence it is these prices that should be used. Second, in buying and selling, the agency will in fact affect prices (indeed, this is the whole point of the exercise). But without knowledge of demand and supply elasticities we are unable to quantify the extent to which this will happen. However, this second point will tend to mean that any loss suffered by the agency will be *understated* in this exercise. That is, we are assuming it buys all its stock at the ruling market price, when in fact it will be buying at least part of it at higher prices as its action forces prices up. Costs will, therefore, be higher than we have stated them. Equally, when the agency sells, it will lower the market price, so that revenue will be overstated by our exercise.

It will be apparent that the agency has the following gains and losses in present value terms, with 1961 the base year:

Cycle 1	Gain	+	726,408
	Loss		− 1,112,052
	Net Loss	(£) −	385,644
Cycle 2	Gain		+ 1,189,283
	Loss		− 1,931,336
	Net Loss	(£) −	742,053
Cycle 3	Gain		+ 1,106,039
	Loss		− 1,400,166
	Net Loss	(£) −	294,127

TABLE 16–25

OPERATION OF A BUFFER STOCK SCHEME, UNITED KINGDOM, 1961–74

Cycle 1	Buy (Tons)	Sell (Tons)	Price (£)	Costs (£)	Discount Factor at 10%	Expenditure & Revenue (£)
Aug. 61–July 62	26,651		18.0	2.6	1.0	− 549,011
Aug. 62–July 63	28,353		18.0	2.6	0.91	− 531,505
Aug. 63–Sept. 63	1,701		18.0	2.6	0.90	− 31,536
Total	56,705					−1,112,052
Oct. 63–Sept. 64		17,721	17.7	2.6	0.83	+ 22,097
Oct. 64–Sept. 65		28,353	20.4	2.6	0.75	+ 378,513
Oct. 65–Mar. 66		10,632	20.0	2.6	0.68	+ 125,798
Total		56,701				+ 726,408
Cycle 2						
Apr. 66–Mar. 67	46,844		19.1	2.6	0.65	− 660,735
Apr. 67–Mar. 68	79,275		18.2	2.6	0.56	− 923,395
Apr. 68–Dec. 68	32,431		17.6	2.6	0.53	− 347,206
Total	158,550					−1,931,336
Jan. 69–Dec. 69		79,275	18.4	2.6	0.49	+ 613,747
Jan. 70–Dec. 70		79,275	19.1	2.6	0.44	+ 575,536
Total		158,550				+1,189,283
Cycle 3						
Jan. 71–Dec. 71	97,200		16.3	2.6	0.40	− 734,832
Jan. 72–Dec. 72	97,200		15.9	2.6	0.37	− 665,334
Total	194,400					−1,400,166
Jan. 73–Dec. 73		97,200	16.9	2.6	0.33	+ 458,687
Jan. 74–Dec. 74		97,200	24.8	2.6	0.30	+ 647,352
Total		194,400				+1,106,039

SOURCE: See Table 16–7a.

According to this exercise, then the buyer agency would have made losses of at least £1.4 million in thirteen years. Clearly, if this is correct, a buffer stock scheme would have been a substantial loss maker. This conclusion is in keeping with earlier work on the operation of such schemes in the United Kingdom, and with the general observation in other commodity control schemes that buffer stock agencies are highly suspect when handling charges are significant.

A possibly more reassuring picture emerges from the exercise carried out by Tractionel for the operation of such a scheme in Belgium (Tractionel, 1976). The essential difference is that their scheme is evaluated on an *ex ante* basis, which requires them to estimate future prices. Further, it operates only with the lower grades of paper as we would assume a buffer stock agency would do. Having considered all the costs of establishing such a scheme and the likely quantities it would deal with, the authors consider three possible "scenarios" for future prices in Belgium.

They then select the one they consider most likely and use this. Most important, they include as a credit to the scheme the savings in disposal costs—that is, is routed by the buffer stock agency to be recycled. These "indirect" receipts are so important that they comprise something like 50 percent of total benefits to the scheme in the early years and over 30 percent in later years. Of course, this proportion will be high in downswings (disposal cost savings not being cyclical) and lower in upswings.

Table 16–26 shows the results.

It will be seen that, in terms of a comparison of sales and costs, the scheme would lose substantial amounts of money. However, the

TABLE 16–26

OPERATION OF A BUFFER STOCK SCHEME IN BELGIUM
(In Millions of Francs)

Year	Costs	Revenue from Sales	Indirect Revenue	Net Profit
1977	20.2	10.4	9.5	0.3
1978	21.7	11.9	10.7	0.9
1979	23.0	12.9	11.9	1.8
1980	25.2	13.9	13.2	1.9
1981	26.6	15.4	14.4	3.3
1982	27.2	18.1	15.1	6.0
1983	28.6	19.2	15.8	6.3
1984	29.2	19.5	16.5	6.8
1985	29.8	20.6	17.2	8.0
1986	31.3	23.6	17.9	10.2

SOURCE: Adapted from various tables in Tractionel (1976, vol. 2).

crediting of disposal cost savings to the scheme gives it a social profit. As far as the United Kingdom exercise reported above is concerned, taking disposal costs as being £2 per ton on average in the United Kingdom, we would need to credit the scheme with the following amounts (see Table 25).

Cycle 1   £107,966
Cycle 2   £184,062
Cycle 3   £149,688
(in present value terms discounted to 1961).

References to Table 16–25 show that such credits reduce the overall (minimum) loss of £1.4 million to just over £1 million.

However, crediting buffer stock schemes with disposal cost savings is only valid in certain circumstances. If the stock scheme does not affect the overall supply of waste paper, then the disposal costs saved in the period when the agency is buying up waste paper are lost in the next period when the agency sells its stocks. Nevertheless, if the discount rate is positive, discounting back to the beginning of the cycle will result in a small credit to the scheme since disposal costs are shifted forward in time. If the buffer stock agency has the effect of increasing the overall supply of waste paper by encouraging greater local authority participation in the waste paper market, then there may be some disposal cost savings. (For further details, see Hallwood [1977].)

To a considerable extent, the conclusion on the use of buffer stock schemes to stabilize waste paper markets must be one of "not proven." Essentially, without knowledge of the elasticities involved, accuracy is not possible. To date, estimates of price elasticities of supply and demand for waste paper have been suspect, while for the United Kingdom it is impossible to secure estimates by grade because of the apparently "secret" nature of these prices. It is hoped to make some attempt at measurement, however, in later work. Nonetheless, the initial analysis suggests that the oft-mooted argument that munici-palities will not come into the waste paper market without stabilization, while it may reflect a collective view, could be misplaced. We must be careful to place the right interpretation on this finding, however. There can be no question that municipalities have lost money in the past in supplying a fluctuating market. All that we are arguing here is that they may still lose money supplying the market at all (with known disposal costs); the choice context must be carefully defined.

INTERNATIONAL TRADE AND WASTE PAPER

Finally, we turn to trade as an instrument for raising the recycling rate. We noted at the outset that trade in waste paper and in the final product (paper and board) explained the observed disparities between utilization rate as a demand indicator and the recovery rate as a supply indicator. Trade thus equilibrates supply and demand, just as we would expect. In this respect, while trade *can* be destabilizing (and thus contribute to the variations observed in waste paper markets), it seem clear that trade in waste paper serves a stabilizing function. Pearce (1976c) demonstrates that the prices of waste paper, by grade, tend to move simultaneously in different countries, although of course some disparities exist the farther the geographical distance. But the European and United Kingdom markets are clearly very closely linked. Actual disparities observed between utilization and recovery rates are thus a composite measure of the impacts of both types of trade on

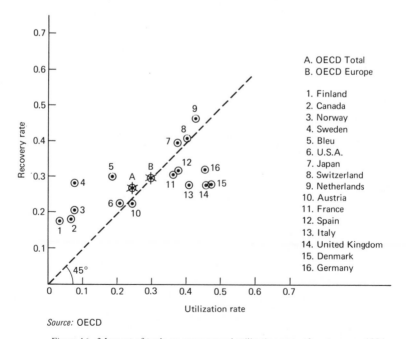

Source: OECD

Figure 16–3 Impact of trade on recovery and utilization rates of waste paper, 1974

recycling activity. Figure 16–3 illustrates these effects for sixteen OECD countries.

In a closed economy as we have seen, the utilization rate would be equal to the recovery rate, and the point representing this situation would be on the 45° line. The distance between the point and the origin would show the proportional level of recycling activity in that country. However, where trade exists, a point may be shifted to the left or right of the 45° line; the direction and magnitude of the shift will depend upon the combined effect of trade in paper and board and waste paper. Canada, Norway, and Austria, for example, are net importers of waste paper and net exporters of paper and board. Both types of trade will increase the relevant utilization and recovery rates, but it is the magnitude of the trade that will determine whether the point will be to the left or the right of the 45° line.

In order to establish how each type of trade affects the recovery and utilization rates, Figure 16–4 has been constructed.

Each country is again represented by a point, but its position is

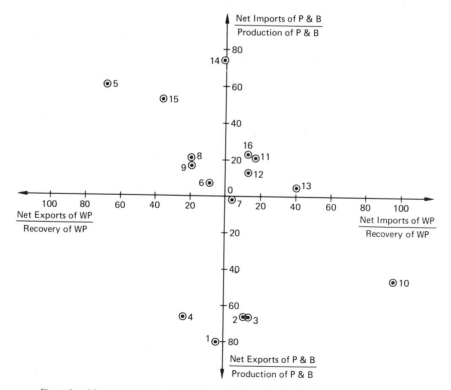

Figure 16–4 Direction of trade, 1974 (Key as in Figure 16–3)   P & B = paper and board

determined by the proportion of trade to domestic production of paper and board and recovery of waste paper. Each quadrant represents one of the four possible combinations of trading patterns. If Figure 16–4 is used in conjunction with Figure 16–3, it is possible to establish a detailed picture of the impacts on trade for any of the sixteen countries. Austria (point 10) provides an interesting example. Figure 16–3 has Austria lying close, but to the right of the 45° line, suggesting that the level of trade is small. However, Figure 16–4 shows that Austria's position is due to the very large trade in waste paper (particularly imports), causing the utilization rate to be high. Austria's large net export trade in paper and board has also tended to push its recovery rate up. The combined effect of the two types of trade flows in 1974 was such that Austria is represented by a point close to the 45° line, the trade in waste paper marginally outweighing the impact of the net export trade in paper and board. The possible alternative impacts of trade on the utilization and recovery rates are shown in Table 16–27.

The pattern which emerges from Figure 16–4 is clearly related to the availability of pulp. The major pulp producing countries—Finland, Canada, Norway, and Sweden—can be easily identified as a group shown by the points 1, 2, 3, and 4. The cluster is quite distant from and to the left of the 45° line but close to the origin. Figure 16–4 confirms that each of these is a major exporter of paper and board,

TABLE 16–27

Trade Impact Matrix

Increase in	Change in		Decrease in	Change in	
	U	R		U	R
Paper/Board exports	—	↑	Paper/Board exports	—	↓
Paper/Board imports	—	↓	Paper/Board imports	—	↑
Waste Paper exports	↓	—	Waste Paper exports	↑	—
Waste Paper imports	↑	—	Waste Paper imports	↓	—

Source: See Table 16–7a.

the impact of this particular type of trade flow outweighing the waste paper trade effect. A second distinct group of countries, those with small indigenous supplies of pulp, can also be identified in Figure 16–3. This second group is represented by the European countries numbered 11 to 16. The location of this second group in Figure 16–3 is the result of the combined effects of a net import trade in paper and board and, with two exceptions, a net import trade in waste paper (see Figure 16–4.) Both types of trade lead to high utilization rates and low recovery rates (see Table 16–19) and hence a grouping to the right of the 45° line. The two exceptions are the United Kingdom and Denmark (points 14 and 15) which are net exporters of waste paper. The effects of this trade flow, however, are negated by the large net import trade in paper and board production. A third group of countries (numbers 5 to 10) are generally scattered along and reasonably close to the 45° line in Figure 16–3. It will be seen from Figure 16–4 that this is because these countries fall in the two quadrants where the impacts of trade work against each other and the magnitudes of the trade flows are of the same order, thus bringing the utilization and recovery rates close together. The Belgium/Luxembourg Economic Union (point 5) is the only exception, because the two trade flows, although yielding opposite effects, do not cancel each other out. Point 5 is pushed farther away and to the left of the 45° line by the impact of the large net export trade in waste paper conducted by Belgium-Luxembourg which tends to depress its utilization rate.

CONCLUSIONS

This paper has ranged widely across a number of issues relating to increased recycling of waste paper. Against the background of actual recycling rates, we discussed the general desirability of increased recycling. Since timber is a renewable resource, and since there exists the feedback loop (which means that less demand for timber will result in less afforestation), the "resource conservation" argument is a complex one to use in defense of increased recycling. Certainly, one would hope that no *existing* and currently noncommercial stock will be used to meet rising demand. Equally, the pollution impact of recycling depends critically upon the establishment of standards to contain water pollution from the use of de-inked fiber and other upgrading techniques. If this is achieved, the environmental gains appear distinctly positive. No attempt has been made here, however, to estimate the costs of securing this kind of protection. Taking the paper out of the municipal waste stream seems unlikely to have significant effects on municipal collection costs, but disposal costs should be unambiguously positive. Just how great these savings are depends very much on what the feasible level of extra household recycling is. We have adopted a rate of 25 percent based on the supposition that collections in towns of less than 30,000 inhabitants would be uneconomic. We certainly know that collections in towns of less than 20,000 inhabitants appear distinctly uneconomic (see the evidence surveyed in Pearce [1976c]), but we have seen varying estimates of the "minimum feasible size" for collection, including one that would make it uneconomic for populations less than 60,000 persons. If, however, the 25 percent rate is feasible *and* economic, disposal cost savings would not appear very significant. If, however, all paper products were charged for the total external cost they impose in terms of collection and disposal costs, then the effect might be significant.

But whether extra recycling is desirable depends in turn upon whether what can be collected from households matches the grade qualities required in future demand. As far as the United Kingdom and the EEC are concerned, a general excess supply of waste paper is likely to materialize in the 1980s. Much depends here on investment in upgrading technology, however, and exactly when in the period up to 1990 any new upgrading plants become operative.

We also noted a distinctly unsatisfactory state of affairs with respect to demand studies. Estimates of elasticities exist but seem suspect. Estimates of future demand also exist, but few seem to have been placed on a systematic economic basis outside the United States. We reported one exercise of our own, which is an attempt to refine United Kingdom forecasts.

Estimating demand and supply is crucial to the issue of policy. In the United Kingdom, and elsewhere, exaggerated claims about the future demand for waste paper have been used to pressure government for special aid for the paper and board industry to stockpile wastepaper. There have been few dissenting voices to these demands, apart perhaps from private merchants who fear that municipalities might enter the market for the higher grades, traditionally their preserve. Our view, however, is that much of this pressure has been misplaced.

In the first place, future demand will not reach the exaggerated levels forecast in some official United Kingdom documents. In the second place, stockpiling schemes need careful scrutiny before they are adopted. It will be interesting to see how those schemes that exist actually progress—all experienced difficulties in the early stages— but in the meantime, serious appraisals are called for. While we cannot be assertive about our own views, we would suggest the strong possibility that stabilized markets might merely reduce the losses previously sustained by the local authorities and voluntary agencies who have traditionally acted as the "residual suppliers" whenever the market booms.

Finally, we have drawn attention to the role of trade in secondary materials. The wider issues have been investigated elsewhere, but we think it useful to emphasize the role of trade as a stabilizing mechanism, not least because there are increased signs that, in a resource-conscious world, some nations will seek to place controls on trade in secondary materials, just as they have on other materials. Indeed, some already have.

NOTES

1. See Pearce (1976a). For example, if a country *imports* waste materials, should this count as contributing toward a *higher* recycling rate or a *lower* rate? In so far as trade in waste materials can be shown to be "good" (if more recycling is an object of social policy), the source of the material should be irrelevant.

2. See U.K. Waste Management Advisory Council, *First Report,* (HMSO, London 1976), where it is stated that wood pulp imports cost £270m in 1974. The authors of the report were apparently unaware that waste paper is a substitute, at best, only for mechanical pulp. A more realistic figure is given in this paper. One might also add that most UK commentary is conducted on the false basis of assuming that balance of payment savings are directly additional to other savings.

3. The 25 percent figure is suggested in Massus (1974) and is based on a study of the economic viability of collection schemes in the EEC. In general, schemes relating to municipalities with populations below 30,000 are distinctly uneconomic. The 25 percent figure is then obtained by estimating the number of households in municipalities of this size and above. The figure is also similar to several suggested for the USA.

4. The exercises reported here use a single growth rate for total paper and board production—i.e., 3 percent per year for the EEC and 1 percent for the United Kingdom. A separate investigation was carried out applying different

342   THE ECONOMICS OF WASTE PAPER RECYCLING

growth rates to the different product components of total paper and board. This is, of course, technically a more legitimate operation. In practice, however, the results did not differ significantly from those secured by applying the overall growth rate so that, for simplicity of exposition, we have presented the more simplistic approach here. It is also self-evident that output forecasts should be based on input-output tables which have technical coefficients responding to future relative prices. To some extent, relative price changes are subsumed in the use of the 1980 matrix in Massus (1974), but we make no pretense that the forecasts allow fully for relative price shifts, simply because no exercise exists which has predicted such shifts for EEC countries.

5. It seems evident that the forecasts can be improved with suitable waste paper price data. No such data are published in the United Kingdom although they are collected, so that this refinement has not been possible. See R. K. Turner and R. Grace (1977), "Forecasting the Demand for Waste Paper," *Conservation and Recycling* (forthcoming).

6. Those studies that have reported elasticities secure very low values indeed. See A. Miedema op. cit.; and also R. Anderson and R. Spiegelman, "The Federal Tax Code as a Deterrent to Recycling" (mimeo), Environmental Law Institute, Washington, D.C., 1976; and R. Anderson, "Federal Policies towards the Use of Scrap Materials," paper presented to the 1976 American Economics Association Meeting. As the authors of the papers admit, there are reasons for supposing that true elasticities are not being revealed by the techniques of estimation used. Nonetheless, the low elasticities of supply would explain the severity of price changes in response to comparatively small shifts in demand.

7. Note that *consumer's* surplus is increased under the stabilization scheme as shown in Figure 1. One ignores welfare measures here and concentrates on revenue because it is in terms of revenue that stabilization schemes are being publicly debated. This may seem regrettable from the welfare economist's standpoint, but it is at least realistic.

BIBLIOGRAPHY

BIS Marketing Research, Ltd. (1975). *Business opportunities in waste paper and board—The next 10 years in Western Europe,* London.
Bower, B. T., (1971). Residuals management in the pulp and paper industry, *Natural Resources Journal,* October.
———, (1973). Residuals in manufacture of paper, *Journal of Environmental Engineering Division,* February.
——— (1975). Studies in residuals management in industry. In E. S. Mills (ed.), *Economic analysis of environmental problems,* Columbia University Press, London.
Darnay, A., and Franklin, W. (1972). *Salvage markets for materials in solid wastes,* U.S. EPA, Washington.
Grace, R., Turner, R. K., and Walter, I. (1976). Environment, international trade and recycling of waste materials. Paper read to International Trade

Session of Southern Economics Association Meeting, Atlanta, Georgia, November.

Hallwood, P. (1977). The external benefits of buffer stock schemes in secondary materials. PSERC/MRP Discussion Paper 77–01, Leicester University.

A. D. Little, Inc. (1975). *Analysis of Demand and Supply for Secondary Fiber in the US Paper and Paperboard Industry,* 3 Vols.

Massus, M. (1974). *Waste paper in the EEC.* 2 vols. European Commission, Brussels.

Miedema, A., (1976). *The case for virgin material charges: A theoretical and empirical evaluation in the paper industry.* Research Triangle Institute, North Carolina.

Page, Talbot (1976). *An economic basis for materials policy.* Johns Hopkins Press, Baltimore.

Pearce, D. W. (1976a). Environmental protection recycling and the international materials economy. In I. Walter (ed.), *Studies in international materials economy,* Wiley, New York.

———— (1976b). "The Economics of Waste Disposal in the United Kingdom," *Resources Policy,* December.

———— (1976c). The economics of waste recycling and the mechanisms to reduce price fluctuations in the secondary materials area: A case study of waste paper. Interim Report to OECD Environment Directorate.

———— and R. Grace (1976). "Stabilising Secondary Materials Markets: The Case of Waste Paper." *Resources Policy,* June.

B. Slatin (1975). "Economic Structure of the Paper Industry," *TAPPI,* vol. 58, July.

F. Smith (1975). "A Solid Waste Estimation Procedure: Materials Flows Approach." US EPA, Washington.

Tractionel (1976). *Les Vieux Papiers en Belgique,* vols. 1–3, Belgian Ministry of Economic Affairs, June.

Turner, R. K. and Grace, R. (1976). Social policy towards recycling paper wastes. *Resources Policy,* December.

———— (1977). Waste paper: Forecasting the demand for waste paper, *Conservation and recycling* (forthcoming).

U.K. Waste Management Advisory Council (1976). *First report,* HMSO, London.

U.S. EPA (1975). *Resources recovery and waste reduction, 3rd report to Congress,* Washington.

CHAPTER 17

Summary and Overview

Michel Potier

For a conclusion to this publication, I was asked to summarize the discussions following the presentation of the various reports contained in this volume. Rather than attempt a full and detailed account, I shall try to highlight the main general conclusions which I feel have emerged.

I believe they can be grouped around these four ideas:

- Recycling is but a single possible feature of a waste management policy;
- The range of instruments, which governments are now using or propose to use to encourage recycling, is extremely varied;
- There is a considerable gap between theory and practice as regards liberalization of the trade in secondary materials;
- A change is needed in public outlook and behavior.

RECYCLING IS BUT ONE POSSIBLE FEATURE OF A WASTE MANAGEMENT POLICY

For some people this would appear to be self-evident; yet, at a time when the press widely supports an "all we need to do is recycle" policy, it does not seem an altogether obvious conclusion. One of

344

the merits of this symposium will have been to show that while recycling may in some ways create new prospects, it is netiher a panacea nor an end in itself.

The advantages of recycling are well known. To begin with, recycling and re-use techniques can promote large energy savings in cases where the waste or scrap can be used as fuel, or provide raw materials, at a lower cost than the primary source. In addition, recycling can have a favorable impact on the environmental quality because it helps to reduce the need for extraction from increasingly poor grade ore and because the recycling process itself in most cases little pollutes the natural environment.

This being granted, there is no evading the basic question, which is: why recycle? In other words, before adopting the principle of recycling, the objectives should first be defined and a careful study made of the various instruments that can help to achieve them.

1. If the prime objective comes under the heading of a *management and disposal policy for urban waste,* Joan Wilcox clearly shows that many variants are possible, such as controlled dumping, incineration, pyrolysis, recycling, and so forth, the advantages of which can be measured by such yardsticks as economic costs, externalities, the recovery of raw materials and energy, or soil rehabilitation.

2. But if, instead, the object is to *conserve raw materials,* the merits of recycling must be set against such other variants as increased product life, a lower absolute level of consumption, the promotion of technologies making economical use of raw materials, and the replacement in manufacturing processes of scarce materials by more plentiful kinds capable of performing the same service.

In the case of the motor vehicle, for example, a study made by G. Leach for the OECD shows that, in 1970, the weight of all vehicles in the world could be estimated at 231 million tons, 85 percent of which consisted of iron and steel, 4.5 percent of aluminium, copper, lead, and zinc combined, and the remainder of other materials.

In 1970 these quantities represented 47 percent and 51 percent respectively of the world's total production of these metals. On the assumption that the average life of a vehicle is nine to eleven years, this would mean that motor vehicles account for about 5 percent of the annual production of such metals. On a world scale, this figure is a small one, but for certain countries it may represent a very large proportion of the metal consumed. In the United States, for example, it is estimated that the shares of total production absorbed by the manufacture of motor vehicles are as follows: steel, 20 percent; aluminium, 10 percent; copper, 7 percent; nickel, 13 percent; zinc, 35 percent; lead, 50 percent; and rubber, 60 percent. The potential for saving metal by recovering and recycling motor vehicles is impressive.

Actual savings are already substantial because, even before 1973, in the United States, 85 percent of scrapped vehicles were being recycled by scrap and spare parts' dealers. Further progress could be made through the development of vehicle-shredding machines and magnetic separators for sorting ferrous, nonferrous and nonmetallic materials, so that recovery rates of 90–95 percent might well be achieved.

While these figures may possibly be representative for the United States, they do not necessarily reflect the viability requirements of some European countries. In Germany, Mrs. Lichtwer's report indicates that the market works well without any government intervention. In France, on the other hand, a car shredder must produce at least one hundred tons of ferrous scrap a day to be an economic proposition.

3. One school of thought holds that there is no point in promoting recovery and recycling beyond a certain limit and that it would be better to encourage manufacturers to build longer life into their products while redesigning them so that they can be disassembled, repaired, recovered, or recycled more easily after giving more years of service. In other words, the question could be whether *to campaign for more intensive recycling or for longer product life.* Even if there is no easy answer to this question, it needs to be put. It was precisely in order to find answers to it that the Waste Management Policy Group of the OECD Environment Committee decided to make a detailed study of the comparative pros and cons of recycling and longer life for three products: cars, refrigerators, and a small household appliance yet to be selected. To me these three products seem to be particularly well chosen, since they will probably go to show that the policy options to be recommended are not necessarily the same in each case or appliance at all times. It is not my intention to anticipate the results of this study; I merely wonder whether extending the life of motor vehicles is a desirable option for the environment as a whole. To me this is far from obvious. Extending vehicle life could mean keeping cars in use that consume increasing quantities of energy,

which would therefore cause ever more pollution and noise and whose pollution control devices would deteriorate as time went by. Such a policy could also introduce considerable delays in putting new, less polluting, and quieter vehicles on the market. In other words, savings on the materials side would well be lost in the form of pollution and other disamenities.

Last under this heading, I agree with Dr. C. Wolbeck, who in his contribution stressed the important but limited part played by re-cycling in a general waste and environment management policy, and showed how an absolute reduction in consumption at the level of demand for raw materials coupled with the introduction of low-con-sumption technologies could do more to help conserve raw materials than recycling itself.

4. Another question to be considered is the extent to which *it may be better to re-use than recycle*. In the packaging area, for ex-ample, the re-use of containers would enable these to be recovered whenever health and sanitary standards permit. It is precisely this possibility that the Waste Management Policy Group of the OECD Environment Comniittee is currently investigating by comparing the environmental impact of certain technical processes and of certain producer and consumer habits adopted with regard to various types of container and beverage. It is certain that the failure to take externalities into account in our costing and pricing systems during recent years has added to the proliferation of throw-away packaging, which ac-counts for an increasing share of the volume of waste that has to be disposed of. The question, therefore, is whether corrective action should include the recycling or the re-use of beverage containers. The first results of work so far done suggest that it is the returnable glass bottle system that would reduce combined economic and social costs to the lowest level. The answer to this question might be dif-ferent for different products.

A WIDE VARIETY OF INSTRUMENTS ARE NOW USED OR PROPOSED BY GOVERNMENTS IN ORDER TO ENCOURAGE RECYCLING

From most of the reports presented in the symposium, it is clear that market forces alone cannot fully promote the waste recycling, even if recycling is regarded as desirable, and that government intervention is often necessary. This may take several forms, classifiable under the headings of regulations, economic incentives, and administrative instruments, which vary greatly from one country to another. Robin Bidwell has given an excellent account of these in his report, and I need not cover the ground again.*

I would, however, like to stress three points which seem to me to be particularly important:

• First, the fact that there is no single, ready-made solution. Most types of action which aim to promote recycling, as Robin Bidwell clearly shows, are undertaken on two levels: at supply level by trying to organize the product markets and recovery channels, and at demand level by introducing incentives to promote the re-use or recycling of certain products.

But it is no easy task to determine in advance what form of action will be most suitable. The various case studies presented at this symposium clearly illustrate this point. Donald Fink thus shows that, for the nonferrous metals industry, the degree of competition affecting the primary and secondary industries appears to have no great impact on the recycling ratio. From this he deduces that any action designed to promote the recycling of nonferrous metals should be undertaken at the demand level. More importantly, with some forms of action, there can be no certainty, *ex ante,* that the desired result will be achieved. The reports of John Butlin and David Pearce, for example, challenge to some extent the usefulness of so-called stabilization funds or buffer stocks which in theory are intended to damp down the widely fluctuating prices for secondary materials and for waste paper in particular. Actually, buffer stocks may even have destabilizing effects if supply and demand elasticities are at certain levels. In the absence of any thorough knowledge of price elasticities in relation to the demand for secondary materials and the supply, and as to the elasticity of substitution of secondary for primary materials in conjunction with various manufacturing processes, the particular difficulty of forecasting the success of such systems in advance will hence readily be realized;

• Second, the growing part played by economic incentives and,

---

* Readers who are interested will find further information in a recent OECD report entitled "Waste Management in OECD Member Countries" (Paris, 1976), which gives a comprehensive list of measures taken by OECD countries in this field.

in particular, by taxes or charges in recycling policies. The inventory of waste management measures in the OECD countries shows that most governments have used or plan on using financial incentives to promote recycling.

1. These incentives sometimes take the form of grants. In Sweden, plant for recycling or neutralizing dangerous wastes is thus eligible for a grant. In France, grants are available in respect of equipment for eliminating toxic and dangerous industrial wastes, and producers may be refunded treatment costs. In Canada, several provincial governments pay grants for the collection of abandoned vehicles (British Columbia).

2. Incentives may also be in the form of a charge. In view of the large quantities of waste oil discharged into the environment every year, the scale of the damage this causes and the various possibilities for re-using such oil, economic incentives, as Mr. Irwin has shown, have been introduced in various countries in order to encourage recycling. The 1975 European Communities Directive is modeled, to some extent, after the German pattern and envisages the possible introduction of a system of charges to cover the collection and processing of waste oil. It should be noted, however, that such a system is not a true pollution charge system as economists understand the term, since the charge is not based on pollution or damage, and since essentially its ultimate purpose is to finance the collection and treatment of waste oil.

3. In his report, F. Smith discusses the more ambitious proposal of a charge on products. This is a very tempting idea with two main objectives: first, to induce producers and consumers, through the pricing system, to cut down the flow of waste generated by production and consumption processes and, second, to provide a way of raising money to finance waste management programs. The practical implementation of such a system involves many problems which F. Smith clearly points out:

a. To what categories of product should such a charge be applied? Should all types of products contributing to the flow of municipal wastes be included or only certain very limited categories such as packaging, paper, and tires?

b. What should be the level of, and basis for, such a charge? In principle, the charge should reflect the cost to society of disposing of the waste, including the cost of any damage caused. But as we know that in practice a simple approximation must suffice, what specifically is that approximation? Would it be better to base the charge on volume or weight?

    c. What adjustment should be made to allow for a producer's recycling effort?

    d. To what use would the money collected in this way be put?

    e. What would be the impact of a charge on products in terms of waste levels, the recycling ratio, the price to the consumer, and the distribution of income?

    f. What would be the cost of administering such a system?

The United States Environmental Protection Agency already has part of the answer to many of these questions. As these are highly complex problems which are difficult to answer, the analytical work carried out by the Solid Waste Management Office of the Environmental Protection Agency is remarkable and deserves mention as a model for countries which are increasingly drawn to taxes or charges as a major policy instrument.

• Third, the need for greater harmonization in sectoral industrial policy. The wide variety of measures taken in different countries, particularly as regards the financial incentives already referred to (grants and taxes or charges), threatens some distortion of competition in certain sectors of activity. Here again, prevention would be better than cure. The various countries should, therefore, do everything they can to ensure that the cost of waste disposal is fairly shared through general application of the principle that the producer of waste must pay for its disposal.

THERE IS AN APPRECIABLE GAP BETWEEN THE THEORY AND PRACTICE OF LIBERALIZING TRADE IN SECONDARY MATERIALS

Professor Pethig's report shows how the liberalization of "waste trade flows" between countries benefits all sides. Similar conclusions were reached by I. Walter in earlier studies. In other words, theory teaches that it would be in the interests of all trade partners—buyers and sellers of waste and scrap—to liberalize the trade, because markets would be bigger, thus making certain recycling operations more attractive and ultimately leading to sizable savings in natural resources.

But how do we find trade to be actually conducted between OECD member countries? The striking fact is that export restrictions have been or are now applied by most OECD member countries on ferrous and nonferrous metal scrap. The measures concerning nonferrous metal waste and scrap relate mainly to aluminium, copper, lead, zinc, nickel, tin, tungsten, and molybdenum. Some countries go to the extreme of an outright ban on exports, mainly of ferrous and copper scrap. The measure most frequently resorted to is the export license granted on a case-by-case basis after thorough scrutiny of each separate export application. Some countries, like the United States, have introduced export quota or licensing systems as a transitional measure, paving the way from severe restrictions to more liberalized trading. Even more striking is the fact that, in most cases, no time limit is set; generally speaking, the measures are introduced for an indefinite period. In Sweden, controls on nonferrous metal exports go back to 1928, in Switzerland to 1939, and in the United Kingdom to the start of World War II. What major concerns does the retention of these controls betray? The reason most frequently given is to conserve home supplies in the event of a shortage. Although three other reasons—to stabilize home prices and curb inflation, to protect a particular manufacturing industry, and to guard against the depletion of nonrenewable indigenous resources—are sometimes also put forward, these do not appear to be the vital factors. What should be inferred from these observations?

If governments fail to apply the theory, it is not, in my view, because they consider it to be wrong but rather because they attach more weight to security as regards their supply of both primary and secondary raw materials. In other words, by forfeiting the advantages of higher recycling ratios which liberalizing the trade in secondary raw materials would afford, they purchase some degree of security of supply by maintaining export controls, often of indefinite duration.

THE NEED FOR A CHANGE IN PUBLIC OUTLOOK AND BEHAVIOR

Apart from export controls on secondary raw materials, many other obstacles hinder the progress of recycling and re-use. These obstacles —which this economics-oriented symposium has too little stressed— may be of an institutional, sociological, and psychological nature.

They are bound up with the behavior of individuals and the way institutions in our consumer society operate. Producers and consumers have been encouraged to draw unreservedly on our natural resources, whose economic value has been incorrectly assessed. While admittedly this has meant larger markets and low-cost mass production, it has also induced and encouraged waste. Awareness and condemnation of this waste are relatively recent phenomena. In this context, it is not enough to react against the behavior of producers and consumers who fail to husband scarce natural resources, but the nature and hierarchy of needs which the economy is designed to meet and the means for meeting them in a new perspective—waste reduction— must be re-assessed.

These changes in outlook and behavior can come about only if the most industrialized market-economy countries—those best representing the consumer society—make a major effort

- to improve the state of our knowledge about natural resources and their use;
- to steer the production system toward processes and techniques that are both cleaner and more sparing of raw materials;
- to guide consumers toward less polluting and less wasteful forms of consumption;
- to ensure that the public is better informed and becomes more closely involved;
- to make the objectives of economic development better understood and to encourage their broad public discussion.

This is a brief picture of the four key ideas which to me seem to emerge from the symposium. Those taking part are bound to point out that I have failed to include many important factors. I trust that they will not interpret any such omission as intentional on my part, but rather as evidence that the delightful setting at Bellagio caused my attention to wander at the very instant when some important point was raised during the course of our discussions.

Trade in Secondary Materials: A Theoretical Approach

Rüdiger Pethig

1. ASSUMPTIONS AND DEFINITIONS

The production technology for the private consumption good i $(i = 1, 2)$ is given by the function $Q^i: D_Q{}^i \to IR_+$, where the domain $D_Q{}^i$ is defined below and where $q_i = Q^i(a_i, m_i, s_i)$ denotes the quantity of good i that can be produced when the labor input is a_i, the basic material input is m_i, and the by-product (secondary material) is s_i. Q^i has the following properties.[1]

(i 1): $D_Q{}^i \subset IR^3$ is convex

(i 2): $(a_i, m_i, s_i) \notin D_Q{}^i$, if $a_i, m_i < 0$ or if $s_i < \beta^i(a_i, m_i)$, where $\beta^i: IR_+{}^2 \to IR_-$ is a strictly monotone decreasing function with $\beta^i(a_i, m_i) = 0$ for $a_i = 0$ or $m_i = 0$

(i 3): $(a_i, m_i, s_i) \in D_Q{}^i$, $a_i = 0$ and $m_i \geq 0$ implies $Q^i(a_i, m_i, s_i) = 0$

(i 4): Q^i is differentiable and concave

(i 5): $Q_s{}^i\big|_{(a_i, m_i, s_i)} < 0$, if $s_i \geq 0$

In (i 2) we establish the convention that the input variables m_i and a_i are nonnegative, whereas s_i is not restricted in sign. If $s_i < 0$, the quantity $(-s_i)$ of secondary material is generated in the production of good $i;$ if $s_i > 0$ the sector i uses the quantity s_i as an input. This sign agreement will prove particularly convenient in the analysis of the next section. Furthermore, by (i 2) we exclude increasing returns to scale in the generation of secondary material. (i 5) makes precise that, in the technologies Q^i, the secondary material is no productive input. Instead, $Q_{s_i}|_x < 0$ for some $x \epsilon D_{Q^i}$ indicates that the technology Q_i includes some secondary material abatement (or disposal) facilities such that, with increased disposal of secondary material, q^i declines for fixed a^i and m^i, implying that part of these resources must have been used up for the abatement of secondary material.

Figure A–1 illustrates the domain of Q^i, projected into the (a_i, s_i) plane for arbitrarily given $m_i = \bar{m} > 0$. The curve OA is the graph of the function $s_i = \beta^i (a_i, \bar{m})$, and curves such as BCD are isoquants of the comsumption good i such that q_i increases with increasing distance of the isoquant from the origin.[2] Figure A–2 shows the graph of the function $q_i = Q^i (\bar{a}, \bar{m}, s_i)$, that is, all combinations of q_i and s_i that can be produced with fixed positive inputs $\bar{a}$ and $\bar{m}$.

It is an important implication of the property (i 5) (and of the differentiability of Q^i) that, starting at $s_i = 0$ (in Fig. A–2, the production of good i cannot be increased for given a_i and m_i unless more secondary material is generated ($s_i < 0$). This defines the technological by-product property of the secondary material, which is a necessary condition for any economy to suffer from pollution.

The production possibilities in the basic material industry consist of

(i) a virgin material technology described by the differentiable and concave production function $M^v : IR_+ \rightarrow IR_+$, where $m_v = M^v(a_v)$ is the basic material produced by the labor input a^v and $M^v(0) = 0$.

(ii) a recycling technology given by the production function $M^\rho : D_{M^\rho} \rightarrow IR_+$, where $D_{M^\rho} \subset IR_+^2$ is defined below and $m_\rho = M^\rho(a_\rho, s_m)$ is the quantity of basic material produced when the labor input is a_ρ and the input of secondary material is s_m. M^ρ is assumed to have the following properties.

(m 1): $D_{M^\rho} \equiv \{(a_\rho, s_m) \epsilon IR_+^2 | s_m \leq \beta^m(a_\rho)\}$ is convex, where β^m is a strictly increasing function with $\beta^m(0) = 0$

(m 2): M is differentiable and concave

(m 3): $x, \bar{x} \epsilon D_{M^\rho}, \bar{s}_m > s_m, \bar{a}_\rho = a_\rho$ and $M_{s^\rho}|_x = 0$ implies $M_{s^\rho}|_{\bar{x}} < 0$

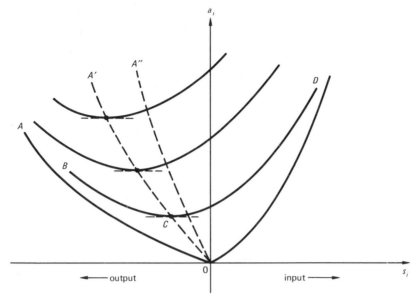

Figure A–1 Joint Production of a Consumption Good and Secondary Material I

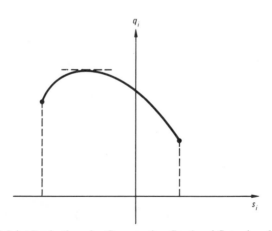

Figure A–2 Joint Production of a Consumption Good and Secondary Material II

(m 4): For every $s_m \epsilon \{s_m | (a_\rho, s_m) \epsilon D_M{}^\rho\}$ we have

$$\max_{(a_\rho, s_m) \epsilon D_M{}^\rho (s_m)} \frac{M^\rho(a_\rho, s_m)}{s_m} = \text{constant}$$

where $D_M{}^\rho(s_m) \equiv \{(a_\rho, s_m') \epsilon D_M{}^\rho | s_m' = s_m\}$

(m 5): $s_m = 0$ and $a_\rho > 0$ implies $M^\rho(a_\rho, s_m) = 0$

Above we have listed some straightforward properties of M^ρ such as the impossibility of virgin material production (m 5) and the impossibility of recycling without labor input (m 1). When combined with (m 3), condition (m 1) also restricts the disposal of secondary material: with given labor input one can neither recycle arbitrarily large amounts of basic material nor neutralize [3] arbitrarily large quantities of secondary material.

The basic material reclaimed from one unit of secondary material cannot be arbitrarily increased by increasing the labor input. It is assumed that, since the content of basic material in the secondary material is limited, there is a maximum ratio m_ρ/s_m independent of the scale of production (m 4).

Fig. A–3 illustrates M^ρ. The line OA is the graph of β^m and the line $OA''\,'$ consists of all points $(a_\rho,\ s_m)$ that satisfy the maximum condition in (m 4). If in Fig. A–3 the graph of β^m were given by OA' (or OA'' or $OA''\,'$) instead of OA, we would have examples for recycling technologies without secondary material abatement processes. An important feature of many secondary material markets appears to be a low degree of market organization and information as well as high costs of collection and transportation, at least high relative to the low unit-value of the secondary material (see I. Walter [1975]).

In order to incorporate such market imperfections into our model in a simple (and admittedly rudimentary) way, we assume that the purchase (collection, etc.) of secondary material s_m by the recycling sector requires the labor input

$$a_s = ts_m \tag{1}$$

where the positive constant t is interpreted as a "transactions input coefficient" in a broad sense. Analytically, we can treat (1) as a part of the recycling technology. Hence we replace the function M^ρ by the function M^r, where (by definition) M^r is linked to M^ρ as follows:

For every $(a_\rho, s_m) \epsilon D_{M^\rho}$, if $a_r = a_\rho + ts_m$, then $M^\rho(a_\rho, s_m) = M^r(a_r, s_m)$. Correspondingly, the domain of M^r is $D_M \equiv \{(a_r,\ s_m)\epsilon IR_+{}^2 | a_r = a_\rho + ts_m$ and $(a_\rho, s_m)\epsilon D_{M^\rho}\}$.

Suppose that, in Fig. A–4, $BCDE$ represents an isoquant (for $m = \bar{m}$) of the function M^ρ, and OA is the graph the linear function

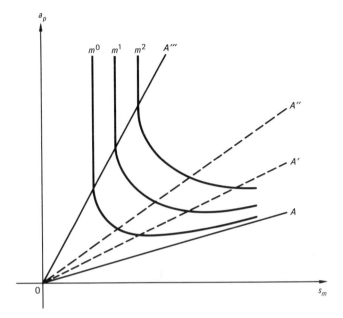

Figure A–3 Recycling Technology I

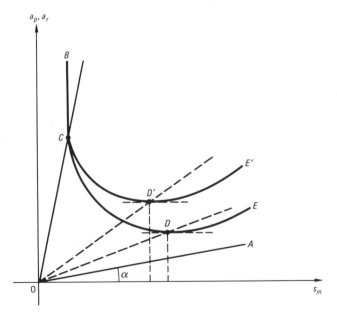

Figure A–4 Recycling Technology II

of (1), that is, $\tan \alpha = t$. Then $BCD'E'$ is the isoquant for $\bar{m}$ of the function M^r constructed by adding vertically OA to $BCDE$.

For analytical purposes, it is convenient to combine the functions M^v and M^r to obtain a single function M. It is easy to show that this function M is concave and quasi concave and has the same domain as M^r.

Fig. A–5 illustrates how the production isoquants of M are constructed from those belonging to M^v and M^r. Let $PFGH$ be the isoquant for $m = 10$ associated with M^r and let $M^v(a^4) = 10$. Then the isoquant for $m = 10$ belonging to M is given by $ERFGH$. We now show how an arbitrary point, say R in Fig. A–5, on EF is generated: The quantity a^2 of labor is used in the virgin material production to obtain $M^v(a^2) = 5$ and the input bundle $(a^1, \; s_m{}^1)$ yields $M^r(a^1, \; s_m{}^1) = 5$ according to the recycling technology. Hence the

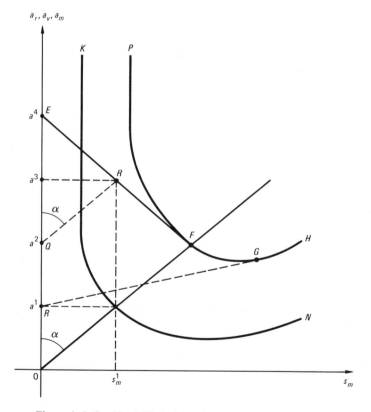

Figure A–5 Combined Virgin Material and Recycling Technology

coordinates of R are $a^1 + a^2 = a^3$ and $s_m{}^1$, and the output at R is $m = 10$.

If the virgin material sector is very productive so that, for example, in Fig. A–5 we have $M^v(a^1) = 10$ (instead of $M^v(a^4) = 10$), the M-isoquant for $m = 10$ is RGH, a line with positive slope everywhere. In this case the virgin material technology is said to dominate the recycling technology. This concept can be made precise as follows: If there is $(a_r', s_m') \epsilon D_M{}^r$, $M^r(a_r', s_m') = M^v(a_v) = m^o$, such that $a_v < a_r'$, then M^v is said to dominate M^r at m^o. If this condition holds for every $m^o > 0$, then we say that M^v dominates M^r.[4] Note that the dominance of M^v over M^r may be partly or even completely due to transaction costs on the secondary material market that had been incorporated into M^r.

From the construction of M, it is clear that every point (m, a_m, s_m) satisfying M can be split up into two points (m_v, a_v) and (m_r, a_r, s_m), satisfying M^v and M^r respectively, as well as the equations $m_v + m_r = m$ and $a_v + a_r = a_m$. Hence for every $(a_m, s_m) \epsilon D_M$, a unique recycling ratio [5]

$$R = R(a_m, s_m) \equiv \frac{(M^r[a_r, s_m])}{(M[a_m, s_m])}$$

is defined, where a_r is chosen so that

$$M^r(a_r, s_m) + M^v(a_m - a_r) = M(a_m, s_m).$$

Denoting $S^m \equiv \frac{s_m}{a_m}$ the secondary material intensity in the production of basic material and defining $\hat{S}^m \equiv \frac{dS^m}{S^m}$ and $\hat{R} \equiv \frac{dR}{R}$, we summarize the preceding arguments in Lemma 1.

Lemma 1. Let M be homogeneous of degree one.

(i) Then $\dfrac{\hat{R}}{\hat{S}^m} \{\lessgtr\} 0$, if $R \{\leqq\} 1$.

(ii) Then the reclaiming ratio $\dfrac{M^p(a_p, s_m)}{s_m}$ is a monotone decreasing function of S^m.

Proof.   Obvious.

We now complete the description of the economy. The aggregate supply of secondary material that is generated in the consumption good industries is $s_1 + s_2$, while the demand is s_m. We define the aggregate excess supply as $e \equiv - (s_1 + s_2 + s_m)$. If e is a proper excess supply of secondary material ($e > 0$), e is assumed to be emitted into the environment,[6] causing environmental deterioration, which is measured by the decline of a real valued environmental quality index u. Formally we introduce a decreasing strictly concave function $U:IR_+ \to IR$, where $u = U(e)$ is the environmental quality index that results from releasing $e \geq 0$ units of secondary material into the environment. With increasing e, the index u decreases and eventually becomes negative. However, for convenience we choose a function U with $U(0)$ positive and large enough to ensure that $U(e)$ is positive for all attainable emissions e.

Finally, the demand side of the model is given by a strictly increasing quasi concave welfare function $W:IR_+^2 \times IR \to IR_+$, where $w = W(q_1{}^d, q_2{}^d, u)$ is the welfare index resulting from the consumption goods demand $q_1{}^d, q_2{}^d$ and from the environmental quality u.

2. ASSUMPTIONS AND DEFINITIONS

The production possibility set T of the economy is defined as the set of all triples (q_1, q_2, u) such that the resource constraints

$$\bar{a} - a_1 - a_2 - a_m \geq 0 \qquad \text{(initial endowment } \bar{a} > 0)$$
$$e + s_1 + s_2 + s_m \geq 0 \qquad\qquad\qquad\qquad (2)$$
$$m - m_1 - m_2 \geq 0$$

and the equations $q_i = Q^i(a_i, m_i, s_i)$ for $i = 1,2$, $m = M(a_m, s_m)$ and $u = U(e)$ are satisfied.[7] The properties of the set T are of particular interest since T is the consumers' choice set as a subset of the domain of W. For analytical reasons, it is convenient to study the set $\bar{T} \equiv \{y | 0 \leq y \leq \hat{y} \text{ and } \bar{y} \epsilon T\} \supset T$, instead of T. This substitution will not affect our results, since W is assumed to be strictly monotonically increasing and, therefore, all that matters in the present model is the set of upper boundary points in T.

Lemma 2. $\bar{T}$ is convex and compact.

Proof. Let y, y' $\epsilon \bar{T}$ and associate to y and y' the factor allocations $v \equiv ((a_i), (m_i), (s_i), a_m, s_m)$ and $v' \equiv ((a_i'), (m_i'), (s_i'), a_m', s_m')$, respectively. $\bar{T}$ is convex if $y^\lambda \equiv (\lambda y + (1 - \lambda)y') \epsilon \bar{T}$ for $\lambda \epsilon [0,1]$. The factor allocation $v^\lambda \equiv \lambda v + (1 - \lambda)v'$ satisfies the first two inequalities of (2). In fact, it fulfills (2) completely, since by concavity of M it follows that $M(a_m{}^\lambda, s_m{}^\lambda) - m_1{}^\lambda - m_2{}^\lambda \geq m^\lambda - m_1{}^\lambda - m_2{}^\lambda \geq 0$. Consequently, $y'' \equiv [Q^1(a_1{}^\lambda, m_1{}^\lambda, s_1{}^\lambda), Q^2(a_2{}^\lambda, m_2{}^\lambda, s_2{}^\lambda), U(e^\lambda)]\epsilon T$. Concavity of Q^1, Q^2, and U implies that y'' is component-wise not less than y^λ. Thus $y^\lambda \epsilon \bar{T}$. $\bar{T}$ is compact, if T is compact. The compactness of T follows from standard arguments.

$$QED$$

Fig. 11–2 in Chapter 11 illustrates the production possibility set T.[8] At the maximum possible environmental quality (point A), the production possibility frontier is BC. The maximum output levels of good 1 and good 2 are attained at environmental quality levels OG and OF respectively. Thus in Fig. 11–2, good 2 is the environment intensive commodity.

After we have shown the feasible allocations (q_1, q_2, u), we wish to specify which allocations are selected when the welfare is maximal, when the economy is in competitive equilbrium with environmental laissez-faire, and, finally, when a competitive equilibrium is supplemented by an environmental price and standard policy. We, therefore, assume that in the economy described above, there are perfectly competitive markets for the two (private) consumption goods, for labor, basic material, and—possibly—for the secondary material. The market prices are denoted p_1, p_2, p_a, p_m, and p_s respectively. The market clearing conditions for the consumption goods are $q_i - q_i{}^d \geq 0$ ($i = 1,2$), and the resource constraints (2) are now also interpreted as market clearing conditions for labor, basic material, and secondary material.

All production sectors maximize profits as price-takers, that is, they solve the problems

$$\max_{(q_i, a_i, m_i, s_i)} \min_{\alpha_i} \quad L_i = G^i(q_i, a_i, m_i, s_i) + \alpha_i[Q^i(a_i, m_i, s_i) - q_i] \quad (3)$$

where $G^i(q_i, a_i, m_i, s_i) \equiv p_iq_i - p_aa_i - p_mm_i - p_ss_i$, and

$$\max_{(m, a_m, s_m)} \min_{\alpha_m} \quad L^m = G^m(m, a_m, s_m) + \alpha_m[M(a_m, s_m) - m] \quad (4)$$

where $G^m(m, a_m, s_m) \equiv p_mm - p_aa_m - p_ss_m$.

The consumption sector solves

$$\max_{(q_1{}^d, q_2{}^d)} \min_{\alpha_y} \quad L^c = W(q_1{}^d, q_2{}^d, \bar{u}) + \alpha_y[\bar{\bar{Y}} - p_1q_1{}^d - p_2q_2{}^d] \quad (5)$$

where $u \equiv U(\max[O, - (\hat{s}_1 + \hat{s}_2 + \hat{s}_m)])$,

$$Y \equiv p_a\bar{a} + \Sigma_i G^i(\hat{q}_i \, \hat{a}_i, \hat{m}_i, \hat{s}_i) + G^m(\hat{m}, \hat{a}_m, \hat{s}_m)$$

and where the "hat" variables are the solutions to (3) and (4).

According to (5), the consumers take the "prevailing" u as given. This is a consequence of the assumption that the environmental quality is a pure public consumption good.

Definition 1: The vectors $p^o \equiv (p_1^o, \ p_2^o, \ p_a^o, \ p_m^o, \ p_s^o) \epsilon IR_+^5$ and $x^o \equiv ((q_i^o), \ (q_i^{do}), \ (a_i^o), \ (m_i^o), \ (s_i^o), \ a_m^o, \ s_m^o, \ m^o, \ e^o, \ u^o) \epsilon IR^{15}$ constitute a competitive equilibrium (without environmental policy), (i) if x^o satisfies (2) and $q_i \geq q_i^d$ and (ii) if x^o is a solution to (3), (4) and (5) for p^o.

It will be shown later that there is a class of economies for which the equilibrium prices p_1^o, p_2^o, p_a^o, and p_m^o will be strictly positive, and that, if also $p_s^o > 0$, then $s_1^o + s_2^o + s_m^o = - e^o = 0$. In this case the secondary material is a scarce pure intermediate good as well as the basic material, and competitive equilibrium coincides with a perfectly clean environment in the absence of environmental policy.[9] Alternatively, the equilibrium allocation x^o may be such that $e^o > 0$. In this case, environmental disruption $(U(e^o) < U(0))$ occurs at $p_s^o = 0$, and it may be desirable to reduce the laissez-faire emission e^o and thus increase the environmental quality. In the following we only consider one particular environmental policy instrument: the Baumol-Oates (1971) version [10] of the so-called environmental price and standard system.

We suppose that, as a result of a political decision process, the society has determined that the environmental quality (aggregate emission) must not be less than (exceed) some standard $\bar{u}$ [$\bar{e} \equiv U^{-1}(\bar{u})$]. This environmental policy target is assumed to be accomplished by levying a tax $p_s < 0$ on secondary material, with the government's tax revenue $p_s e \leq 0$ being redistributed to the consumption sector as a lump sum transfer.

This type of environmental policy can be easily incorporated into the model without excluding the possibility of laissez-faire equilibria with $p_s^o \geq 0$.

Definition 2: Let $\bar{e} \geq 0$ be an emission standard. The vectors x' and p' constitute an $\bar{e}$-feasible competitive equilibrium

- if x' satisfies $\bar{e} \geq e'$, $q_i' \geq q_i^{d'}$ $(i = 1, 2)$ and (2)
- and if for $p = p'$ the vector x' is a solution to (3), (4) and (5),

where in (5) $\bar{\bar{Y}}$ is substituted by $\hat{Y} \equiv \bar{\bar{Y}} - \max[0, -(\hat{s}_1 + \hat{s}_2 + \hat{s}_m)]p_s$.

Definition 3: An $\bar{e}$-feasible competitive equilibrium (p', x') is $\bar{e}$-efficient, if there is no $\bar{e}$-feasible equilibrium (p'', x'') such that $q_i^{d''} \geq q_i^{d'}$ for $i = 1, 2$ with the strict inequality holding for at least one good.[11]

Next we define the Lagrangean

$$
\begin{aligned}
L^W = L^W(x, \lambda) &\equiv W(q_1^d, q_2^d, u) + \Sigma_i \lambda_i[Q^i(a_i, m_i, s_i) - q_i] \\
&+ \lambda_m[M(a_m, s_m) - m] + \lambda_s[-s_1 - s_2 - s_m] \\
&+ \Sigma_i \bar{\lambda}_i[q_i - q_i^d] + \lambda_a[\bar{a} - a_1 - a_2 - a_m] \\
&+ \bar{\lambda}_m[m - m_1 - m_2] + \lambda_e[e + s_1 + s_2 - s_m] \\
&+ \lambda_u[U(e) - u] + \bar{\lambda}_e[\bar{e} - e]
\end{aligned}
\tag{6}
$$

and we further consider the problems

$$
\max_x \quad \min_{\lambda^{(\bar{e})}} \quad L^W(x, \lambda) \tag{7}
$$

$$
\max_{x^{(u)}} \quad \min_{\lambda^{(u)}} \quad L^W(x, \lambda) \tag{8}
$$

$$
\max_{x^{(u)}} \quad \min_{\lambda^{(u, \bar{e}, e)}} \quad L^W(x, \lambda) \tag{9}
$$

where $x^{(u)} \epsilon IR^{14}$ is equal to

$$
x \equiv ((q_i), (q_i^d), (a_i), (m_i), (s_i), a_m, s_m, m, e, u) \epsilon IR^{15}
$$

except that u is omitted, and where $\lambda^{(\bar{e})}$ is equal to

$$
\lambda \equiv ((\lambda_i), (\bar{\lambda}_i), \lambda_m, \bar{\lambda}_m, \lambda_a, \lambda_s, \lambda_e, \lambda_u, \bar{\lambda}_e) \epsilon R^{11}
$$

except that in $\lambda^{(e)}$ the component λ_e is put identically equal to zero. The vectors $\lambda^{(u)}$ and $\lambda^{(u, \bar{e}, e)}$ are defined correspondingly.

Finally, let $(x^+, \lambda^+) \epsilon IR^{26}$ be defined alternatively by the vectors $(x, \lambda^{(\bar{e})})$, $(x, \lambda^{(u)})$, or $(x, \lambda^{(\bar{u}, \bar{e}, e)})$ which solve (7), (8), or (9) respectively, and which, by the Kuhn-Tucker Theorem,[12] satisfy

$$
\left.\frac{\partial L^W}{\partial \xi}\right|_{x^+, \lambda^+} \leq 0 \qquad \left.x^+ \frac{\partial L^W}{\partial \xi}\right|_{x^+, \lambda^+} = 0
$$

$$
\left.\frac{\partial L^W}{\partial \rho}\right|_{x^+, \lambda^+} \geq 0 \qquad \left.\lambda^+ \frac{\partial L^W}{\partial \rho}\right|_{x^+, \lambda^+} = 0
\tag{10}
$$

where ξ is equal to x or $x^{)u\zeta}$ and ρ is equal to λ, omitting, respectively, $\bar{\lambda}_e$ or λ_u or $(\lambda_e, \bar{\lambda}_e$ and $\lambda_u)$.

Theorem 1: Suppose the assumption of Section 1 hold, and consider a vector (x^+, λ^+) satisfying $(a_i^+, m_i^+, s_i^+)\epsilon$ interior $D_Q{}^i$ and $(a_m^+, s_m^+)\epsilon$ interior D_M.[13]

(i) Let (x^+, λ^+) solve (7). Then there exist prices $p \ \epsilon \ IR^r$ such that (p, x^+) is a competitive equilibrium (decentralizing the welfare maximizing allocation x^+).

(ii) Let (x^+, λ^+) solve (8). Then there exist prices $p \ \epsilon \ IR^5$ such that (p, x^+) is an $\bar{e}$-efficient competitive equilibrium.

(iii) Let (x^+, λ^+) solve (9). Then there exist prices $p \ \epsilon \ IR_+{}^5$ such that (p, x^+) is a competitive equilibrium (without environmental policy).

Proof: Ad (i): By the first sentence of Theorem 1 and by (10) the vector (x^+, λ^+) satisfies

$$\begin{aligned}
\lambda_i^+ Q_v^{i+} - \lambda_v^+ &= 0 \qquad (v = a, m; i = 1, 2) \\
\lambda_i^+ Q_s^{i+} - \lambda_s^+ + \lambda_e^+ &= 0 \\
\lambda_m^+ M_a^+ - \lambda_a^+ &= 0 \\
\lambda_m^+ M_s^+ - \lambda_s^+ + \lambda_e^+ &= 0
\end{aligned} \tag{11}$$

and

$$\begin{aligned}
q_i^{d+} - q_{i+} &= 0 \\
\bar{a} - a_1^+ - a_2^+ - a_m^+ &= 0 \\
m^+ - m_1^+ - m_2^+ &= 0 \\
- s_1^+ - s_2^+ - s_m^+ &\equiv e^+ \geq 0.
\end{aligned} \tag{12}$$

Consider the price vector $p \equiv (p_1 = \lambda_1^+, \ p_2 = \lambda_2^+, \ p_a = \lambda_a^+,$ $p_m = \lambda_m^+, \ p_s = \lambda_s^+ - \lambda_e^+)$ and solve (3) and (4) for p. By the Kuhn-Tucker Theorem, the corresponding Kuhn-Tucker conditions are necessary and sufficient for a solution to (3) and (4).[14] In particular, the Eqs. (11) belong to these conditions. Therefore, we know that the production plans $(q_i^+, a_i^+, m_i^+, s_i^+)$ for $i = 1, 2$, and (m^+, a_m^+, s_m^+) maximize profits at prices p.

The Kuhn-Tucker conditions obtained from solving (5) for p, for $U(e^+)$ and for

$$\hat{Y}^+ \equiv p_a\bar{a} - p_s e^+ + \Sigma_i \, G^i(q_i^+, a_i^+, m_i^+, s_i^+) + G^m(m^+, a_m^+, s_m^+)$$

are necessary and sufficient for a solution of (5). Consider now the Kuhn-Tucker conditions

$$\hat{W}_{q_i} - \hat{\alpha}_y p_i = 0 \tag{13}$$

that are associated to the solution $(\hat{q}_1{}^d, \hat{q}_2{}^d, \hat{\alpha}_y)$ of (5). This solution satisfies $\hat{Y}^+ = p_1 \hat{q}_1{}^d + p_2 \hat{q}_2{}^d$, since by assumption $W_{q_i} \gtrless 0$. Further, it follows from the definition of G^i and G^m that $\hat{Y}^+ = p_1 q_1{}^+ + p_2 q_2{}^+$ and from the definition of p_i that

$$\frac{\hat{W}_{q_1}}{\hat{W}_{q_2}} = \frac{\hat{W}_{q1}{}^+}{\hat{W}_{q2}{}^+} .$$

All this implies when combined with the equations $q_i{}^{d+} = q_i{}^+$ from (12) that $(\hat{q}_1{}^d = q_1{}^{d+}, \hat{q}_2{}^d = q_2{}^{d+}, \hat{\alpha}_y = 1)$ is a solution to (5) relative to p. Hence p has the desired properties.

Ad (ii): Equilibrium prices p can be constructed as in the proof of Theorem 1 i. (Note that $\lambda_u{}^+ \equiv 0$ implies $\lambda_e{}^+ = \overline{\lambda}_e{}^+$.) Eqs. (10), when derived from solving (8), also yield $\bar{e} \geq e^+$. Hence (p, x^+) is an $\bar{e}$-feasible competitive equilibrium. It remains to show that (p, x^+) is $\bar{e}$-efficient. This follows from the fact that the Kuhn-Tucker conditions associated with the solution of

$$\begin{aligned}
\max_{x} \min_{\lambda} \quad L(x, \lambda) &\equiv \Sigma_i \lambda_i [Q^i(a_i, m_i, s_i) - q_i{}^+] \\
&+ \lambda_m [M(a_m, s_m) - m] + \overline{\lambda}_m [m - m_1 - m_2] \\
&+ \lambda_a [\bar{a} - a_1 - a_2 - a_m] + \lambda_s [- s_1 - s_2 - s_m] \\
&+ \lambda_e [e + s_1 + s_2 + s_m] + \overline{\lambda}_e [\bar{e} - e]
\end{aligned} \tag{14}$$

are a subset of the Kuhn-Tucker conditions in (10).

Ad (iii): Again, equilibrium prices p can be constructed as in the proof of Theorem 1 i. Note that $p_s = \lambda_s{}^+ - \lambda_e{}^+ = \lambda_s{}^+ \geq 0$.

QED

Suppose that in Theorem 1 iii the equilibrium is such that $e^+ = 0$. Then this equilibrium (p, x^+) also satisfies the Theorems 1 i and 1 ii. In this case (except for $p_s = 0$), the secondary material is a scarce pure intermediate good as is the basic material. Also, the production possibility set $\bar{T}$ does not look like that depicted in Fig. 11–2, since the equilibrium (p, x^+) is not only $\bar{e}$-efficient for $\bar{e} = e^+ = 0$ but also for every $\bar{e} > 0$. Therefore in Fig. 11–2 in Chapter 11, the plane ABC is equal to the plane $OD'E'$ instead.

If, on the other hand, the economy is such that $e^+ > 0$ in an equilibrium (p, x^+) of Theorem 1 iii, then the three parts of Theorem 1 do not coincide. Suppose that $e^+ > 0$ in (x^+, p) of Theorem 1 i or 1 ii. Then $\lambda_s^+ = 0$ and hence $p_s = -\lambda_c^+$. From (10) we obtain $\lambda_c^+ = -\lambda_u^+ U_c^+ + \bar{\lambda}_c^+ > 0$. In the case of Theorem 1 i, one has $\lambda_c^+ = -\lambda_u^+ U_c^+ > 0$, since $\lambda_u^+ = W_u^+ > 0$, $\bar{\lambda}_c \equiv 0$ and $U_c^+ < 0$, whereas in the case of Theorem 1 ii one has $\lambda_c^+ = \bar{\lambda}_c^+ \geq 0$, since $\lambda_u \equiv 0$. Hence in an equilibrium with a price and standard system, a necessary condition for $p_s < 0$ is that the emission standard is binding. Furthermore, $p_s < 0$ is always associated to a welfare-maximizing equilibrium. It follows that if an economy suffers from pollution in its (unique) laissez-faire equilibrium, then there is a misallocation of resources in the sense that the associated equilibrium allocation x^+ is not welfare maximizing.[15]

Fig. 11–2 in Chapter 11 shows the production possibility set of an economy as it was characterized in the preceding paragraph. The point H may be the allocation (q_1, q_2, u) associated with the equilibrium under laissez-faire. The equilibrium allocations for alternative emission standards may be represented by points on the line $HKLM$ on the production possibility frontier. One of these points, say L, is associated with the welfare-maximizing equilibrium.

3. COMPARATIVE STATICS
OF THE CLOSED ECONOMY
In order to apply the so-called hat calculus,[16] the following assumptions are introduced in addition to those already stated in Section 1:

(a 1): The functions Q^1, Q^2 and M are linear homogeneous and strictly quasi concave.

(a 2): The welfare function W is homothetic with respect to q_1^d and q_2^d and yields continuous demand functions $D^i: IR_+^3 \rightarrow IR_+$, where $q_i^d = D^i (\pi_{21}, Y, u)$ is the ith consumption good demanded at prices π_{21}, income $Y = q_1 + \pi_{21} q_2$ and at environmental quality u.

(a 3): Let $x_i \equiv (a_i, m_i, s_i)$ and $x_m \equiv (a_m, s_m)$ be associated with an allocation $x \epsilon IR^{15}$. If x is the economy's initial equilibrium allocation, then x_1, x_2, and x_m are points in the interior of D_Q^1, D_Q^2, and D_M, respectively.

(a 1) is a standard assumption in traditional pure trade theory. In the present context, however, the homogeneity assumption on M

appears to be restrictive, since decreasing returns to scale in the virgin material sector are a basic and natural proposition in (exhaustible) resource economics. But even under (a 1), one could generate the effect of decreasing returns in the virgin material industry by parametrically reducing its labor productivity. We do not pursue this line of argument here, however.

The homotheticity assumption on W (a 2) serves only to simplify the analysis by reducing the impact of demand conditions on the equilibrium allocations. Similarly, (a 3) is introduced to avoid complications which would be caused by boundary solutions. (a 3) implies that Q^i (M) is such that there exist nonempty subsets of its domain where the isoquants are negatively sloped (positively sloped), since otherwise either x_i for $p_s > 0$ or x_m for $p_s < 0$ would be boundary points in the respective domains.

Under assumptions (a 1)–(a 3), the model of Section 1 is described by the subsequent Eqs. (15)–(22). The price equations are

$$c_{ai}p_a + c_{mi}p_m + c_{si}p_s = p_i \tag{15}$$

$$c_{am}p_a + c_{sm}p_s = p_m \tag{16}$$

where $$c_{ai} \equiv \frac{a_{i.}}{q_i}, c_{am} \equiv \frac{a_m}{m},$$

and so on.

The quantity equations are

$$c_{m1}q_1 + c_{m2}q_2 = m \tag{17}$$

$$c_{a1}q_1 + c_{a2}q_2 + c_{am}m = \bar{a} \tag{18}$$

$$c_{sm}m + c_{s1}q_1 + c_{s2}q_2 = \bar{s} - e \tag{19}$$

where $\bar{a} > 0$ and $\bar{s} \geq 0$ are the initial endowments of labor and secondary material, respectively. $\bar{s}$ is introduced primarily for the technical reason that the relative rate of change $d(\bar{s} - e)/(\bar{s} - e)$ is defined for $e = 0$. Note that $\bar{s} > 0$ modifies slightly the definition of e.

The coefficients c_{ji} are determined by the eight functions c_{ji} ($j = a, m, s; i = 1, 2, m; i \neq j$), such that at given prices and given t

$$\begin{aligned} c_{ji} &= C_{ji}(p_a, p_m, p_s) \quad \text{(for } j = a, m, s; i = 1, 2) \\ c_{am} &= C_{am}(p_a, p_s, t) \\ c_{sm} &= C_{sm}(p_a, p_s) \end{aligned} \tag{20}$$

are the minimum "input" requirements [17] per unit of output. The variable t in (20) denotes the transactions coefficient which was already introduced in Eq. (1). If this coefficient is changed parametrically, we can study the effects of alternative degrees of market organization (or changing collection and transportation techniques) in the market for secondary material.

Finally, we take into account the conditions for equilibrium in the consumption goods markets and Walras's Law and thus complete the description of the model

$$q_1 = D^1(\pi_{21}, Y, U(e)) \tag{21}$$

$$q_2 = D^2(\pi_{21}, Y, U(e)) \equiv \pi_{12}[Y - D^1(\pi_{21}, Y, U(e))]. \tag{22}$$

We first turn our attention to the price equations (15) and (16). By the "hat" calculus we obtain

$$\rho_{ai}\hat{p}_a + \rho_{mi}\hat{p}_m + \rho_{si}\hat{p}_s = \hat{p}_i - [\rho_{ai}\hat{c}_{ai} + \rho_{mi}\hat{c}_{mi} + \rho_{si}\hat{c}_{si}] \tag{15.1}$$

$$\rho_{am}\hat{p}_a + \rho_{sm}\hat{p}_s = \hat{p}_m - [\rho_{am}\hat{c}_{am}{}^{\pi} + \rho_{sm}\hat{c}_{sm}] - \rho_{am}\hat{z} \tag{16.1}$$

where $\rho_{ai} \equiv c_{ai}\pi_{ai}$, $\rho_{sm} \equiv c_{sm}\pi_{sm}$, and so on,

$$\hat{c}_{am}{}^{\pi} \equiv \frac{1}{c_{am}} \frac{\partial C_{am}}{\partial \pi_{sa}} d\pi_{sa}, \quad \hat{z} \equiv \frac{1}{c_{am}} \frac{\partial C_{am}}{\partial t} dt$$

and

$$\hat{c}_{am}{}^{\pi} + \hat{z} = \frac{dc_{am}}{c_{am}} \hat{c}_{am}. \tag{23}$$

Cost minimization (for given t) implies that the bracketed terms in (15.1) and (16.1) are equal to zero. Hence (15.1) and (16.1) become

$$\rho_{ai}\hat{p}_a + \rho_{mi}\hat{p}_m + \rho_{si}\hat{p}_s = \hat{p}_i \tag{15.2}$$

$$\rho_{am}\hat{p}_a + \rho_{sm}\hat{p}_s = \hat{p}_m - \rho_{am}\hat{z}. \tag{16.2}$$

Solving (16.2) for $\hat{p}_m$ and substituting $\hat{p}_m$ in (15.2) yields

$$\theta_{ai}\hat{p}_a + \theta_{si}\hat{p}_s = \hat{p}_i - \rho_{mi}\rho_{am}\hat{z} \tag{15.3}$$

where for $v = a, s$,

$$\theta_{vi} \equiv \rho_{vm}\rho_{mi} + \rho_{vi} = r_{vi}\pi_{vi} \quad \text{and} \quad r_{vi} \equiv c_{vm}c_{mi} + c_{vi},$$

r_{ai} is the gross labor coefficient of the ith sector and must be distinguished from the net labor coefficient c_{ai}. Similarly, we denote r_{si} and

c_{si} as the gross and net secondary material coefficients respectively. For $v = a, s$ we have $r_{vi} \geq c_{vi}$.

We now subtract (15.3) for $i = 1$ from (15.3) for $i = 2$ to obtain

$$\hat{\pi}_{21} = |\theta| \hat{\pi}_{sa} + (\rho_{am}\rho_{m2} - \rho_{am}\rho_{m1})\hat{z} \qquad (15.4)$$

where
$$|\theta| \equiv \begin{vmatrix} \theta_{a1} & \theta_{s1} \\ \theta_{a2} & \theta_{s2} \end{vmatrix} = \theta_{a1} - \theta_{a2} = \theta_{s2} - \theta_{s1},$$

$$\hat{\pi}_{21} \equiv \left(\frac{\hat{p}_2}{p_1}\right) = \hat{p}_2 - \hat{p}_1$$

and

$$\hat{\pi}_{sa} \equiv \left(\frac{\hat{p}_s}{p_a}\right) = \hat{p}_s - \hat{p}_a.$$

Lemma 3. Suppose $p_s \neq 0$. Then $p_s|\theta| \lesseqgtr 0$

(i) if and only if $S_g^2 \lesseqgtr S_g^1$,

(ii) If $S_n^2 \lesseqgtr S_n^1$, $J_{ma}^2 \begin{Bmatrix} \geq \\ \leq \end{Bmatrix} J_{ma}^1$ and $S_n^i \leq 0$,

where for $i = 1, 2$ $J_{ma}^i \equiv \dfrac{c_{mi}}{c_{ai}}$, $S_g^i \equiv \dfrac{r_{si}}{r_{ai}}$, $S_n^i \equiv \dfrac{c_{si}}{c_{ai}}$ and $S^m \equiv \dfrac{c_{sm}}{c_{am}}$.

Proof. Lemma 3 i follows from

$$|\theta| = \theta_{a1}\theta_{s2} - \theta_{a2}\theta_{s1} = \frac{p_a p_s}{p_1 p_2}(r_{a1}r_{s2} - r_{a2}r_{s1})$$

$$= \frac{p_a p_s}{p_1 p_2}(S_g^2 - S_g^1)r_{a1}r_{a2}.$$

To prove Lemma 3 ii, we make use of the definitions of r_{si} and r_{ai} and obtain

$$(r_{a1}r_{s2} - r_{a2}r_{s1}) = c_{a1}c_{a2}(S_n^2 - S_n^1)$$
$$+ c_{a2}c_{am}c_{m1}(S_n^2 - S^m) + c_{a1}c_{am}c_{m2}(S^m - S_n^1)$$
$$= c_{a1}c_{a2}(S_n^2 - S_n^1) + c_{a1}c_{a2}c_{sm}(J_{ma}^2 - J_{ma}^1)$$
$$+ c_{a1}c_{a2}c_{am}(S_n^2 J_{ma}^1 - S_n^1 J_{ma}^2).$$

Since the variables S_n^i are non-positive and the variables J_{ma}^i nonnegative, the right-hand side of the last equation above is positive under the conditions listed in Lemma 3 ii.

QED

Before we give an economic interpretation to Lemma 3, we reconsider the coefficients c_{si} and r_{si}. Note that recycling takes place if $r_{si} - c_{si} > 0$. We may look at r_{si} as the ith sector's "gross per unit excess demand" of secondary material, where according to the usual sign convention negative values indicate an excess supply. This excess demand is composed of c_{si}, the sector's per unit supply of secondary material as a by-product and its per unit demand $c_{sm}c_{mi}$ being calculated indirectly via the sector's per unit demand for basic material.

For intersectoral comparisons of secondary material generation, it is convenient to substitute r_{si} and c_{si} by $S_n{}^i$ and $S_g{}^i$, denoting sector i's net and gross secondary material intensities. We say that the production of good 1 is more intensive in its gross (net) generation of secondary material than the production of good 2 if $S_g{}^1 < S_g{}^2$ ($S_n{}^1 < S_n{}^2$). If in addition $r_{s1} + r_{s2} < 0$, then $S_g{}^1 < S_g{}^2$ implies that good 1 is relatively more intensive in its use of the environment as a waste receptor.

According to Lemma 3, the gross intensity ranking uniquely determines the sign of $p_s|\theta|$, but the net intensity ranking is neither necessary nor sufficient for the sign of $S_g{}^1 - S_g{}^2$. Qualitatively, this result is comparable to that of Batra and Casas, who showed that the net and gross intensity rankings may not coincide in the presence of pure intermediate goods.[18] But Lemma 3 exhibits two major differences from their results: First, their sufficient conditions for the identity of net and gross factor-intensity rankings do not carry over in the present model; and second, in the present context, the sign of $|\theta|$ not only depends on the gross secondary material intensity ranking, but also on the sign of p_s.

Observe, however, that p_s as a sign-determining variable preserves (rather than disturbs) the monotonicity of the functional relation between π_{21} and π_{sa} whose slope is given by (15.4). Suppose that sector 1 is relatively secondary material intensive ($S_g{}^1 < S_g{}^2$). Then π_{21} is a strictly monotonically increasing function of π_{sa} regardless of the sign of p_s, since by Lemma 3 and by (15.4) for $\hat{z} = 0$

$$\frac{d\pi_{21}}{d\pi_{sa}} = \frac{\hat{\pi}_{21}}{\hat{\pi}_{sa}}\frac{\pi_{sa}}{\pi_{21}} = \frac{p_s|\theta|}{p_a\pi_{21}} > 0.$$

Another relationship between relative prices can be studied by solving (16.2) for $\hat{p}_a$ and substituting $\hat{p}_a$ in (15.2):

$$\frac{\theta_{ai}}{\rho_{am}}\hat{p}_m + \frac{(\rho_{am}\rho_{si} - \rho_{sm}\rho_{ai})}{\rho_{am}}\hat{p}_s = \hat{p}_i + \rho_{ai}\hat{z}. \qquad (15.5)$$

From (15) and (16) it follows that $\rho_{ai} + \rho_{mi} + \rho_{si} = 1$ and $\rho_{am} + \rho_{sm} = 1$. By these restrictions, the bracketed term in Eq. (15.5) is equal to $\theta_{si} - \rho_{sm}$. We use this information when (15.5) for $i = 2$ is subtracted from (15.5) for $i = 1$ and obtaiñ:

$$\hat{\pi}_{21} = \frac{|\theta|}{\rho_{am}}\hat{\pi}_{sm} - (\rho_{a2} - \rho_{a1})\hat{z}. \qquad (15.6)$$

Further, we combine (15.6) and (15.4) to have

$$\hat{\pi}_{sa} = \frac{1}{\rho_{am}}\hat{\pi}_{sm} - \hat{z}. \qquad (15.7)$$

By this result, changes of the relative price of secondary material have the same sign regardless of whether labor or basic material is used as numeraire.

We now investigate some implications of the Eqs. (17)–(20). Solving (17) for m and substituting m into (18) and (19) yields for $v = a, s$

$$r_{v1}q_1 + r_{v2}q_2 = v^o \qquad (18.1)$$

$$\lambda_{v1}\hat{r}_{v1} + \lambda_{v2}\hat{r}_{v2} + \lambda_{v1}\hat{q}_1 + \lambda_{v2}\hat{q}_2 = \hat{v}^o \qquad (18.2)$$

where $\quad a^o \equiv \bar{a}, s^o = \bar{s} - e, \hat{a}^o = \hat{a}, \hat{s}^o = (\bar{s}/s^o)\hat{s} - (e/s^o)\hat{e}$

and $\lambda_{vi} \equiv r_{vi}q_i/v^o$.

With the help of Eqs. (20) it can be shown similarly to Batra (1973, p. 199 n.) that

$$\hat{c}_{ai} = (\rho_{si}\sigma_{sa}{}^i + \rho_{mi}\rho_{sm}\sigma_{am}{}^i)\hat{\pi}_{sa}$$
$$\hat{c}_{mi} = (\rho_{si}\rho_{am}\sigma_{sm}{}^i - \rho_{ai}\rho_{sm}\sigma_{am}{}^i)\hat{\pi}_{sa} \qquad (24)$$
$$\hat{c}_{si} = - (\rho_{ai}\sigma_{sa}{}^i + \rho_{mi}\rho_{am}\sigma_{sm}{}^i)\hat{\pi}_{sa}$$

$$\hat{c}_{am} = - \rho_{am}\sigma_m\hat{\pi}_{sa} + \hat{z}, \hat{c}_{sm} = - \rho_{sm}\sigma_m\hat{\pi}_{sa} \qquad (25)$$

$$\hat{r}_{ai} = \frac{(\alpha_i + \beta_i)}{\theta_{ai}}\hat{\pi}_{sa} + \frac{\rho_{am}\rho_{mi}}{\theta_{ai}}\hat{z} \qquad (26)$$

$$\hat{r}_{si} = - \frac{(\alpha_i + \beta_i)}{\theta_{si}}\hat{\pi}_{sa}$$

where in (26) $\alpha_i \equiv \rho_{si}\rho_{ai}\sigma_{sa}{}^i + \rho_{am}{}^2\rho_{si}\rho_{mi}\sigma_{sm}{}^i + \rho_{sm}{}^2\rho_{ai}\rho_{mi}\sigma_{am}{}^i$ and $\beta_i \equiv$ $\rho_{sm}\rho_{am}\rho_{mi}\sigma_m$, where σ_m is the elasticity of substitution between labor and secondary material in M, and where $\sigma_{am}{}^i$, $\sigma_{sm}{}^i$, $\sigma_{sa}{}^i$ are partial elasticities of substitution associated with the production functions Q^i.

From (24)–(26) and (15.7) we easily obtain

$$\hat{S}_g{}^i = -\frac{\alpha_i + \beta_i}{\rho_{am}\theta_{ai}\theta_{si}}\hat{\pi}_{sm} + \frac{\alpha_i + \beta_i - \theta_{si}\rho_{am}\rho_{mi}}{\theta_{ai}\theta_{si}}\hat{z} \qquad (27)$$

$$\hat{S}^m = \hat{c}_{sm} - \hat{c}_{am} = -\frac{\sigma_m}{\rho_{am}}\hat{\pi}_{sm} + (\sigma_m - 1)\hat{z} \qquad (28)$$

$$\hat{S}_n{}^i = -\gamma_n(\hat{\pi}_{sm} - \hat{z}) \qquad (29)$$

where $\gamma_n \equiv (\rho_{ai} + \rho_{si})\sigma_{sa}{}^i + \rho_{mi}(\rho_{am}\sigma_{sm}{}^i + \rho_{sm}\sigma_{am}{}^i)$.

Furthermore, using Eq. (28) we can write for (18.2)

$$\gamma_a\hat{\pi}_{sa} + \lambda_{a1}\hat{q}_1 + \lambda_{a2}\hat{q}_2 = \hat{a} - \gamma_z\hat{z} \qquad (18.3)$$

and

$$-\gamma_s\hat{\pi}_{sa} + \lambda_{s1}\hat{q}_1 + \lambda_{s2}\hat{q}_2 = s^o \qquad (18.4)$$

where

$$\gamma_z \equiv \frac{\rho_{am}(\theta_{a2}\rho_{m1} + \theta_{a1}\rho_{m2})}{\theta_{a1}\theta_{a2}} > 0$$

and for $v = a, s$

$$\gamma_v \equiv \frac{\lambda_{v1}(\alpha_1 + \beta_1)}{\theta_{v1}} + \frac{\lambda_{v2}(\alpha_2 + \beta_2)}{\theta_{v2}}.$$

Lemma 4. $\gamma_a > 0$ and $[p_s s^o > 0 \Rightarrow \gamma_s > 0]$.

Proof. $\gamma_a > 0$ if for $i = 1, 2$ $(\alpha_i + \beta_i) > 0$. $\alpha_i > 0$ and $\beta_i > 0$ can be proved essentially as in Batra (1973, p. 199 n), taking into account that, in contrast to Batra's case, the signs of the variables ρ_{sm} and ρ_{si} are unrestricted and observing that (as in Batra's model) all partial elasticities of substitution of the type $\sigma_{jj}{}^m$ $(j = a, s)$ and $\sigma_{jj}{}^i$ $(i = 1, 2; j = a, s, m)$ are negative by the assumption that M, Q^1 and Q^2 are quasi concave functions.

$\alpha_i > 0$ follows if in Batra's proof (1973, p. 201) the inequality (written in the notation of this paper)

$$\sigma_{sa}{}^i > \frac{-\rho_{mi}\sigma_{sm}{}^i\sigma_{am}{}^i}{(\rho_{si}\sigma_{sm}{}^i + \rho_{ai}\sigma_{am}{}^i)}$$

is substituted by

$$\rho_{si}\sigma_{sa}{}^i > \frac{-\rho_{si}\rho_{mi}\sigma_{sm}{}^i\sigma_{am}{}^i}{(\rho_{si}\sigma_{sm}{}^i + \rho_{ai}\sigma_{am}{}^i)}$$

(both of which coincide, of course, for $\rho_{si} > 0$).

$\beta_i > 0$ since $\rho_{am}\rho_{mi} > 0$ and $\rho_{sm}\sigma_m = -\rho_{am}\sigma_{aa}{}^m > 0$.

From these results the remaining part of Lemma 4 is straightforward.

QED

Subtracting (18.4) from (18.3) leads to

$$\hat{q}_2 - \hat{q}_1 = \sigma_s|\theta|\hat{\pi}_{sa} - \frac{1}{|\lambda|}(\hat{a} - \hat{s}^o - {}_z\hat{z}) \tag{18.5}$$

where

$$|\lambda| \equiv \begin{vmatrix} \lambda_{a1} & \lambda_{a2} \\ \lambda_{s1} & \lambda_{s2} \end{vmatrix} = \lambda_{s2} - \lambda_{a2} = \lambda_{a1} - \lambda_{s1}$$

and where

$$\sigma_s \equiv \frac{\partial(q_1/q_2)}{\partial\pi_{21}}\frac{\pi_{21}}{q_2/q_1} = \frac{\hat{q}_2 - \hat{q}_1}{\hat{\pi}_{21}} = \frac{\gamma_a + \gamma_s}{|\lambda|\ |\theta|}$$

is the elasticity of substitution between the goods 1 and 2 on the supply side (compare Jones (1965)).

Lemma 5. $|\lambda|\ |\theta| > 0$ if and only if $|\theta| \neq 0$ and $p_s s^o > 0$.

Proof. Lemma 5 immediately follows from

$$|\lambda| = \frac{q_1 q_2}{a^o s^o}(r_{a1}r_{s2} - r_{a2}r_{s1}) = \frac{p_1 q_1 p_2 q_2}{p_a a^o p_s s^o}|\theta|.$$

QED

The final step needed to study the full comparatic statics of the model is to show the effects of changes in prices and endowments on the demand for consumption goods. From (22) and (23) that represent the demand side of the model we have

$$\hat{q}_i{}^d = \eta_{ip}\hat{\pi}_{21} + \eta_{iy}\hat{y} + \eta_{iu}\eta_{ue}\hat{e} \tag{22.1}$$

where

$$\eta_{ix} \equiv \frac{\partial D^i}{\partial x}\frac{x}{q_i{}^d}$$

for $x = \rho(= \pi_{21}), Y, u,$

and where

$$\eta_{uc} \equiv \frac{dU}{de}\frac{e}{u}.$$

The assumption (a 2) that W is homothetic with respect to q_1^d and q_2^d implies that $\eta_{1y} = \eta_{2y} = 1$. Using this property and the Eqs. (22.1) and (15.4) we can show that

$$\hat{q}_2^d - \hat{q}_1^d = -\sigma_D|\theta|\hat{\pi}_{sa} + (\eta_{2u} - \eta_{1u})\eta_{uc}\hat{e} - \sigma_D\rho_{am}(\rho_{m2} - \rho_{m1})\hat{z}$$
$$(22.2)$$

where

$$\sigma_D \equiv \frac{\partial(q_1^d/q_2^d)}{\partial\pi_{21}}\frac{\pi_{21}}{q_1^d/q_2^d} = \eta_{1p} - \eta_{2p} > 0$$

is the elasticity of demand substitution (compare Batra (1973, p. 26)).

The equilibrium conditions on the markets for basic material, for labor and secondary material are given by Eqs. (17), (18) and (19).[19] We assume that the markets for consumption goods have also been cleared initially. Furthermore, these markets should be in equilibrium again after some exogenous changes in $\bar{a}$, $\bar{s}$, e and t, that is, we require $\hat{q}_2 - \hat{q}_1 = \hat{q}_2^d - \hat{q}_1^d$. Hence we equate (22.2) and (18.5) and obtain

$$\hat{\pi}_{sa} = \frac{B}{(\sigma_S + \sigma_D)|\theta||\lambda|} \qquad (30)$$

where

$$B \equiv \hat{a} - (\bar{s}/s^o)\hat{s} + [\eta_{uc}(\eta_{2u} - \eta_{1u})|\lambda| + e/s^o]\hat{e}$$
$$- [\gamma_z + |\lambda|\sigma_D\rho_{am}(\rho_{m2} - \rho_{m1})]z.$$

Theorem 2 (i) [Secondary material as a pure intermediate product]. Let the economy satisfy at its initial equilibrium $S_g^2 \neq S_g^1$ and $p_s > 0$, $\bar{s} > 0$. Then

α) there are no economically interesting sufficient conditions for a unique sign of

$$\frac{\hat{\pi}_{sa}}{\hat{z}}, \frac{\hat{\pi}_{sm}}{\hat{z}}, \frac{\hat{R}}{\hat{z}}, \frac{\hat{S}_g^i}{\hat{z}}, \frac{\hat{\pi}_{21}}{\hat{z}}, \frac{\hat{q}_2 - \hat{q}_1}{\hat{z}}$$

β) for $\hat{v} = \hat{a} - \hat{s}$, $\hat{a}$:

$$\frac{\hat{\pi}_{sa}}{\hat{v}}, \frac{\hat{\pi}_{sm}}{\hat{v}}, > 0, \frac{\hat{R}}{\hat{v}}(=) < 0,^{20}$$

$$\frac{\hat{S}_g^i}{\hat{v}} \lessgtr 0, \qquad \text{iff } r_{si} \gtrless 0^{21}$$

$$\frac{\hat{q}_2 - \hat{q}_1}{\hat{v}} \begin{cases} > 0, \text{ iff } S_2^g \gtrless S_1^g & \text{and} \quad \sigma_S \gtrless \dfrac{1}{|\theta|\,|\lambda|} \\[2mm] < 0, \text{ iff } S_2^g \gtrless S_1^g & \text{and} \quad \sigma_S \lessgtr \dfrac{1}{|\theta|\,|\lambda|}, \end{cases}$$

$$\frac{\hat{\pi}_{21}}{\hat{v}} \gtrless 0, \qquad \text{iff } S_g^2 \gtrless S_g^1$$

(ii) [Environmental price and standard system]. Let the economy satisfy at its initial equilibrium $S_g^2 \neq S_g^1$ and $p_s < 0$, $s = 0$. Then

(α) the same as in α) of Theorem 2 i;

(β)
$$\frac{\hat{\pi}_{sa}}{\hat{a}}, \frac{\hat{\pi}_{sm}}{\hat{a}} > 0, \frac{\hat{R}}{\hat{a}}(=) > 0$$

$$\frac{\hat{S}_g^i}{\hat{a}} \lessgtr 0, \qquad \text{iff } r_{si} \lessgtr 0$$

$$\frac{\hat{q}_2 - \hat{q}_1}{\hat{a}} \begin{cases} > 0, \text{ iff } S_2^g \gtrless S_1^g \text{ and } \sigma_S \lessgtr \dfrac{1}{|\theta|\,|\lambda|} \\[2mm] < 0, \text{ iff } S_2^g \gtrless S_1^g \text{ and } \sigma_S \gtrless \dfrac{1}{|\theta|\,|\lambda|} \end{cases}$$

$$\frac{\hat{\pi}_{21}}{\hat{a}} \gtrless 0, \text{ iff } S_g^2 \lessgtr S_g^1$$

(γ)
$$\frac{\hat{\pi}_{sa}}{\hat{e}}, \frac{\hat{\pi}_{sm}}{\hat{e}} < 0, \frac{\hat{R}}{\hat{e}}(=) < 0, \text{ if } [\varphi_1 \text{ or } \varphi_2]$$

$$\frac{\hat{S}_g^i}{\hat{e}} \lessgtr 0, \qquad \text{if } [\varphi_1 \text{ or } \varphi_2] \quad \text{and} \quad r_{si} \gtrless 0.$$

$$\frac{\pi_{21}}{e} \gtrless 0, \text{ if } \{\varphi_1, \frac{\hat{q}_2 - \hat{q}_1}{\hat{e}} < 0, \text{ if } [S_g^1 < S_g^2 \text{ and } \eta_{1u} > -\frac{\tau_2}{\eta_{ue}} < 0],$$

or if $[S_g^2 < S_g^1$ and $\eta_{2u} > \dfrac{\tau_1}{\eta_{ue}} < 0]$

where $\varphi_1 : S_g^1 < S_g^2$ and $\eta_{1u} > -\tau_2/\eta_{ue}|\lambda| < 0$ and

$$\varphi_2 : S_g^2 < S_g^1 \quad \text{and} \quad \eta_{2u} > \frac{\tau_1}{\eta_{ue}|\lambda|} < 0 \text{ with } \tau_i \equiv \frac{p_i q_i}{Y}.^{21}$$

Proof. The proof of Theorem 2 is straightforward from Lemmata 1 and 3–5 and the other intermediate results derived above in this section. It suffices, therefore, only to indicate the general scheme of how the results can be obtained. For example, we have

$$\frac{R}{a} = \frac{R}{S^m} \frac{S^m}{\pi_{sm}} \frac{\pi_{sm}}{\pi_{sa}} \frac{\pi_{sa}}{a},$$

where the sign of R/S^m is determined by Lemma 1 i and that of S^m/π_{sm} with the help of Eq. (28) and the fact that $\rho_{sm}\sigma_{ss}{}^m = -\rho_{am}\sigma_m$ $\lessgtr 0$ for $p_s \gtrless 0$. Further, the sign of π_{sm}/π_{sa} can be determined from (15.7) and that of π_{sa}/a from (30) and Lemmata 4–5. Calculating $(q_2 - q_1)/v$ $(v = a - s, a)$ we must take into account the direct effect of v on $q_2 - q_1$ in (18.5) and the indirect effect that v has on $q_2 - q_1$ in (18.5) via π_{sa} as determined by (30). Note finally that the conditions φ_1 and φ_2 in Theorem 2 ii γ are formulated with the help of the equation $\tau_1\eta_{1u} + \tau_2\eta_{2u} = 0$ as derived from (22). The rest of the proof is left to the reader.

QED

Theorem 2 summarizes the main comparative static results for the closed economy which will be of interest for the discussion of trade in secondary material in the next section.

In addition to the direction of changes in the rate of recycling, it would be interesting to know whether in absolute terms the virgin material production and/or the production of basic material in the recycling sector expanded. A necessary condition is to know the sign of m that follows from the "hat" equation associated to Eq. (17) when combined with (18.3) and (18.4). However, $\hat{m}$ is a fairly complex function of a, z, s^o and π_{sa} so that no straightforward sufficient conditions for a unique sign of m could be found.

3. TRADE IN BASIC AND SECONDARY MATERIAL

Our model contains five commodities that can potentially be traded. If, however, trade in more than two goods is introduced, the well-known problem of indeterminacy may arise. Since we are interested here in international markets for secondary material and recovered secondary material, we avoid these difficulties by restricting the subsequent analysis to trade in basic and secondary material only.

Let us first consider a country (the home country) that is small in the sense that the other country (rest of the world) accepts arbitrarily large trade flows at given prices $\pi_{sm}{}^+$. From standard pure trade theory, we expect the basic results that (i) trade flows are nonzero if $\pi_{sm}^+ \neq \pi_{sm}$, where π_{sm} is the home country's autarchic price ratio of secondary and basic material, (ii) that the pattern of trade is determined by the comparative price advantages, that is, that the home country exports the secondary material, if $\pi_{sm} < \pi_{sm}^+$ and finally, that (iii) the home country gains from trade if $\pi_{sm}^+ \neq \pi_{sm}$.

This conjecture is clearly intuitive. But there is no easy way to demonstrate it diagrammatically since the structure of the model is fairly complex and none of the traded goods is directly subject to consumers' preferences. In particular, when gains from trade are calculated in the present context, one must take into account welfare effects due to possible changes in environmental quality that may occur when trade is introduced. Since Melvin (1969) showed in a single-primary-factor framework with intermediate products that not every country necessarily gains from trade, it is also an open interesting question whether in our model the price differentials in points (i) and (ii) of the conjecture above are sufficient as well as necessary conditions. Moreover, in the case of environmental management at least one of the price ratios π_{sm}, π_{sm}^+ will be negative so that one may ask to what extent the notion and the role of comparative price advantages extends to such cases. For all these reasons, we will rigorously qualify and prove the above conjecture.

Before the theorem is stated, some formal concepts must be introduced. We define the Lagrangean

$$
\begin{aligned}
L^t = L^t(x_t, \lambda_t) \equiv\; & W(q_1^d, q_2^d, u) + \Sigma_i \lambda_i [Q^i(a_i, m_i, s_i) - q_i] \\
& + \lambda_m [M(a_m, s_m) - m] + \lambda_s [\bar{s} + \alpha_s s_t - s_1 - s_2 - s_m] \\
& + \Sigma_i \bar{\lambda}_i [q_i - q_i^d] + \lambda_a [\bar{a} - a_1 - a_2 - a_m] \qquad (31) \\
& + \bar{\lambda}_m [\alpha_m m_t + m - m_1 - m_2] \\
& + \lambda_e [e - \bar{s} - \alpha_s s_t + s_1 + s_2 + s_m] + \lambda_u [U(e) - u] \\
& + \bar{\lambda}_e [\bar{e} - e] + \lambda_\pi [\delta(\pi_{sm}^+) \pi_{sm}^+ \alpha_s s_t + \delta(\pi_{sm}^+) \alpha_m m_t],
\end{aligned}
$$

where $x_t \epsilon IR^{17}$ and $\lambda_t \epsilon IR_+^{12}$ are defined as x and λ in Eq. (6) but enlarged by the components s_t, m_t and respectively, λ_π. The variables s_t and m_t denote trade flows of secondary and basic material. They are not restricted in sign unless assumed otherwise. α_s and α_m are variables that can only attain the two values $(+1)$ and (-1). $\delta(\pi_{sm}^+)$ is defined as

$$
\delta(\pi_m^+) \equiv \begin{cases} -1, & \text{if } \pi_{sm}^+ \geq 0 \\ +1, & \text{if } \pi_{sm}^+ < 0. \end{cases}
$$

Further, we denote by P^o the saddlepoint program:

$$\max_{x_t{}^{)u(} } \min_{\lambda_t{}^{(u)}} L^t(x_t, \lambda_t)$$

by P^1 the program:

$$\max_{x_t{}^{)u(} } \min_{\lambda_t{}^{(u, \bar{e}, e)}} L^t(x_t, \lambda_t)$$

and we define the programming problems (for $j = 0, 1$)

$P_2{}^j$: [P^j subject to $\alpha_s = \alpha_m = + 1$],
$P_3{}^j$: [P^j subject to $s_t = m_t = 0$],
$P_4{}^j$: [P^j subject to $\alpha_m = - \alpha_s = + 1$ and $\pi_{sm}{}^+, s_t, m_t \geq 0$],
$P_5{}^j$: [P^j subject to $\alpha_s = - \alpha_m = + 1$, and $\pi_{sm}{}^+, s_t, m_t \geq 0$],
$P_6{}^j$: [P^j subject to $\alpha_s = \alpha_m = -1, \pi_{sm}{}^+ < 0, s_t, m_t \geq 0$],
$P_7{}^j$: [P^j subject to $\alpha_s = \alpha_m = + 1, \pi_{sm}{}^+ < 0, s_t, m_t \geq 0$].

Theorem 3. Let the home country be such that for $\pi_{sm}{}^+ \epsilon IR$ the problems $P_2{}^o - P_7{}^o$ and $P_2{}^1 - P_6{}^1$ have a unique solution satisfying

$$(a_i, m_i, s_i) \epsilon D_Q{}^i \text{ and } (a_m, s_m) \epsilon D_M.$$

(i)   Suppose the small country implements an environmental price and standard system at $\bar{e} \geq 0$ and the autarchic equilibrium emission satisfies $e = \bar{e}$. Then (α) trade takes place according to the comparative price advantages and (β) the small country gains from trade if and only if $\pi_{sm} \neq \pi_{sm}{}^+$.

(ii) Suppose the small country implements an environmental price and standard system at $\bar{e} > 0$, but the autarchic equilibrium is such that $e < \bar{e}$.[22]
      α) If $\pi_{sm}{}^+ > 0$, Theorem 3 i α and 3 i β hold.
      β) If $\pi_{sm}{}^+ < 0$, the home country may lose from trade.

(iii) Suppose the small country does not enforce an environmental price and standard system and its autarchic equilibrium emission satisfies $e > 0$.
      α) If $\pi_{sm}{}^+ > 0$, Theorem 3 i α and 3 i β holds.
      β) If $\pi_{sm}{}^+ < 0$, there does not exist a trading equilibrium.[23]

Proof. Ad. i α: First we realize that $P_3{}^o$ is equivalent to problem (8). Hence, if $(x_t{}^3, \lambda_t{}^3)$ solves $P_3{}^o$, then by Theorem 1 there exist prices $p^3 \epsilon IR^5$ such that $(p^3, x_t{}^3)$ is an $\bar{e}$-efficient (autarchic) equilibrium. It has been shown in the proof of Theorem 1 that $\pi_{sm}{}^3 \equiv p_s{}^3 / p_m{}^3 =$

Rüdiger Pethig   379

$(\lambda_s{}^3 - \lambda_c{}^3/\lambda_m{}^3)$. By the same kind of arguments that have been used to prove Theorem 1, it can be shown with the help of the solution $(x_t{}^2, \lambda_t{}^2)$ of $P_2{}^o$ that there exists an $\bar{e}$-efficient competitive trading equilibrium $(x_t{}^2, p^2)$ for the small country such that

$$\pi_{sm}{}^2 \equiv (\lambda_s{}^2 - \lambda_c{}^2/\lambda_m{}^2) = \pi_{sm}{}^+.$$

To prove the last equality sign, we use the two uhn-Tucker conditions (associated with [31])

$$\frac{\partial L^t}{\partial s_t} = (\lambda_s - \lambda_c)\alpha_s + \lambda_\pi\delta(\pi_{sm}{}^+)\pi_{sm}{}^+\alpha_s \leq 0 \qquad (32)$$

and

$$\frac{\partial L^t}{\partial m_t} = \bar{\lambda}_m\alpha_m + \lambda_\pi\delta(\pi_{sm}{}^+)\alpha_m \leq 0 \qquad (33)$$

which are satisfied as equalities for the solution $(x_t{}^2, \lambda_t{}^2)$ of $P_2{}^o$, since s_t and m_t are not sign-restricted.

Next we want to establish that for $\pi_{sm}{}^+ > 0$ the pattern of trade follows the existing comparative price advantage. Let $(x_t{}^4, \lambda_t{}^4)$ be the solution to $P_4{}^o$ such that $s_t{}^4 = m_t{}^4 = 0$. Then (32) and (33) yield $\pi_{sm}{}^4 \equiv (\lambda_s{}^4 - \lambda_c{}^4/\lambda_m{}^4) \geq \pi_{sm}{}^+$. We obviously have $x_t{}^4\epsilon F_4{}^o \cap F_3{}^o$, where $F_3{}^o$ and $F_4{}^o$ are the feasibility sets of the problems $P_3{}^o$ and $P_4{}^o$. Hence $(x_t{}^4, \lambda_t{}^4)$ solves $P_3{}^o$. By assumption, the solution is unique, so that $\pi_{sm}{}^4 = \pi_{sm}{}^3$. Since $\lambda_m = \bar{\lambda}_m > 0$ and since by (33) $\lambda_\pi > 0$, this result implies $[\pi_{sm}{}^3 < \pi_{sm}{}^+ \Rightarrow s_t{}^4, m_t{}^4 > 0]$ where from $\alpha_m = -\alpha_s = 1$ it follows that the secondary material is exported and the basic material is imported. Now it must be shown that the converse is also true, that is, that $[s_t{}^4, m_t{}^4 > 0 \Rightarrow \pi_{sm}{}^3 < \pi_{sm}{}^+]$. Suppose, therefore, that $(x_t{}^4, \lambda_t{}^4)$ solves $P_4{}^o$ with $s_t{}^4, m_t{}^4 > 0$. In this case by (32) and (33) $\pi_{sm}{}^4 = (\lambda_s{}^4 - \lambda_c{}^4/\lambda_m{}^4) = \pi_{sm}{}^+$, and it remains to show that $\pi_{sm}{}^3 < \pi_{sm}{}^4$. Suppose on the contrary that $\pi_{sm}{}^3 = \pi_{sm}{}^4$. It follows easily that, in the equilibria $(x_t{}^3, p^3)$ and $(x_t{}^4, p^4)$, the relative prices π_{am} and π_{sa} must also be the same. Hence all equilibrium coefficients c_{ji} $(j = a, m, s)$ and c_{jm} $(j = s, a)$ are the same. Equilibrium on the markets for basic and secondary material and for labor requires

$$c_{m1}{}^3q_1{}^4 + c_{m2}{}^3q_2{}^4 = m^4 + m_t{}^4$$
$$c_{s1}{}^3q_1{}^4 + c_{s2}{}^3q_2{}^4 + c_{sm}{}^3m^4 = \bar{s} - s_t{}^4$$
$$c_{a1}{}^3q_1{}^4 + c_{a2}{}^3q_2{}^4 + c_{am}{}^3m^4 = \bar{a}$$

with $m_t^4 = \pi_{sm}^+ s_t^4$, and by (22.2) (for $\hat{\pi}_{sa} = 0$) market clearing for the two consumption goods requires $q_i^4 = bq_i^3$ ($i = 1, 2$), where b is a positive variable. We clearly know that by assumption these six equations above have a solution for $b = 1$ and $s_t^4 = m_t^4 = 0$, but they cannot be solved for s_t^4, $m_t^4 > 0$ and any $b \geq 0$. Therefore s_t^4, $m_t^4 > 0$ implies $\pi_{sm}^3 < \pi_{sm}^4 = \pi_{sm}^+$. Using P_5^0, one can show by symmetric arguments that $[\pi_{sm}^3 > \pi_{sm}^+ > 0 \leftrightarrow s_t^4, m_t^4 > 0]$. Correspondingly, with the help of P_6^0 and P_7^0 one argues for $\pi_{sm}^+ \leq 0$. Thus Theorem 3 i α is proved.

Ad i β: We first consider the case $\pi_{sm}^+ > \pi_{sm}^3 > 0$ (and $\bar{e} = 0$). Then by Theorem 3 i α s_t^4, $m_t^4 \neq 0$ and hence $x_t^4 \neq x_t^3$ and $x_t^4 \notin F_3^0$. But we want to show that $W(q^3) < W(q^4)$, where $q^3 \equiv (q_1^{d3}, q_2^{d3}, u^3)$ and $q^4 \equiv (q_1^{d4}, q_2^{d4}, u^4)$ and $u^3 = u^4 = U(o)$ by π_{sm}^+, $\pi_{sm}^3 > 0$. We denote by $F_j^{pr}(u) \subset IR_+^2$ the projection of F_j^0 ($j = 3,4$) into the space of the variables q_1 and q_2 for given u. Suppose first that $(q_1^4, q_2^4) \in F_3^{pr}(u^3)$. Then $W(q^4) \leq W(q^3)$, since (q_1^3, q_2^3) maximizes $W(., u^3)$ on $F_3^{pr}(u^3)$. On the other hand $W(q^4) \geq W(q^3)$, since (q_1^4, q_2^4) maximizes $W(., u^3)$ on $F_4^{pr}(u^4)$ and $F_4^{pr}(u^4) \supset F_3^{pr}(u^3)$ since $F_4^0 \supset F_3^0$. Hence $q^4 = q^3$. But by (18.5) and (15.7) there exists no $b \geq 0$ such that $(q_1^4, q_2^4) = (bq_1^3, bq_2^3)$ if $\pi_{sm}^4 \neq \pi_{sm}^3$. This contradicts the supposition that $(q_1^4, q_2^4) \in F_3^{pr}$. Hence $W(q^4) > W(q^3)$. . . .

Now we suppose that $0 < \pi_{sm}^+ > \pi_{sm}^3$, but $\pi_{sm}^3 \leq 0$ and $0 < e^3 = \bar{e}$. In this case q^3 and q^4 are clearly such that $u^3 < u^4 = U(o)$. Let $(q_1^{4'}, q_2^{4'})$ maximize $W(., u^3)$ on $F_4^{pr}(u^3)$ and denote $(q_1^{4'}, q_2^{4'}, u^3) \equiv q^{4'}$. From the arguments of the preceding paragraph, it follows that $W(q^{4'}) \geq W(q^3)$. Hence also $W(q^4) > W(q^3)$ for $F_4^{pr}(u^4) \supset F_4^{pr}(u^3)$. The rest of the proof of Theorem 3 i β is straightforward.

Ad ii: Theorem 3 ii α is proved as Theorem 3 i β. To show Theorem 3 ii β, we suppose that (x_t^7, λ_t^7) is the solution of problem P_7^0 with the associated trading equilibrium (x_t^7, p^7). Clearly, $\pi_{sm}^7 = \pi_{sm}^+ < 0$ and $e^7 = \bar{e} > e^3$. Let $(q_1^{7'}, q_2^{7'})$ maximize $W(., u^3)$ on $F_7^{pr}(u^3)$ and denote $(q_1^{7'}, q_2^{7'}, u^3) \equiv q^{7'}$. Similar to the proof of Theorem 3 i β, we show that $W(q^{7'}) \geq W(q^3)$. But in contrast to the preceding proof, even if $F_7^{pr}(u^3)$ is a proper subset of $F_7^{pr}(u^7)$, it is possible that $W(q^7) \gtrless W(q^3)$ for $u^7 < u^3$.

Q.E.D.

Ad iii: Theorem 3 ii can be proved essentially as Theorem 3 i if P_k^0 is replaced everywhere by P_k^1, $k = 2, 3, 4, 5$, considering the equivalence of P_3^0 and problem (9). Theorem 3 ii β follows from the fact that problem P_i^1 has no solution since by assumption the space of emission e is unbounded.

Theorem 3 is restricted to the small-country case, but with some minor modifications (see note 23), the results can be extended to the two-country case where the equilibrium prices on the international market for secondary material are determined endogenously. The existence of a bilateral trading equilibrium can be shown by standard arguments: We transform the two-country trade model into a closed economy with two consumers and six producers where all commodities except basic and secondary material are regarded as (if they were) different products and where the consumers' preferences are defined only over the space of the two "domestic" consumption goods and the "domestic" environmental quality. The existence of equilibrium for this economy follows from a fixed point argument as that of a standard Debreu economy.

Notes

(References relate to Chapter 11.)

1. For a more detailed interpretation of a similar technology, compare Pethig (1975, p. 100 f.)

2. The line OA can be moved up to coincide with OA' or OA'' which would mean that $Q_S^i \leq 0$ everywhere on D_Q^i.

3. *Waste neutralization* (waste treatment, waste disposal) is defined as a technical process by which a waste product (causing pollution when discharged) is transformed into a nonobnoxious product (which does not enter explicitly the analysis here). M^ρ can be said to include a waste treatment technology, if there is $x \epsilon D_M{}^\rho$ such that $M_S{}^\rho|_x < 0$. Correspondingly, we may define waste treatment in the consumption good sector i by $Q_S^i < 0$. It is possible to separate analytically the waste treatment technology from the production of consumption goods (see, for example, Siebert [1976, I]) and basic material. But along the lines indicated in Pethig (1976, I) it can be shown that Siebert's gross concept basically coincides with the approach of integrated technology followed here.

4. If M^v is strictly concave, M^v may dominate M^r for low values of m, but there may be some $m^o > 0$, such that $M_S|_x > 0$ for every x with $M(x) > m^o$. The increasing scarcity of virgin material could also be studied with the help of M. Suppose, initially M^v dominates M^r but the labor productivity in the virgin material production decreases successively (by parametric shifts of the function M^v). Then the dominance of M^v over M^r must vanish eventually.

5. See D. Pearce (1974, p. 89). This ratio must be strictly distinguished from the ratio $\dfrac{-s_m}{s_1 + s_2}$. These two ratios coincide at zero but not at one. If the latter is one the former may well be less than one.

6. It is an important property of the model that the sets of "regular" goods and waste products are not disjoint by assumption. Whether secondary material is a waste product ($e > 0$) is determined endogenously in the model. This approach is due to Mäler (1974, p. 46 n.); see also Pethig (1976, III).

7. Note that in T the production possibilities of basic material are only implicitly considered. In contrast, Walter (1975, p. 16) considers a transformation space including explicitly basic material. However, an important difference to our approach is that Walter assumes that basic material is a (final) consumption good (i.e., an argument of the welfare function). For an interesting different analysis of the shape of the transformation curve in an economy with pure intermediate goods, see Batra and Casas (1973).

8. A proof and an illustration of a convex production possibility set in an economy without recycling is given in Pethig (1975). See also Walter (1974) and Siebert (1977).

9. Naturally, if more than one by-product is introduced (as, e.g., in Pethig [1976, III]), some may have positive prices and others zero prices, and there may still be environmental disruption.

10. Compare also Tietenberg (1973, II) and Pethig (1975, 1976 II).

11. Compare also Pethig (1975). An $\bar{e}$-efficient equilibrium implies that the environmental quality $U(\bar{e})$ is achieved at "least cost." For this concept, see Baumol and Oates (1971), Ruff (1972), and Tietenberg (1973, II).

12. See, for example, Intrilligator (1971). The Kuhn-Tucker Theorem in its standard version requires $x \geq 0$, which in the present case may be violated by s_i and u. u has been normalized to be nonnegative in the relevant part of its domain. But we keep s_i unrestricted in sign even though there is also a lower bound for s_i in the relevant domain. We simply avoid the discussion of boundary solutions with respect to s_i by restricting the analysis to cases where

$$\frac{\partial L^W}{\partial s_i}\bigg|_{x^+,\, \lambda^+} = 0$$

(see Theorem 1). Note further that in contrast to all other components of λ the variable λ_c need not be nonnegative since the associated constraint is always equal to zero by the definition of e. See van Moeseke (1974).

13. This technical assumption can be removed without qualitative changes in the results. However, it helps to keep the arguments simple and still allows us to study a sufficiently interesting class of economies.

14. It is also possible that in an equilibrium of Theorem 1 i and (1 ii) $e^+ = 0$ and $p_S < 0$. This is the special case of a prohibitively high emission tax.

15. This is no general result, since we excluded a class of boundary solutions that may not be exceptional. It is shown in Pethig (1977) that competitive laissez-faire allocations can be welfare maximizing even if $e^+ > 0$ and if U and W are strictly increasing functions in all their arguments.

16. This technique is developed by Jones (1965) and was adopted by many authors since then, mainly in trade theory. In particular, it proved a powerful tool in trade theory with pure intermediate products in Batra and Casas (1973) and Batra (1973). In this section we heavily rely on their analysis.

17. Of course, c_{si} is no regular input-output coefficient, since s_i is an output quantity. But, nevertheless, at given prices p_a, p_m and p_s there is a uniquely defined cost minimizing by-product coefficient c_{si}.

18. Compare Batra and Casas (1973, p. 304). The difference between their results and our Lemma 3 is due to the by-product property of the secondary material. Note also that the gross coefficients r_{si} ($i = 1, 2$) may be nonpositive. (If $p_s > 0$, then at most one of them can be negative). But the sign of r_{si} does not influence most of the following results.

19. If $e > 0$ in Eq. (19), this variable is interpreted either as the laissez-faire emission or the fixed emission standard. Correspondingly, $\hat{e} \neq 0$ is an endogenous variation of the equilibrium emission as response to some exogenous shock in the first case or an exogenous variation of the emission standard being an environmental policy instrument.

20. I. Walter (1974, p. 14) argues that only a small amount of an increased waste flow ($\hat{s} > 0$) would be recycled. If $p_s > 0$ initially and $\hat{s} > 0$, $\hat{a} = 0$, then $\hat{\pi}_{sm}$, $\hat{\pi}_{sa} < 0$ according to Theorem 2 i β. But in contrast to Walter's statement in our model, the total increased waste flow will be recycled unless p_s drops to zero. Even in this case, the recycling rate increases.

21. Note that $\eta_{1u} = \eta_{2u} = 0$ is sufficient for the second part of ρ_1 and ρ_2. This case was treated in Pethig (1975, Lemma 4) in a model without basic material.

22. Since the emission standard is not binding, the environmental policy is inactive in the autarchic equilibrium. Hence $\pi_{sm} \geq 0$ and $e \geq 0$. A situation where $\pi_{sm} = 0$, $e > 0$ but $e < \bar{e}$ in autarchy can be illustrated by Fig. 11–2, if the point H represents the equilibrium point and if $\bar{e}$ is such that $U(\bar{e})$ corresponds to OF. The idea of the hypothesis of Theorem 3 ii is that the country decides to stop the decline of environmental quality at $U(\bar{e})$ by adequate emission taxes whenever in the course of trade the emission should increase.

23. This result is economically insignificant, since it is due to the small country assumption of fixed world prices. It disappears in the two-country case. Besides, it can be taken as an additional motivation for the hypothesis of Theorem 3 ii.